Springer Texts in Business and Economics

D1726943

More information about this series at http://www.springer.com/series/10099

Peter Eichhorn • Ian Towers

Principles of Management

Efficiency and Effectiveness
in the Private and Public Sector

 Springer

Peter Eichhorn
OPINIO Forschungsinstitut
Mannheim, Germany

Ian Towers
SRH Hochschule Berlin
Berlin, Germany

ISSN 2192-4333   ISSN 2192-4341   (electronic)
Springer Texts in Business and Economics
ISBN 978-3-319-89007-4   ISBN 978-3-319-70902-4   (eBook)
https://doi.org/10.1007/978-3-319-70902-4

Printed on acid-free paper

This Springer imprint is published by Springer Nature
The registered company is Springer International Publishing AG
The registered company address is: Gewerbestrasse 11, 6330 Cham, Switzerland

Foreword

The title of the German edition of this book is *Das Prinzip Wirtschaftlichkeit.* We have chosen two words for the title of the English edition to capture the idea of *Wirtschaftlichkeit*: *efficiency* and *effectiveness*. Efficiency is a measure of the relationship between inputs and outputs, and effectiveness is the degree to which targets are reached. 'Efficiency' and 'effectiveness' do not, however, completely capture the meaning of *Wirtschaftlichkeit*, which always carries with it the concepts of *economic efficiency* and *economic effectiveness*. Economic efficiency exists when the relationship between the quantity of inputs needed to produce goods or services and the number of goods or services actually produced is favourable, and economic effectiveness exists when the desired output is in fact produced.

Business administration as an academic discipline in Germany has always concerned itself with economic efficiency and effectiveness (and it could be argued that this has played a role in the success of German companies over the last 50 years). The German approach started to develop at the end of the nineteenth century, and it roots can be found in accounting, which has led to an emphasis on decision-making based on facts and figures. This book reflects this, while at the same time building on the Anglo-American approach to management studies whose roots go back to the scientific management theories of Frederick Taylor. We believe that the combination of the strengths of the German and Anglo-American methods is a valuable aspect of the book.

A further feature of the book is that it does not just focus on firms. Economic efficiency and effectiveness apply to all economic agents, whether they be households, hospitals, sports clubs, municipal authorities, universities, charities, government ministries or multinational enterprises. Unlike most books on management, we also cover topics from the discipline of economics, because in order to manage an economic agent well, it is necessary to understand the overall framework in which is it active.

Also unusual for a management textbook is that we review theories of knowledge and approaches to research, because we believe that in order to understand the academic disciplines of business administration and economics, it is necessary to have a grasp of how they are structured and how they can be developed. This is also relevant for managers because they too need to learn and expand their knowledge as well.

Economic efficiency and effectiveness do not focus only on monetary aspects. Activity within the economy involves the transformation of inputs into outputs; the inputs and outputs generate external effects in the form of outcomes and impacts. Our holistic approach takes into account the social and ecological environment, where costs and benefits emerge that go beyond what can be measured in purely monetary terms.

The chapters share a common structure. There is an opening vignette which takes one of the chapter's themes and provides an illustration of it in real life. Since precision is important, the relevant terms are defined and the appropriate instruments are presented during the course of the chapter. Each chapter ends with some applied examples of what has been discussed and some questions to test comprehension. Throughout the book is a continuing project in which the reader is put in the position of owning their own business—a cafe serving only fair-trade and organically grown vegetarian food and drinks—and must make decisions about what the chapter has discussed. We have decided not to include references in the text; the reader is directed towards the literature (both in English and German) that we recommend for further reading.

The first chapter lays the foundations by describing the fields of business administration, economics and their related fields of study. It also explores methodology and terminology. The second chapter deals with the fundamentals of economic activity and economies. The four basic types of economic agents are discussed in the third chapter, with examples of mixed forms. The various principles related to economic efficiency and effectiveness are discussed in the fourth chapter, and in the following chapter, we consider goals and input factors in all their complexity and describe measurement methods. Chapter 6 provides a conceptual basis for the establishment and measurement of the economic efficiency and effectiveness of an economic agent's activities, including external effects. Chapter 7 provides more detailed insight into the various calculation methods, and the following chapter discusses how they can be applied to various activities in the value chain.

The final chapter emphasises the importance of economic efficiency and effectiveness for management, beginning with strategic management and looking at the three different phases of the management process. Last but not least, there is a German-English and English-German glossary of terms.

The basis of this book is the fourth edition of *Das Prinzip Wirtschaftlichkeit, Basiswissen der Betriebswirtschaftslehre* by Peter Eichhorn and Jochen Merk, the fourth edition of which was published by Springer Gabler in 2016, which was revised for this English version by Peter Eichhorn and Ian Towers. The initial translation from German to English was by Barbara Geier, London, England, Sarah Lauren Harris, Toronto, Canada, Mark King, Ober-Ramstadt, Germany and Paolo Rondo-Brovetto, Klagenfurt, Austria.

Our hope is that our focus on efficiency and effectiveness, and on *economic* efficiency and effectiveness, will help readers to understand how best to transform inputs into outputs, in both the private and public sectors, while at the same time considering the outcomes and impacts of economic activities.

Mannheim, Germany   Peter Eichhorn
Berlin, Germany   Ian Towers

Contents

1 Understanding Economic Activity 1
   1.1 Introduction 2
   1.2 The Objects of Cognition 5
   1.3 Business Administration 9
   1.4 Related Disciplines 14
   1.5 Neighbouring Disciplines 18
   1.6 Understanding the World and Business Administration 20
   1.7 Research 23
   1.8 Cognitive Methods 26
   1.9 Examples and Exercises 29

2 Economies and Needs 35
   2.1 Needs 36
   2.2 Fulfilment of Needs 40
   2.3 Economic Systems 49
   2.4 The Economic Constitution 53
   2.5 Examples and Exercises 59

3 Individuals and Institutions in the Economy 63
   3.1 Economic Agents 64
   3.2 Households 70
   3.3 Firms 73
   3.4 Associations 76
   3.5 Administrations 80
   3.6 Mixed Types 85
   3.7 Examples and Exercises 88

4 A Principle for Action 93
   4.1 Metaeconomic Foundations 94
   4.2 Basic Principles of Economic Efficiency 96
   4.3 The Economy of Needs 102
   4.4 The Economy of Returns 103
   4.5 The Economy of Self-Interest 104
   4.6 The Economy of Common Interest 106

4.7   The Individual Economy 107
4.8   The Aggregate Economy 107
4.9   Examples and Exercises 109

5   Goals, Production Factors and Results 115
5.1   Goal Setting 116
5.2   Input Factors 127
5.3   Factor Input 138
5.4   Types of Result 143
5.5   Measurement of Results 146
5.6   Examples and Exercises 151

6   The Conceptual Basis 157
6.1   Measuring Quantities and Monetary Value 158
6.2   Outpayments and Receipts of Payment 161
6.3   Expenditures and Revenues 167
6.4   Expenses and Income 171
6.5   Costs and Outputs 179
6.6   External Costs and Benefits 194
6.7   Assets and Capital 207
6.8   External Assets and Liabilities 212
6.9   Examples and Exercises 214

7   Calculating Economic Efficiency 221
7.1   Ratio Calculations 222
7.2   Static Methods for Capital Budgeting 225
7.3   Dynamic Methods for Capital Budgeting 229
7.4   Optimisation Methods 232
7.5   Forecast Analyses 234
7.6   Examples and Exercises 235

8   Economic Efficiency in Practice 243
8.1   Procurement 244
8.2   Transport 246
8.3   Inventory Management 247
8.4   Manufacturing 249
8.5   Administration 252
8.6   Marketing 256
8.7   Examples and Exercises 257

9   Managerial Methods 263
9.1   Management 264
9.2   Planning 281
9.3   Execution 291
9.4   Supervision 300
9.5   Examples and Exercises 306

Glossary English—German 313

Glossary German—English 337

Bibliography 359

Index 363

List of Figures

Fig. 1.1   Objects of experience and of cognition in the economic sphere   4
Fig. 1.2   A tiered system of economic entities and economies   10
Fig. 1.3   Disciplines of business administration   13
Fig. 1.4   The building blocks of experienced reality   21
Fig. 1.5   The elements of science   24
Fig. 1.6   Methods of discovery   25
Fig. 1.7   The components of research   26
Fig. 1.8   The cognitive methods of research   29

Fig. 2.1   Examples of needs   39
Fig. 2.2   Typology of goods   41
Fig. 2.3   Four alternative methods of need fulfilment   42
Fig. 2.4   Public tasks and operational activities   44
Fig. 2.5   Aggregating individual preferences   47
Fig. 2.6   Instruments for needs control   48
Fig. 2.7   Types of market economy   51
Fig. 2.8   Types of planned economy   52
Fig. 2.9   Instruments for governmental environmental protection politics   56
Fig. 2.10 Administrative and fiscal law regulations   57
Fig. 2.11 Types of eco-tax   57
Fig. 2.12 Areas of environmental law   58

Fig. 3.1   Criteria for classifying economic agents   67
Fig. 3.2   The four basic types of economic agent   69

Fig. 4.1   Economic efficiency, efficiency and effectiveness   100
Fig. 4.2   Categories of economic efficiency   109

Fig. 5.1   Types of goal   119
Fig. 5.2   The goal system of economic entities   122
Fig. 5.3   Overview of goal functions   123
Fig. 5.4   Components of a goal concept   125
Fig. 5.5   Components of goal setting   127
Fig. 5.6   A universal system of production factors   130
Fig. 5.7   The four areas of nature   135

Fig. 5.8   Negative effects of use of the earth 136
Fig. 5.9   Cost types associated with the appropriation of nature 137
Fig. 5.10   Overview of diseconomies 138
Fig. 5.11   Characteristics of diseconomies 139
Fig. 5.12   Cost determinants 144
Fig. 5.13   Potential sources of weaknesses 145
Fig. 5.14   Ten steps from meaning to realisation 147
Fig. 5.15   Measurement and valuation of effects 148

Fig. 6.1   Calculating the closing balance 161
Fig. 6.2   Short-term coverage ratios 163
Fig. 6.3   Long-term coverage ratios 164
Fig. 6.4   Ratios and the golden rule 164
Fig. 6.5   Cash flow calculation 166
Fig. 6.6   Characteristics of expenditures and revenues 168
Fig. 6.7   Cash conversion cycle 170
Fig. 6.8   General forms of financing 171
Fig. 6.9   Types of expenses and income 172
Fig. 6.10   Categories of expenses and income 173
Fig. 6.11   Differentiating expenses and expenditures, income and revenues ... 174
Fig. 6.12   Structure of income statements 176
Fig. 6.13   Two income statement formats 177
Fig. 6.14   From annual surplus to net surplus 177
Fig. 6.15   EBIT and EBITDA calculation 178
Fig. 6.16   Categories of costs and outputs 180
Fig. 6.17   Categories of costs and outputs 181
Fig. 6.18   Examples of financial ratios 183
Fig. 6.19   Factors of production and cost types 184
Fig. 6.20   Chart of accounts 185
Fig. 6.21   Further categories of cost types 186
Fig. 6.22   Cost centres 186
Fig. 6.23   Basic structure of an overhead allocation sheet 187
Fig. 6.24   Cost estimate sheet for goods 189
Fig. 6.25   Cost estimate sheet for services 190
Fig. 6.26   Costing methods 190
Fig. 6.27   Components of an operating statement 191
Fig. 6.28   Combinations of costing systems 192
Fig. 6.29   Methods of calculating the operating result 193
Fig. 6.30   Valuation methods for external costs 196
Fig. 6.31   Valuation methods for external benefits 197
Fig. 6.32   Ecological accounting in the accounting system 198
Fig. 6.33   Types of accounting in companies 199
Fig. 6.34   Human resource accounting 200
Fig. 6.35   Outcome-impact result statement 208

Fig. 6.36   Structure of balance sheet 210
Fig. 6.37   Flow balance sheet 211
Fig. 6.38   Outcome-impact balance sheet 213

Fig. 7.1   Examples of ratios 223
Fig. 7.2   RoI ratio system 223
Fig. 7.3   Value added calculation—production approach 229
Fig. 7.4   Value added calculation—use approach 229
Fig. 7.5   Linear regression forecast 237
Fig. 7.6   Moving average forecast 238

Fig. 8.1   The circular economy 253
Fig. 8.2   Recovery and/or recycling of waste 254

Fig. 9.1   Functional system 265
Fig. 9.2   Hierarchical system 266
Fig. 9.3   Hybrid system 266
Fig. 9.4   Goal matrix with factors and functions 270
Fig. 9.5   The elements of management systems 272
Fig. 9.6   Process steps of management 275
Fig. 9.7   Management process as activity circuit 275
Fig. 9.8   Primary and secondary circuits in the management process 276
Fig. 9.9   Kinds of knowledge 278
Fig. 9.10   Skills for the application of knowledge 278
Fig. 9.11   Controllership in the management process 282
Fig. 9.12   Basic strategies 283
Fig. 9.13   Growth strategies 283
Fig. 9.14   SWOT analysis 284
Fig. 9.15   Portfolio analysis matrix 285
Fig. 9.16   Balanced scorecard 286
Fig. 9.17   Earnings planning 288
Fig. 9.18   Components of an acquisition plan 289
Fig. 9.19   Budget system of a multi-level concern 291
Fig. 9.20   Organisational structure 293
Fig. 9.21   Components of human resource management 296
Fig. 9.22   Indicators in personnel controllership 298
Fig. 9.23   Aspects of financial controllership 300
Fig. 9.24   Year-end auditing in a multi-level concern 304
Fig. 9.25   BCG matrix 311

Understanding Economic Activity

The Scientist must set in order. Science is built up with facts,
as a house is with stones. But a collection of facts is no more
a science than a heap of stones is a house.

Henri Poincaré (1854–1912)

Opening Vignette

Natalie Schmidt was sitting in the lounge of her parents' house. She was concentrating so much on her mobile phone that she did not hear her mother, Sarah, come into the room and gave a little jump when Sarah asked, "Well, have you decided yet?" Natalie looked up and said hesitantly, "No... not yet. I just don't know. There are so many things to think about."

"Before we talk about this other matter," replied her mother, "have you finished painting your room. I can see by the amount of paint in your hair that you have been painting, but is it actually done now?"

"I'm happy to say it's almost finished. I say 'almost' because I ran out of paint."

Sarah was shocked. "Are you kidding? I gave you enough to paint two rooms! What happened? You do know paint's not cheap, don't you?"

Natalie got defensive. "Of course I know. It's just that, well, I spilled a little bit." Sarah gasped, so Natalie quickly added, "Not a lot. And I cleaned it all up so you can't see a thing!" She followed her mother who had rushed into her bedroom and was relieved hear Sarah say, "All right, at least there's no paint on the floor, so you did a good job cleaning up. But you've spread the paint on far too thickly, there must be about three coats on that wall when you only need to do two coats with the paint I gave you. That's why it's not cheap."

They returned to the lounge. Natalie looked at her mother and said, "You seem a bit annoyed." "I am a bit annoyed. You haven't done a good job with painting your room. You've wasted a lot of paint and you haven't even completed the job. We couldn't afford to be like that in the factory where I work. We have to be efficient,

© Springer International Publishing AG 2018

P. Eichhorn, I. Towers, *Principles of Management*, Springer Texts in Business and Economics, https://doi.org/10.1007/978-3-319-70902-4_1

otherwise we'd lose a lot of money, and we have to be effective, otherwise we'd lose even more money. Now, back to the decision you have to make: are you going to study economics or business administration?"

1.1   Introduction

We deal in this book with efficiency (German: *Zweckmäßigkeit* or *Leistungsfähigkeit*), and effectiveness (German: *Zielorientierung* or *Wirksamkeit*) and economic efficiency (German: *Wirtschaftlichkeit*) and economic effectiveness (German: *wirtschaftliche Zielerreichung*). *Efficiency* generally refers to the relationship between resources and results. In a narrow sense, we are talking about the relationship between the input factors—resources, people, ideas, materials or services—and the goods and services that are the result of a process of transformation. Inputs and outputs can be measured in monetary or quantitative terms in order to calculate the *economic efficiency* of the entire transformation. In a broader sense, we take into account the external (non-market, i.e. meta-economic) effects that are experienced as outcomes and impacts. For example: a transformation process can produce not only finished goods but also pollution—therefore the outputs in this case include outcomes in the form of emissions which may have unwanted and negative impacts on the environment, which in turn negatively impacts health.

Effectiveness expresses the extent to which targets and goals have been met. It can be defined as the ratio between the actual and the desired result of the use of a given allocation of resources. Here too we must differentiate between two aspects—economic and meta-economic. *Economic effectiveness* measures, for example, the actual labour costs of a particular transformation process against the planned and expected costs for the total revenue generated. This approach can be similarly applied to political, social, technical or other actual and target goals.

The differences are shown in Eqs. (1.1), (1.2), (1.3) and (1.4).

$$Efficiency = \frac{Goal}{Means} = \frac{Benefit}{Cost} = \frac{Output + Outcome + Impact}{Resources\ used} \tag{1.1}$$

Equation 1.1 Efficiency

$$Effectiveness = \frac{Actual}{Planned} = \frac{Actual\ benefit}{Planned\ benefit}\ or\ \frac{Actual\ results}{Planned\ results} \tag{1.2}$$

Equation 1.2 Effectiveness

$$Economic\ efficiency = \frac{Output}{Costs}\ or\ \frac{Sales\ revenues}{Costs}\ or\ \frac{Output}{Input} \qquad (1.3)$$

Equation 1.3 Economic efficiency

$$Economic\ effectiveness = \frac{Actual\ costs}{Planned\ costs}\ or\ \frac{Actual\ profit}{Target\ profit} \qquad (1.4)$$

Equation 1.4 Economic effectiveness

A further consideration is the relationship between inputs and outputs. One approach—the principle of maximum result (Eq. 1.5)—is that given a certain input, the output should be as large as possible, e.g. how far can a car be driven on a single tank of petrol? A second approach—the principle of minimum means (Eq. 1.6)—is that the input should be as small as possible to produce a desired output, e.g. how little petrol do you need to travel from Munich to Stuttgart?

$$Max! = \frac{Output}{Input} \qquad (1.5)$$

Equation 1.5 Principle of maximum result

$$Min! = \frac{Input}{Output} \qquad (1.6)$$

Equation 1.6 Principle of minimum means

Human activity aimed at satisfying needs with scarce goods takes place in the economy through economic agents. Figure 1.1 presents the different types of economic agent and economy in anticipation of their discussion later in this book. The reader should turn to Sect. 1.6 for a discussion of what we mean by object of experience; in short, it is an element in the world as we perceive it. As Sect. 1.2 shows, objects of cognition are the things we study.

We can differentiate between the economic efficiency and effectiveness of the individual economic agents and that of the aggregate of all economic agents in an economy, which is a geographic area where economic activities take place. Depending on its scope, economic efficiency measures the relationship between individual or aggregate economic input and individual or aggregate output. Relationship is not understood here in a strict sense as a quantitative measure but rather as the result of a complex set of **causes and effects, goals and means in the economic sphere**.

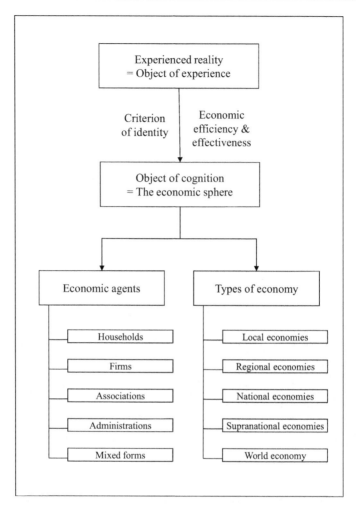

Fig. 1.1 Objects of experience and of cognition in the economic sphere

This book deals with economic agents, specifically business entities, which are organisations that are established and managed according to commercial or non-commercial law to sell or offer products or services. The former group consists, for example, of firms and partnerships while the latter group includes hospitals, charities and voluntary associations. The academic discipline *business administration* brings together theory and practice in the **study of business entities.** It deals with their internal and external environments, and the relationships between them. It concentrates on the functions of leadership, management, procurement, transport, storage, production, research and development, human resource management, administration, sales, investment, finance, taxation, accounting, auditing, marketing and more.

The **study of economies**—the academic discipline is economics—addresses all other economic relationships. An interesting issue is what level of aggregation is relevant, and this depends on the relation between the state and economic activity. The state becomes visible in institutions at various levels of government, from a small local authority to an international institution representing a community of countries. Economic activity can be aggregated accordingly, meaning that it is possible to discuss the local economy, the regional economy, the national economy, the supranational economy and the world economy: these are objects of cognition. In view of the development of internationalisation processes, the extension of cities beyond national borders and the globalisation of firms and other types of organisation, the concept of the national economy may soon belong to the past. Issues of local, regional, international and world economies are already closely entwined and will become even more so in the future.

1.2   The Objects of Cognition

1.2.1   Economic Entity

An **economic entity** is **autonomous in its decisions** and actions and has **factors of production permanently at its disposal.** The degree of autonomy—in planning and producing, for instance—and permanence of the availability of factors of production—e.g. people, machines and capital—must be examined on a case by case basis. Is the plant of an industrial enterprise an independent economic unit in itself or simply a part of one? What of the branch of a bank or of an insurance company, the hospital belonging to a non-profit institution, the building authority of a country, the land registry office of a city? These examples make it clear that the concept of economic entity is not limited to firms active in a market economy, for economic entities exist in market economies and planned economies, in the primary, secondary and tertiary sectors. They pursue different goals in the different ways and are owned by individuals, groups of individuals, other companies, cities, states, churches, associations and foundations.

The common denominator is that they (should) aim for economic efficiency and effectiveness in the combination of the factors of production. The principle of input and output is a general and abstract construct that is valid for any kind of economic entity, no matter what the inputs and outputs are. It is however also possible to think about economic entities in a more concrete way and acknowledge that what they do and how they do it have internal and external influences, with the consequence that their economic behaviour depends on their goals and on their environment—a custom motorcycle manufacturer in the United States will have some similarities with a mass-producer of motorcycles in China, but there will also be very many differences.

1.2.2   Local Economy

The term *local economy* describes the economic activities of all **economic agents in a municipal (or rural) area**. It includes not only private enterprises but also the households of the inhabitants, churches, communities, associations, public administrations, municipal-owned and state-owned enterprises. The local economy is the smallest economy that is analysed, and is significant from a theoretical as well as from a practical point of view because local economic agents often cooperate, compete against each other or are interdependent in a variety of other ways. There are, for example, interactions between a city administration and local enterprises, between suppliers, and between these and the city administration. A prosperous or a stagnant local economy is reflected in the local markets for labour, capital, goods and services, as well as in the private households, the public household and in the state of the natural environment.

Individual economic agents are affected by local laws and regulations, political developments and other local issues. Subsidies from the city can be important for companies, while all business entities are interested in the presence of potential customers (clients, guests or patients), suppliers, qualified personnel, transport infrastructure, educational institutions, recreational opportunities and prospects for the future development of the community.

Economic entities—and especially business entities—need to find **information** on local land planning, economic structure, employment, population development, production, aggregate income, economic growth, real estate prices, prices of the factors of production and other products, tariffs, taxes, public procurement, waste disposal and environmental protection. **Sources of information** are first of all the local administration; other sources include local experts, consulting firms and banks, while a company can of course carry out its own research, but this is really only necessary if public information sources are out of date, lack detail and provide no view of future developments.

1.2.3   Regional Economy

A regional economy is a **grouping of the local economies in a specific geographic area**. The size of the region depends, of course, on how it is defined—it may be neighbouring communities in the countryside (e.g. the northern part of Bavaria), or a state (e.g. Brandenburg). Typical examples are metropolitan areas on the one hand, such as the Ruhr, and regions lacking in infrastructure and with slow rates of development on the other, like the eastern part of Saxony. Just as in a local economy, individual economic agents and to the regional economy are closely linked, as the former try to exploit a region's strengths and cope with its weaknesses. The regional economy is an object of cognition for the fields of both business administration, which deals with aspects which are relevant for individual business entities, and economics, where the concern is to develop ideas and proposals for regional and economic policy.

Economists are mostly interested in the roles cities play in the region, cooperation between different localities, mobility within the region, development policies, migration, rural development, land planning, energy and water supply, traffic links, subsidies, industrial parks, infrastructure projects, waste disposal and the protection of the natural environment.

1.2.4   National Economy

The national economy is the original object of cognition of economics. Economics, whether historical or current, theoretical or applied, concerns itself with the **economic order of a country** (economic system), the network of relationships between the various actors in the economy (e.g. firms, private households, the state and foreign countries) and between economic branches (primary production, manufacturing and service sectors), the general state of economic processes (national accounts). Economic policy is concerned with laws and regulations (regulatory policy), economic processes and economic structures.

Although markets and competition, money and currencies, financial and social policy, employment, the economic cycle and growth remain their main themes, economists have recently started to pay more attention to issues related to the regional economy as a subsystem of the national economy, to supranational economic issues—dealing with the effects of Brexit on the European economic and monetary union, for example—and relationships with other supranational economies (e.g. ASEAN and Mercosur—see Sect. 1.2.5) and the global economy.

Economics as an academic discipline can provide insights both for business administration as a discipline and for economic entities. Lessons can be drawn from how economies develop—companies should consider economic trends in investment decisions, for example.

1.2.5   Supranational Economy

Supranational economies are **economic areas with a single economic policy that is followed in member states**. The community of states agrees to common economic goals, principles and measures and in doing so the member states surrender the relevant sovereign rights. The European Union is the most integrated supranational economy; others include the European Economic Area, the Association of South-East Asian Nations (ASEAN) and Mercosur, the South American counterpart. The forms of cooperation between member states range from coordination in individual areas (such as agriculture) and the financing of development projects all the way to the integration of currencies. In recent years trade agreements have been proposed which share some characteristics of supranational economies, but which cover even larger geographic areas. The most relevant are:

- The North American Free Trade Agreement (NAFTA) whose signatories are Mexico, the US and Canada. Signed in 1992, its goals are the elimination of barriers to investment and trade.
- The Transatlantic Trade and Investment partnership (TTIP) was a proposed agreement between the EU and the United States. Its goals were the removal (or at least reduction) of barriers to trade between the partners. There was much opposition to it in the EU and the agreement was never ratified.
- The Trans-Pacific Partnership (TTP) is an agreement between countries with access to the Pacific Ocean with similar aims as TTIP. China was never involved; the US signed the agreement under President Obama, but in January 2017 President Trump signed a memorandum to withdraw from it.
- The Comprehensive Economic and Trade Agreement (CETA) covers free trade between the EU and Canada. It was in the process of ratification in mid-2017.
- The Trade in Services Agreement (TISA) is a proposal covering service industries, with over 50 countries being represented. It has not yet been ratified.

Supranational economies help expand the activities of individual economic entities beyond national borders. The European Union, for example, guarantees the freedom of movement of workers, the freedom of establishment, and the freedom of movement of services, goods, capital and payments. ASEAN and Mercosur in contrast do not allow the freedom of movement of workers to the same degree. These developments mean increased competition on the national market as foreign companies can compete; motivated by this, individual economic entities are forced to improve their performance.

1.2.6 World Economy

Globalisation as we know it today has developed in the last 30 years as the result of the development of supranational economies and the kind of trade agreements mentioned in the previous section. In practical terms, globalisation means that economic entities are able to pursue their activities around the world. Technical progress has made possible the worldwide exchange of information, capital, services, goods and people. It has led to growing similarities between cultures—cinema, television, music, fashion and even food are less culturally specific than 50 years ago. One needs only to drive from Beijing airport to the city centre to see how popular American fast food is. Globalisation has opened up national and supranational economies and let them grow closer. Further reasons for this worldwide economic development include the active participation of newly industrialised countries in world trade, the opening up of China and the political change in other former socialist countries which have embraced the market economy. Also significant has been the rapid rise of neoliberalism as a political-economic philosophy. After the Second World War there were early moves towards the deregulation of trade—the General Agreement on Tariff and Trades (GATT), the formation of the World Bank and the Organisation for Economic Cooperation and Development (OECD).

The opportunities to be active on a world scale have given rise to ever larger enterprises, mainly in the form of multinational corporations which are organised as networks and build strategic alliances with their suppliers. Globally active firms choose to deploy their resources and carry out their activities anywhere in the world where they can find favourable conditions. Raw materials, other inputs, equity and debt capital, executive and skilled personnel are sourced and employed worldwide; production is located where labour is cheap or has skills that are difficult to find. The choices in location, transport, warehousing, production, disposal, research and marketing are global. They favour those countries which are seen as attractive by enterprises, for example because they have lower levels of taxation, fewer environmental burdens, less burdensome regulation and bureaucracy or even less workers' participation in decision-making. For example: Facebook has its European headquarters in Ireland because the data protection rules in that country are not as strict as in other European countries, the corporate tax rate is lower, and there is a ready supply of qualified multi-lingual staff.

Beginning in the 1970s political forces in Europe and the US were able to win wide acceptance for policies like privatisation and deregulation which encourage globalisation. This is the logic of neoliberalism, putting in the forefront the interests of large enterprises and transferring power from the state to the enterprises themselves. Instead of being active, a "minimal" state only reacts to global developments. This process creates winners (such as large enterprises) and losers (e.g. countries which lose economic activity and cannot use their production capacity). Individual economic entities and whole economic areas (local, regional, national, supranational and global) have new opportunities but face new risks. This requires the creation of new worldwide regulatory frameworks, for example in areas such as the protection of competition or of the natural environment—there is still much progress to be made in these respects.

The objects of cognition described above form a tiered system of economic agents as shown in Fig. 1.2. The small circles represent the individual economic entities. Figure 1.2 does not show the interdependencies between the objects of cognition but these relations exist and are very complex. They range from the horizontal (e.g. between economic regions), to the vertical (e.g. between the national economy and regional economies), to the diagonal (e.g. between the national economy of one country and one of the regional economies of a neighbouring country). The relations can be bilateral or multilateral, regulated or determined by market forces and can be characterised by cooperation or competition.

1.3 Business Administration

1.3.1 Tasks

Business administration (sometimes known as *management studies* or simply *management*) as an academic field has two prime tasks: **it analyses economic entities** (such as small and large companies, hospitals, charities, and government

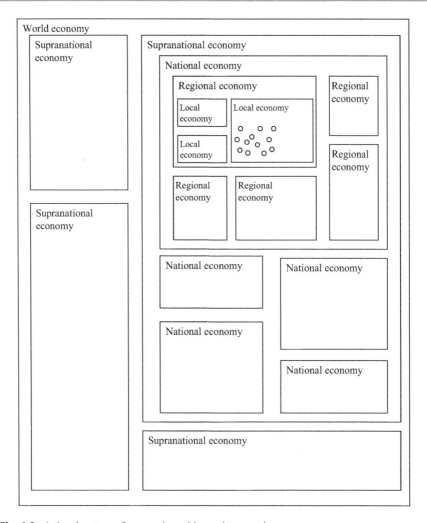

Fig. 1.2 A tiered system of economic entities and economies

agencies) and **communicates the results of its analyses.** Like other academic
disciplines, it has its own approaches, goals and methods (see Sect. 1.8). It is
concerned not only with the economic aspects of economic entities—their goals,
principles, decisions and decision-making, behaviours, structures and processes
etc.—but also with the environment in which they find themselves, and the
relationships and dependencies between them and the market, society, the state
and nature. There are interfaces to other disciplines such as economics, political
science, law, the social sciences and the environmental sciences.

Compared to other areas, business administration as a subject is characterised by
its efforts to do more than build **theories**; it is equally concerned with **practicality**.

In other words, theory and practice are intertwined and there is a constant endeavour to create transfers from theory to practice and vice-versa. This is why business administration as an area of academic endeavour must carry out both basic and applied research and be based on scientific methods but at the same time prepare those who study it for the world of work.

Given their number and diversity, the field of business administration cannot restrict itself to just a few types of economic entity. Historically, scholars have concerned themselves with privately-owned, profit-oriented manufacturing companies (the supply side) and with private households in their role of consumers (the demand side). While more work is being done today than a few years ago on the service industries, they still receive relatively little attention from business administration academics, while the agricultural sector receives even less. Still under-researched from a business administration point of view are private households seen as economic entities that have to deal with issues like generating income, spending and investing, decision-making, book-keeping (for tax!) and the division of labour. The same is also true of non-profit economic entities like unions, associations, institutions of higher education, chambers of trade, churches, hospitals, social insurance organisations, social welfare institutions with their services and their establishments. Similarly neglected are federal, regional and municipal administrations, with the services they provide, the facilities, libraries, museums, schools, theatres, technology parks they own, and the courts of justice, prisons and parliaments they run. This neglect is one reason for the oft-criticised management issues in all these institutions!

Since all economic entities have to deal with management issues, the number of potential recipients of the knowledge and skills needed for their management is nearly unlimited. Management knowledge does not have the same value in all situations; a commercial enterprise exposed to strong competition in a mature market will place a very high value on it because it can be crucial for the survival of the enterprise. On the other hand, management knowledge plays a minor role if the pursuit of a concrete goal (for example cultural sponsorship) is financed by a generously endowed foundation. Generally speaking, whether professional managers (by which we mean people for whom managing is their main responsibility) are needed alongside architects, chemists, computer experts, economists, engineers, journalists, sociologists, theologians etc. depends on the goals, the types of activity, the size, the market form, the type of product and the financing of the economic entity. Management education must provide the knowledge and competencies required by specialists in different functions, such as procurement, budgeting, controlling, logistics, personnel management or marketing, and also the knowledge and competencies required by senior executives, who, being generalists, often need economic, legal and technical knowledge. A further concern of management education is the training of the next generation of academics in the field.

The study of management in Germany has a long history, going back to the middle of the seventeenth century, but really grew in importance at the end of the nineteenth and beginning of the twentieth century when specialist colleges were established in Leipzig (1898), Cologne and Frankfurt (1901), Berlin (1906), Mannheim (1907) and Munich (1910), as well as in other cities. These were either integrated later into existing universities or formed the basis of a new university. German management studies have always had a very strong basis in accounting and operations management. In recent years, many developments from English-speaking management studies have been integrated, both in terms of their content and linguistically—*budgeting*, *consulting*, *outsourcing*, *marketing* and *reengineering* are examples of words that now form part of the German language.

1.3.2 Taxonomy

The subjects that fall within the discipline of business administration can be classified according to various criteria. In Germany, one of the first classifications was based on the area of activity: banks, trading companies, industrial enterprises, hospitals, transport enterprises or insurance companies. Evidence of this **institutional** classification is to be found in the names of business administration professorships at German universities. The most common classification today is **based on functions**, i.e. on the activities of economic entities, which, although they can be very different, must nevertheless concern themselves with functions like accounting, auditing, finance, human resource management, logistics, marketing, operations management, organisational behaviour and taxation.

A third, newer, taxonomy— sectoral classification—takes as its starting point issues that are relevant for society and the economy as a whole, and tries to find the best way, from the point of view of business administration, to deal with them. For example, educational management deals with problems like how to make sure that the right quantity and quality of human resources is available and that they have the correct skills and competencies. Healthcare management has the goal of delivering complex medical and related services in a cost-effective way. Social management searches for strategies, structures and processes for social care institutions and environmental management is concerned with the protection of the natural foundations of life. These sectoral disciplines have in common that they connect the fields of business administration and economics—educational management and educational economics, healthcare management and health economics, social management and the economics of social care, environmental management and environmental economics. Each pair is closely related in terms of teaching and research, with each discipline contributing to the overall understanding of the sector.

Public management and non-profit management are special cases in business administration. They can be identified as functional disciplines, because they deal with public tasks and their efficient and effective execution. However, since the other functional disciplines focus on areas like sales, production and procurement that relate to the internal tasks of economic entities, and public and non-profit management focus on the internal aspects of the entities that perform public tasks, we classify them as sectoral disciplines. Public tasks derive from political goals, which are set in the general or public interest, and can be the duties of a

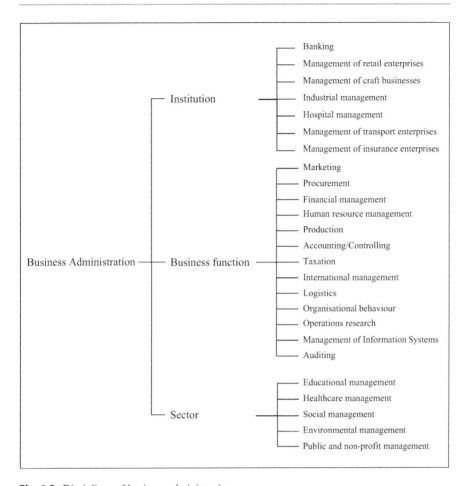

Fig. 1.3 Disciplines of business administration

governmental body or other public services. These can be delivered in non-market (as is the case for national defence) or market form (e.g. through outsourcing). Public tasks are performed by federal, central, regional and local institutions, institutions of higher education, social insurance institutions and other organisations such as unions, churches, foundations, associations and companies charged with the execution of a public task. This is why public and non-profit management are very closely related disciplines.

Figure 1.3 shows the different disciplines that together form the field of business administration.

1.3.3 Concepts

In business administration, the search for truth is almost without exception directed towards the joint principles of economic efficiency and effectiveness. A number of approaches have emerged which try to discover ways in which these principles can be understood and applied.

The **decision-oriented approach** concentrates on the problems of information gathering, the formulation of possible alternatives for action, and the use of quantitative methods as support tools.

The **systems approach** views businesses and other organisations as goal-oriented social systems, whose regulatory and control mechanisms are studied and then used to shape future events.

The assumption that some economic agents are more efficient and effective than others dominates the **comparative approach**, which emphasises comparisons of various kinds (e.g. planned vs. actual output) within an economic entity and between economic entities.

The **behavioural approach** focuses on the behaviour of individuals and groups given certain objectives and constraints; this approach analyses conflicts between individual and institutional goals, incentive systems, and so on.

The **labour-oriented approach** is closely related to the behavioural approach. It concentrates on employees and working conditions, on cooperative leadership styles and on better participation in decision-making processes. This approach serves as a counterweight to traditional business administration which generally looks at issues from the point of view of capital. In the English-speaking world there exists the Critical Management Studies approach, which, as its name implies, challenges conventional views.

The **environment-oriented approach** explores the integration of economic entities in their social and natural environment, and their (corporate) social responsibility. It is concerned with finding and operationalising ways of measuring what economic entities do regarding their social and natural environment.

A more recent approach is the **institutional economic perspective**. Based on institutional microeconomics, it is being increasingly adapted by researchers, principally in marketing, organisational behaviour and human resource management. The rise of this approach and the development of evolutionary perspectives on market processes, the use of resources and corporate functions suggest a growing interest in general business administration.

1.4   Related Disciplines

1.4.1 Economics

The most closely related discipline to business administration is economics. Both deal with real phenomena (which is why we talk about them as empirical disciplines) and have economic efficiency and effectiveness as objects of cognition.

Economics is concerned with **economic processes within economic entities** (which are represented individually in abstract form or grouped with others) **and in the national economy**. In contrast to business administration, which aims at describing, explaining and predicting decisions and actions from the point of view of an individual economic entity, economics has its main focus on economic aggregates. Economics explains economic relationships and predicts economic events by building hypotheses for propositions of a general nature that can be verified.

Economics is normally divided into microeconomics and macroeconomics. The focus of **microeconomics** are rational economic agents acting as producers and consumers. Their behaviour (as sources of supply and demand) is the object of the theory of the firm and of budget theory. Partial analysis in microeconomics deals with price formation on a single market or on the relationships between upstream and downstream market stages. Total analysis looks at the relationships that exist at a given time between all enterprises and households in all markets. Competition theory, which includes the analysis of the mechanisms and processes of coordination among market participants, is also part of microeconomics.

Macroeconomics analyses economic relationships on the basis of aggregation, for example of households, firms, the state and foreign countries on the one side and income, consumption, savings and investment on the other. Of interest are the generation and distribution of income and assets, employment, the economic cycle and price levels, growth and external trade. Macroeconomics is not concerned with the behaviour of individual economic agents.

A new discipline, **mesoeconomics**, has developed between microeconomics and macroeconomics. It deals less with individual economic entities or aggregates and more with industries, groups or regions. Mesoeconomics, like the two other fields of economics, is more concerned with the theoretical than the practical.

1.4.2   Economic Policy

Economic policy deals with the form the economic system takes and its influencing factors, with economic processes and with the structure of the economy. It shows the possibilities and limits of interventions in the economy, meaning that it provides tools that governments can use as they develop their (practical) economic policies. For this reason, some scholars maintain that economic policy is a field of academic endeavour where it is difficult to remain objective and neutral.

The core of **regulatory policy** (i.e. the policies concerned with the form of the economic system) is competition policy, which has the aim of keeping markets functioning properly. In a social market economy, great importance is attached to regulatory policy, social policy and environmental policy, since they help correct the effects of pure market forces on infrastructure, society and ecology. Regulatory policy in a planned economy consists primarily of imposing the decisions and concepts of a central administration on all economic agents.

Growth policy is concerned with shaping and influencing the complete economic process through indirect measures rather than rules and regulations. Unlike in a market economy, it is possible in a planned economy to directly control what economic agents do. Growth policies aimed at a constant improvement of the supply of goods in the economy normally cause structural changes, so that they must be accompanied by **structural policy**. Sectoral structural policies can be developed for areas such as agriculture, energy, housing, industry and transport, and regional structural policies can also be produced. Depending on the type of monetary instruments used, fiscal policy (in particular budget and tax policy), monetary policy, credit policy and currency policy are developed and implemented.

1.4.3   Public Finance

This discipline covers **theory and policies relating to the state economy**, i.e. central, regional and local authorities and their budgets. The main areas of research are revenues and expenditures policies, and their effect on the allocation of capital and labour in the economy, the distribution and redistribution of income and assets, and the maintenance of economic stability.

Economic theory, economic policy and public finance are traditionally the main components of economics. Discussions on issues that concern specific sectors have given rise to a number of more specialised disciplines, the main ones of which are described next.

1.4.4   Educational Economics

Educational economics studies the economics of basic, professional, higher and continuing education and training. The theoretical and practical interests of educational economics concern the **contribution of the educational system** (primary, secondary, tertiary and other) **to the national product and economic growth**. Researchers investigate, for example, the relationship between training, investment in education and income, trying to find the return on education—an attempt to describe the correlation between investment in education and its yield. A production theory of the educational system has been developed, which deals with the problems of measuring educational output and the possibilities for strengthening competition in the educational market. The goal is to provide the basis for educational policy and the planning of educational measures. The principles, methods and tools of empirical social research are particularly useful in this context.

The corresponding discipline in business administration is **educational management**, which deals primarily with functional aspects relevant to educational institutions, such the optimal size of schools, the planning and financing of school buildings, the adoption of modern media in education, the costs of school administration, incentive systems for educators and students, leadership styles, public relations and so on.

1.4.5   Health Economics

The goal of health economics is to investigate the impact of the health system on the national economy. It analyses health, seen as a good, through health indicators. How should healthcare services be supplied and demanded? How can the **behaviour of actors** in the healthcare system be managed, such as physicians, nurses, pharmacists, providers of emergency services, hospitals, health insurers, professional associations, regulatory bodies, pharmaceutical companies and unions? How should the **interfaces** of the healthcare system be managed, for example between inpatient and outpatient services, diagnosis and therapy, prevention, care and after-care? How can the cooperation between different parts of the system be improved? What are the benefits of health research, health education, early recognition of diseases, the fight against addiction, self-care, fees for the provision of services? The answers to these questions are sought by the discipline of public health.

Healthcare management is concerned with issues such as factor procurement, service provision and delivery in the various economic entities within the health sector. More specifically, it deals with such decisions as: in-house or external procurement (make-or-buy, outsourcing, contracting out), efficiency (lean management, lean production), management structure, organisational structure, comprehensive (Total Quality Management) or partial quality assurance (via certification), vertical or horizontal cooperation, health centres or specialised clinics. On top of this come budgeting, controllership, financing and the marketing of state-owned, municipal, non-profit hospitals and of private commercial hospitals and other health facilities.

1.4.6   Social Economics

Social economics is particularly difficult to define since social issues are intrinsic to all areas of economics, so it is helpful to adopt a narrower definition in order to describe it. Social economics describes, explains and characterises social phenomena from an economics point of view. This happens primarily through the **theory of social policy**, which articulates the basic values of society and strives for the improvement of the life conditions of individuals that are not well situated and in need of protection. At the core of social economics are risks to life, and the economic needs which may then develop.

Social management deals with the management of the various kinds of economic entity that are active in this field, such as homes for the young and for the elderly, professional training centres, welfare centres, charities, social insurance bodies, youth and social welfare institutions, as well as the social services provided by for-profit enterprises.

1.4.7 Environmental Economics

Environmental economics is an area of growth within the whole field of economics; it links knowledge about economics with the ecological challenges the world faces. **External effects**, i.e. effects outside market mechanisms, restrict economic growth, so the view that the **natural elements** (earth, water, air and space) are a further factor of production alongside the traditional ones is gaining recognition world-wide. It is as important to think about the natural environment as about efficiency and effectiveness on the supply side, while on the demand side, consumption cannot be understood without taking it into consideration. It is necessary to go beyond input-output ratios when measuring the size of outcomes and impacts by looking at the pollution caused by industry and traffic and its effect on people, animals, vegetation and nature in general. Only knowledge of causal relationships and the size of external diseconomies make it possible to design adequate measures of environmental policy.

Environmental management explores and explains ecological issues at the level of the individual economic entity. Firms, private households, associations and public institutions—if they are concerned with environmental protection—can (and should) regularly verify the extent to which their activities (e.g. procurement, transport, storage, production, disposal, marketing, research and administration) are carried out in an environmentally friendly way. Relevant information is provided by environmental accounting and auditing.

1.5 Neighbouring Disciplines

While all economics and business administration disciplines are directly concerned with the various aspects of economic efficiency and effectiveness, there are various disciplines which, although they have other objects of cognition and deal with different questions, are able to provide useful support as well as data and facts to the economic and management sciences. The neighbouring disciplines outlined below offer a wider view by having premises, influences, and understandings that go beyond the purely economic and so prevent the other approaches from becoming too narrow.

Business informatics is a special area of informatics dealing with electronic data processing in production and administrative processes in economic entities of all kinds. It is becoming increasingly important, especially in these days of big data and the internet of things.

The themes of **business psychology** are the experiences and the behaviour of individuals engaged in economic activities. It deals with how people perceive their economic environment, with their attitudes, with the motives guiding them, with how, if at all, it is possible to predict their opinions and behaviours. Psychology is used as a tool primarily in human resource management and marketing, and now increasingly in the financial industry—behavioural economics and behavioural finance study the effects of psychological factors on economic decisions.

Economic criminology is concerned with major economic crime—offences connected to professional or corporate activities. Such crimes include the establishment of fake companies, fraud on capital investments, credit fraud, cheque fraud, currency fraud, illegal employment, subsidies fraud, insurance fraud, tax crimes, customs fraud, false accounting, computer criminality, environmental offences, obstruction to competition, bankruptcy fraud. Individuals' offences, such as small theft, moonlighting or tax evasion is not included. Researchers look at the economic crimes of individuals and at organised economic crime.

The task of **business education** is to determine what knowledge is needed to understand and be active in work, business and the economy, and ways in which this might be organised. The concern of didactics is how the required knowledge can best be transferred.

Thanks to the insights of **business ethics**, there is now a widespread belief that economic activities do not necessarily have to follow the maxim of laissez-faire or that those involved should have a purely egocentric view of the world. The main principle of business ethics is that market logic cannot apply to all aspects of life and that economic activities must take into account social and ecological needs.

Economic geography explains how economic activities are organised spatially. Typical issues are the interdependencies between purchasing, transport, storage, production, disposal and sales by industrial enterprises and the locations where these activities take place and the demands that are made on these locations. Land is a location factor—it is a source of raw materials, a basis for road and rail transport, a carrier of energy and water distribution networks, a place where waste can be deposited, a place for culture and life, and a good for public consumption.

Economic history analyses the economic development of countries, regions, cities, industries and companies. It attempts to locate economic activity in the wider context of processes of social, political, technical and scientific change. Economic historians investigate topics such as household economy in the ancient world, the exchange of money in the middle ages, the trading firms of the Medici, Fugger and Welser families, mercantilism, liberalism, industrialisation, war economies, and currency reform.

Economics and business journalism is the production and delivery of information on economic events through the various on-line and traditional media. News on economic policies, industries, unions, associations of enterprises, individual enterprises, bankruptcies, trade exhibitions, market processes, stock quotes, people in management positions, income and assets statistics are typical subjects.

Economic and business law encompasses all the laws that are relevant for participants in economic processes, be they natural or legal persons. It includes the rules for the exchange of goods and services on markets between producers, traders and consumers by defining the framework within which contractual relations can exist, as well as the legal relations between the participants in economic processes and the state. All areas of economic activity are included in its reach, from truth in advertising to minimum wage.

Economic sociology applies sociological knowledge to topics that concern the economy as a whole and individual economic entities. It explores the division of labour as a relationship between individuals, and the overall relationship between the economy and society. Industrial sociology analyses roles and conflicts in the industrial society; organisational sociology deals with the relations between people and organisations and between people within organisations, similar to administrative sociology in public institutions.

Economic and business statistics capture and describe economic events in numbers. Statistics are gathered about populations, enterprises, workplaces, agriculture, industries, exports, traffic, incomes, consumption, prices, finance, tax, money and credit statistics, as well as national statistics. The resulting data allow the assessment of individual economic entities, industries, local, regional and national economies.

1.6   Understanding the World and Business Administration

We have just provided an overview of the areas that are involved in the study of economics, business and management, and in this book we will be addressing many topics related to these areas. Before going any further though, we want to take a step back and talk about themes that are not normally part of any economics, business or management textbook, but which are important because they lie at the root of how we act in the world. It is important to think critically about what we do as scholars, as managers, as humans, and why we do it, so in this section we address the perception of reality, the search for truth and how we try to learn about what we are studying. As we cover topics later in the book, you may find it interesting to refer again to these sections. For example, a great deal of marketing is concerned with our perceptions of ourselves, of products and services. When top managers develop a new strategy, it will be based on the ways in which they perceive the world. Their thought processes play a role in determining the decisions they make. Product managers carry out research into new products for new markets—they are trying to reach the truth. Companies that carry out research and developments activities usually are carrying out applied science (but not always).

We are firmly of the belief that this part of the chapter provides a valuable background for helping you to understand what is happening below the surface when you are thinking, talking or taking action. Indeed, we suggest that readers spend some time finding out about their own styles of perceiving, thinking and learning. Understanding these things about ourselves helps us to understand others better.

In addition, what we say below about research is not just relevant for scholars and students. Managers—no matter where they work—are always involved in research, so an understanding of the principles involved does in fact have a practical benefit, even if this does not seem obvious at first. For evidence of this, look at Sect. 1.9.

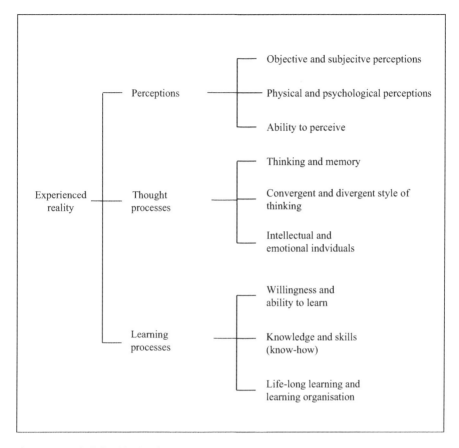

Fig. 1.4 The building blocks of experienced reality

1.6.1   Experienced Reality

How we experience and perceive reality depends on how we perceive it, how and what we think about it, and how and what we learn. Why do we address this issue in this book? Because our behaviour and our thinking are influenced to a huge extent by our "reality", which may of course be very different from someone else's "reality". In order to be able to make good decisions, to work with others, we need to understand how we build our "reality", because our "reality" has a major impact on everything we do. Figure 1.4 shows the components that contribute to how we experience reality—and experienced reality is the starting point of human activity.

1.6.2   Perceptions

We perceive the world in which we live through our senses. Objects, living things and situations stimulate feelings and reactions. The five senses (hearing, seeing, smelling, tasting and touching) are different from person to person. This leads to multiple perceptions of reality. Since we would like to know whether our perceptions are right and how others perceive the world, we must look for the common features of subjective perceptions. It is possible, under certain conditions, to generalise the common features of **subjective** perceptions and derive **objective** perceptions from them. Senses are, however, unreliable: what appears to be an objective perception can be based on a mistake and may need to be revised. Our imprecise and limited perception of reality shuts us off from a truthful representation of reality. Reality is what we perceive it to be.

How the world is perceived is a very complex process. Beyond **physical** and **psychological** perception, which takes place selectively given the enormous number of stimuli in the environment, there are processes of thinking and learning. Perception, thinking and learning are influenced by the innate characteristics of every person (sex, age, genetic inheritance) and by their processing in the human conscience. Each of us has attitudes, which may be understood as our points of view of real phenomena, as well as motives, to be understood as forces that lead us into taking (mental or physical) action. We can look at this from the other side: perceptions, thinking and learning processes shape attitudes and motives. Reactions to our perceptions are varied: adaptation, opposition, reinforcement, speeding up or stopping.

1.6.3   Thought Processes

Thought can be described as the consequence of the desire to seek knowledge or as the processing of perceptions. Thought is therefore developed in processes in which short-term and long-term memory play an important role. **Memory** can be seen as a repository that allows for perception and thought. But we must be aware that we can only perceive and think about what we are able to perceive and think about.

Thoughts develop in an orderly or disorderly fashion. There can, of course, be a mixture between systematic, disciplined, continuous, straight and convergent thought and non-systematic, undisciplined, free, intermittent and divergent thought. The condition for a convergent **style of thought** is the availability of hard, concrete information, whereas a divergent style of thought is possible with less explicit information. Different styles of thought are based in different parts of the brain, and the development of these parts contributes to each person's preferred way of perceiving and thinking. A convergent style of thought is associated with a detailed and real description of the environment and conclusions are reached in a logical way. A divergent style of thought has intuitive, vague features and conclusions are more likely to be based on feelings.

If we classify individuals according to their dominant style of thought—keeping in mind that both styles can co-exist, even on an equal basis—we can identify the intellectual type and the emotional type. The former is analytical, follows logic, is objective, takes herself out of the equation, is cold towards things and other people, plans, plans and supervises, takes goal-oriented and results-oriented decisions. The latter is guided by feelings, attaches importance to values, is subjective, includes herself, is involved with other people and even with objects, improvises, is flexible and spontaneous, does not like to take decisions and if so, they are based on "gut feeling". Both types have their own breadth of interests, experience, energy and creativity. Individuals' decision-making styles will reflect these styles of thought.

1.6.4 Learning Processes

Perception and thought are reinforced by learning. Learning, too, develops in processes, namely through experience and practice. Learning processes can be managed through education and learning programmes. Simple learning happens by imitation or by reflex, while intelligent learning takes place when an individual discovers a course of action which promises a successful outcome.

Learning requires **willingness and ability**. The will and ability to learn can coincide or diverge. The latter is the case when someone is willing to learn but, for whatever reason, is not able to learn or on the other hand able to learn but not willing to do so. Successful learning requires a certain amount of both qualities.

The result of learning is better know-how or more knowledge and better skills. The acquisition of **knowledge and skills** takes place in schools, colleges and universities—but also in the home and at work. In an increasingly knowledge-based society, the importance of general, technical and management knowledge as well as of intellectual, communicative, technocratic, physical and psychological skills cannot be overestimated. Basic education is often not enough for know-how and skills must be deepened and widened: life-long learning is the response to a rapidly changing environment. A learning organisation tries to counteract the obsolescence of the know-how of its members.

1.7   Research

1.7.1   The Search for Truth

The question of whether cognitive perception and its processing lead to true insights applies to both **pure and applied science**. The difference between the two is based on whether extending knowledge is an end in itself of the research, or answering needs and pursuing the common good. In our current understanding, pure and applied sciences are not alternative, but complementary. It is impossible to draw a border between the two, since assertions arising from pure research end up being

Fig. 1.5 The elements of science

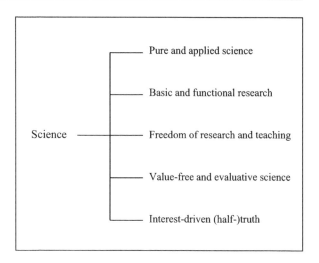

used in practice, and conclusions drawn from applied research head in the opposite direction.

Research is entrusted with the search for the truth; we make a distinction between **basic and functional research**. The former aims at fundamental knowledge, the latter at knowledge which can be used in practice. Both types of research can be encountered in the natural sciences, humanities, social sciences and economic and management sciences. Research serves social and technical progress, and this means not only research on the future or on the impact of technical progress, but also historical research, without which one cannot fully investigate, explain and evaluate the developments and connections of today.

In many countries it is taken for granted that there should be **freedom of research and teaching**. Indeed, this concept is anchored in the Basic Law of the Federal Republic of Germany—Article 5 Para. 3 states "Arts and sciences, research and teaching shall be free. The freedom of teaching shall not release any person from allegiance to the constitution." Limits to research are usually based on ethical considerations.

A further issue is the independence of assertions from value judgements. Difficulties arise in particular in applied research and teaching since the search for the truth cannot be exclusively value free, however desirable some might feel this to be. Applied research must deal with the fact that people have views on its value, sometimes based on ethics. Applied research is therefore only to a certain extent **value-free** and is indeed primarily an **evaluative science**. A researcher beholden to truth will try to uncover the viewpoints from more than one subjective position. It is essential her perceptions are as value-free as possible, that she be aware of them and make clear her subjective position. In practice though, it is quite common to observe the establishment of half-truths, which aim to serve particular interests, not science or research.

- Observation and gathering of information (e.g. market analyses)

- Evaluation of published writings (literature analyses)

- Surveys of archive materials, reports, laws, plans and catalogues (document analyses)

- Interviews and written enquiries

- Experiments, case studies and business simulations

- Primary data and evaluation

- Secondary data (e.g. benchmarking, financial ratios analyses)

- Building and evaluating models

- Application of mathematical methods

Fig. 1.6 Methods of discovery

Figure 1.5 shows the elements that contribute to science as a way of seeking the truth.

Three modes of thinking guide researchers in the search for the truth—the investigation of causes, relationships and effects: making discoveries, finding rationales and understanding decision-making. Each can contribute to learning.

1.7.2   Discoveries

Discoveries occur when **unknown facts are identified**, either in relation to more theoretical or more practical matters. As far as theoretical matters are concerned, the researcher tries to contribute to the logic of discovery and to the theory of cognitive progress. Practice-oriented discoveries draw empirically based conclusions on real phenomena. Conclusions are well-founded when—given the same premises—other independent researchers with similar competencies also draw them. As far as economics and business administration are concerned, new learnings arise from discoveries which are either empirically validated or derived from logic. In this kind of research, there are normally no such laws as those in mathematics or in the natural sciences, but rather uniformities, propositions and tendencies, which are valid only on the basis of certain (arguable but not necessarily proven) assumptions.

Figure 1.6 provides an overview of the most important methods of discovery.

1.7.3   Rationales

The search for the rationale for an assertion involves understanding what it is saying and finding an explanation; it involves the investigation of assumptions and hypotheses with regard to their empirical verifiability, the logical implications and the value of the methods. Starting from the knowledge of facts, rationales explain relationships, with a main interest being the ability to make links between

Fig. 1.7 The components of research

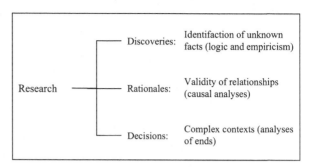

cause and effect; these **causal analyses** ask, "what if?" If the same effects recur, we can speak about patterns or (natural) laws depending on how well founded the rationale is.

1.7.4 Decisions

Decisions made by an individual have effects and results, and so it is necessary during the process to consider ends and means. The goal of the **analysis of ends** is to direct the use of resources appropriately. While looking for rationales helps us to explain relationships between causes and effects, this analysis captures the logical and actual relationships between means and ends and hence is a support for decision-making.

Two ways of decision-making can be identified: **normative** decision theory looks for rules to take rational decision-making; rationality in decision-making and action is a basic assumption. **Descriptive** decision theory deals with the actual decision-making process. This theory seeks to derive valid conclusions from empirical observations. The problem normative decision theory tries to solve is how rational decision-makers should make decisions, while descriptive decision theory is interested in how people actually make decisions, why they behave in a certain way and what decisions can be expected.

Figure 1.7 shows the cognitive interests of research.

1.8   Cognitive Methods

1.8.1 Method Diversity

Cognitive methods are aligned with research interests. Discoveries, rationales and decisions can be analysed in purely theoretically, or in practical contexts. In other words, the way in which the problem is formulated and its possible solutions indicate whether the wish is to generate pure or applied knowledge.

Terms such as "theory and practice" and "research and practice" sometimes create difficulties and mislead us into using "theory" and "research" as synonyms.

Although this might be legitimate in normal language, science distinguishes between pure and applied disciplines. "Theory" has a narrower meaning than "research". Within academic disciplines we can differentiate between **theory** and **policy**. Business administration for example distinguishes between investment theory and investment policy, sales theory and sales policy, finance theory and finance policy.

Having set adequate premises, the theorist derives functional connections between causes and effects (**deduction**). These assertions are logically correct in regards to the premises, but not necessarily true. **Induction** is the inference of general rules from empirically observed facts.

The search for empirically based truthful propositions in the form of discoveries, rationales and decisions is based on **three stages of analysis**: description, explanation and prediction. Through the **description** of perceptions we can formulate propositions that are specific to a particular place and time. Besides descriptive questions of the kind "What is it?" or "What was it?", a further interesting question is "Why is it so?"

Explanation looks for an answer to that question, moving beyond considerations of specific time and place. As long as explanatory propositions withstand empirical test so that they are true, they result in a law, and a number of logically connected laws build a theory.

Prediction is closely linked with explanation. Here we have to reverse the process. Instead of making a hypothesis according to which a given cause will generate certain empirically verifiable effects, here we predict the occurrence of a certain event. If, for example, the hypothesis that examination results are influenced by the amount of time spent studying is valid, we can make a proposition which predicts that the more a student studies, the better their exam results. This proposition also has a hypothetical character and needs to be confirmed by reality.

If what has been predicted does not occur, the hypothesis has been refuted by reality, which is called **falsification**. According to Karl R. Popper (1902–1994), empirical propositions must be formulated in such a way that they may fail to withstand reality. As long as a hypothesis is not falsified or contradicted, it has to be considered (for the time being) true. On the other hand, the **verification** or confirmation of a hypothesis does not ensure its truthfulness. Necessary for this would be the verification of the validity of the hypothesis with all possible real circumstances to which it can be applied, and this is normally impossible for reasons of time, cost and practicality.

1.8.2   Modelling

Reality's complexity is such that it is impossible to comprehend it completely. This is why we make do with building a **simplified image of reality**—a model. A few items are extracted from the multitude of actual phenomena and although they are not separate and isolated in reality, their use in a model can produce knowledge. Generally, the **ceteris-paribus method** is used: one variable—the control or dependent variable—is isolated from a complex of variables and by keeping all other variables constant (the independent variables) it is possible to investigate the influence of the control variable on an outcome.

Partial and global models differ in their frames of reference: they can be static or dynamic, depending on whether they refer to a single or several time periods. **Explicative and decision models** are chosen according to the problem being addressed. Different types of model have different assumptions about outcomes: **deterministic models** imply absolute certainty; **stochastic models** imply probability and **game-theory based models** do not even assign a probability to possible outcomes.

1.8.3 The Issue of Values

Unlike mathematics and to a much greater extent than the natural sciences, the humanities and in particular social, and economic and management sciences are confronted with the problem of values. In economic and management science normative conditions and subjective evaluations are introduced, so that objective knowledge becomes subjective knowledge. In the interests of scientific objectivity, the researcher should strive to be neutral, but if this is not possible, should declare her own biases openly.

In methodological debates, extreme positions often turn out to be one-sided and questionable. There is no position of "either...or" when it comes to values in the academic discipline of business administration, for there is only "both...and." While generally recognising the premise of neutrality, yet knowing that it can never be fully achieved, we should accept that value judgements and ideology exist and can be criticised. Common ground can be found in dialogue where experts come together, leading to the establishment of agreed values through **processes of communication.**

1.8.4 Terminology

Gaining knowledge and transferring it require the availability of concepts and their proper use in language through having the right terminology. Concepts and terms are not an end in themselves, but serve as means for the goals of knowledge and communication. It is necessary to define concepts as tightly and as closely as possible so that participants in a communication process understand each other.

Difficulties arise from the confusion between colloquial and specialised language. Concepts used in colloquial languages tend to spread fast. On the contrary, only experts—sometimes even only those with similar views or belonging to the same school—are familiar with specialised terms, so that knowledge transfer requires a "translation". As the authors found during the preparation of this English language version of a Geman book, translating to and from a foreign language is never simple. Sometimes, one language does not use the same concept as the other

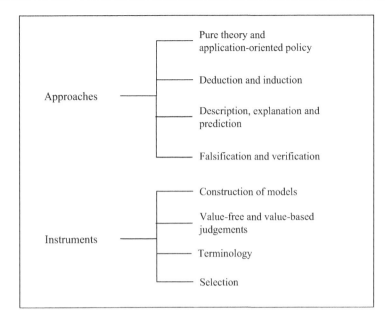

Fig. 1.8 The cognitive methods of research

language (e.g. *Formalziel* and *Sachziel*) and sometimes there are false friends like the German word *Controlling*, which does not mean the same as the English word *controlling*.

1.8.5 Selection

It is not possible to study everything, so we must make a selection based on whatever criteria we decide to use—what we choose are the objects of cognition (or areas of study) as discussed in Sect. 1.2. The criteria we have used in this book are economic efficiency and effectiveness. Figure 1.8 provides an overview of the cognitive methods of research on which our work is based.

1.9 Examples and Exercises

1.9.1 Economic Modelling

Situation
A German bicycle company purchases groupsets (a collection of components, including gears, brakes and chain) from a Japanese company. As part of procurement planning, the company must decide when to order the groupsets and how big the orders should be.

Solution

The managers of the company come to the conclusion that the best method to answer their procurement question is to build a decision model. In order to do so, they need to make certain assumptions:

1. The annual requirement is known and can be divided into equally sized order quantities.
2. The purchase price per groupset remains unchanged (volume discounts are not possible).
3. The daily requirement is constant, i.e. parts are taken from inventory uniformly. This means that on average half the order quantity is always in stock.
4. The warehouse stock is always replenished when there are no parts on hand.
5. The order costs are fixed.
6. The storage capacities are sufficient for the optimal inventory.
7. The company has sufficient financial resources.

This model has the advantage of simplicity and the necessary data can be collected easily. However, its simplicity is also a problem, because the managers need to ask themselves if it is realistic.

Questions

- What would change if assumption 2 were wrong and prices increased?
- Are there any other assumptions that you would make?
- Think of a recent purchase you made of an expensive item. What assumptions did you make before you made the purchase?

1.9.2 Information Sources

Situation

E-Vehicle AG is planning to build a plant in Mannheim for the production of its newly developed emission-free electric vehicle "Zero E". The model has been tested successfully for a year and a half. The investment would amount to around 200 million Euro. About 370 jobs would be created.

Solution

Up-to-date and detailed information on the local economy is an important basis for making decisions on location. One source of information is local government. The city of Mannheim provides a wealth of information about the location on its website (Stadt Mannheim 2017, www.mannheim.de/wirtschaftentwickeln). In addition, state, federal, research institutes and associations provide local (also regional, national and international) information. For example:

Employees by industry

As of 30.06.	2015	2014	2013
Total	180,273	178,114	174,861
Total production	51,194	52,071	49,797
– Manufacturing	40,058	40,468	358,591
– Construction industry	8060	7805	7589
Total services	128,110	125,817	128,842
– Trade; Maintenance and repair of vehicles	26,185	25,806	25,750
– Transport and storage	9708	9381	9241
– Catering	4935	4632	4505

Source: Bundesagentur für Arbeit

Job Market

	2016	2015	2011
Total jobless	9157	9489	9442
Jobless as percentage of workforce in Mannheim	5.7	6.0	6.1

Source: Statistisches Landesamt Baden-Württemberg—Annual average. http://www.statistik. baden-wuerttemberg.de/Arbeit/Arbeitslose/03033015.tab?R=KR222

Property Market

As of 30.06	2016	2015	2014
Amount on market in sqm (Rental + transactions to end users)	78,000	55,000	45,000
Office space im million sq,m.	2.0	2.0	2.0
Unrented space (percent)	4.5	5.2	5.6
Avg. rent €/sq.m./month	11.8	11.4	10.7
Office space under construction (thousand sq.m.)	11,000	38,000	11,000

Source: Gesellschaft für Immobilienwirtschaftliche Forschung e,V,, Jahresabgleich—Büromärkte Deutschland 2016

New businesses

	2015	2014	2014
New businesses started	2771	2893	3219

Source: Statistisches Landesamt Baden-Württemberg

Communications

Mannheim is well situated for road transportation:

- E35 Arnheim-Cologne-Frankfurt-Mannheim-Basel
- E50 Prague-Mannheim-Paris
- A5 Frankfurt-Mannheim-Karlsruhe-Basel
- A6 Nuremberg-Mannheim-Saarbrücken-Paris
- A61 Venlo-Bonn-Koblenz-Speyer A5

- A65 Karlsruhe-Landau-Ludwigshafen
- A67 Arnheim-Cologne-Frankfurt-Mannheim A3

Mannheim is 30 minutes away from Frankfurt Airport, and the following cities can easily be reached by train:

- Stuttgart 35 min
- Frankfurt (Main) 40 min
- Cologne 1 h 30 min
- Basel 2 h 10 min
- Munich 3 h
- Hannover 3 h
- Paris 3 h 10 min
- Berlin 4 h 30 min

Questions

- Find similar information about your home town. How easy was it to find it?
- What other information about Mannheim would E-Vehicle AG need before deciding to open a factory there?
- Is all the information about Mannheim presented above relevant? What reasons do you have for your opinion?

1.9.3   MyCompany Project

As you work your way through the book, you will take part in an activity where you plan your own business. The goal is that you can apply the contents of each chapter to your company.

Today, people have less and less time to prepare food for themselves and so are spending more on eating outside the home. At the same time, there is growing awareness that food should be healthy, that farm animals are sometimes not treated very well and that agri-business does a lot of damage to the natural environment. For these reasons the business is we have chosen is a cafe serving only fair-trade and organically grown vegetarian food and drinks.

As this chapter discussed, research involves gathering and analysing information, and it is essential to do the same before starting any business. You need to find out:

- The size of the market. How has it developed?
- The competitive situation. How many potential competitors are there in your neighbourhood? Who are the direct competitors?
- Information about the formalities of starting a business. What steps do you need to go through? Which permits are necessary? Is it possible to get advice?
- Costs. How much is rent? How much do people working in cafes earn? Does any national or city government agency offer financial assistance?

- What else might be important?

What are you going to call your company? You need to make sure that the name is not used by anyone else. How can you do that?

1.9.4 Self-Test Questions

– *What are the characteristics of an economic entity?*
– *What is the difference between a regional and supranational economy?*
– *What is meant by the term globalisation?*
– *What is the subject matter of business administration?*
– *How can the various areas within business administration be classified?*
– *What are the key features of the normative and descriptive decision theory?*
– *What is the difference between business administration and economics?*
– *What are the most important neighbouring disciplines of business administration and economics?*
– *What are the most important methods used in discovery during the research process?*
– *What is the purpose of modelling in business administration research?*
– *What is the relationship between perceptions, thought processes and learning processes?*

Economies and Needs

We require little when we are unhappy; happiness in turn makes us insatiable.

Words of Wisdom

Opening Vignette

Miriam Hoffman got onto her scooter and drove the five kilometres to the nearest shopping centre in Hellersdorf. She could still not quite believe that she lived in this suburb on the outskirts of Berlin after living for many years in the Neukölln area. "How did I end up here?" she asked herself. She answered her own question: "The situation I found myself in and my needs."

Neukölln had been a working-class area and in the 1960s had become the home to immigrants from many countries, firstly from Turkey and then more recently from different places in the Middle East. Rents had remained low during all this time. Neukölln lies next to Kreuzberg, which had been the trendier area when Miriam moved from Cologne to Berlin in 2005. Miriam had lived in an area in Neukölln that was on the border to Kreuzberg and she had experienced how the neighbourhood had changed.

First, students and artists looking for cheap places to live and work moved in. New bars opened to serve the students, and the artists opened spaces where they could show their work. More students came to drink in the bars, and more artists arrived to use the galleries and studios that had been opened. This influx made the area attractive to people who had more money than the artists and students, and who were looking for somewhere interesting and alternative to live.

The part of Neukölln where Miriam lived started to become known as Kreuzkölln, reflecting its location, and word of its attractiveness began to spread. When some friends from England had visited, they had shown her some websites that positively raved about that part of the city. As wealthier residents started to

© Springer International Publishing AG 2018　　　　　　　　　　　　　35
P. Eichhorn, I. Towers, *Principles of Management*, Springer Texts in Business and
Economics, https://doi.org/10.1007/978-3-319-70902-4_2

move in, rents started to rise. "Too many people want to live here now," she told herself in 2012, "but it won't last."

But it did last. International investors had been fairly uninterested in Berlin for a long time. Property prices were much lower than in any other major German city, which meant that rents were comparatively low and this made Berlin property a relatively unattractive investment for property owners and developers. This started to change towards the end of the 2000s, and areas like Kreuzkölln were the first to provide evidence of this as the process of gentrification started. Developers began to buy properties in the area, renovate the apartments in them and then either rent them for much more or sell them to the kind of affluent purchaser that could afford them. Property developers constantly flipped the buildings they owned, with Miriam's building changing hands three times in two years.

The latest of them started renovating her building—putting up balconies, redoing kitchens and bathrooms—and offering the apartments for sale. Miriam's apartment was bought by two lawyers and she was forced to move out. She tried to find another apartment in Kreuzkölln, but it was simply impossible—rents were so high. She went to the public viewings of a couple of apartments whose rents were still reasonable, but she was discouraged both by the unbelievably long queues of people waiting to view the empty flats and by the very poor condition they were in. She had no choice but to move out of Kreuzkölln.

Miriam asked a friend for advice, hoping for a brilliant suggestion. Ludwig thought for a second and then confirmed what was obvious. "You'll have to do what Greta and I did. Move out of the area. You've visited us in Hellersdorf, it's OK there and rents are lower than where you are now. Lots of people are doing it, I saw Heinrich there last week." "Lower rents because nobody wants to live there," replied Miriam. "That's partly true perhaps," replied Ludwig, "but there's also quite a lot of choice, so it's easier to find a place and much less stressful."

That conversation had taken place 2 months ago, and Miriam reflected, it had indeed been much easier to find an affordable apartment than in Kreuzkölln, where it was more or less impossible. "Supply and demand—that's how the market works," she said to herself as she parked her scooter and prepared to do some shopping.

2.1 Needs

2.1.1 Shortage of Resources

Business activity is driven by the tension between unlimited needs and the fulfilment of these needs on the one hand and the limited supply of goods on the other. A **need is the perception that something is lacking,** and the ultimate goal is the relief of this feeling. This perceived lack is the result of the inaccessibility of a good of a certain kind, quantity and/or quality. The reason may have natural origins or be influenced by others—we eat when we feel hungry and we buy new clothes to look fashionable. From the standpoint of economic efficiency and effectiveness, limited goods must be distributed in such a way that the largest possible fulfilment of needs is achieved.

Goods provide the means necessary for need fulfilment. All goods that are limited in quantity but suitable and available for the intended purpose are **economic goods**. These include tangible goods such as land, buildings, machinery, office equipment, tools, raw materials and supplies as well as intangible goods such as laws and services.

In practical terms only economic goods exist, for what were traditionally seen as **free goods,** such as air and water, are now being used as economic goods. Space and time are scarce goods, whose combination with factors of production and other goods is not straightforward. Valid information and relevant data, the creativity of employees, the willingness of negotiating partners to compromise and the attention of television viewers are also scarce goods. If it is not possible to increase the amount available of these goods, they have to be used more efficiently and more effectively so that needs can be met.

2.1.2 Types of Needs

When individuals or societies have needs, there then exists a demand for goods to satisfy them, but the argument that total needs are the sum of active demands **within the market** is unconvincing, because by only considering needs that can be satisfied by buying something, it ignores needs that can be satisfied **through non-market activities**. These are activities that we do not directly pay for, such as activities that take place in households, government offices or in courts or volunteer services. The creation and delivery of such services must also be efficient and effective.

We also do not see it as helpful to classify needs as **objective** and wants as **subjective**. Should one nevertheless wish to do so, one can understand needs as relating to a physical and/or psychological state, and wants as being an economic category.

Given the nature of humans as individual and social beings, we can identify **individual and collective needs**. The former are felt personally, the latter by society. To which category particular needs fit is not intrinsic to them, but rather depends on the characteristics of the state, law, civil society and the environment where the need is being experienced. How the need is characterised is significant from an economics point of view because it determines the way in which the need will be met. Taking education as an example—everybody needs to be educated so that they can live and work. Society also has a need for education, because if employees do not have the appropriate skills and competencies, nothing can be produced. In this case, individual and collective needs are met through the provision of education by the state: individuals themselves do not have to find teachers to educate them.

The characteristics of governmental, legal, social and economic frameworks originate in the **need for organisation** that develop when people come together in communities and societies. **Needs for controlling** develop to deal with coexistence itself should function; they are concerned with how things can and should run and take the formal form of laws, rules and regulations and the informal form of expected patterns of behaviour.

Needs can also be differentiated on the basis of whether they are those of economic entities, local, regional, national or supranational economies or the global economy. When compared to the needs of individuals, **institutional and societal needs** do not arise from the feeling that there is a lack of something, but from a more rational process that determines as objectively as possible that something is lacking, with the objective of obtaining what is missing. Businesses and other types of organisation have human resource needs, capital needs, needs for space, needs for information etc. In local economies there is a need for school places and jobs, property, cultural facilities, transportation, etc. Within regional economies it is necessary, for example, to establish plans for meeting the needs for hospital beds, the requirements for higher education, energy needs and the disposal of hazardous waste. Needs that must be met at the level of national economies include the money supply, pensions, telecommunications, transport and so on. A supranational economy such as the European domestic market has needs like tax rate harmonisation, compensation funds for the agricultural sector and common legislation regarding the freedom to set up subsidiaries and freedom of services in member states. In the global economy there is a need for food and medical care in developing countries, disarmament, global postal services etc. Figure 2.1 provides examples of needs at the various levels of the economy.

The definition of needs and the gathering, appraisal and satisfaction of these needs—no matter at which level the need exists—is done by economic entities, be they companies, universities, public authorities or international organisations. Needs can be obvious, but often they are not so a wide range of instruments exists to determine which needs exist. A company, for example, can carry out an analysis of its weaknesses which will, of course, depend on the company's goals: if customer service is to be improved, then any informational, human resource or financial limitations should be identified and, where appropriate and possible, removed. Wherever needs are established—in individual economic entities or at higher levels of the economy—management activities should follow.

2.1.3 Need Creation

It is not easy to answer the question of whether a need actually exists or not. Indeed, it is often impossible to draw the line as to where a vital need begins and ends. When one considers physical needs such as food, clothing and shelter, it is necessary to take into account the various forms these take, bearing in mind socio-cultural considerations that influence what the minimum for existence is, and what this means in terms of quantity and quality. Oranges, radio, television, refrigerators and mobile phones are part of the basic lifestyle for all but the very poorest in affluent societies, whereas in other societies such items count as luxuries.

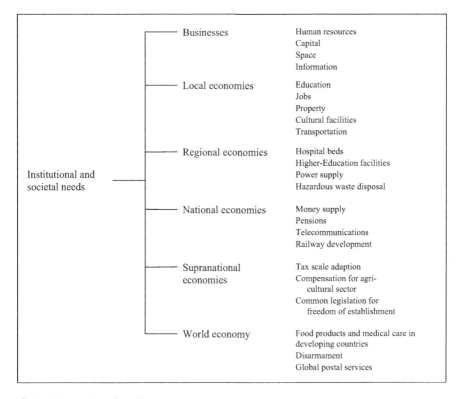

Fig. 2.1 Examples of needs

Even within an affluent society distinctions can be made: some people feel they must have a BMW or Mercedes while others are happy to take the U-Bahn even if they can afford an expensive car. **Does an individual really know his or her needs?** Are an individual's needs for things like education, culture, cleanliness, sport, mobility and travel real or imagined? What is a true need and for whom? Who stimulates true and false needs?

We cannot afford to satisfy every need, either as individuals or as a society, so it is necessary to prioritise them. How societies prioritise needs is often a political decision, but individuals have to prioritise for themselves. Of the many approaches that have studied how we prioritise, Adam H. Maslow's (1908–1970) original hierarchy of needs model is one of the most widely known. He distinguishes primary physiological needs (shelter, clothing) from secondary needs of safety (health, financial security), belonging (friendship, family), esteem (being respected) and finally self-actualisation (achieving one's full potential). He argues that individuals begin by satisfying needs at the lowest level, and then move to the next level after all needs at the lower level have been met. The model has been criticised because Maslow suggests that people do not satisfy needs higher up in the pyramid until all below have themselves been met. In addition a single item can meet needs at more than one level—a T-shirt with the name of a band on it satisfies physiological needs, but also shows other that the wearer is a fan of that band, which is meeting a social need. Nevertheless, the model has many strengths and is widely used.

There are of course other relationships at play here. How can the various prioritised and coexisting individual needs within the hierarchy be met at the general level of the economy and society? Need creation and need fulfilment may, for example, occur because a company wants to make a profit or a political party wants to win an election. An economic challenge is to align **personal needs** (of employees, customers, voters) with **institutional needs** (of a company or political party). Need creation is in effect demand creation, and represents a way in which individual and institutional needs can be harmonised.

Need research is concerned with the discovery and creation of needs and their fulfilment. The tools of need research have in common that their first task is to meet the need for information. The following **five instruments** are used in internal and external **need research**:

- A vulnerability analysis can help determine weaknesses in companies, individuals, different areas of business operations, facilities etc. This is a part of a SWOT analysis as discussed in Chap. 9.
- Market research is concerned with finding out about supply and demand, consumer preferences and motivations etc.
- Empirical economic and social research can be used for example to identify the positions, bargaining power and behaviour of negotiating parties so that their room for manoeuvre in pay negotiations can be assessed.
- Electoral research and political behavioural research aim to understand citizens' political perceptions, attitudes, motives and wishes.
- Legislative and impact research (e.g. on taxation) helps determine which legal and administrative measures are necessary so that specific public duties can be fulfilled.

2.2 Fulfilment of Needs

2.2.1 Types of Goods

The production, supply and use of goods and services to fulfil needs are the result of economic activity. Goods used to produce other goods are **factors of production**. Such factors form the **input**; they are then combined (production), and this process results in an **output** (products and/or services). These outputs may be used immediately or stored for later use. **Diseconomies** are to be avoided—machines that are not being used, defective products, waste or other harmful emissions are examples. Management's goal for the production of goods is to produce value-added goods and to avoid the production of diseconomies. Added value is in itself a good when this characteristic fulfils a given need. The fundamental characteristics of the good

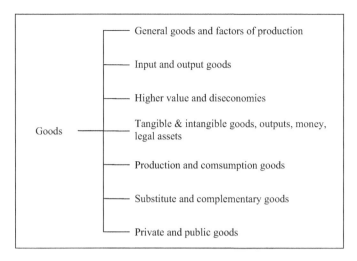

Fig. 2.2 Typology of goods

itself need not change, but the water that a consumer receives in a bottle has added value due to its transportation and the fact that it has been bottled adds convenience.

We said that goods are used, but it is important to keep in mind that goods do not disappear once they have been used up. As physicists tell us, nothing physical in our world simply vanishes, so consumption is itself in effect part of a process of transformation. The book you are reading has been printed and is an input; you are reading it, transforming you (we hope!) into a more knowledgeable person; and if you recycle the book, it becomes paper waste (output), which itself is the input for recycled paper, and so on. In terms of ecology, the transformation of a good from having higher value to having a lower value takes place when the resources that have been transformed into a product "vanish into thin air".

A classification of goods is shown in Fig. 2.2.

Material goods are tangible and can be stored (frozen pizzas, laptops), unlike **intangible goods** such as a haircut. In addition, there **monetary assets,** as well as **legal assets** (like patents, copyright, contracts etc.) and **environmental assets** (climate, sun, lakes, forests etc.).

Goods can be classified based on their use. There are **production** and **investment goods** and **commodities and consumer goods**. Such classifications can be helpful in accounting, as when determining requirements for capital on the one hand, and amortisation and depreciation of goods on the other hand. Consumer goods can be further classified, depending on their use, into consumer durables and non-durable goods. Economists also talk of **substitute goods** (e.g. car and tram), where either one can be used, and **complementary goods** (e.g. printer and ink), where both goods are required to achieve the desired goal.

Based on the differentiation between individual and collective needs, we can identify **private goods** and **public goods**. In essence, private goods fulfil individual needs, whereas public goods satisfy collective needs. Figure 2.3 illustrates how

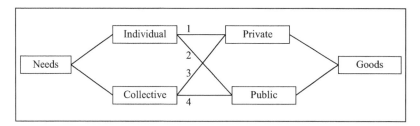

Fig. 2.3 Four alternative methods of need fulfilment

these types of good complement each other. Private goods include products from the local bakery that will be used to fulfil the requirements of a single person's breakfast (no. 1). In contrast, public goods such as fire services, coast guards and police fulfil a collective need for security and protection (no. 4). As there are many points at which these types of goods overlap, it is sometimes difficult to draw a clear boundary between them. There are of course individual needs that are fulfilled using public goods, such as the demand for cultural activities that is met by publicly owned theatres (no. 2). Private goods can also be used to satisfy collective needs. Self-employed physicians provide emergency medical services, for instance, and car workshops check the roadworthiness of cars (no. 3).

In the first instance it depends upon time and place as to which the best goods are to satisfy specific needs. The **Theory of Public Goods** deals with the characteristics that distinguish public goods from private goods. The rationale for having public goods dates back in public finance literature to Richard A. Musgrave (1910–2007) who was among the first to introduce the concepts of non-excludability and non-rivalry. Non-excludability refers to the financial or technical impossibility of preventing individuals from consuming the good—anyone can watch a fireworks display. Non-rivalry indicates that the use of a good by one individual does not prevent another from using the good—only one person can wear a shirt, but anyone can use a park. If both characteristics are present, this is a **pure public good**, such as national defence. This is different from **merit goods,** which are goods that the market does not offer or cannot provide in sufficient quantities, such as educational services, basic research, environmental protection agencies and medical emergency services.

We have so far discussed goods with a focus on their characteristics; to this we can add a **Theory of Public Tasks** that centres on institutions, where the central questions are: which public tasks develop to deal with need fulfilment? And which economic entities can best carry them out? The starting point for public tasks is the public interest, which political parties, interest groups, opinion leaders and others all seek to identify. From here—sometimes contradictory—political objectives are set which represent the desired situation. We are talking here about a complex set of goals, which may have to do with any one or more of such areas as education, energy, finance, health, youth, communities, small businesses, security, social issues, national issues, environment, defence, economic issues and the political objectives of various legislative bodies, governments, ministries or councils. Public tasks then develop out of these political objectives and they lead to actions; the tasks are expressed in the form of laws, acts, decrees, charters and other forms of legislation, government statements and programmes, legal decisions or the decision of those who carry out public tasks. We see the end results in educational, research and defence programmes, for example.

The two central aspects to public tasks are their **definition** and **fulfilment**. As already seen in the discussion of the four alternative methods for need fulfilment (Fig. 2.3), public tasks need not necessarily be administered or carried by public bodies. Other economic agents may also play a role—from households who look after their own children and non-profit organisations that act as broadcasters to companies that provide transport services. What they do and how they do it depends on how the tasks are defined, how they are compensated and also on the nature of the contract. The economic agents have to organise themselves so they can carry out the tasks for which they are now responsible, which means that they must plan the procurement of the necessary resources, the details of the product and/or service they are to provide, timelines and so on. Then based on these considerations, they plan and carry out their own internal operations.

Figure 2.4 details how public tasks become operational activities, showing the feedback loops which are always in place.

The circumstances in which these activities take place and the ways in which the stakeholders act greatly influence whether or not needs are fulfilled in a manner that is efficient and effective. Typically, the work involved in public tasks is shared between **many participating parties**. Who is involved in determining the necessary characteristics, quality and quantity of national or local tasks? Who checks that the tasks are being carried out and makes sure that all is well from the organisational and financial perspective? Doing all this is the responsibility of parliaments, local councils and their representatives, ministries and supervisory authorities (e.g. a local government responsible for waste disposal), the funding bodies (such as an insurance company that is entrusted with the financing of long-term care), the economic entities that are actually performing the task, public auditors and courts of justice.

These issues do not play much of a role in **privatisation discussions**, being often simply ignored from an ideological perspective as discussion focusses more on the privatisation of public tasks and less on the transfer of task fulfilment responsibilities to the private sector. **Public-Private Partnerships** exist where the tasks themselves remain within the public sector but are executed by private companies on behalf of the public sector. We see this in areas like education, waste management, health services, postal services, social care, transportation, housing and so on, where certain public tasks are outsourced to private partners who are responsible for carrying them out in a satisfactory manner in return for compensation. The other aspects of these tasks, such as political and administrative planning, supervision and controllership—all of which have costs associated with them— remain the responsibility of the public authority.

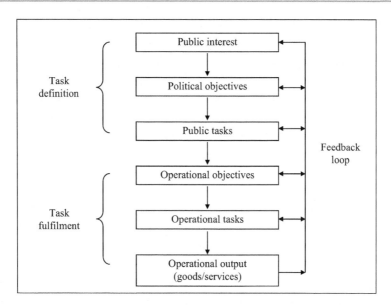

Fig. 2.4 Public tasks and operational activities

2.2.2 Provision of Benefits

Based upon the **Theory of Value** as outlined by Adam Smith (1723–1790) and other classical economists, a given good has both an exchange value and a use value. The exchange value, in essence the price, is based upon the costs required for production of the good. The exchange value for water is small and this is reflected in the price. On the other hand, its use value is very high. The difference between these two values cannot be explained by trying to establish the exchange value objectively so we also have to take into account the subjective value that the consumption and enjoyment of a good brings—this is **the benefit**, which **is the value of a good for satisfying needs**. Goods should therefore provide benefits. Just as needs cannot be described precisely, it is also difficult to provide a precise answer to the questions of which goods provide which benefits and to which extent. In addition, benefits depend upon circumstances, on time and place—a glass of water is worth more to a person lost in the desert than to someone in a bar. Quantitative and qualitative aspects of benefits of course also vary from person to person; a good which appears useful to one person (a cigarette to a smoker) may be perceived as dangerous by another, and this makes it problematic to assert that a good has an overall benefit just on the basis of benefit it has for an individual.

Other theories of value have been developed since Adam Smith, of course. Representative of the older ones is the **General Theory of Marginal Utility** developed by Hermann H. Gossen (1810–1858). His first law states that the consumption of an increasing quantity of a good creates a decreasing supplementary benefit (marginal utility) and may indeed create an aversion to the good. For example, if you are thirsty, you drink water so that you are no longer thirsty; the first few sips have a greater benefit than later sips, and once you get full, drinking more water will make you feel ill. His second law focusses on the maximisation of utility rather than on measuring utility in a numerical sense and according to it economic agents spend their income on various goods in order to maximise utility. For example, if a person has 200€, she will allocate the money among her various wants in a way that produces the maximum utility given her resources, taking all wants into account. Each of the goods provides her with the same amount of marginal utility.

The somewhat more recent **Ordinal Utility Theory** was developed by Vilfredo Pareto (1848–1923). Here the form of utility is of greater interest than the degree of utility. There are many possible bundles of goods with comparable benefits, and consumers rank not the individual goods in the bundles, but the bundles themselves.

A less theoretical but more practical approach suggests that purchasing decisions and voting (and other such behaviours) can serve as **indicators of benefits**. The first of these is related to market processes, and the others to decisions made by the majority. Analysing behaviour as an indicator of utility should be done with caution, as the analysis must be done in terms of who or what benefits and who or what is hurt, i.e. whether or not a person or thing is capable (financially or technically) of providing a benefit or preventing damage. When there are several possible ways of generating benefits, the most efficient and effective alternative should be chosen, but this in turn does not mean that efficiency and effectiveness should be the only measures.

2.2.3 Optimum Welfare

Individual economic agents are economically active in order to satisfy their own needs; ideally, this coincides with the satisfaction of others' needs. This individualistic (as well as liberal) concept of market economy was described in Adam Smith's "The Wealth of Nations", written in 1776. To summarise Smith's work: **self-interest is the driving force behind the common good**. He argues that each individual ought to act in enlightened self-interest and that as long as this happens in a framework of basic rights and liberties established by the state, the "invisible hand" will create general prosperity.

Smith was one of the fathers of economics, and since his time this social science has developed a theoretical construct in the search for the common good: the welfare of a country, region or community is maximised when the **social welfare function** takes its greatest value. The social welfare function allows us to consider what social conditions should look like, and its value is dependent upon the extent to which society's social welfare objectives have been met. There are of course limitations: all societal objectives cannot (yet) be determined and the extent to which objectives have already been met is also difficult to establish. One way round these difficulties is to view economic welfare as being dependent upon the quantity of goods available to society and how they are distributed.

The establishment of an **economic welfare function** is not easy because the total welfare function can only be partly derived from individual welfare functions. Kenneth J. Arrow (1921–2017) was one of the first to point out the difficulties implicit in aggregating individual preferences or group preferences to generate a consistent total welfare function. Arrow demonstrated the impossibility of determining a consistent order of preference from majority decisions. This can be illustrated using a simple example. Three groups are sitting in a local pub. They are trying to decide how to spend the rest of their evening. Their preferences are as follows:

Group I

Most preferred: (A) watching football on television
Moderately preferred: (B) watching a televised boxing match
Least preferred: (C) not watching television.

Group II

Most preferred: (B) watching a televised boxing match
Moderately preferred: (C) not watching television.
Least preferred: (A) watching football on television

Group III

Most preferred: (C) not watching television.
Moderately preferred: (A) watching football on television
Least preferred: (B) watching a televised boxing match

The barkeeper would like to end the disagreement between the three groups. He can offer two alternative solutions:

Solution 1
A choice between football (A) and boxing (B)—groups I and III would prefer football to boxing.

Solution 2
A choice between watching football (A) and not watching television at all (C)—groups II and III would prefer not watching television.

Combining these two results gives the following order of preferences: (1) no television, (2) watching football, (3) watching the boxing match.

To ensure that the best decision has been made the barkeeper allows the groups to vote a third time:

No television (C) versus the boxing match (B)

One might assume that the greatest preference would be for not watching television (C), however the results show something different. Groups I and II

Fig. 2.5 Aggregating
individual preferences

Order of preferences		For:	Against:
Group I	A > B > C		
Group II	B > C > A		
Group III	C > A > B		
		For:	Against:
1st Vote	A : B	I & III	II
2nd Vote	A : C	I	II & III
Expectation	C > A > B		
3rd Vote	B : C	I & II	III

would prefer the boxing match (B) over not watching television (C). This is contrary to expectations.

Figure 2.5 illustrates the impossibility of aggregating individual preferences to an uncontested total welfare function:

Individual welfare functions in a pluralistic society are either very different from each other or unknown. It is, however, possible to make a statement about economic welfare without having to use a welfare function. It is enough to assume (a) that a worthwhile goal is to increase the quantity of all existing goods, and (b) welfare can no longer be increased once an increase of the welfare of one individual serves to decrease the welfare of another individual (this is the Pareto criterion).

In the economics literature there is discussion about the satisfying of (marginal) conditions guaranteeing welfare maximisation or optimisation. The argument is advanced that economic measures which improve the situation of an individual to a lesser (marginal) or greater (total) extent should implemented as long as this happens without worsening the relative situation of another individual. The **compensation principle** captures this idea: the harm caused to the disadvantaged individual should be compensated for by the individual who gains an advantage. Benefits must outweigh costs.

2.2.4 Needs Control

There is always a tension between needs and the goods that satisfy them, i.e. between demand and supply. Unlimited needs are faced with limited goods, so we need to take needs as the starting point for resolving this challenge. It is necessary to set priorities regarding the type, quantity and quality of needs, and their distribution should also be considered. We discussed above the different types of need and their nature leads us to conclude there are two possibilities: global need management or a more differentiated one. These possibilities match those in other spheres—in the political-economic context one refers to micro, meso and macro control, companies have strategic and operative planning, and there are overall budgets and budget line items.

Fig. 2.6 Instruments for
needs control

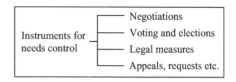

Need control is necessary in economies when the "free play of forces" has a negative effect on welfare—market failure, cutthroat competition, exploitive monopolies, no liability for product defects, poorly managed waste disposal, negative external effects etc. When the market is not capable of acting as a control mechanism, there are four instruments of control:

- Negotiations: for example, when employers and employees agree labour relations contracts about compensation; an industry association voluntarily agrees to actions that will be taken by their members, as when an automotive producers body sets up processes that their members must follow for the disposal of old cars.
- Voting and elections: in elections voters make choices based on the economic concepts of the parties; a regional assembly decides how much to invest in hospitals.
- National, regional or local regulations with requirements and prohibitions that set binding specifications.
- Appeals and calls for particular behaviours in order to reduce or prevent desirable needs, such as campaigns to encourage people to stop smoking.

The instruments are shown in Fig. 2.6.

Comparable instruments are available for **individual companies**. The concept of the profit centre creates an internal market to which the needs for input factors are initially directed before the company releases anything on the external market. In-house there are such needs as budget funds, diversification, market research, equipment maintenance and so on—these are managed via agreements, votes (e.g. on the supervisory board), specifications, directives or non-binding appeals to goodwill, and this is always done with a view to achieving the relevant goals. Companies that are committed to shareholder value meet in the first instance the demands of the shareholders for higher share prices, while on the other hand, community-based or cooperative enterprises influence the needs of often economically disadvantaged parties such as the unemployed, trainees, the disabled, children, the ill, individuals requiring care, recipients of social assistance and so on.

2.3 Economic Systems

The **economic system** is the way in which economic life and its related activities are organised in a national economy. We can differentiate between models of economic systems on the basis of the interdependencies and transactions between the various system elements. When analysing a system, we often use the term **economic order**; how it is organised is the outcome of the **regulatory process**. This regulatory process is steered by politics, and among its tasks is determining the rules for competition among economic actors. At the same time, processes are put into place that deal with the economy and growth and in addition, there are structural policies that are concerned with the various sectors of the economy

2.3.1 Market Economy

Characteristic of the market economy as an economic system is that the providers and buyers of goods and services are autonomous in their decision making and are in a state of competition with each other. The term **competition economy** can also be used; this emphasises the fact that providers strive to make a profit and are involved in price competition. We talk about the **private sector** when market participation is based on possessing private property. A **free market economy** exists when the providers and buyers enjoy complete freedom in making decisions such as choice of profession, school or place of work; when there is freedom of trade, there exists the ability to set prices and set up subsidiaries, and there is also freedom of association and of contract. An **open market economy** exists when these freedoms extend beyond a single national economy; relevant freedoms in this context include the free movement of goods, services and capital with other national economies. Cornerstones of an open market economy are the principle of most-favoured-nation, no trade restrictions and a ban on discrimination. Since the 1970s most countries have followed the path of liberalisation in order to create such an economy—opening up markets, introducing processes of deregulation (i.e. a reduction of bureaucracy and regulatory overhead), integration, harmonisation, establishing external trade initiatives, and cutting back subsidies, taxes and duties.

If an economy is allowed to operate with very few restrictions it is said to be extremely liberal, reflecting a "laissez faire" philosophy, which means that just about anything is allowed. This can lead to economic anarchy and social chaos, with few winners and many losers. It is generally agreed today that a firm hand is needed to establish ways in which to protect existing freedoms, meaning that the preferred alternative to a completely free market (which has never existed, even during Victorian times), is a **mixed market economy**. Such an arrangement is based on economic actors enjoying fundamental freedoms in their relationships with each other, society as a whole and the natural environment, but with some restrictions, the extent of which is always a matter of debate between different interest groups. In the search for finding the correct balance, many advocate "more market and less state", or "as much market as possible and as little state as necessary". There is a continuum; the United States economy is organised on the basis that the state should play as small a role as possible, while the state is much more active in the Scandinavian countries, for example. Some people call for social justice or emphasise the boundaries of growth as they argue that the economic order should emphasise social justice or sustainable development. These demands can be met by organising economic activities so that one of the following emerges: a **social market economy** (such as in Germany), an **ecological market economy**, or, combining both aspects, a **socio-ecological market economy**. These are theoretical constructs and rarely found in practice, but Costa Rica could arguably be said to have more of an ecological market economy than other nations, while Denmark has more of a social market economy than, say, Australia.

It is of vital importance to be aware that the market—within the constraints established by governments or similar bodies at the national and international level—determines how the goods that are produced are distributed to economic agents, and this in turn determines how income is distributed. The state and the many public authorities and institutions create the structures in which the market operates, decide on the extent of competition and intervene (or not) in times of market failure. Among the many areas of activity where they are active are promoting and subsidising research and technological development, supporting business start-ups, developing policies for industrial sectors and generally encouraging businesses of all kinds in all areas of the economy in many business activities. States make long-term plans for their economies, setting goals and priorities. In some economies, the state is less directive about what it wants companies to do (eg **planification** in France), while **interventionist states**, as Japan is argued to be, are more directive.

In a **socialist market economy**, decentralised economic entities drive supply and demand, but their room to manoeuvre is significantly restricted. Private ownership is limited in its extent, being found mainly in households' consumption and living arrangements and small businesses although there may also be a degree of private ownership of medium-size companies. The must usual form of ownership in agriculture are cooperatives. Companies in the coal and steel, health care, and transportation industries are generally owned by socialist market states, as are banks and insurance companies. The ratio of expenditure of state owned and run companies and bodies compared to the gross national product is very high (70–80%). Nevertheless, it is still essentially through the mechanism of the market that economic activities are coordinated. The former Yugoslavia had such an economic system.

Figure 2.7 summarises the different types of market economy.

2.3.2 Planned Economy

In contrast to a market economy, a planned economy is an economic order in which the objectives and strategies, structures and processes of a national economy are determined by one or more central authorities. The economy is steered through plans, which generate norms and targets that must be met by the actors in the

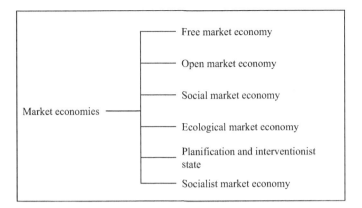

Fig. 2.7 Types of market economy

economy. We can distinguish between **partially** and **totally planned economies,** depending on whether the planning system concerns itself only with individual sectors or regions or the entire national economy.

Another classification of planned economies is based on the extent to which central bodies provide direction and establish targets. In **economies with indicative planning**, the state does not compel, but uses its influence to direct behaviours and actions by economic entities, while in **command economies**, central state bodies produce detailed plans that are binding. Planned economies do not require socialism or communism to exist. Both of these political systems, where private property plays a subordinate role, take advantage of planned economies, but it is theoretically possible for a planned economy to exist in an economic order with private property.

A pure planned economy is as unfeasible as a pure market economy. The centralised directives and obligations in a planned economy must allow for an element of individual freedom in economic activities. In a **mixed planned economy**, small scale individual private business activities are possible; small businesses producing tangible and intangible goods or selling them to consumers and other businesses can exist, as can small scale farming. This was the case in the German Democratic Republic and other countries to the east of the Iron Curtain.

Figure 2.8 illustrates the different types of planned economy.

2.3.3 A Third Way?

Market and planned economies represent the extremes on a continuum of ways in which economic activities can be ordered in a society. Many have tried to find a **third way** which would combine the advantages of these economic systems while at the same time avoiding their disadvantages.

Over time, the following advantages of **market economies** have emerged: they encourage a strengthening of individual initiative, commitment, motivation and

Fig. 2.8 Types of planned
economy

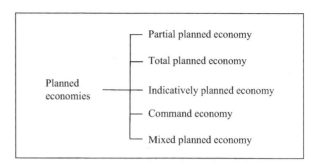

personal responsibility. They promote competition and a willingness and ability to
react to the market. They lead to the production of cost-effective goods, high
productivity, and these in turn contribute to high incomes and a generally high
level of satisfaction of needs. In short, market economies produce affluent societies.
Their disadvantages are clear. Long-term recessions and costly economic crises,
destructive competition, mass unemployment, extreme economic disparity, social
tension, unsatisfactory public services and a low level of public and community
spirit are very frequently found.

Planned economies too have their advantages. They offer the standardised
provision of public services, a high degree of manoeuvrability which allows them
to react quickly to emergency situations (man-made or having natural causes),
prevent unnecessary production (e.g. of luxury items) and consumption of goods
(through rationing). On the other hand, there is a significant amount of evidence of
problems (not that some of these problems cannot be found in market economies, but
not to such a great extent). Their bureaucracies are complex and sluggish, advantage
is taken of the weaknesses in their administrations, corrupt officials, an unwilling-
ness to take responsibility, and low entrepreneurial spirit and attitudes of dependency on the state. The goods tend to be hard to differentiate from each other and not
available in the quantities needed. Labour as a factor of production is very strictly
controlled, meaning that there may be no freedom to choose a profession and no
freedom of association, of contract or movement. Capital may be poorly invested
and other serious mistakes made because the central authorities themselves make
errors.

The third way would be a combined market and planned economy. As desirable
as this may be, it is not even theoretically possible because a given economic
system has fundamental characteristics and in the case of planned and market
economies these cannot coexist because the way economic activities are ordered
is based either on people being free to act in the market or on their following plans
that have been established by a central authority. Mixing the two is possible: a
market economy can have elements of a planned economy and vice-versa, but in
each case, the underlying order remains unchanged. Market economies dominate in
the twenty-first century, and in the next section we discuss their most important
features.

2.4 The Economic Constitution

2.4.1 The State

The economic constitution is based on all the laws and regulations that relate to business and these determine the ways in which the various actors in the economic system interact; the central role of the state in developing and setting standards and norms that determine how the economy works is evident. The systems that coordinate economic activities are the outcome of the complex relationships between the form of the state, state authority, state territory, state sovereignty and powers, political parties and lobby groups, all of them being influenced by the power of the media. The most appropriate option for a market economy is a liberal state because it limits government authority and emphasises individual freedoms, whereas an authoritarian type of state is most appropriate for a planned economy, as it possesses extensive authority over economic entities.

2.4.2 The Legal System

The legal system of a state determines the **principles of the rule of law** on which the state bases its actions. Under a liberal rule of law, paramount are the guarantee of individual freedoms and human rights, the protection of minorities, the prevention of the misuse of power through a balance of powers, an administration that acts lawfully, equality, the assurance of legal certainty, the principle of proportionality and prohibition of disproportionality in actions, as well as the maintenance of rule of law by independent courts of justice.

The question as to whether and to what degree the legal system determines the way in which economic activities are arranged, thereby determining a particular economic system, must be examined on a case by case basis. There are three possible answers. The state's (written or unwritten) constitution can: (a) allow only the presently existing economic system; or (b) accept (as in Germany) that the current economic system is one of several possible systems among many; or (c) remain neutral so that a completely different economic system would be possible. It is important to remember that theory and practice need not be identical in this regard. The legal system must not be overwhelmed, and in any case it only provides a basic framework, because ethical behaviour, voluntary self-restraint and how we interact with others are also important factors in determining how an economic system functions in practice.

2.4.3 The Social Order

An economic order that is based purely on the mechanism of the market would be counter-productive because it would ignore the necessity of striking a balance between the interests between different groups, regions and generations, as well as between man and nature. The goal should be to achieve a fair and just society, a principle which is enshrined in Article 20 of the German constitution: "The Federal Republic of Germany is a democratic and social federal state." Article 20 has of course influenced Germany's **social market economy**, whose aims are to avoid the "ugly face of capitalism" (as former British Prime Minister Edward Heath (1916–2005) said) through a free, but still regulated, market economy which allows the economically disadvantaged to lead a dignified life and benefit from the general level of prosperity. The term *social* represents solidarity, the collective and pluralism.

The concept of **solidarity** is reflected in five social insurance programmes that were established by the German government. These contributions-based schemes are: public compulsory health insurance, long-term care insurance, unemployment insurance, accident insurance and pensions. There also exist other forms of social assistance for specific circumstances, such as family allowance, housing allowance, study grants and loans, as well as the reimbursement of school fees, tuition costs and school supplies. The rights of individuals within a system of social solidarity are matched to responsibilities; owning property brings with it obligations in respect of the social good. There is great deal of debate about the degree of solidarity. On the one hand there are those who advocate a system that provides only the most basic services in order to reduce the demands on it—and consequently costs—to a minimum. Others fear this will cause social unrest and lead to people not receiving the services they need.

Collectivity refers to a social partnership between employers and employees with such characteristics as free collective bargaining, employee participation (e.g. workers' councils, representation on the company board), wages being paid in the event of illness or injury, job security and protection against the unjustified termination of employment. German employers' bodies sometimes criticise this, arguing that small or struggling companies suffer through collective labour agreements that cover a whole industry. They also say that worker participation is a disadvantage for companies based in Germany. The success of the German economy would appear to indicate that this particular criticism is not well founded.

Plurality in the market economy seeks to ensure social equity. It emerges from the processes in which many and various industrial, non-profit and government organisations meet and deal with the interests of individuals and institutions. Plurality is achieved through the harmonious coexistence of small and large companies, mixed-economy and public enterprises of different sizes, with different legal forms, with different interests. The relationships and interactions between these economic actors are the basis of plurality.

2.4.4 The Ecological Order

A country will develop an **ecological market economy** when it sets the protection of nature and the environment as a priority and actually acts on it. The basis of an ecological market economy lies in what is to be found in the constitution, in laws, regulations and administrative rulings as well as in relevant court rulings. Environmental objectives, principles, instruments, departments, institutions authorised to act in this field and penalties for non-compliance all come from these sources.

Objectives   Germany is one of the countries that has gone furthest down this path. Article 20a of Germany's basic constitution states, "Mindful also of its responsibility toward future generations, the state shall protect the natural foundations of life and animals by legislation and, in accordance with law and justice, by executive and judicial action, all within the framework of the constitutional order."

Significantly more concrete than these state objectives is the concept of sustainability. This approach was adopted at the 1992 conference organised by the United Nations in Rio de Janeiro but it has still not been ratified by every country. Sustainable development aims to satisfy the needs of the present generation without disadvantaging future generations. **Sustainable development** can be achieved by:

- Exploiting nature and its resources with consideration for how it can recover and renew itself,
- Placing limitations on the use of pollutants based on how well they can be absorbed by the environment,
- Taking of risks in the use of technology in so far as these risks can be measured and managed
- Frugal use of natural resources.

Follow-up conferences have been held on a regular basis, with the most recent taking place in Paris in December 2015. At this conference, the twenty-first to have been held, 196 countries agreed to reduce emissions by reducing their carbon output "as soon as possible" with the aim of keeping global warming below 2 °C (although countries like the Republic of Seychelles wanted a target of 1.5 °C). Newly elected US President Trump (born 1946) announced in June 2017 that the US would withdraw from the Paris Agreement with the argument that ecological objectives conflict at least in part with objectives such as growth, mobility, competition and development. Our view is that nature is the good with the highest value of all and that the cost of using it should reflect the demands that are being made of it.

Principles   The **precautionary principle** states that damage to the environment should be avoided as far as possible. For instance, a priority should be to avoid waste, but should this not be possible, the next best thing is to reuse the waste, and then—only if reuse is not possible—dispose of the waste using the most environmentally-friendly methods possible. The circular economy should be the goal of all actors in the national economic system. The **polluter pays principle** seeks to assign to those that (might) cause damage to the environment the costs required to avoid harm in the first place or to remedy the damage once it has occurred, even though it may be difficult to determine the origin of a problem or the extent of a given organisation's contribution to environmental damage. An

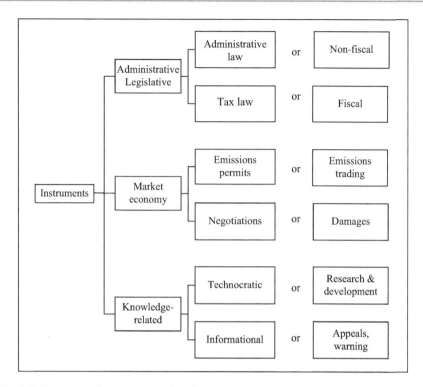

Fig. 2.9 Instruments for governmental environmental protection politics

alternative in such circumstances is to follow the **burden sharing principle**, where costs are met by the government using revenues gathered from the broader community. Under the **cooperation principle**, stakeholders are involved in the relevant processes with the goal of allowing wider input into decision making about environmental issues, leading to an improved quality of decisions and a broader consensus.

Instruments Administrative, legal, market-related and analytical instruments exist (see Fig. 2.9). Administrative and legal instruments include requirements and prohibitions in areas like production and emissions, in the shape of regulations, statutory processes and recommendations; court cases and damages are measures of performance (see Fig. 2.10). These essentially non-fiscal instruments are complemented by financial stimuli such as tax relief and deterrents (e.g. an eco-tax: see Fig. 2.11). **Market economy** instruments may also be used in this area, as shown by the example of the trading of emissions permits. For instance, emission rights for sulphur dioxide for power plants are traded on the Chicago commodity futures exchange and on the European Energy Exchange in Leipzig, Germany. Knowledge-related instruments may be technocratic (research and development)

Approach / Type of regulation	Input-oriented	Output-oriented
Performance-related	Requirements & prohibitions concerning resources & production processes	Requirements & prohibitions concerning products
Financial	Financial levies & tax relief on resources & production processes	Financial levies & tax relief on products

Fig. 2.10 Administrative and fiscal law regulations

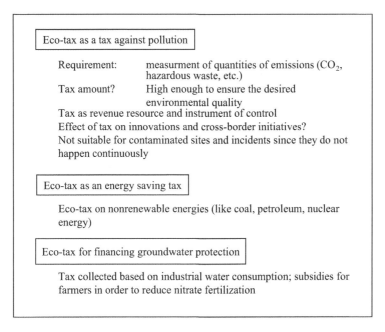

Fig. 2.11 Types of eco-tax

or informational (appeals and pleas for desired behaviours, warnings against unwanted behaviours).

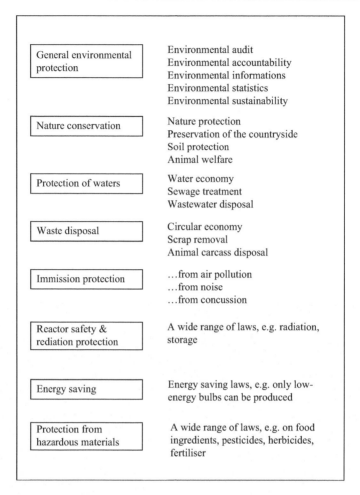

Fig. 2.12 Areas of environmental law

Scope Many areas of human existence and activity are affected: people, animals, plants; land, water, air and space; general environmental care, management of natural habitats, water protection, waste disposal, emission protection, nuclear reactor security, radiation protection, energy-preservation initiatives and protection from hazardous materials. Environmental legislation includes constitutional law, administrative law, eco-tax law, criminal law, civil law, international law and European environmental community law.

The most important areas of environmental law are illustrated in Fig. 2.12.

Responsible Parties Aside from various levels of government, most countries have national, regional and local environmental bodies. There are also special offices, institutes, state-owned and municipal enterprises that take on various environment-related tasks and responsibilities such as research, occupational health and safety inspection, food analysis, protection of natural habitats, water protection, land use planning and waste disposal.

Sanctions When the environment is damaged, the consequences are outlined in the relevant legislation dealing with liability and compensation; environmental crimes are punished with fines and/or imprisonment. Endangering the environment may itself be a crime regardless of whether damage actually occurs.

2.5   Examples and Exercises

Here we present two cases that demonstrate some of the concepts we have discussed. In the first case we show the relationship between national and international government actions and business decisions. It deals with how EU regulations have created a market on which firms can become active; the goal is to meet collective needs within social market economies. The second case deals with the provision of public goods and how this can best be organised, taking into account concepts like non-rivalry and non-exclusivity.

2.5.1   A Market-Based Instrument for Environmental Policy

Situation
In the Kyoto Protocol adopted in 1997, the participating States undertook to reduce or limit their climate-damaging greenhouse gas emissions. The European Union pledged to reduce its emissions by eight per cent by 2008 compared to 1990 levels. In 2012, the signatories agreed to extend the Kyoto Protocol to 2020. The European Union has announced a 20 per cent reduction in emissions by 2020. Even greater reductions were agreed at the Paris Conference of 2015.

The targets of reduced emissions must be achieved through national and EU instruments. The European Emission Trading Scheme (EU ETS) is the EU's central climate protection instrument for meeting the Kyoto Protocol. The basic idea of this trading system is based on Ronald H. Coase's (1919-2013) thoughts on the problem of social cost and targets the internalisation of external effects.

Solution
The EU ETS has existed since 2005 and includes the trading of certificates which allow their holders the emission of carbon dioxide. It is the first international trading system for emissions permits and is currently the largest. Some 12,000 companies from the energy and energy-intensive industries (e.g. steelworks, refineries) participate in the EU ETS, as well as around 2500 aerospace companies.

Principle of "Cap and Trade"

First, an upper limit is set as to how much CO_2 can be emitted at most. This upper limit, which is as narrow as possible, is the **cap**. The companies that participate in emissions trading as a result of the statutory provisions are then allocated a certain number of emission allowances from the cap; this number is based on Europe-wide rules of allocation. One emission allowance is equivalent to one tonne of CO_2. By limiting the available allowances, companies are given specific targets for the reduction of their emissions. The allowances are **tradable** and thus serve as a kind of credit note. By converting CO_2 into tradable credits, one tonne of CO_2 is given a concrete value and this value is determined by the market on which they are traded.

Every year companies have to surrender a number of emission allowances based on their actual emissions. If a company reduces its output enough that the amount of its actual emissions is less than the number of emission rights it possesses, it can sell the remaining emission allowances it no longer requires on the market. In the opposite case, it has to buy allowances to comply with its emission obligations. If the company does not meet these requirements, penalties are levied. These were initially 100€ per tonne of carbon dioxide; this number is adjusted to reflect increases in consumer prices. Companies that do not reach their goals must meet them the following year. A company can also purchase allowances on the market if this is less expensive than implementing its own measures for reducing CO_2. This also means that reduction measures are implemented where they make the most economic sense.

Example

Companies A and B emit the same amount of carbon dioxide and each has now to reduce its amount by 500 tonnes—a total of 1000 tonnes CO_2. Company A is able to significantly reduce its emissions by investing in modern technology but Company B is not ready or able to do so, so its emissions remain constant. As a result of emissions trading, it is more economical for company A to reduce its emissions of CO_2 by 1000 tonnes and to sell its unused emission rights for 500 tonnes to company B, which itself has not implemented any emissions reduction. In this way, the overall ecological target is achieved, since the total emissions of these two companies were reduced by 1000 tonnes CO_2.

Questions

- Company B is still polluting—is this ethically acceptable?
- What other ways exist that could get companies to reduce their emission of carbon dioxide?
- Should companies in developing countries have to behave in the same way?

2.5.2 Provision of Public Goods

Situation

A city council is planning a fireworks display to mark the end of a festival. The leader of the council has a degree in economics and decides that the principles of non-rivalry and non-exclusivity should apply to the fireworks display: She argues that the enjoyment of the fireworks by an individual spectator does not decrease even if another spectator sees the fireworks. Similarly, it is not possible to exclude people from viewing the fireworks.

The leader of the council has been provided with the following information:

- The cost of the fireworks is 100,000€.
- Each of the 100,000 inhabitants of the city is willing to pay 4€ to see the fireworks, bringing in 400,000€.

Since the benefits of the fireworks display are more than the costs, she decides to go ahead.

The issue: Who should provide the fireworks?

There are two alternatives:

(A) A private company could offer the fireworks and sell tickets for 2€ per person. This price is under the amount of 4€ that individuals are prepared to pay. However, no one would buy a ticket, since everyone could behave as a "free rider" and watch the fireworks for free.

(B) The city could levy a tax of 1€ each inhabitant, bringing in revenues of 100,000€. With this amount, the city could hire the private enterprise to arrange the fireworks. The inhabitants could enjoy the fireworks and enjoy a consumer surplus of 3€.

Questions

- Which alternative would you choose?
- There is a third alternative: the council could arrange the fireworks itself. What are the arguments for and against this?
- Do you think there are some public tasks that should never be carried out by private companies? Which ones?

2.5.3 MyCompany Project

Your fair-trade and vegetarian café is going to be supplying food and drink. As you start to think about your business plan, you realise that there are some basic questions that you need to answer.

- What needs are you going to be satisfying? Think about Maslow's hierarchy of needs—does an organic chocolate brownie satisfy only physiological needs? How can you find out about demand for your product and what consumers are looking for?
- What needs do you have in the cafe?
- What benefits are you going to be supplying?
- Your cafe is (probably) in a market economy of some kind. How are you as a business person running a cafe affected by the state? Could your type of cafe exist in a planned economy?
- The chapter discusses the ecological order. Which principles and instruments would apply to you?

2.5.4 Self-Test Questions

- *What is a need?*
- *What are the differences between individual and collective needs?*
- *What are examples of needs in local economies?*
- *What is Maslow's hierarchy of needs?*
- *Which instruments in need research do you know?*
- *What distinguishes private and public goods?*
- *What are substitute and complementary goods?*
- *What four methods exist for need fulfilment?*
- *What is the core of the Theory of Public Tasks?*
- *Which economic entities can carry out public tasks?*
- *What is Gossen's first law?*
- *Why is it difficult to aggregate individual preferences?*
- *What kinds of market economy are there and what characterises them?*
- *What are the advantages and disadvantages of a planned economy?*
- *What characterises the social market economy?*
- *Why can there never be a 3rd Way?*
- *What is meant by the concept of collectivity in the context of the social market economy?*
- *What are the basic objectives of the ecological order?*
- *Which principle is the eco-tax based upon?*

Individuals and Institutions in the Economy

3

> *Always recognise that human individuals are ends, and do*
> *not use them as means to your end.*
>
> Immanuel Kant (1724–1804)

Opening Vignette

Susanne Ebert came down from her bedroom to join the rest of her family for the evening meal. As they ate, the conversation turned as usual to what each of them had been doing that day. Susanne started off the conversation. "Today we had economics at school and learned that I'm an agent!" "Not a secret agent, though," remarked her father in an attempt at humour. "No, of course not! We are economic agents, where you work is an economic agent, where mum works is an economic agent, where David studies is an economic agent, my school is an economic agent and when I go later to the volleyball club, that's an economic agent as well!"

Her father smiled (rather patronisingly, Susanne thought) and said, "Look Susanne, I work for the civil service in the Ministry of Family Affairs. If I'm honest, all we do is move pieces of paper around, write reports, take decisions and see that things get done. We're not interested in making a profit, we aren't selling anything, so we are definitely not economic agents!" "How wrong you are!" replied Susanne. "The ministry spends money, it has to make sure things get done so the economy can keep running, so of course it's an economic agent."

Her brother Stefan interrupted her. "Listen," he said, "I'm a student at the Humboldt University in Berlin. It gets most of its money from the Berlin government, so how can that be an economic agent? It's not trying to make any money, although obviously the private universities do in fact aim to make a profit. These private places are economic agents, not the public universities."

Susanne was starting to lose her temper with her older brother. "Look, any person or organisation or body or administration or foundation or just about anything that plays a role in the economy is an economic agent. Mum has her

© Springer International Publishing AG 2018   63
P. Eichhorn, I. Towers, *Principles of Management*, Springer Texts in Business and
Economics, https://doi.org/10.1007/978-3-319-70902-4_3

own medical practice, she buys stuff, she provides a service that the people need, so she's an economic agent. And what about us as a family? We buy things as a household and we provide services that society needs as well, just about like any other business!"

Stefan interrupted her again. "You're joking of course! What services do we provide that society needs? We're just a household of people. Sure we buy things, but we're not selling anything."

Now Stefan's mother started to look somewhat annoyed. "Just a minute, young man!" she exclaimed. "Who looked after you when you and your sister were babies? I did, that's who. I didn't get any money for it, but don't tell me that looking after children isn't an activity that need not be carried out!" "Quite right, mum," declared Susanne. "We learned today that economic agents are people and organisations that have an effect on the economy, not just those that are trying to make a profit." She turned towards her brother and said in a somewhat haughty tone, "Even my volleyball association is one and so is your students' union."

3.1   Economic Agents

3.1.1   The Variety of Economic Agents

After discussing in previous chapters the economy as an object of analysis and examining why economic activity exists, we now present the economic agents that are responsible for this activity. Taking a simple view of economic life, we can identify individuals and institutions that are consumers and/or producers of goods and services in a multitude of areas and in different ways. Their goals, legal forms and sizes vary widely. It is easy to grasp the sheer number of economic agents by looking at a telephone directory or online directory, where you will find individuals, a huge number of large and small companies, voluntary organisations, associations, and—often unnecessarily forgotten in books like this—different kinds of public and semi-public bodies. These are all **economic agents**. But some of them—for instance government authorities, cultural institutions, research institutes, sports clubs—do not carry out their activities for a primarily economic purpose because their main objective is not economic in nature. Although they are **atypical economic agents**, they still organise their activities based on the division of labour and they too must possess the financial resources that allow them to purchase the factors of production that enable them to produce their output and so to play an active role in the economy. If the provision of goods or services takes place without payment—as is the case for many of the services provided by public institutions—some form of tax payments provides the finance. It is of vital importance to recognise that the principles of economic efficiency and effectiveness apply to all economic agents, regardless of their individual characteristics.

3.1.2 Typology of Economic Agents

We need to develop a typology of economic agents because it is easier to study them if we can group them according to some basic characteristics and features. Once we have done this, we can focus on the features that differentiate one from another, and this then allows us to discuss the possibility of more efficient operational forms and processes.

We can classify economic agents based on the **economic sector** in which they are active. We normally distinguish three sectors: primary, secondary and tertiary. Economic agents in the primary sector are involved in the production and extraction of raw materials; the agriculture, forestry, fishing and mining industries are typical of this sector. Business activities in the secondary sector are centred on the transformation of the outputs of the primary sector into goods. Industries that are in the secondary sector include energy and water, automotive, machinery, chemical industry, electronics, aerospace, construction, plastics, textiles, printing, and so on. Economic agents in the tertiary sector supply services; typical examples are banks, insurance companies, trade and retail, hotels, travel agencies, transport, real estate, professions like accounting and the law, hospitals, homes for the elderly or the handicapped, schools, colleges and universities, associations and federations, public administrations, courts and tribunals. Economies shows a tendency to develop over time, with most economic activity initially in the primary sector, then in the secondary sector, and finally in the tertiary sector. In the post-industrial society seen in the most economically advanced nations, more than half of the working population is active in the tertiary sector. Some authors now even refer to a quaternary sector based on information services and a quinary sector that is based on human services (e.g. providing temporary workers).

A further classification is that between **market and state** economic agents, although as will be discussed later, there are some overlaps here. We can distinguish between entities which are market oriented, commercial and profit-driven and those which are part of the bureaucracy, owned by the state in a planned economy, public or exist to implement rules and regulations. This classification, leaving aside any implication that economic agents of the first kind are good and those of the second kind are bad (see the discussion of neoliberalism in Chap. 1), is not only unclear, but also confusing. Many enterprises act according to the rules of the market although they are not primarily profit driven and are in fact following other goals, as is the case when the state hands tasks over to entrepreneurs, in which case they are carrying out a public function whose primary goal is not to make money. Examples of this are air traffic controllers, surveyors, companies that certify the safety of products and chimney-sweeps (in Germany). Other non-state economic agents discharge public duties in the field of legal protection, for example (lawyers and solicitors) or work as professionals with a publicly defined function (like auditors). Additionally, private companies may receive a concession from the state to operate in a certain field. One example of this is transport, where the state may require companies to guarantee the provision of certain services of public transport on given routes with a given frequency.

The main goal of most public bodies or public-private partnerships is not to grow or to produce profit, but rather to reach some substantive goals. Even in those cases where the generation of a profit is the primary goal, this cannot be achieved without taking into account the restrictions that have been put into place by the state (such as opening hours, health and safety standards and the minimum wage). When we look at the state itself, we observe that it is not simply a set of bureaucratic units exclusively driven by rules. Federal, state or local authorities too have to be concerned with the acquisition and investment of financial resources, and with dealing with supply and demand. They are involved in activities like the promotion of technology, the operation of business parks, the management of natural resources and of infrastructure, the running of lotteries, casinos and spas, transport services and a great deal more. The state also runs the central bank and owns or part-owns whole enterprises. This all goes to show that the state plays a major role in the market and emphasises that the "market or state" classification of economic agents is limited in its usefulness.

Categorising on the basis of **production and consumption** is also unconvincing. Business entities that produce—typically firms—are often seen as the only possible object of study by management experts and academics, so they ignore the economic agents that are the objects of analysis in public finance and public economics. However, every company or public body, and even every private household, produces goods or services and needs to consume resources in order to be able to do so.

A classification based on the **dominant factor of production** distinguishes between labour-intensive and capital-intensive economic agents, depending on whether labour costs or capital costs are the most significant. Since capital is embedded in tangible assets, financial investments and in stocks of materials, this classification can distinguish between capital-intensive, labour-intensive or material-intensive businesses. Further differentiations are also possible; we could, for instance, identify energy-intensive business entities. Overall, however, this classification is not particularly helpful as there are many companies in which more than one factor of production is significant, i.e. is responsible for a sizeable proportion of total costs, as in the case of airlines, where fuel costs, staffing costs and aircraft costs are all very high.

The dominant factor of production is frequently a decisive criterion when deciding on location, so it is possible to develop a categorisation based on **location dependency**. The location may be primarily determined by requirements for low cost or specialised labour, raw materials or energy, or companies may need to be close to their markets.

Using **type of good** as a criterion leads to a differentiation between business entities which produce goods and those which produce services. The former can be further categorised on the basis of the phase of the production process in which they are active: extraction of raw materials (e.g. mines), production of industrial goods (e.g. steel mills) and production of consumer goods (e.g. mobile phones). The latter can be distinguished on the basis of which factors of production are most important for their production (e.g. financial services companies or personnel services companies), which functions they support (e.g. purchasing, storage, transport, disposal, marketing or administration), which type of service they provide or in which branch they operate (consulting, planning, information, research, teaching, health, social services, safety, maintenance, and so on). A classification on the basis of types of good does not imply exclusivity because the production of goods can be preceded, accompanied, or followed by the production of services.

The type of good is linked to the **production method**. We can distinguish between business entities on the basis of whether they rely primarily on intellectual or manual labour and on the basis of production method—mainly manual, mechanical or automated; custom, series or mass production; few or many stages of work; cell production, assembly line, or fixed position layout; high or low contact (for services). In the real world it would be difficult to find a business to which just one of these criteria applies because in many cases there are mixed forms of production which involve more than one of these features (e.g. mainly mechanical series production and mainly mechanical custom production).

We can use **size** to distinguish between economic agents and this can be measured in many ways. The measure can be monetary in nature, like total assets, value added, sales, income, payroll, capital, budget, tax revenues, membership fees or foundation assets. Size can also refer to a quantity, like the number of employees, members, clients, students, patients, hotel rooms and so on. These measures are not universally relevant. For example, total assets as a measure is relevant for banks, revenues and number of employees for commercial or industrial enterprises; the size of farms is measured by acreage or number of animals; transport companies are measured by the number of passengers, ports by the tonnage moved, hospitals by the number of beds, hotels by the number of overnight stays, municipal administrations be the number of inhabitants or the budget, universities by the number of students. There is rarely a single measure that tells the whole story—it is generally necessary to use several to create meaningful groupings. Figure 3.1 presents the criteria for a typology of economic agents.

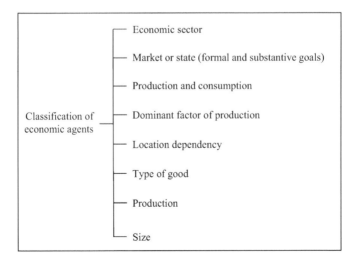

Fig. 3.1 Criteria for classifying economic agents

3.1.3   Legal Form

The legal form of an economic agent plays an important role in determining its rights and duties, and the limits of its activities. (Note that laws vary from country to country; this section deals with the situation in Germany.) Economic agents can be persons or institutions. This distinction is similar to, but not identical with, the legal distinction between natural and legal persons. **Natural persons** in this context are individuals with rights and duties (where duties derive from rights) and who are legally responsible and have the legal capacity to act. From an economic point of view they are of interest mainly because of the role they play as households in the supply and demand of goods and services; a narrow view of the activities includes only those where money is involved, while a wider view includes all activities—e.g. buying food compared to looking after a baby.

Groups of persons or associations of persons without a legal form are also economic agents and therefore relevant for readers of this book. These are for example households composed of more than one person, associations of various kinds, or groups of individuals running some kind of activity together. Typical in this case is that a functional grouping can be easily recognised but those involved cannot be said to be part of a formal organisation. A natural individual person has rights and duties, can sign contracts and own capital, but a group of friends, for example, does not have a legal personality and can do none of those things.

Institutions can be divided into those with or without legal personality. **Institutions with legal personality** are legally independent, with assets of their own which they use to achieve their goals and for which they bear liability; they are legal entities. There are legal personalities of private or of public law in Germany. The former includes associations or foundations that have registered with the relevant bodies, as well as listed companies, limited companies and co-operatives; the latter includes public institutions.

The choice of legal form has many implications. It affects the way in which the economic agent is organised, its legal position and its supervision by the relevant authorities. Other areas where the legal form is relevant include:

- the way in which owners, members or bearers of other rights exercise influence
- the autonomy of management
- the participation of natural persons in strategic decisions
- the opportunities for financing
- audit obligations
- the tax burden
- transparency

Apart from purely economic aspects, the autonomy of the institution, its standing in the political and social system and the protection of consumers also play an important role in the choice of legal form. The legal form for entities that carry out certain economic activities is prescribed by law, as is the case with banks and law firms, for example.

3.1.4 Basic Types

There are **two overarching criteria** which apply to all economic agents: objectives (the effort to achieve a desired situation) and financing (the effort to remain independent in a money-based economy). These criteria mean that four basic types of economic agent can be identified. **Households** strive for self-fulfilment and are financed by their revenues (in the form of income, pension, state benefits etc.). The main goal of **firms** is either the achievement of profit from sales revenues or the achievement of a certain performance while covering costs. **Associations** are economic agents which satisfy the needs of a group and are financed by membership fees or other types of contribution. **Administrations** meet collective or public needs, and are financed by taxation.

Fig. 3.2 gives examples and provides some insight into the diversity and variety of economic agents.

Basic types / Characteristics	Households	Firms	Associations	Administrations
Goals	Self-fulfilment	Achievement of profit Producing output while covering costs	Meeting group needs	Meeting public needs
Financing	Income	Sales revenues	Fees Contributions	Taxes
Examples	Single-person household Multi-person households	Professionals Commercial enterprises Tradesman firms Insurance companies Industrial enterprises Banks Hospitals Transport companies	Trade unions Chambers of commerce Social insurance institutions Sports clubs	Federal administrations State administrations Municipal administrations Church administrations (in countries with church taxes, e.g. Austria, Germany, Switzerland)

Fig. 3.2 The four basic types of economic agent

3.2   Households

3.2.1   Self-Fulfilment

The original economic agent is the individual (it is interesting to note that the word *economy* comes from the Greek word *oikonomos*, which means "one who manages a household"). In order to satisfy their basic needs, the individual establishes a domestic unit which provides the basic **economic infrastructure** for the self-fulfilment of that individual. Self-fulfilment is a complex endeavour, not analysed in detail here, but we can refer to its basic conditions: the availability of food, clothes and shelter, safety, the opportunity to socialise and gain the respect of others. Self-fulfilment takes place through physical and mental activities. The private household is the first place where needs are met. Consumption takes place here as does the reproduction of labour which is then used inside or outside the private household.

Households are **the starting point for the activities of other economic agents**. Even in ancient times, self-support was not the only activity within households, for goods were produced for exchange or sale. In such cases a distinction must be made between a household and a business, even if they coincide as they frequently do today when we think about freelancers working from home—a distinction which is important for taxes because it is necessary to distinguish between work which is performed "privately" for the household and work which is done to earn money—cooking a meal for the family versus designing a webpage. Households can supply labour to other households (for example housekeeping services) and to all other economic agents. Beyond offering paid labour, household members perform unpaid work. Although this kind of work is not to be found on the labour market, it has a great economic impact in fields such as the social services, healthcare, education, sports, the protection of the environment, culture and politics. Examples of these kinds of activities include looking after elderly parents, taking care of a sick child, teaching a child to read, playing football with the family, recycling old newspapers, going to the cinema and taking part in elections, thereby influencing policies.

Households also make financial resources available to other households (for example in the form of alimony, rents or gifts), they invest capital in enterprises and buy their products. They make payments to associations (e.g. in the form of membership fees) and administrations (in the form of taxes etc.), and require their services (counselling, permits, teaching, infrastructure, protection, safety, etc.).

From an economic point of view, it is interesting to observe how the self-fulfilment of households influences the flows of goods and services and of payments, and this has a clear impact on other economic agents. **Determinants** of the economic activity of households include: size and composition; age, education, employment and income of its members; social position; consumption, mobility and leisure patterns; type of housing.

3.2.2   Types of Income

In non-barter economy, the existence and the autonomy of households depends on income, of which there are different types.

Income from agriculture and forestry derives from the operation of a farm or from forest management. Income generating activities include growing fruit and vegetables, animal husbandry and breeding, beekeeping and even hunting. When looking at these activities, it is often difficult to distinguish the household from the business, a problem which may be of great interest to tax collectors.

Income from business activities derives from the profits of businesses which belong, entirely or partially, to the household, or from any other form of participation in a business activity for which a member of the household bears some form of entrepreneurial risk.

Income from self-employment comes from work done when one is not in an employment relationship. Many types of work can be done by the self-employed—scientific, artistic, educational and so on. Among the self-employed are those who are often said to be members of a profession (e.g. physicians, dentists, lawyers, architects, nurses and accountants) and those who are often referred to as freelancers, such as journalists, programmers and translators. Individuals may have an employer and at the same time generate some income from self-employment on the side.

Income from employment can be earned at any of the four kinds of economic agent in our classification. It can take the form of wages, salaries, bonuses, pensions, any form of benefit and can be paid in money or in kind.

Income from capital assets derives from investments in shares or other forms of participation in private enterprises, or from investment funds, life insurance policies, interest on deposits, etc.

Income from rents and leases comes from the granting of the use of land, buildings or parts of buildings, ships, copyrights or related rights to other economic agents. This includes the value of using one's own residence to earn revenue.

Other revenues include benefits received by the household for educational or social purposes, alimony payments, and unemployment insurance.

Revenues from the sale of capital assets is **not considered income**, nor is the payment of health or accident damages by an insurance company. The same applies to lottery wins, inheritances, donations and awards.

3.2.3   Use of Resources

Households' resources can be used for consumption or for investment. **Consumption by private households** consists in the purchase of goods and services to satisfy the needs of its members. The consumption of the goods can take place over a shorter or a longer period of time—food is consumed soon after purchase, while furniture and cars last longer.

The main categories of consumption are:

- food, beverages and tobacco,
- clothing and shoes,
- house and apartment rents and energy (excluding fuel),
- furniture, household appliances and similar goods,
- goods for health and body care,
- goods for education, entertainment and leisure (excluding hotel services) and
- other personal needs, hotel services and other kinds of goods.

The **investment expenditures of households** lie in the purchase of real estate (land, buildings or apartments) and capital investment in various forms. These expenditures, as opposed to those for consumption goods, have an impact on the household assets. Investments are financed by savings, by current income and by debt. The amount of current income, i.e. the financial strength of the household, determines whether the household is in a position to employ its resources not only for consumption but also to increase its assets.

Past decisions on the allocation of resources influence current ones. They determine payment obligations (e.g. rent or interest payments) and—subtracted from all other income (derived from employment, investments and so on)—the **surplus**, on the basis of which new decisions can be made. When (and if) private households work on their **budgets**, it is in the context of expected income and payments.

3.2.4   Accounting

Even households are not exempt from the need for accounting due to the financial relations they have with other economic agents. The bookkeeping and accounting duties of households derive from the need to determine their **taxation**. Taxpayers whose income comes from employment, and whose tax payments are made directly by their employers, do not need to keep accounts. A different situation arises when certain expenditures are deducted from gross income to lower taxable income so that the tax burden is reduced: in this case the taxpayer has to supply evidence of those expenditures through their accounts—one cannot simply present the tax office with a pile of bills.

At the level of national accounting, where the transactions between economic agents belonging to different sectors of an economy are captured, data from households' economic activities are included the figures for private households. If a household member works as a freelancer or rents apartments, their income will be included in those of private households in the national accounts, because these are not viewed as the activities of a firm. Furthermore, private non-profit organisations are also counted as private households in government economic statistics (at least in

Germany). In our classification, on the other hand, we always distinguish between economic agents on the basis of the question: are they engaged autonomously in an economic activity using one or more factors of production? We therefore consider the self-employed and non-profit organisations to be autonomous economic agents rather than "just" households.

3.3 Firms

3.3.1 Profit Orientation

We define firms as those economic agents which try to achieve a profit through the sale of goods and services in a **market economy**. The self-employed also fall into this category, as mentioned in the previous section, because from our point of view (though not from a tax or regulatory perspective) their activities are **typical of a firm**—their services are offered for revenue and should generate profit, although in a few cases profit is not the primary goal.

Besides the typical profit-oriented firms there are a number of **atypical firms**, which strive neither for the highest possible profit, nor even for an adequate one. These may consider profit desirable but not really achievable (e.g. research and development subsidiaries, or local public transport enterprises) or they may be content with minimal profit or even just with being able to cover costs (e.g. non-profit hospitals or public enterprises which supply water). The main goal of these enterprises is meeting needs, rather than the achievement of a profit. At the same time however, they want to be as efficient and effective as possible in terms of generating the maximum output from the given inputs, and they generally want to at least cover their costs. When their revenues do not match costs, subsidies become a necessity in order to preserve assets and keep the enterprise functioning. Such subsidies will normally be provided when it is decided that it is in the public interest to keep the enterprise going—perhaps to facilitate the provision of education, for research or technological development, to support the development an industry or of a region, to protect jobs, to maintain competition, or for health-related, cultural, ecological or social reasons. Public theatres, libraries, hospitals, research institutes, transport authorities and state universities are all given subsidies for these reasons.

Another kind of atypical firm is that which operates in a **planned economy**. Instead of having objectives of its own, such a firm strives to achieve the overall economic objectives of the economic system as laid out in a plan, rather than its own particular objectives.

3.3.2 Sales Revenues

Sales revenues result from the economic exploitation of a firm's output and are the basis of its existence. Even if it receives subsidies on a regular basis, a firm cannot continue to exist in the long term without revenues from sales. In principle, revenues from sales are closely related to the costs incurred by the firm to procure the factors of production, to produce its output, to sell it to other economic agents and to realise a profit. Once costs are calculated on the basis of different cost elements and cost centres, it is possible to determine the **lower price limit**, taking into account the market situation. When there is no full competition between firms but rather a weakened competitive climate—because of market failure or because the market is subject to regulation (e.g. in the transportation sector)—the **asking price** set by the firm needs to take into account not only costs but also economic and political considerations. Costs offer only a general orientation when a **flat fee** is set, by law or in a contract (such as television licences or nursing rates in hospitals).

Sales revenues come from the sale, leasing or rental of products, their by-products and waste, from the sale of services or from the sale of the outcomes of specific projects. They are shown as an earnings item in the income statement. Operating income is also affected by the quantity of finished or semi-finished products held by the firm, by internally produced assets (vehicles, tools, etc.) and by other sources of income. Together, these represent the overall performance of the firm. After subtracting operating expenses (materials, personnel, depreciation), we determine the **operating result**, which will be an operating profit or loss. Next, we can include non-operating income (e.g. income from investments and interest) and non-operating expenses (e.g. interest paid) to establish the firm's **result of ordinary business activity**. After including extraordinary income (e.g. the sale of a building owned by the firm for a price higher or lower than its value is accounted for in the financial statements) and extraordinary expenses (such as outpayments made necessary by fire damage) and subtracting taxation, we arrive at the **profit or loss for the year**.

A firm must buy the machines and the raw materials, rent a factory and hire people before it can even start production, so costs generally precede sales revenues because the factors of production need to be acquired and used before goods and services can be brought to market. We discuss income statements in more detail in Chap. 6.

This form of calculating and representing financial results applies to industrial firms. For trading and service firms, banks and the professions, revenues do not come from the production and sale of goods, but from trades or from the sale of financial services, from interest, commissions, or from the sale of consulting services.

The **total revenue** of a firm can be split up by business unit, product, customer, region, branch, plant, subsidiary and so on. Some parts of firms involved in more than one area of business will generate more revenues than others and some will have higher expenses—the difference between sales revenues and expenses determines the contribution of each area to the overall financial result of the firm. There are cases in which an area that makes a surplus supports a loss-making area. This may even be planned, because the areas which make losses are necessary to support others, or because the products are just in the process of being introduced to the market and prices need to be kept low. Another case of planned deficits are those of public sector enterprises (such as transport authorities) which fulfil a public duty while producing a service, but which cannot charge their customers or users the full cost.

Some firms, such as professional football clubs, have both economic and non-economic goals and it is often difficult to separate them. This is important mainly for tax reasons, because **sales revenues resulting from commercial activities** generally lead to various kinds of tax being levied while turnover related to charitable or religious goals, for example, is non-taxable (in Germany).

3.3.3 Entrepreneurs

In normal language usage, entrepreneurs are people who show initiative, are creative, like taking decisions, work hard and are ready to take risks. These entrepreneurial characteristics can be found in all facets of life, where they assume different but always important functions. According to Joseph A. Schumpeter (1883–1950) entrepreneurs have the role of pioneers and determine the pace of innovation and of technical progress in an economy: they invest capital, take risks and expect a return. Besides **owner-entrepreneurs** there are entrepreneurs who operate with capital which is not their own and are employed as managers.

Managers have many different roles: they lead and they take decisions on how to combine production factors (see also Chap. 9). It is not easy to define who is a **manager-entrepreneur**—it is clearly the case for the members of the top management boards of companies but can also extend this view to include not only the top management of firms, but also middle and lower management. According to this relatively new perspective, **everyone who works in a firm** should be regarded as an **entrepreneur** and they should think and behave as entrepreneurs at their place of work. This view is particularly relevant in companies where everyone performs a recognised role and participates in the economic benefits of the firm's success.

The professions have a special situation. A doctor's practice, for example, is from a business administration point of view a firm, and the doctor is at the same time a physician and an entrepreneur. In her role as an entrepreneur she takes all important decisions, hires and supervises personnel, procures furniture, equipment and pharmaceutical goods, organises the factors of production and the performance of services, deals with the finances, does the bookkeeping and prepares accounts (or delegates these functions to others) and checks them. This entrepreneurial work is relevant when considering efficiency and effectiveness. The calculation of the financial results of the practice should include (fictional) compensation to the doctor for their entrepreneurial/managerial activities, in addition to interest on equity and a reward for the risk incurred.

Entrepreneurs become employers as soon as they hire a second person. Natural persons or legal entities can be employers, just as they can join employer associations and participate in wage negotiations with trades unions.

3.3.4   Employees

Employees are natural persons who have a contract to perform work; they are not able to decide themselves what they do and how they do it because they are in a situation of dependence. A labour contract for paid employment is one of many possible kinds of service contract, which can also be made with professionals such as lawyers, tax consultants or doctors. Service contracts usually specify exactly what the outcome should be and in most, but not all, cases how it should be achieved. The employee of company usually has much less discretion in deciding on outputs and methods compared to an outside consultant. This is relevant for the courts who have been asked to determine whether those who drive for the company Uber or deliver food for the company Deliveroo are independent contractors or employees; the result will affect things like sick pay and holiday entitlement of the workers (employees are entitled to these, contractors are not). **Types of employee** can be identified on the basis of function, institution, position and employment relationship; examples are technical employee, factory worker, office employee, trainee, intern and so on.

In order to pursue common interests, employees can establish **unions**. They normally negotiate work conditions, including payment, for large numbers of workers with employers (or associations of employers). Germany has the concept of **co-determination**, which is the participation of employees through elected representatives in the decision-making processes of a firm. It applies to companies and administrations with at least five employees. Workers' councils are initially concerned with matters such as working hours, holiday planning, health and safety at work and the basis of the compensation system. They also have a right to be informed about and participate in decision-making processes related to business issues, as when a firm needs to lay workers off because business is not going well.

There is a right to equal participation in corporate decision-making in companies with over 2000 employees which have the legal form of a corporation. The employees' representatives are members of the supervisory board where they have an equal say to that of the owners' representatives.

3.4   Associations

3.4.1   Special Tasks

Associations are economic agents which, despite their importance for the economy, society and the state, have been somewhat neglected by the disciplines of business administration and economics. Associations are organisations with (free or compulsory) membership. Members can be individuals or institutions who join with the aim of being able to perform certain activities or achieving a certain goal. Depending on the kind of duties and the legal form, we can distinguish between associations of private law and associations of public law (this is the situation in Germany and regardless of local legal considerations, the points we make apply to associations in all countries).

In **associations of private law** we observe either the dominance of collective interests (professional associations, citizens' initiatives, trades unions, self-help groups, consumer associations), of social needs (traditional associations, hobby clubs, cultural and sport associations, or associations of people with similar opinions) or of visions and goals for others (for example associations of citizens, cultural associations, support associations, environmental associations, parties, political associations and social associations). Their goals and tasks are often mixed, which makes a clear typology of associations of private law impossible.

Associations of private law organise the interests, the needs or the wishes of their **members**. There are of course also associations of associations; these are, in a certain sense, associations of a higher order and are sometimes designated as federations.

Associations of private law perform their tasks in **different fields**. In the fields of labour, law, technology and the economy we find employers' associations, professional associations, industry associations, labour unions, associations of communes, associations of taxpayers and of consumers. In the fields of education, church, culture and science, we find school, college and university associations, scientific associations, religious and philosophical associations. In the fields of leisure, society, health and the environment we find associations for home care, gardening, human rights, environmental protection, sports, animal protection, mutual understanding between peoples. In the social field, we find associations for foreigners, refugees, families, young people, children, senior citizens.

The duties of associations have two dimensions: internal and external. The **internal tasks** consist for instance in providing relevant information to members, in individual counselling and support (e.g. in technical, financial, legal or tax issues), in education and training, in the conciliation of diverging interests, occasionally also in research or in the assignment of research work to third parties.

External tasks consist of activities like public relations work and advertising of the association's goals and activities, the organisation of exhibitions and similar events, cooperation with other associations and organisations, with local and state authorities and European institutions, and also in the representation and defence of their own interests, i.e. lobbying.

Associations of public law such as chambers of industry, chambers of commerce, and chambers of agriculture also meet the needs of a specific group. Lawyers, physicians, architects and accountants are typical professions that have their own professional body with statutory membership. All associations of public law perform **duties for the state** and can therefore take severe action against members in order to enforce the law on behalf of the state (e.g. disbarring doctors or lawyers). Their duties include the representation of the interests of the members, the promotion of professional education, the administration of exams, the recruiting of experts for various tasks, the supervision and enforcement of professional standards and duties, the management of conflicts, the preparation of expert opinions, the provision of expert advice, the maintenance of up-to-date lists of members and the provision of education and welfare institutions, not only for members but also for their families.

Beyond those responsible for the self-administration of the professions, there are corporations of public law in the field of **social insurance**, and in the field of the administration of **natural resources**, such as water, forests, coastal areas or mines.

Our main interest in associations lies in the way in which their tasks are defined and how they can carry out their tasks in an efficient and effective way. There are therefore three areas to which we must pay attention: first, financing, the procurement and use of resources and accounting; second, their size and area of responsibility; and third, decision-making processes and what is involved in their management.

3.4.2 Membership Fees

Characteristic of associations is that they are financed by membership fees. The **yield from contributions** determines what an association can do, like revenue does in households, but unlike firms, whose scope is dictated primarily by their capital assets.

Starting from the duties to be performed, the association must find potential new members (if membership is not compulsory), persuade them to join and raise membership revenue. Often associations do not realise that these activities take place in competition with other associations, nor do they take competition into consideration when trying to attract new members. Indeed, sometimes the opposite of member acquisition takes place, since some associations (e.g. exclusive clubs) hold their membership numbers deliberately low. It may be that the priority is not as large a membership or as high revenues as possible, but rather a good mix of members in relation to the association's duties. This can mean going so far as to create financial and other obstacles (e.g. waiting lists, exams, age limits) to membership. There is often a discussion about whether policies that limit membership are discriminatory, and how far can they go. It was only in 2016, for example, that the members of the private Royal Troon golf club in Scotland voted to allow women to join. Associations of public law, in most countries, must abide by non-discrimination policies.

The decision on amount, structure, payment schedule and maturity of membership fees is either taken internally by decision-making bodies, or, when membership is compulsory, is taken externally or even prescribed by law. This decision is inherently different from price-setting decisions in firms, which seek to determine a minimum acceptable price through a cost calculation; associations determine membership fees on the basis of what they intend to do or even on what they have done in the past.

Besides membership fees as their main source of financing, associations have other forms of revenue. They often receive **allowances** from households or firms, or from other associations and in some cases they receive **grants** from the state, religious groups, foundations and similar organisations. Associations can also generate revenues from rents or sales, when they provide services, organise events, operate educational institutions, nurseries and kindergartens, youth centres and nursing homes, hospitals, foster homes, fire brigades, water works, and so on. However, in these cases, associations are behaving as entrepreneurs and if this kind of activity is the primary source of financing, the association then turns into a firm, raising issues related to taxation.

The **management of financial resources** depends on the amount and timing of the payment of membership fees to the association and on the payments it must make—these should in normal cases be balanced and temporary surpluses can be invested and deficits must be covered by loans. As a precaution it is possible to build up some reserves, consisting of a small amount of cash for short-dated payments (up to 1 year) and some interest-yielding investments as coverage for the medium term (up to 5 years). Reserves must be invested while bearing in mind three principles which are normally not easy to reconcile: safety, high yield, and availability in case of need.

The **financial management and accounting** of most associations consists of a budget, simplified bookkeeping and a final account (more on accounting can be found in Chap. 7). Such an approach is sufficient for many associations in that it permits basic financial planning and reporting, but does not go far enough to support achieving improved efficiency and effectiveness though the organisation's structures and internal processes. The advantages of double-entry bookkeeping with income statements and balance sheet are quite evident, and not just for larger associations.

3.4.3 Regionalisation

Normally associations follow the regional principle, meaning that their activities, the discharge of their duties and their membership are contained within a specific geographical area. Their **catchment area** can be large (e.g. pension insurance institutes) or small (e.g. company pension scheme) in geographic terms, membership can be open (like in sports associations) or closed (e.g. chambers of commerce), it may be organised with a single geographic structure, be divided in territorial subsections or both (for example a union or an employers' association with central offices and local branches), and its borders may be those of a country, a region, a province, a country, a city or any other administrative unit.

The regional structure of large associations, in particular of corporations of public law, is an important issue because it has an impact on the efficiency and the effectiveness of their operations. One side of the issue is internal efficiency, which implies that a large, centralised structure is preferable as it provides economies of scale. The other side is the fact that the proximity of services to members can improve service quality and decrease members' costs (such as travel costs) as decentralised structures facilitate access. Managers of associations need, then, to find the **optimum balance** where costs are minimised while services are maintained at an acceptable level in terms of quantity and quality. This usually leads to a structure where there is a coordinating headquarters and decentralised local offices.

3.4.4   Decision Making

Since associations have certain tasks and duties, members or their representatives must take major decisions. The establishment of associations and internal decision-making follow democratic principles according to which every member has one vote and the majority decides on the composition of the governing bodies and their duties. Associations typically have **two governing bodies**: a general assembly, in which every member is entitled to participate, and a management board.

The general assembly debates matters of general concern for the association, approves and modifies its statutes, chooses and discharges the members of the management board, determines membership fees, authorises the budget and approves the final accounts. The management board prepares the general assembly and carries out decisions once they are adopted, represents the association towards third parties and takes care of normal operations. These responsibilities can also be delegated to one or more senior managers. The management board can elect a smaller executive board, with a president as its speaker. For special duties or activities of the association committees or expert groups are sometimes set up which are normally not official bodies of the association.

In principle, decision-making processes in associations are democratic. Laws regulating associations require that members participate in their development, but there is now a tendency towards what can be termed a **professionalisation of strategic duties**. Information advantage, flexibility in action and reaction, competitive and performance pressures are leading to a shift in decision-making from the general assembly to the board, and the former only formally rubber-stamps the latter's deliberations. Associations' main decision-making bodies are often incapable of defining goals and strategy so this decision-making deficit is made up for by professional managers whose primary tasks were originally intended to be the execution of strategy rather than its formulation.

To this day, business administration disciplines still owe us a better understanding of the special demands of the management of associations. The interdependencies between self-organisation and the executive function, substantive goals and financial objectives, volunteer and paid work are as yet mostly unexplored.

3.5   Administrations

3.5.1   Public Tasks

The concept of *administration* is ambiguous. From an institutional point of view, it encompasses only one of our four kinds of economic agents but from a functional point of view, administration is an activity performed by all economic agents. In this last sense, administration is a **principal function** in administrations and associations, and a **secondary function** in firms, where areas like procurement, production or sales dominate. The administrative function can be relatively autonomous or closely linked to top management and other functions, such as the administration of warehousing and distribution, or to the organisation of factors of production (e.g. the finance function or human resources management). When it is the main function in the economic agents which we call administrations, it is instrumental to the activity of governing.

Administration could be defined on the basis of constitutional law, which divides state power into three branches: the legislative, the executive and the judiciary. Administration would then be linked to the executive branch. We view this distinction as not helpful and accordingly define administrations as those economic agents which meet the general needs of a population or a community and are financed through public charges, normally, but not exclusively, in the form of taxes. This general goal is based on the existence of a **public interest** and which can be subdivided into different **political goals**, such goals related to education, energy, food, public finance, health, industrial, agricultural, small and medium sized firms, security, social and environmental policies. Public tasks, in the form of specific activities aimed at achieving desired goals, are derived directly from political goals.

Public tasks and duties can be classified according to which person or institution may, should or must carry them out (normative concept); or according to who really does carry them out (descriptive concept). The "public" in the definition of public tasks represents **the general public and the common good**, terms that are rather imprecise. Do only people in a specific place belong to the general public, or all citizens and (non-citizens?) living in Germany? Are people in neighbouring countries included? Do only people who are now alive belong, or also future generations? What is the meaning of common good? Is it the sum of personal value preferences or is it an equilibrium between individuals and institutions which goes beyond private interests?

In the absence of exhaustive, realistic and consistent theories, practice has developed models in which the public duties in a democratic state are defined by legitimate political authorities. The **requirements of public duties**, such as equality, fairness, equal treatment, the rule of law, objectivity, and social justice, make it in some cases imperative that the state (at local, regional or national level) fulfils them directly.

Public tasks are numerous and complex, relevant to everyone from birth to death in nearly all important aspects of life. **The fulfilment of public tasks** takes place through administrations, but also through public associations and enterprises as well as private economic agents. Even when third parties are put in charge of a public duty, the final responsibility for it lies with a public administration. If the latter assign a mandate to perform a certain duty, they must also ensure that it is carried out not only in accordance with the law, but also with the political wishes of the relevant decision-makers. If services are produced internally by an administration, it must use and manage its own means and factors of production; if they are produced externally, the administration becomes a contracting body or a purchasing authority. Its role changes from that of a direct producer to that of planner, supervisor and quality manager of the performance of public duties carried out by an external contractor. If the contractor is a private economic agent, there is a privatisation of the discharge of public duties, not a privatisation of the public duties themselves. It is important to underline this because this fundamental distinction is sometimes neglected in discussions on privatisation.

3.5.2 Public Charges

Public tasks are primarily financed through public charges which provide the revenues administrations need to perform public duties. General needs are covered by general financial means, i.e. taxes. **Taxes** are recurring or non-recurring payments which do not correspond to the specific provision of a service. Besides the acquisition of revenues, taxes also serve the purpose of directing the behaviour of tax-paying private firms and households, thereby contributing to the achievement of political and non-fiscal goals.

Taxes provide **covering funds** to public administrations. The revenues they produce are seldom earmarked for specific duties or activities and are used to cover expenditures in general, not just specific ones. It is possible for taxes to be allocated to specific tasks—the German government spends the money raised by a tax on petrol on road building and maintenance and the Quebec government allocated some tax revenues specifically to cover the deficit incurred by the 1976 Montreal Olympics.

Other public charges take the form of contributions and fees which are payments for a specific service provided by an administration. **Contributions** are charged to cover spending on the production, procurement, expansion and renovation of public facilities; examples are the contributions for connection to public utilities networks or for access from private property to the public road network. Spa towns raise a spa tax on visitors which is allocated to the facilities used by the visitors, and private economic agents may also have to make a contribution for facilities if they derive an economic benefit from them, or if the facilities prevent possible damage (as when a public institution operates a system of dams which prevent flooding in a city). It is not necessary that the private economic agents actually use the facilities to have to make a contribution; it is enough that the possibility of use exists.

Fees are divided in two categories: administrative fees and utilisation fees. **Administrative fees** are paid for official acts or other services which are required by third parties, such as issuing a marriage certificate. The basis for the calculation of administrative fees varies: from the number of photocopies required to reproduce a document in a public archive to the value of real estate when registering a change of ownership. Administrative fees may greatly exceed the actual cost of providing the services, or they may be much lower than the cost, which is often not even roughly known, let alone known precisely.

Utilisation fees are levied for the usage of a public facility and their basis is actual usage. Should actual usage be difficult to measure exactly, estimated usage can be the basis for the determination of utilisation fees—the city of Berlin does not know how much rubbish an individual inhabitant throws away, but charges a fee based on the size of the apartment. The revenues from utilisation fees should cover the full costs as far as possible (e.g. for sewage disposal, recycling, swimming pools).

Contributions and fees as special public charges, together with socially acceptable prices for private transactions (e.g. for public transport tickets, entrance prices, electricity prices, rents and leases) are **administered prices**. On the one hand, they are an important source of revenue for public administrations; on the other hand, they are an instrument that can be used to manage the demand for public services. The latter is based on the necessity to meet general needs as defined and established in political processes. Although general needs are felt by individuals, it is often not feasible to have them met solely through market mechanisms.

Administered prices for public tasks generate revenues for administrations and also for public enterprises given the responsibility of carrying out such tasks. It is also possible to spin-off parts of administrations and turn them into public enterprises with the responsibility of carrying out public tasks. Administrations can even outsource to private economic agents who, under supervision, make them available to the public at administered prices which need to be approved and are not set by the market, such as is the case with the tariffs of electricity, gas, water, public transport and social care services.

3.5.3 Partial Market Entities

Territorial authorities are responsible for public administration, encompassing all levels of government and defined by the geographical area for which they are responsible—national, regional or local. In democratic states, they include a **political body**, elected by the population of the area in which the administration is active. Territorial authorities are together responsible for the welfare of the population; the areas in which they are active are determined by law and by the decisions of their political organs. Territorial administrations concurrently cover all levels of government. Each level—small town, province, region, national state or a supranational entity—has specific tasks, which it defines itself or are defined by another, higher, level of government. This sometimes causes conflicts of competency, in which institutions from more than one level of government want, or do not want, to be responsible for a certain area of policy.

Administrations are different from other economic agents primarily, but not exclusively, in their goals and in their financing. Similar to other economic agents, administrations procure factors of production, combine them and offer the goods and services that they then produce so that they can achieve their goals. The **procurement of factors of production** in administrations is similar to that of other economic agents: e.g. recruitment of personnel, awarding contracts for the purchase of goods and services and borrowing money. Differences exist when **factors of production are combined**, a process in which administrations normally have more rules to follow than other economic agents. The essential difference, however, lies in the way in which revenues are obtained, since administrations **offer their goods and services** in large part without requiring payment. In this sense, they cannot really be considered as full participants in the market: they do procure factors of production on markets, but most of their outputs are made available to third parties through non-market mechanisms and so, following Hanns Linhardt (1901-1989), we refer to them as partial market entities. Administrations normally do not exchange goods and services for payment; the financing of administrative bodies active in the fields of labour, construction, public finance, internal affairs, justice, agriculture, police, social affairs, environment, defence and so on is achieved through the imposition of taxes on all taxpayers. Taxpayers are those individuals and economic agents whom tax laws characterise as being liable to tax. Whether taxpayers use the services provided by administrations is not relevant to the amount of taxes they have to pay.

Purchase decisions determine the quantity, quality and provider of products on free markets. For administrations, though, the kind of services provided, their quantity and quality, depend on **political decisions** which in turn are influenced and determined in general and local elections and in the elected bodies of the territorial public institutions.

Although the supply of services by administrations and their financing through taxation are two distinct processes, far apart from each other and governed by political decisions, one principle is relevant to both: **the principle of value-for-money**. According to this, each administration must strive to provide a maximum of services with the financial means available. Administrations which are bound by the value-for-money principle must always be able to answer the cardinal question: which alternatives are available, in the framework of political goals and the law, for the more cost-efficient and cost-effective provision of goods and services?

3.5.4 Need for Improvement

The commonly made distinction between administrations and business prevents many people from seeing administrations as economic entities, an oversight that this book addresses. From the point of view of business administration, administrations are economic agents that need to be efficient and effective in the ways they function and deliver services. Even though some laws specifically require efficiency and effectiveness, reality does not match expectations. Some new approaches, such as **Public and Non-Profit Management**, try to reinforce the economic character of administrations, which they view as service units, arguing that public duties should be met in an economic way, and that administrations should be tested to establish how business-like are their internal conditions, their external environment and the laws and rules which govern their activity. These approaches seek to introduce market elements (but not markets) into administrative systems and encourage the application of modern management methods to administrative activity. This is happening mainly in the following areas:

The **volume of public tasks** is analysed and questioned, core duties are separated from marginal and supporting duties, strategic goals are differentiated from operative goals and the "principal-agent" principle is emphasised. This means addressing such questions as whether public tasks should be discharged directly by administrations or by third parties under supervision, and whether administrations should own property and equipment or rent it.

As far as **administrative goals** are concerned, the new approaches deal with the influence of political decisions on goals related to the procurement of factors of production, operational activities and the satisfactory delivery of the goods and services produced. Demand for public goods and services plays a much more important role here.

There is an effort to build more efficient and effective structures and procedures in **administrative organisation**, and to encourage performance-oriented behaviour by **administrative personnel**—some new laws and regulations have been and are being introduced for this very reason, although it is not easy to change the working conditions of civil servants. The modernisation of public administrations aims at a reduction of bureaucracy (lean administration) through such initiatives as the outsourcing of certain functions (e.g. data processing, printing, cleaning, mainte-nance, and so on), the granting of autonomy to institutions (e.g. hospitals, nursing homes, theatres, museums, utilities) and the contracting out of service production processes to third parties. The remaining core duties are carried out in performance centres and by specialised departments which bear not only the technical, but also the economic responsibility for the results they achieve. The coordination of activities and the preparation of budgets are tasks of the top management of public administrations. Planning, administrative and authorisation procedures are improved by greater use of techniques such as project management and teamwork.

Budgeting and accounting are evolving to include the most modern techniques—double-entry bookkeeping, cost accounting and cost-benefit analysis, for example. These developments mean that **financial management** includes **performance management** and the **accounting system** becomes an **information system**.

3.6   Mixed Types

The four basic types of economic agent do not always appear in their pure form and a single economic agent can take more than one of the basic forms over its lifetime. There are however some mixed forms that can generally be associated with a basic type as the following examples demonstrate.

3.6.1   Self-Employed

As noted in Sect. 3.2.2, it is necessary to distinguish between freelancers and professionals. In the classic sense, professionals have occupations where they are subject to strict rules of entry and a code of ethics—typical examples are doctors, lawyers and accountants. Freelancers are people who sell services but are not committed over the long-term to a particular employer; in other words, they are self-employed. The activities of the full-time self-employed are autonomous, profit-oriented, and for the long run. Typical of this type of economic agent are, in addition to those already mentioned, architects, healers, masseurs, sculptors, painters, musicians, writers, translators, management consultants, auditors and technical experts of various kinds. Even if these activities are classified as professional (in the sense of being carried out for payment) activities by civil and tax law, they unmistakably show the main features of firms in their objectives and their financing. The fact that the self-employed also belong to households does not prevent their classification as firms. The nature of the activities generally makes possible a clear distinction between those belonging to the private life of the individual and activities which belong to the work life of the self-employed—tax law takes this distinction into account.

3.6.2 Foundations

The origin of a foundation lies in the decision of one or more benefactors to relinquish capital or other assets which are then invested with the aim of preserving or (hopefully) increasing their value. The resulting interest and any other revenues are distributed in alignment with the goals set by the benefactors. The foundation, since it binds the use of its assets to a goal for the long run, is—in legal terms—a household (in German law); it remains a household even if the foundation owns a firm.

If the foundation itself is used as a form of firm and its goal is the management of a firm which has been entrusted to it, then it is an **economic foundation** and can be classified as a firm in our taxonomy. If the foundation holds shares in companies and controls the holdings, it is a **holding foundation** which normally has economic and non-economic (cultural, educational, political etc.) goals. A holding foundation can provide for members of the family of the benefactor. In a **foundation company**, the assets are not shareholdings in firms, but rather the firms themselves and in this case the foundation is the entrepreneur and its sole goal is the management of the firms, with the consequence that the foundation's assets become an end in themselves. The earnings of foundation companies can be used for non-economic goals or also as a source of future support for members of the benefactor's family.

3.6.3 Sports Clubs

A large number of associations are active in the field of sports. The goal of the typical sports association is the encouragement of the practice of sports by members, who pay contributions to the association and sometimes also share its costs. Even if associations obtain extra revenue from the sale of tickets, drinks and food and from the rent of facilities which they may own, they are not firms. This sort of **economic activity**, far from being forbidden, contributes to achieving the **non-economic goals** of the association.

The transition to the form of a firm takes place when the revenues from other sources exceed the contributions of the members. Large sports clubs (Bayern Munich, Borussia Dortmund, Union Berlin), which sell television and other rights and advertising space, fall into this category.

3.6.4 Hospitals

There are public, non-profit, and commercial hospitals. The latter are obviously firms: they are profit-oriented and are financed mostly by payments for their services. Public hospitals, which belong to local, regional and national public bodies, and non-profit hospitals (which may belong to churches) have some of the characteristics of firms and they also have some of the features of administrations. Alongside the effort to at least cover their costs, they have the **goal** of answering health care needs; university hospitals support research and education; teaching hospitals support the training of physicians and nurses. The **financing** of their current costs comes mainly from revenues in the form of fees for services or rates per day of stay. The fees are covered directly or indirectly by public and private health insurance providers. The capital for investment in public and non-profit hospitals is made available by the territorial authorities which in turn take it from the payments they receive. Sometimes commercial hospitals also receive investment support from public bodies, provided they accept the provisions and conditions of public health care investments.

Similar to public and non-profit hospitals as a mixed type are **nursing homes and residential homes** for the elderly. They are financed partly on the basis of nursing rates and partly by other contributions from their owners (e.g. churches). For the sake of completeness, it must also be mentioned that nursing homes and residential homes for the elderly as well as other firms in the health care field receive financial means from their owners (for special services or to cover losses) and from third parties in the form of donations.

3.6.5 Theatres

Some municipal and regional authorities in Germany, usually the larger ones, own theatres. The **rationale** is that theatres fulfil public tasks in the field of culture, in principle presenting classic and experimental theatre rather than popular entertainment. It is possible to distinguish between two types of theatres: theatres which are part of a municipal administration and theatres that are autonomous public enterprises. Both types are **financed** primarily through taxes, which would be evidence that they are administrations; however, when they have an independent legal personality, they do show entrepreneurial tendencies, marketing aggressively, diversifying their programmes to include lucrative shows, underlining their role as an economic factor. They use sophisticated systems for management.

Similarly, **orchestras, music schools and museums** are undergoing a metamorphosis from being administrations to being firms. Various factors play a role in this process: fewer contributions by the authorities and the introduction of professional management. It is important to note, however, that these developments are taking place in economic agents that are part of the public sector, and are not to be confused with privatisation, which happens when tasks of the state in the cultural field are relinquished to private economic agents.

3.7   Examples and Exercises

Here we present two cases that deal with economic agents. First we look at British Railways. Ensuring that transport services exist is one of the tasks of the government, which does not automatically imply that the organisations with the responsibility of actually running the trains must be owned or run by the state. Ownership and running of the railways in the UK was handed over to private companies in 1994, and since then things have not gone very well as the case shows. Associations are economic agents whose main reason for existence is not making money, and in our second case we look at an association that plays an important role in the lives of Turkish women in Berlin.

3.7.1   Who Should Run the Railways?

British Rail is in crisis. This is clear to anyone who has the bad luck to be at a London train station during the rush hour. The platforms are crowded, the trains too, and punctuality and cleanliness leave a lot to be desired.

British Rail, once a state enterprise, was privatised in 1995. Since then, several companies have been operating the rail network, which they divided up into regions. The result is a shattered rail network which is divided into three: one firm owns the track, other firms run the trains and another group of firms lease the trains out. So passengers traveling from London to Aberdeen ride in trains that the operator Great North Eastern Railways leases from another operator. The trains run on rails that belong to Railtrack. Railtrack has the responsibility of maintaining and improving the rail infrastructure, as well as making sure that the timetables of all 23 different railway operators can actually be met.

No one feels responsible for the entire network. The rail network, the trains and stations are now much worse off than before their privatisation. In addition, there are major financial difficulties for the operating companies, which are not cost-effective despite price increases, cost cutting and an ever-growing number of passengers.

The government is having to subsidise the railway companies to make sure that they can continue to provide the services that are necessary for the economy. Subsidies have tripled over the last 20 years and are now in the region of £6 billion per year. The government also has to subsidise the building of new railways, such as

Crossrail in London, because private firms are not willing or able to invest the huge amounts of money needed for such projects because they are essentially loss-making. Crossrail will cost £16 billion.

Questions

- What arguments can be made for governments to outsource public tasks—like rail transport—to private companies?
- Compare the situation of rail transport in Britain to that in Germany and France. How much privatisation has there been in those countries?
- What would you do if you were the British Minister of Transport?

3.7.2   The Role of Associations

The Turkish Women's Organisation Berlin (Türkischer Frauenverein Berlin e.V./ Berlin Türkiye Kadınlar Birliği) is the oldest such organisation in Berlin. It was founded in 1975, and as part of the celebrations for its fortieth anniversary held a gala dinner, whose list of attendees showed how important the organisation is. It has five principles:

- Solidarity and community make us strong
- Women are not alone
- Every person has the right to learn and continue their education
- Integration begins by learning the language
- We stand for the social and personal rights of women

Its goals are to support women from the Turkish community and to help them with the integration process. It pays particular attention to women and girls who:

- are in a financial or family crisis situation
- have family, partner and parenting problems
- have health problems or questions
- are affected by violence
- need help with authorities
- have legal problems
- have moiney problems
- have a low level of education
- do not speak or understand German well

In this organisation, women can get consulting, life coaching and German language courses. The organisation also provides social support and helps out with legal issues. Also offered are many social activities, such as going to concerts and the theatre. Members also hold discussions on topics of contemporary interest.

Financed by the Berlin Senate, it has two full-time qualified social workers who provide counselling, advice and support, as well as providing the services of many volunteers who teach, coach and offer advice. This organisation is meeting the needs of a large number of women in the Turkish community who face many problems. In comparison with women without a migration background, women from the Turkish community are likely to be poorer, worse educated, more frequently the victims of violence (inside the family and outside) and subject more to racial and sexual discrimination. These issues, together with the low level of language skills of this group, partially explain why a smaller proportion of women from the Turkish community are employed than is the case with people with other migration backgrounds. The Turkish Women's Organisation Berlin is clearly helping individual women with their problems, and is making an impact at that level.

Questions

- In what ways is this association an economic agent?
- How could you measure the success of the organisation?
- How can the leaders of the organisation make sure that it is run in an efficient and effective way? Can you run an organisation such as this like a business?

3.7.3   MyCompany Project

It should be clear that what kind of economic agent your company is: a firm. One of the main characteristics of firms is that they are profit-oriented.

- Think about your company—is profit your only motivation?
- What other goals might your cafe have?
- If you become successful, would you set up a foundation? What might its goals be?

When you set up your own company, you are an entrepreneur.

- What are the most important characteristics of entrepreneurs?

Think of some entrepreneurs, like Richard Branson, Mark Zuckerberg, Elon Musk, or anyone you know who has started a successful business.

- How did they do it?
- What made them successful?

The chapter discussed associations.

- Which associations would you join? Why?

The chapter also discusses administrations.

- What if anything would you as a café owner have to do with the national government and the bodies that it runs?
- Why would you deal with the local administration?
- To which public administrations would you need to make payments and why?

3.7.4 Self-Test Questions

- *What is the difference between typical and atypical economic agents?*
- *Give examples of typical and atypical economic agents.*
- *What are the criteria for a typology of operational units?*
- *What are the weaknesses of the classification of economic agents according to the criterion of market and state?*
- *What are the four basic types of economic agent?*
- *What characterises the goals and financing of the four basic types?*
- *What types of revenues of households can be distinguished?*
- *How is the operating profit or loss calculated?*
- *Define associations and give examples.*
- *Describe how decisions on membership fees of associations are made?*
- *What is the decision-making process in associations?*
- *What are the public tasks of administrations based upon?*
- *Identify different public charges.*
- *How can hospitals be characterised as a mixed type of economic agent?*

A Principle for Action

4

To think is easy. To act is hard. But the hardest thing in the world is to act in accordance with your thinking.
Johann Wolfgang von Goethe (1749–1832)

Opening Vignette

Alois and Meret had gone to the 40th birthday party of Meret's boss. She worked in investment banking and prided herself on her logical and rational way of thinking. It must have been a case of opposites attract, because Alois was quite different. A university lecturer in the history of art, he was, by his own admission, only half as logical as Meret, but, as he liked to say, twice as creative and able to think "outside the box" (a term Meret hated). He had told her on innumerable occasions that real artists didn't think like computers, but dealt with emotions and feelings. She always responded that while there was a place for emotions in private life, there was no place for them in the world of finance. Meret always held that the best decisions were the ones you thought through, not those were you just used your "gut instinct". "People aren't like that," Alois would say, "they're not algorithms!".

After a while, an entertainer was introduced and he announced that they would be playing a game. It consisted of the following: each guest must write a number between 0 and a 100 on a piece of paper. The notes would be collected and the average of the numbers then determined. The entertainer explained, "Whoever is closest to two-thirds of the average with her or his number has won. What number are you going to write pick?"

"Easy" said Meret to Alois. "The average must be 50 because each guest can choose any number! Half will chose above 50 and half below 50. So two-thirds of 50 is 33—that's what I'll choose!"

"Hold on a second," Alois warned her. "If everyone is as rational as you, they'll all think about putting 33 and two-thirds of that is 22. But then again, everyone will think like that, won't they? That is if they're rational as you say they are."

© Springer International Publishing AG 2018

P. Eichhorn, I. Towers, *Principles of Management*, Springer Texts in Business and Economics, https://doi.org/10.1007/978-3-319-70902-4_4

"Hmm, I suppose so," replied Meret. "Then that means the average should go down towards zero." Both entered their number, neither telling the other which number they had chosen. Ten minutes later the entertainer came in with the result. "And the winning number is. . . . . .!" Neither Meret nor Alois came close to winning. "But," Alois said, a little arrogantly to Meret's ears, "we were both wrong, so I'm right about people not being rational. Aren't I?"

4.1   Metaeconomic Foundations

4.1.1   The Principle of Rationality

Economic action is often considered to be equivalent to rational action. Some people go so far as to identify rationality as an economic principle and the rationally behaving individual with the *homo oeconomicus*. Carl Menger (1840–1921) was one of the first to use the term *metaeconomics*. It represented a new kind of economics, one which relies very heavily on mathematical models and as a consequence is purely rational. This notion must be dismissed: economic action can be rational but also irrational, as recent developments in behavioural economics indicate.

Rationality can be subdivided into **economic and metaeconomic rationality**. These two forms of rationality can be alternative to each other, or complementary, or, in a few cases, unconnected. The most common form of relation between the two is the alternative, or trade-off. What is economically rational can be irrational from the point of view of art, democracy, education, health, justice, politics or technology. For instance, an individual entrepreneur may find it entirely rational to export weapons to North Korea, but this is arguably irrational from a political standpoint. Another example: it is metaeconomically rational to buy cheap food, but irrational if it effects one's health.

Conversely, action inspired by metaeconomic rationality can be against economic rationality as is the case in the following example: state universities in Germany do not charge fees, so from the metaeconomic view it is rational to study at one in order to save money. However, these savings are irrational from view of a student who can learn better in a private university with smaller classes and so would get better results (with the assumption, of course, that she can afford the tuition fees).

Even if actions are deemed economically rational, we need to think about whether this rationality applies just to a single economic actor or to the economy as a whole. Since rationality is ultimately indivisible, we must reconcile perceptions and insights from metaeconomics with economic logic.

4.1.2   Goals and Objectives

When we consider the rationality of a set of actions, we also need to think about the goals of these actions and how they can be best achieved. We can take the case of a mountaineer: the **meaning** of their actions lies in their sporting performance and in the feeling of isolation and freedom, their **goal** is the top of the mountain, their **objective** or **purpose** is to climb the mountain and their **means** are their skills and equipment. There is an obvious functional relation between means and end.

A goal is a desired situation; having an objective implies the goal-oriented deployment of means. The relation of means to end is a question of efficiency, and it can be shown as in Eq. (4.1):

$$Efficiency = \frac{Goal}{Means} \ or \ \frac{Objective}{Means} \ or \ \frac{Target}{Means} \tag{4.1}$$

Equation 4.1 Efficiency

Our mountain climber behaves appropriately if they choose the best combination from a number of alternatives, which include a more direct or less direct route on the mountain on the one hand, and heavier or lighter equipment on the other hand—their choice could be heavy equipment and a less direct route, which would take longer and so they might need to camp. The alternative of light equipment and a more direct route implies a speedier ascent.

This example also illustrates that there are different types of efficiency. A professional mountaineer may very well choose differently from an amateur climber, and a mountain guide might prefer another combination of route and resources, more oriented to the wishes and abilities of his customers. Simplifying somewhat, we can identify **an economic and a metaeconomic purpose**. The mountain guide pursues an economic purpose, the amateur climber pursues a metaeconomic purpose, possibly health or recreational, and the keen climber pursues one or the other purpose, or possibly both at the same time. The choice of means and the choice of route can be made on the basis of economic or non-economic criteria.

There are different kinds of efficiency—technical, political and economic. When ends and means are determined by (mainly) economic considerations, we have a case of **economic efficiency**. Another definition of economic efficiency is the relation between target figures and performance, for instance the comparison between planned and actual output; we discuss this more in Chap. 7.

Economic efficiency does not necessarily imply that the goal to which actions are leading is an economic goal. The goal of conquering a mountain may be purely motivated by the feeling of joy that mountain climbing brings, or it may be the result of the desire to earn an income, or it may be a combination of both. Turning to businesses, **performance or substantive goals** can be set against **financial or formal goals**; the former can be of an economic, cultural, charitable or ecological nature, while the latter consist of numbers such as rate of return, profit margin and costs. Here are some examples:

- An industrial company produces office equipment with a very high level of quality (substantive goals) and pursues a profitability rate of 10% (financial goal).
- A theatre puts on a play (substantive goal) and must cover its costs (financial goal).
- A municipal office is responsible for procurement (substantive goal) and can spend no more than 1 million euros (financial goal).

When non-economic goals influence economic goals, we are again made aware of the problems of the metaeconomic approach.

Mutually connected and dependent goals are elements of the overall system of goals of individual economic agents or multiple economic agents. The inter-dependencies and relative importance of the intermediate and final objectives (i.e. short term, medium term and long term) of an economic entity are similarly complex, as are their relationships with the different possible sets of means (we discuss goals in more detail in Chap. 5). To understand these relationships, we must recognise **the centrality of means and ends to the achievement of goals**. Is the use of inputs reasonable in terms of meeting predefined objectives or are there other possibilities for achieving these objectives? A question we have not yet asked is: are the goals themselves reasonable? Our focus has been on discussing the relationship between means and ends, but not on whether the means or the ends are in themselves desirable or sensible.

As indicated above, **behavioural economics** is concerned with non-rationality in economic decision-making. Like its related discipline, it questions the assumptions of metaeconomics and the *homo oeconomicus*, who is taken to be completely rational. Using insights from psychology and neuroscience, behavioural economists focus on three main topics:

- the fact that people make 95% of their decisions using heuristics, which are mental shortcuts such as "the more expensive the wine, the better it is",
- the use of framing to construct a reality (see Chap. 1's discussion of perception and thought processes), and
- the existence of market anomalies, where prices exist that seem to contradict the hypothesis of efficient markets.

The opening vignette in this chapter is an example of how irrationality can exist in decision making, a concept that is also not unknown to marketers.

4.2   Basic Principles of Economic Efficiency

4.2.1   The Principle of Maximum Result

Purposeful actions imply the best possible relationship between means and ends (inputs and outputs) and this can be achieved by **keeping one of them fixed and varying the other**. Changing them both at the same time is logically impossible, as the following example illustrates. An athlete cannot sprint over a long distance. We can give her a specified time (the input) and then measure the distance she has covered within this allotted time—this is the output. Alternatively, we could set the output (a distance—for example 100 m) and measure the time (the input) she needs to cover it.

The principle of maximum result means achieving the greatest possible output (the purpose) with a given input. Since the purpose is often identified as a goal, and the goal placed in an economic category, we often refer to the principle of maximum result in terms such as goal orientation, benefit orientation, output orientation, revenue orientation and so on. A favourable relationship between means and purpose does not in itself represent a final goal, but is at most an initial or intermediate goal, or in other words, a **basic condition** for the achievement of a goal. For instance: a taxi driver has many costs (fuel, loan payments on the vehicle, licence fees) and so aims to have the maximum number of trips to generate revenues.

The principle of maximum result is shown in Eq. (4.2).

$$Max! = \frac{Output}{Input} \qquad (4.2)$$

Equation 4.2 Principle of maximum result

4.2.2   The Principle of Minimum Means

We follow the principle of minimum means when we try to reach a given end (goal, purpose) with the lowest possible input—e.g. how few workers and machines does a factory need to produce 10,000 T-shirts a day? Using economic categories, the principle of minimum means leads to resource oriented, input oriented, expense oriented or cost oriented approaches. It is difficult to think only in terms of economic efficiency when we look at this principle, because not only direct costs need to be considered. It is important to decide what other internal costs need to be included, nor should external costs be forgotten, such as the effect on the social and natural environment and on the various stakeholders. A complete analysis of economic efficiency has to compare all benefits and costs of any actions.

The principle of minimum means can be expressed as shown in Eq. (4.3).

$$Min! = \frac{Input}{Output} \qquad (4.3)$$

Equation 4.3 Principle of minimum means

In general, it is impossible to say whether the principle of maximum return or the principle of minimum means is a better way to achieve goals. This depends on the way the goal is set and the **accompanying conditions** for the assessment of efficiency. As far as economic efficiency is concerned, it is immaterial which of these principles is followed.

4.2.3   Planned vs. Actual Perfomance

The relation between results (output) and means (input) is not the only one through which we can think about efficiency. Another relation is that between the desired result (target) of the use of certain means and the result that the use of those means actually achieves. Equation (4.4) shows this relationship; the higher the quotient, the more effective the activity.

$$Effectiveness = \frac{Actual\,performance}{Planned\,performance} \tag{4.4}$$

Equation 4.4 Effectiveness

If we assume that 400 units have actually been produced in a certain work process, although 500 should have been (and could have been) produced, based on a comparison with a previous period of time or with another department or with another, similar firm, the calculation is simple: $400 \div 500 = 0.8$. If all the units had been produced as planned, the quotient would be 1, and a production of 600 units results in a quotient of 1.2.

4.2.4   Categorisation

The principles of efficiency remain empty propositions if the numerator and denominator of the relations between purpose and means, and between target and actual performance, are not put into categories. We must go beyond **raw numbers**, and **describe the contexts** for which it is important to make information available. For example, the tax authorities want to levy taxes efficiently, a publisher measures the effectiveness of its advertising of a new (hoped-for) bestseller in terms of sales, and a student hopes to learn effectively.

The choice of categories depends on the kind of conclusion one wants to draw. In administration, aesthetics, construction, criminology, ecology, economy, engineering, literature, medicine, pedagogy and politics (just to mention a few fields) we can use very different categories. A building project, for example, can be reviewed on the basis of architectural, aesthetic, safety and economic categories. The problem consists in bringing together all the different aspects and their analyses. In the best case, a common denominator and a uniform dimension can be found—possibly through different scoring models as used in cost-benefits analysis (see Sect. 6.6.2).

We need to be aware that the **principles of efficiency** capture only one of many possible points of view. In addition to thinking about the inputs and outputs required to build a factory in a purely economic sense, its construction requires consideration of legal aspects as well as of tax implications; safety requirements must be taken into account, as well as practicality, adaptability to production processes, access to transport, ecological impact and so on. So we need to go beyond the concepts of economic efficiency and take into consideration non-economic characteristics in order to gain a general, overall perspective. To enable us to do so, we can use the concepts of efficiency and effectiveness which tell us about the contribution of the actions we take to the achievement of our goals.

Efficiency describes the relationship between actions and their effect, or the relation between employed means and purpose achieved. **Effectiveness** refers to the achievement of goals. Efficiency refers to the relation between input and output, and effectiveness makes it possible to describe the relation between the way things actually are (actual performance) and how we wanted things to be (the target) and to determine whether a certain output has been useful, so it measures the degree of goal-achievement. A simple example: Peter and Maria each own a house with identically sized gardens, each of which needs a new lawn. Peter chooses Louise to work in his garden and Claire works for Maria. Both get the job done to their owner's satisfaction so they can say that their efforts have been effective. However, Louise used 25% more seed than Claire and took 7 h longer: Claire's performance was more efficient than Louise's performance when we look at the inputs (time and seed) and the output (a freshly sown lawn).

By using economic categories to describe input and output we can draw conclusions about economic efficiency, but this does not tell the whole story because efficiency also depends on **outcome** and **impact**. An example from a firm: a company produces and sells cigarettes (inputs are tobacco, labour etc; the cigarettes are the output). There are positive (duty on tobacco) and negative (street cleaning costs increase) outcomes and positive (feeling of satisfaction for the smoker) and negative (health-related) impacts. A second example: at a public broadcaster economic efficiency is determined by the input—the use and cost of resources (staff, actors, studio equipment and so on)—and the output as measured by the minutes of broadcasting produced. The outcome is the quality of the programmes and, obviously related to the quality, the extent to which the goals of

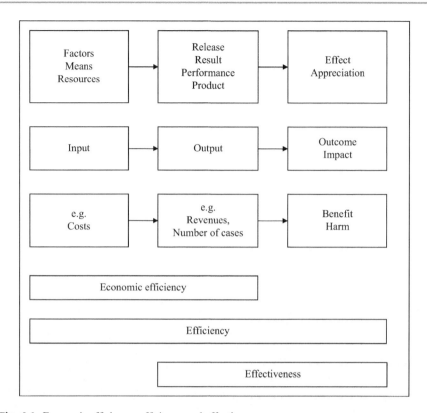

Fig. 4.1 Economic efficiency, efficiency and effectiveness

the programme makers have been met. The impact is the acceptance of the programme by the general public and its satisfaction with it.

The concepts of efficiency and effectiveness often have only economic connotations when used in everyday language, and sometimes even when experts talk about them. But as we have shown, efficiency and effectiveness include, but also go beyond, economic aspects, as Fig. 4.1 illustrates.

We should not confuse the terms economic efficiency and profitability. **Profitability** is the return on invested equity and/or debt capital and describes the rate at which capital grows (or shrinks, in case of negative profitability) when it is invested for a certain period. It can be calculated as a percentage, as shown in Eq. (4.5).

$$Return\ on\ capital = \frac{Profit}{Capital} \times 100 \qquad (4.5)$$

Equation 4.5 Profitability

Economic efficiency is an input-output relationship to which we can attach monetary values and which can be measured as shown in Eq. (4.6).

$$Economic\ efficiency = \frac{Operational\ income}{Operational\ expenses} \times 100 \qquad (4.6)$$

Equation 4.6 Economic efficiency

Combining economic efficiency and profitability generates four possible states:

- economically efficient and profitable (e.g. a farm works economically and is profitable),
- economically efficient and unprofitable (e.g. an advertising agency is well managed, but still makes a loss due to a downturn in the economy),
- economically inefficient and profitable (e.g. a plumber who runs his own company is not good at managing his resources, but has enough jobs to still make a profit), and
- economically inefficient and unprofitable (e.g. a trading concern has too many staff, negotiates bad deals, and so makes a loss).

We can also calculate **return on sales**, which is the relationship between profit and sales revenues, as shown in Eq. (4.7).

$$Return\ on\ sales = \frac{Profit}{Sales\ revenues} \times 100 \qquad (4.7)$$

Equation 4.7 Return on sales

It is important that we think about economic efficiency in broad terms, because any statements that we may make depend on the goals that have been set, and these themselves depend on the system in which the economic activity is taking place. The goal of improving economic efficiency is generally based on the idea that competition forces the lowering of costs, so that profit grows accordingly (assuming that revenues stay the same). This relationship holds in the situation where companies are competing to make a profit, i.e. in capitalism. But different systems are possible, such as one based on the principle of solidarity. In this case goals would be based on satisfying the needs of the commons or other groups as economically efficiently as possible, meaning that economic activity would not be centred on money but on meeting specific—non-monetary—objectives.

4.3   The Economy of Needs

4.3.1   The Principle of Solidarity

Underlying the principle of solidarity is the concept that a community or group is striving for **social equity**. The reasons can be ethical, religious, humanitarian, political, social or given by the state; they can even lie in market failure or in the desire to reduce risks (for which reason solidarity funds, social insurance and pension funds exist). The members of a community or group that is based on this principle make contributions (which may be equal or based on their means) which are used to meet their needs. It may be that everyone's needs are met in exactly the same way (no differences between people or institutions) or there may be differences in the way needs are met, based on specific individual or institutional characteristics.

In principle, then, four cases are possible:

1. Contributions are equal on a per capita or per institution basis, and all are treated the same concerning the employment of resources.
2. There are differences between people and institutions in terms of contributions made and the employment of resources to serve them.
3. Contributions are equal (as in 1) but there are differences in how the resources are allocated (as in 2).
4. Contributions are not raised equally (as in 2) but the resources are allocated equally (as in 1).

Differences in contributions and in allocation of resources can be based on criteria like ethical or social standards, or economic standards such as performance.

Social insurance and pension funds are normally based on a system of proportional contribution and their resources are employed based on need. On the other hand, the system of income tax is based on progressive contributions, which require the financially better-off to contribute a higher proportion of their means to the financing of the activities of the state.

4.3.2   The Priority of Substantive Goals

A common feature of all economic agents that are bound to the principle of solidarity is the priority of meeting their substantive goals (as opposed to their formal goals, which are secondary but nevertheless must exist in a money-based economic system). Substantive goals in a system based on the principle of solidarity centre around meeting the needs of the community for accommodation, education, infrastructure, recreation and so on **without a making a profit or wanting to make a profit**.

Needs must be met in the most economically efficient way, meaning that everything related to meeting needs should be done for as low a cost as possible, from raising funds, through producing the necessary goods and services to delivering them. Economic efficiency in meeting needs has met with little interest in the disciplines of business administration and economics, nor in businesses and governments. Relevant research is overdue, given the **range of problems** concerning the determination of needs, the procurement of factors to meet them, the costs of these factors, the management of quality, issues related to financing and the perspectives of those whose needs are being met.

4.4   The Economy of Returns

4.4.1   The Principle of Competition

The counterpart of meeting needs according to the principle of solidarity is the effort to secure returns in competition with other economic entities. The principle of competition does not require that issues of social equity are taken into consideration; it is rather about the **assertion of interests** against those of competitors. We can distinguish between monetary and non-monetary interests and between economic and non-economic competition. Of the greatest importance in a market economy with free competition are the maximisation of economic returns and product-price competition.

In the case of competition in sports, between political parties or political associations in elections, when building one's career, between cities aiming to attract companies, between artists and scientists for reputation, etc. competition takes place in the **social sphere**. In all these cases the decisive factor is not profitability, but rather extra-economic motives and considerations.

As mentioned above, free competition is not necessarily a feature of the market economy because **limited competition** is also possible. State interventions—spurred by market failures (including negative externalities and information gaps)—can take the form of the direct regulation of state-owned or private enterprises, or also the form of setting the conditions under which whole sectors of the economy must operate, such as happens in the energy sector in most countries, including Germany and the UK, and in the transport, mail and telecommunications sectors. In the former case, the need to carry out public tasks or requirements to provide services are set by the state. In the latter case, the state takes measures that can include limitations to market entry, incentives for innovation, regulations regarding product quantity, quality and prices, safety standards and the extent of liability. Despite these interventions of the state in the market, competition does take place, although it is limited. It takes the form of competition between groups, competition between substitute products, competition on the basis of price and as competition where conditions have been imposed, such as having to pay compensation and offering free use by certain groups or at particular times. Forms of limited competition can be observed in the areas of infrastructure, especially in the energy, transport, mail and telecommunications sectors.

What is important in a regime of free or limited competition, is that the **same conditions** apply to all competitors, i.e. all have the same starting point and all are treated equally.

4.4.2 The Priority of Financial Goals

Financial goals are the priority for most participants in a market economy and consequently they drive the actions of market participants. The financial goal of companies is generating profit and of households generating a surplus of income over expenditure. Theoretical economic models assume that enterprises have the goal of **profit maximisation**, although in the real world most of them aim at a return on employed capital that may be variously described as adequate, satisfactory, average or typical. In reality, profitability competes with other goals such as liquidity and simply staying in business. The maximisation of the return on investment is often linked to an increased risk of insolvency—see Chap. 6 for more on this topic.

Actions that are based on financial and commercial goals are of necessity linked to meeting the needs of other economic agents. This process is an indirect one; needs can only be met if they take the form of **demand**, which comes into existence when needs are complemented by purchasing power.

4.5   The Economy of Self-Interest

4.5.1 The Principle of Equivalence

The concepts *economy of needs* and *economy of returns* refer to the goal-oriented behaviour of economic entities and the concepts *economy of self-interest* and *economy of common interest* refer to the orientation of the goals. The principle of equivalence of **performance and consideration** (counter-performance) applies in the economy of self-interest. In a money-based economy a consideration is (usually) paid in return for work, service, the right to use facilities or goods, and for the lending of money. In order to survive, economic agents are forced to ensure that the flows of goods or services in one direction and payments in the opposite direction are more or less **equivalent**. For instance, a company whose products are very expensive in comparison to those of competitors will probably go out of business because the flows are not equivalent—customers are paying too much for what they are getting.

The flow of goods and services in one direction and the flow of payments in the other direction do not necessarily take place simultaneously. There is no delay when cash is paid and the bought product handed over straight away; when firms, associations and administrations buy, it is usually on credit. Firms can bridge a short-term gap through careful management of liquidity and of cash flow, at the same time making sure that all transactions are booked in the correct accounting period. The principle of equivalence still applies in the case where there is a longer gap between delivery and payment, as when a company borrows a large sum from the bank for immediate use, but pays the loan back over a period of 5 years.

There are problems if money is losing its value at a rapid rate (i.e there is a high rate of inflation), is hard to get hold of or is expensive, because in these cases there is no real equivalence between the flow of goods and services and the flow of payments. In such a situation the flows tend to dry up, or, in extreme cases, a form of **barter economy** emerges, as it did in Germany during the 1920s, when there was a fifteen-fold increase in prices between June and December 1922, and the price of a loaf of bread which cost 250 marks in January 1923 rose to 200,000 million marks by November in the same year.

Flows of goods and services and of payments are in the majority of cases essentially simultaneous, whether we are talking about trading currencies, purchasing goods, the payment of rents, paying for labour and so on. The principle of equivalence also applies to **public charges** as they relate to the provision of a public service, such as treating sewage. An interesting case is offered by the payment for services provided by hospitals: if the full cost of each hospital stay is paid—including the costs of financing the infrastructure, for example—the principle of equivalence applies fully. But when payments simply cover running costs, we have a case of **partial equivalence**. A further example is the payments made by homeowners for road construction—they do not pay the full costs of the work needed to build a road to their home. Similarly, the small administrative fees levied for a government service are not equivalent to the services received, nor are, of course, taxes, whose payment does not imply receiving goods or services of equal value in return.

4.5.1.1 The Goal of Cost Coverage

The economy of self-interest presumes that economic agents **finance their own consumption of resources in the long run**, implying that revenues must at least cover costs. Cost coverage for firms only involves sales revenues from commercial activity, i.e. the result of normal operations, and is not the same as the coverage of expenses or expenditures because these can involve the use of non-operating income or revenues. Some economic agents are bound to the principle of equivalence, like housing cooperatives, public hospitals, old people's homes, pension funds, mutual insurances, public utilities, and other non-profit economic agents. Other economic agents strive for a surplus after costs have been covered, of course, and when this happens the interests of owners, managers, employees, and other stakeholders can be taken into account.

Covering costs is a somewhat empty phrase for a firm, being a grey zone together with the profit goal. The extent to which it can be said that costs have been covered is not fixed, because it depends on many factors, such as the recipient of the cost information (internal external parties or, such as rating agencies, banks, customers or negotiation partners), on how costs are defined (on the basis of cost or financial accounting), on which values are used (purchase price or replacement price), on how costs are accounted for in the cost accounting system (full or direct costs), on planning methods (simple extrapolation or detailed forecasts) and on which period of time costs are assessed (short term break-even point, margin contribution, asset preservation for long-term viability).

The **range of possible variations in cost coverage** can be well illustrated by the example of depreciation and amortisation, which depend on the concept of cost used as well as on the capital structure, reinvestment effects, the maintenance of capital and much more. These topics are covered in more detail in Chaps. 6 and 7.

4.6   The Economy of Common Interest

4.6.1   The Principle of Alimentation

The terms economy of common interest and social economy originally referred to common property, the property of a cooperative or of the state, but today these terms cover all those economic agents that act in the common interest, i.e. primarily for third parties, not themselves. They cover functions in the fields of health, society, justice, the environment, culture, science, politics and administration and they follow the principle of alimentation, meaning they provide **goods and services free of charge**. This is possible through unpaid volunteer work, donations, compulsory contributions, fees and taxes, as well as internal support. In the latter case, for example, a money-making part of an organisation can support the charitable work of another part of the organisation, as is often seen in the corporate social responsibility programmes of companies.

Besides such pure forms of alimentation, we actually find in practice mainly **mixed forms**. Services are not supplied completely free of charge, so that those who use them have to finance part of their costs. Students, for instance, pay reduced prices for room and board to the student services of the university, which are in turn subsidised by the state. Or, the revenues of a local authority department that produces a surplus may subsidise the transport department (a cross-subsidy). The principle of equivalence applies to the users of these services, rather than the principle of alimentation.

4.6.2   Striving for Common Welfare

The principle of alimentation corresponds to working towards the common welfare, i.e. the common good, where the goal is to contribute to social, economic and ecological welfare. The economic agents involved in this—be they private or public—do not aim to make money from their goods and services, but provide them free of charge or at a low price. Financing is based on similar principles: it is voluntary in the case of private economic agents like associations, churches, foundations and unions, but compulsory with public ones, like city, regional and state public authorities.

4.7 The Individual Economy

4.7.1 The Institutional Principle

The economic efficiency of individual economic agents and of a whole economy are two different concepts, so carrying out an economic analysis of a single economic agent is different to a macroeconomic analysis. The institutional principle helps us to more clearly define the objects of economic study and analysis—in our case, economic agents—and this helps us to win insights. How do we recognise an economic agent? As we discussed in Chap. 3, critical in this respect are the factors of production used, the degree of autonomy in decision making and taking action. This led us to identify households, firms, associations and administrations as the core types of economic agent, all of which can—and should—be managed so that they act in an economically efficient and effective way.

4.7.2 The Creation of Added Value

Individual economic entities—private households, foundations, firms, private or public associations, public authorities—have different sets of goals, but one thing unites them: they can only survive by adapting to the environment. Ensuring survival is a long-term goal, and this is achieved when an economic entity adds it own contribution to the value of the factors it acquires from its external environment, and it adds value if its contribution means that it **produces more output than the input it uses**. The outputs can serve the economic agent's own needs or those of others, they can be measurable or not, paid for or free of charge, produced now or later. Added value does not necessarily imply a monetary value, for it can be intangible, such as an increase in the number of jobs, increased safety, better energy conservation, a higher frequency in the provision of a service, increased health and ecological protection. It is at the same time evident that these social and ecological values and goals also always have an economic component.

4.8 The Aggregate Economy

4.8.1 The Principle of Aggregation

The overall economy emerges from the pooling of the individual economic entities within it. Until relatively recently, the overall economy was identified with the national economy, but today issues of national economics have declined in absolute importance compared to those of the global economy and regional economies. Economic agents of similar type form **institutional aggregates** and economic activities of similar type form **functional aggregates**. For example, the highest level of aggregation in national accounts is of all enterprises, all private households and all public bodies, and in these accounts we find total production, income, assets, credit and foreign exchange transactions, imports and exports and so on.

4.8.2 The Growth of Wealth

The goal of the economy as a whole is to increase prosperity; in an extreme case this could take the form of the maximisation of prosperity. The starting point for this is **quantitative growth of the national product**, but this should mean that everyone benefits from the growth, not just an elite. As many social groups as possible, then, should benefit from the growth of the national product according to their contribution, but also on the basis of political decisions that are taken about the distribution of wealth.

Qualitative considerations are becoming ever more important in the context of the economic efficiency of an economy, and economic activity is measured increasingly by its **contribution to the quality of life**. This can be measured indirectly by looking at numbers which allow us to draw conclusions about qualitative aspects of prosperity and related goals. Examples of these social indicators include the rate of unemployment, the index of vocational qualifications, the ratio of teachers to pupils, infant mortality, life expectancy, crime, carbon dioxide emissions, income distribution and so on. The development of a differentiated, informative and normative system of goals for these measures is an ongoing challenge for researchers. The OECD (Organisation for Economic Cooperation and Development) has developed a Better Life Index which ranks countries on the basis of material living conditions (housing, income, jobs) and quality of life (community, education, environment, governance, health, life satisfaction, safety and work-life balance). The top countries in 2017 are Norway, Australia and Denmark, while South Africa, Mexico and Turkey form the bottom three of the (so far only) forty countries analysed.

So we move away from a narrow perspective to a broader one, from **wealth** to **welfare**. We should, strictly speaking, differentiate between economic and social prosperity. **Aggregate economic welfare** considers economic circumstances; welfare economics and cost benefit analyses deal with the effects of individual economic activities on aggregate economic welfare and seek to evaluate them with the support of quantitative and qualitative economic categories. **Aggregate social welfare** goes further and includes goals in the areas of health, the environment, culture, society, law, politics and other extra-economic fields. At present neither theory nor practice provide methods for the measurement of these goals, let alone their expression in monetary terms.

Figure 4.2 provides an overview of what has been discussed in the chapter.

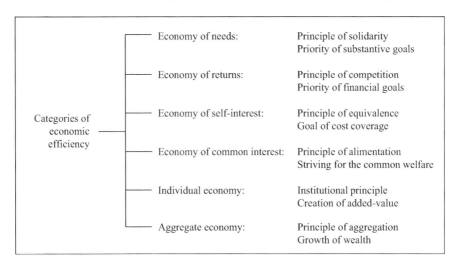

Fig. 4.2 Categories of economic efficiency

4.9   Examples and Exercises

4.9.1   Economic Efficiency

Situation

SAV GmbH is a small bakery company which produces baguettes and rolls for hotels in the Berlin area. Karina Müller has just been appointed general manager and one of her first actions has been to investigate the economic efficiency of the company. She finds out from the head baker that according to the recipes they use, 500 g flour produces ten rolls, and that the flour they use costs 1.00 €/kg (other costs are negligible). The selling price of one roll is 0.05 €. They normally produce 4000 rolls per day.

Problem I

Karina looks at last week's figures and notices that SAV sold 20,000 rolls and that had been 1000 kg of flour had been taken from storage to produce them. What conclusions can she draw from this?

Solution

She can look at the value relationship.

$$\text{Output/Input} = 20,000 \text{ rolls @ } 0.05\text{€/roll} \div 1,000 \text{ kg flour @ } 1.00\text{€/kg}$$
$$= 1,000\text{€} \div 1,000\text{€}$$
$$= 1$$

She can also investigate effectiveness. 20,000 rolls were produced; the recipe calls for 1000 kg of flour to be used and this is what actually happened.

Problem II
SAV is efficient but now she now wants to make the company more profitable by 10%. What are her options?

Solution

1. SAV could bake more with the same amount of flour. She rejects this possibility on the advice of the head baker as the rolls would not taste as good.
2. A second option is to reduce the amount of flour used. She rejects this for the same reason.
3. They could use cheaper, lower quality flour. This option is also rejected.
4. They could try to find a cheaper supplier.
5. They could raise the price by 10%.

They actually find a cheaper supplier, who is willing to sell them the flour for 0.90€/kg.

$$\text{Output/Input} = 20,000 \text{ rolls @ } 0.05€/\text{roll} \div 1,000 \text{ kg flour @ } 0.90€/\text{kg}$$
$$= 1,000€ \div 900€$$
$$= 1.11$$

Karina decides that is close enough to a ten percent increase in profitability.

Questions

• What are the risks in increasing prices?
• What are the risks of moving to a new supplier?
• If Karina had decided to use cheaper flour, how do you think the head baker might react?
• If cheaper, lower quality flour was used, this could mean lower prices. Do you think Karina should consider entering into a new market segment?

4.9.2   The Economic Principle

Consider the following situations. Which principles are being demonstrated?

1. A new version of a 40 in. television uses 15% less energy than the previous one did, while the picture remains as bright and colourful.

2. A large steel producing company is selling steel on foreign markets at a price much lower than its own costs and is sustaining huge losses.
3. Karina, from the previous exercise, found a way to increase output simply by changing the workflow in the kitchen. No costs were incurred and production increased by 4%.
4. An office cleaning company finds that it can reduce the amount of cleaning materials and hygiene products it uses by 7.5% and yet clean to the same standard—customers are still satisfied.

Solution

1. The case demonstrates the principle of minimum means.
2. The economic principle is not being followed in this situation.
3. Here a case of the principle of maximum result.
4. The case also demonstrates the principle of minimum means.

4.9.3 Determining Profitability

Situation

Referenz is a German producer of industrial robots. The following are some basic financial data from 2016 (€ million):

Sales revenues	195
Operating expenses	150
Operating profit	45
Profit (net income)	11
Equity	45

What is the return on equity and return on sales? What is Referenz' economic efficiency?

Solution

$$Return\ on\ capital = \frac{Profit}{Captial} \times 100$$

$$= 11\ \text{million euros} \div 45\ \text{million euros} \times 100$$

$$= 24.4\%$$

$$Return\ on\ sales = \frac{Profit}{Sales\ revenues} \times 100$$

$$= 11\ \text{million euros} \div 195\ \text{million euros} \times 100$$

$$= 5.64\%$$

$$Economic\ efficiency = \frac{Operational\ income}{Operational\ expenses} \times 100$$

$$= 45 \text{ million euros} \div 150 \text{ million euros} \times 100$$

$$= 30\%$$

Such results cannot be viewed in isolation. Comparisons must be made against past performance and competitors.

4.9.4 MyCompany Project

As your business starts, you need to think about what your goals and objectives are, and the meaning of your actions as a cafe owner.

- What are your substantive goals?
- You will definitely have financial goals—what are they? Have they to do with growth, profit, costs?

You will also need to think about your basic approach. Maximum result or minimum means? Let's assume you'll follow the principle of maximum result.

- Does this mean that you will work your employees as hard as possible?
- Would you want to invest in a lot of machines?
- Would you use non-organic milk if it were cheaper? And if no one knew? Explain.
- Apart from economic efficiency, which non-economic characteristics are important for you? How would you measure them?
- Would you rather be economically efficient and unprofitable or economically inefficient and profitable? Why? Can you think of any situation where the first of these two options might make sense? (Hint: think about the fact that you are starting a new business.)

4.9.5 Self-Test Questions

- *What is the relationship between economic and metaeconomic rationality?*
- *What themes does behavioural economics investigate?*
- *What is the relationship between objective and means?*
- *How can efficiency be defined and what different types of efficiency exist?*
- *What are the principle of maximum result and the principle of minimum means?*
- *How can effectiveness be measured?*
- *What factors must be considered in order to draw conclusions about the effectiveness of measures?*
- *What is the difference between effectiveness and efficiency related to each other?*

- *What are economic efficiency, efficiency and effectiveness?*
- *How are profitability and economic efficiency connected?*
- *What is the difference between outcomes and impacts?*
- *What does the principle of solidarity say?*
- *What is of the greatest importance in a market economy?*
- *What is the principle of equivalence?*

Goals, Production Factors and Results

5

> *Having lost sight of our goals,*
> *we redoubled our efforts.*
> Mark Twain (1835–1910)

Opening Vignette

Russell Laurence and Daniel James were members of a small group of activists; the group was called PtP—Protect the Planet. They were both part of the leadership team of the group and had met up in a café to prepare for the next meeting. The group had had some success in the past with media-friendly actions; Russell had climbed to the top of a local landmark and had hung out a banner saying, "Meat is murder!", while Daniel was well-known locally for leading protests against a large manufacturing company that was refusing to clean up some land it had polluted 25 years previously.

The problem was that the group was losing members. One of them had said, "I don't know what we stand for any more! On the one hand we're protesting against factory farming, and on the other hand we're going on about pollution—and that's what we're really about!" Losing members meant losing income, and money was always a problem in any case.

So as the two activists sat down to drink their fair-trade coffee, they were both aware that PtP was facing a crisis. Daniel started off. "I think we need to be clear about what we're trying to do. What are our objectives as a group? What are our goals?" Russell took a sip from his coffee and said, "I agree we've gone in too many different directions. Let's take a moment to think about what we're trying to achieve." Three coffees later they had decided they needed to relaunch the group and had come up with a mission statement. "Having a mission statement sounds a bit corporate to me," Daniel had said, but came to realise that having a short, clear declaration of what PtP was "all about" would be helpful. As Russell had argued, "It

© Springer International Publishing AG 2018
P. Eichhorn, I. Towers, *Principles of Management*, Springer Texts in Business and Economics, https://doi.org/10.1007/978-3-319-70902-4_5

will give us a direction and keep us focussed. And then we won't be pulled into doing a lot of things that aren't connected to each other."

The meeting of the group members took place three days after the coffee shop discussion. Russell and Daniel presented the mission statement, and following a lengthy discussion which involved the consumption of large amounts of organic alcoholic and non-alcoholic drinks, the group had come up with a plan that was based on the mission statement. Lily, one of the older members, commented, "Excellent! Now we've finally been able to set goals and prioritise them. Good work guys!" and Frank, another of the older members, added with a look of determination on his face, "I agree, and this will also make it a bit easier to get new members."

As he cycled home after the meeting, Daniel thought more about the mission statement and became even more convinced that it would mark a turning point in the history of the group: "PtP works to conserve and restore the systems on which all life on the planet Earth depends."

5.1 Goal Setting

5.1.1 Types of Goals

Goals represent a desired situation; individuals and institutions set them to guide their behaviour. Broadly speaking, the members of households in the west—once their basic physiological and psychological needs have been met—strive for personal development and self-actualisation (cf. Maslow's hierarchy of needs discussed in Chap. 2); firms seek profit or at least to break even; associations wish to satisfy the needs of their members; administrations want to meet general public needs. The first two groups' goals are the **coverage of individual needs**, whereas the two other are seeking **to cover the needs of others**. These different types of goals are not in conflict but rather complement and complete each other.

The realisation of one goal often leads to meeting others, so we can distinguish between **original goals** and **derived goals**. Meeting goals often does not only benefit the person or institution who sets the goal. If a member of a household takes part in a yoga class for reasons of personal development (original goal), they are also helping the yoga teacher to meet her goals (derived goals), and if the teacher is renting studio space, she is helping the property owners to meet their (derived) goals, and so on, almost *ad infinitum*. Similarly, associations and administrations must meet their own goals of having adequate resources for them be able to provide services to others.

There are **successive goals**. There can also be **simultaneous goals**, as in the case of charitable institutions and the majority of state and municipal enterprises—profit (or covering their costs) does not take precedence over meeting the needs of their users. Both sets of goals are to be met simultaneously, so we can refer to dual goal setting, but this does not necessarily imply that the goals are of equal importance. The goals may supplement and complement one another, so the achievement of one goal will lead to the achievement of the other—**complementary or compatible goals**. The opposite is also possible: two goals can stand in conflict with each other, when pursuing one will negatively affect the achievement of the other—**competing or incompatible goals**. Furthermore, simultaneous goals are not necessarily interdependent, so the pursuit and achievement of one has no impact on the other—**neutral or indifferent goals**.

The goals of economic agents can be classified by their source. Contrary to generally accepted opinion, it is not always the case that goals are **self-determined**. If we look at public companies, for example, the board of directors can and does set corporate goals, but major shareholders can and do exercise significant influence over goal setting. A shareholder could of course sit on the board of directors, in which case they are not a third party, but sitting on the board is not a prerequisite for exercising influence on firms' goals; banks can be very influential in goal setting, as many companies and individuals who owe them money can attest. Administrations are subject to **goal setting by others** as the goals of government departments and agencies are set by legislation and regulation, from specifying to whom services are to be provided to identifying the objectives to be met during the procurement process (such as favouring suppliers from the region).

Further classifications of goals can be based on organisational characteristics: the goals of departments, divisions, profit centres, branch etc., individual job positions and the employees themselves. The goals of individual employees can be determined by their managers and/or by themselves and therefore have to be aligned with **institutional and individual goals**, between which there can be a greater or lesser degree of conflict. A simple example of this is when a father needs to leave early to pick up his child from kindergarten but whose boss has told him that a report needs to be finished. There can also be conflict between the goals of two different departments in the same company—sales departments want to get new software products on the market as soon as possible while programmers want to get all the problems sorted out first.

We can also differentiate between **global and specific goals**. Particularly in the field of public services, goals tend to be quite general, so specific concrete goals must be determined by individual entities. Overall objectives are generally based on legislation and regulation: energy supply enterprises are obligated to provide a country-wide, safe, cost-effective and environmentally friendly supply; businesses responsible for local public transportation must comply with given regulatory obligations (e.g. routes and frequency of bus services); savings banks must encourage saving and provide credit to the less well-off. Associations are also not completely free to set their own goals, as is the case of charitable organisations, which are not permitted to have purely economic goals. Global goals may be set by a holding company, in which case the companies owned by the holding must determine their own specific goals, strategies and structures.

Managers are generally most interested in their organisation's individual economic goals, which can be categorised on the basis of the **production factor** involved:

- **Labour**: there are personal and socio-political goals for areas such as recruitment, education, training, apprenticeships, corporate identity, job security, job creation, work climate improvement, remuneration policies, profit sharing policies etc.
- Among the relevant goals arising from the use of **capital** are those related to profit and profitability, liquidity, capital maintenance, equity appreciation, capital risk protection, creditworthiness and solvency.
- The use of **material** (e.g. operating resources and raw materials) leads to goal setting in areas like technical advancement, capacity growth, material quality and maintenance.
- Goals exist also for **other** input factors such as **energy** (e.g. energy-saving), **services** (e.g. safety, punctuality), **law** (e.g. patent protection) as well as the **natural environment** (e.g. decreasing emissions).

Discussions of the future often revolve around the concept of sustainable development at both the global and local level, and this involves the balancing of **economic, ecological and social goals**. Economic goals are related to the factors of production already discussed, while ecological and social goals relate to the environment and people. The **triple bottom line** is a concept managers can use as they decide on ways to meet economic goals in ways that do not harm the planet or human beings. A concept that has emerged from corporate social responsibility, the triple bottom line asks managers questions such as: are you willing to make 0.05 € less profit per shirt so that the women in Bangladesh who made them earn enough to live on? Is your company willing to increase its manufacturing costs by 1% so that waste is disposed of in an ecologically sound way? In the long term, the needs of the economy for profitable, innovative and competitive companies can only be met if business entities do not neglect their responsibilities for the social and natural environment.

Operational functions can also be criteria for categorising goals, leading to the identification of **procurement, production and distribution** goals. A further breakdown of goals in manufacturing companies can include those related to warehousing and storage, transportation, production and waste disposal; hospitals' goals include in/out-patient care, diagnosis and treatment, home care and hospital stays; city administrations' goals can be in the areas of city planning, licensing, budgeting and so on.

In the area of goal setting itself we find: **management and execution goals** (explained in detail in Sect. 9.1.2), **strategic and operative goals** as well as goals related to **planning, execution and supervision**. Management and execution goals are generally set for institutions (e.g. companies) or individuals (e.g. managers); strategic goals are fundamental in nature and oriented to the long-term, while operational goals are short-term in nature and are concrete and specific. Planning, execution and supervision goals rely on various management tools and relate to different phases of the management process.

The different types of goal are shown in Fig. 5.1.

Fig. 5.1 Types of goal

5.1.2 Goal Systems

In the search for a taxonomy of goals, a categorisation of **formal and substantive goals** is helpful because it locates them within an economic system. A **formal goal** is a desired state expressed in financial terms; typical examples are income, profit, profitability, cash flow and profit contribution. **Substantive goals** represent the desired state of an activity, and can be expressed in terms of quantity, quality, space and time. Given the unlimited number of human needs and the limited amount of resources, there are an unlimited number of substantive goals, because they are based on meeting all kinds of needs—physical, psychological, sports-related, political, cultural and so on.

Through a connection with formal goals, substantive goals can also be expressed in economic terms; if this does not happen, the financial and business aspects of substantive goals are lost. Formal goals determine economic activity, which in itself does not depend on substantive goals, and this fact may lead to their fetishisation. However, if people and organisations only follow formal goals without taking substantive goals into account, they may be criticised because such an approach can (and often does) lead to social injustice, harm to people's health and ecological destruction. **Business ethics** involves questioning the meaning and value of economic activity and warning us against blindly equating economic activity with rational behaviour. Business ethics provide a bridge between formal and substantive goals by highlighting their mutual dependence.

Ideally, economic entities should pursue both types of goal, but realistically one of the two types will be prioritised—formal goals dominate in firms and substantive goals in public administrations and often in municipally-owned and state-owned enterprises. The formal goals of the profit-driven enterprise revolve around **profitability**, **liquidity** and **security**. There can be an optimum relationship between these goals in a **magic triangle**, "magic" because achievement of all three goals requires a bit of wizardry. It is in fact extremely difficult, if not impossible, to maximise them individually as they stand in competition to one other. For instance: if managers concentrate on achieving the highest possible profitability, liquidity may be under threat, as may be the security of financial and non-financial assets. Excessive liquidity reserves have a negative effect on profitability and limit the growth of a business. Finally, exaggerated protective measures or total risk-avoidance can negatively impact company capital gains, profit and liquidity.

A company's strategy will determine whether it prioritises one of these three goals or treats them all equally. If one **main goal** is selected, the other two goals will act as **constraints**, although they too must be met. Profitability generally has top priority in businesses; the target—what is measured—is profit (short- or long-term, retained or distributed). Even in cases where managers have been accused of setting an increase of their personal income as the main goal, as has sometimes been argued in recent years, profit remains the core theme, around which everything else revolves.

The substantive goals of profit-driven companies can be divided into three categories: economic, social and ecological. **Substantive economic goals** include customer orientation, performance and competitiveness. *Customer orientation* implies that company strategies, structures, operations and processes are aligned to the needs of the customer, i.e. the goods and services provided (the output) are not determined purely by the input for customer retention and winning new customers are the top priorities. Associated with these primary goals are many secondary goals such as focus on target markets, customer care, support services etc. *Performance* is an overall goal related to the production of goods and services, and it can be broken down into secondary goals for productivity, capacity utilisation, employee qualification, inventory turnover, delivery times and so on. *Competitiveness* emphasises meeting secondary goals for things such as price-performance ratio, product quality, market share and growth, brand preference etc.

Good corporate behaviour, social responsibility and employee satisfaction are examples of **substantive social goals**. These goals also have secondary goals. *Good corporate behaviour* includes not breaking the law, upholding the rules for good business practices and control (i.e. corporate governance) and placing limits on the exercise of power (e.g. when faced with weaker contracting parties). *Social responsibility* includes the integration of "various cultures, religions, nationalities, races, ethnic and social groups, gender identities and individuals of all ages" (as stated in Siemens' guidelines; see Sect. 9.1.5), communication with stakeholders and taking into account their interests as well as public acceptance. The goal of *employee satisfaction* includes corporate health management (physical and mental), motivation, and fair treatment in terms of pay and conditions.

The protection of nature and the environment is the central priority of **substantive ecologic goals** such as resource conservation, avoidance of hazardous substances and safe disposal of waste. Verifying the extent to which this kind of goal has been met depends of course—as is the case with all goals—on its operationalisation. *Resource conservation* means pursuing sub-goals such as the frugal use of materials, use of environmentally-friendly substances, avoidance of excess waste, reducing overall weight of products, increasing the lifetime of products and optimal logistics. The use of recycled materials and the development of recycling processes through which the waste of one stage of production becomes the input for another product are also relevant goals, being inherent in the **circular economy**. Further relevant sub-goals related to ecology include the reduction of emissions and immissions during production, transport and storage, during recycling processes for waste materials, during the collection, handling, treatment and disposal of waste. To this list can be added the environmentally-friendly disposal of waste, and the evaluation and monitoring of work sites, vehicles, materials and production with regard to their effect on the natural environment. The great difficulty remains that the goal is to avoid harmful outcomes and impacts on the natural environment but the reality is that damage can only be reduced, not eliminated.

The goals mentioned here are (or should be) the operational goals of an economic agent, but they can also be environmental policy goals at the national and international level. This is also true for refuse and waste disposal issues and the management of environmental damage. Sub-goals include estimates for the degree of liability, cost-related risks and financing issues, contracting experts for incident prevention with available technologies (e.g. automatic alert system in the event of an accident), repair of accidental or continuous pollution, as well as identification of contaminated areas and their decontamination.

Substantive goals are interdependent—the goal of an increase in performance levels and competitiveness must take into consideration the effect on the workforce and occupational safety as well as on emissions and immissions, for example. The optimisation of goals requires that all substantive goals and formal goals are harmonised through the consideration of priorities and of the relations between complementary, competitive and neutral goals—once this is done, a well-defined overall goal emerges. It should be noted that these issues apply to all kinds of economic entity, not just to firms.

To demonstrate this, we can look at the **goal system of public administrations**, where meeting needs and the fulfilment of substantive goals take priority, while formal goals have more of a secondary role. Of all the substantive goals, **substantive social goals** are the most important, above all the legality of the administrations' activities. In order to carry out public tasks legally, administrations must respect the basic principles of equal treatment of citizens, objectivity and the appropriate use of resources. The principle of the welfare state and duty-of-care as an employer ensure that the conduct of public administrations is acceptable to society and employee-friendly. All public administrations, not only environmental authorities, have a constitutional duty to uphold the national goal to protect the environment and natural resources.

In addition to **substantive ecological goals**, public administrations also pursue **substantive economic goals**. *Customer orientation* requires that the services provided meet the needs of members of the public and companies asking for them, which could then involve making changes in the organisational structure of

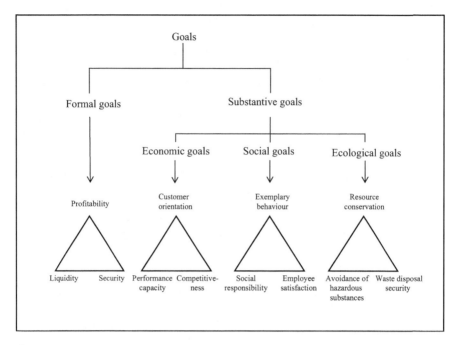

Fig. 5.2 The goal system of economic entities

the authority. Behind the overall goal of *performance level* there are multiple specific goals such as: meeting requirements related to personal freedoms, foreign and domestic security, protection from nuclear accidents, infrastructure improvements, supply guarantee, transportation; planning projects (e.g. land-use, national, regional and urban planning); health and social services; culture and sport, user-friendly services (information, advice, assistance and access); productivity; capacity utilisation and capacity building. *Competitiveness* could also be considered as a goal since, contrary to what many people believe, public administrations compete with each other to attract industries, entrepreneurs, educational institutions, associations, boards, courts, tourists, visitors, students, ideas, public funds, personnel, offices etc. This competition is not just national; European cities are competing to become the new homes of institutions that must move out of London due to Brexit, for instance.

Figure 5.2 provides an overview of the goal system of economic entities. The substantive goals depend on the economic agent and here we are using a manufacturing company as an example; a hospital would have different substantive goals, which would include medical goals, and a state university would have educational goals and different formal goals. For simplicity goals are illustrated using triangles.

5.1.3 Goal Concepts

Economic entities pursue a multitude of goals and because the majority of goals are in some way connected, the type, priority, scope, quality and time-frame of the goals must be determined. The result is the goal concept, which may be implied or explicitly formulated. Even when the goal concept is developed formally, there are often unknown and perhaps even unknowable goals outside the concept which may be crucial. As former US Defense Secretary Donald Rumsfeld (born 1932) said in 2002, "There are things we know that we know. There are known unknowns. That is to say there are things that we now know we don't know. But there are also unknown unknowns. There are things we do not know we don't know."

Given the importance of operationalising goals, and based on the differentiation between of formal and substantive goals, we can identify two interdependent concepts: finance-related and output-related. As Fig. 5.3 shows, the target orientation of **firms** is to maximise the profit from a given revenue, the target orientation of **non-profit organisations** is to maximise output while breaking even, and of **organisations dependent on public subsidies** to minimise costs or losses for a given output.

The **finance concept** of a company specifies the amount of profit, the period it should be earned in, its relationship to capital expenditure and sales revenue, and how this profit will be achieved (based on division, profit centre, product, customer group, sales region etc.). It also determines how the profit will later be used. Similar figures are also needed for other types of economic entities. Instead of thinking about profitability, individual households are concerned with the division of income across their various needs, associations want to know how their income from memberships is made up, and the concerns for administrations include tax revenue per head, per location and per period, as well as tax burdens.

The implementation of the financial concept takes place through payments, the subject of **liquidity planning**. The optimisation of cash flows means that the remaining solvent is achieved through the efficient use of financial resources, i.e. having enough money (in cash, in the bank or available through other means) at the right time and at the lowest cost. In addition to cash flow variables (size and

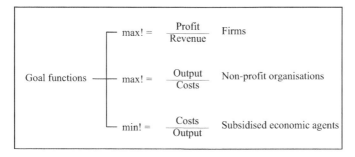

Fig. 5.3 Overview of goal functions

timing), financial concepts include the size (as shown in a balance sheet) of items such as cash holdings, bank deposits, accounts receivable and financial investments (**financial assets**) on the one hand and equity, liability reserves and liabilities (**capital rights**) on the other. The amount and composition of capital needed and its financing is dependent upon the output concept (see below) and the leverage effect. The more debt capital a firm uses to finance its activities, the higher its return on equity—as long as the return on debt equity is lower than the overall return on equity, i.e. when debt capital is cheaper. At the same time though, the higher the leverage, the greater the risk of the loss of the firm's own equity.

The **output concept** (sometimes **performance concept or programme**) of a firm is more than the business purpose as outlined in the articles of incorporation of limited companies, charters of joint-stock corporations and registered co-operatives, or in legislation and decrees for municipal enterprises. Such documents include simple statements like: "The purpose of the company is production of vehicles", or "The company's purpose is to produce and distribute electricity." Included in an output concept are the types of product or service, their extent, quality, features, places, timings and prices.

The output concept is closely linked via costs, prices and revenues to the financial concept. In addition to taking into account technical issues, decisions must be made on the economic and ecological facets of operations related to location, processes, warehousing, transport and waste management etc. The value of the **tangible assets** used in output processes provides a link to the financial concept. The interdependent nature of the output and financial concepts means that both are concerned with the necessary fixed and current assets and their financing.

Figure 5.4 summarises the components of goal concepts.

5.1.4 Mission Statements

Goal concepts—no matter how sophisticated—are not enough. The leaders and as many employees as possible of an organisation need to be convinced by them. The usual next step is therefore to develop a mission statement that has an effect on those both inside and outside the organisation. It captures what the organisation is ultimately "all about" in the form of **guiding principles and axioms** that relate the overall abstract objective of the organisation to more concrete ways of acting. Many business entities have mission statements:

- Oxfam: A just world without poverty
- Bristol-Myers Squibb: To discover, develop and deliver innovative medicines that help patients prevail over serious diseases
- BBC: To enrich people's lives with programmes and services that inform, educate and entertain.

Fig. 5.4 Components of a
goal concept

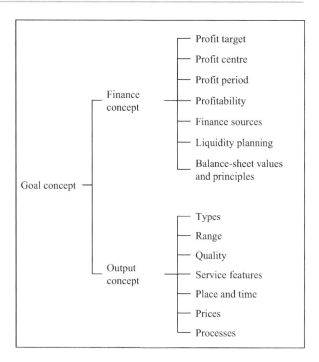

Other economic entities maintain other principles: households, for example,
may follow a religious way of living, associations might hold common interests,
social insurances are "about" the pooling of risks in solidarity, and
administrations are "about" the identification of collective needs and their fulfilment. Recently, even universities have developed sets of guiding principles in
order to raise their profile in the face of competition. A good example is Cornell
University's mission: "to discover, preserve, and disseminate knowledge; produce creative work; and promote a culture of broad inquiry throughout and
beyond the Cornell community."

One component of guiding principles is the **management philosophy**. This is
based on the basic values and norms that are intended be the at the heart of how the
organisation and its staff are managed. Attitudes towards profit, substantive goals,
business partners, customers, apprentices, social contributions, profit and asset
sharing among employees, employee participation, environmental protection, charitable donations and sponsorships etc. must be clarified and developed.

Closely related is **organisational culture**, which helps to develop the ways of
thinking and behaving of the organisation's leaders and employees, and moves
them towards those implicit in the management philosophy, which itself is of
course influenced by the organisational culture. From the perspective of the
organisation is it desirable that the goals that are set correspond to those of all
who are involved. This is crucial for avoiding internal conflicts in interpersonal

relationships and it plays a major role in ensuring that the members of the organisation behave in a consistent way when dealing with those outside it.

Management philosophy and organisational culture should contribute to the establishment of a public identity for the organisation. A clear **corporate identity** (CI) makes it possible to create a relationship between product and producer, and thus helps the company to develop a consistent appearance or **image**. An organisation must use the tools of CI-making to try to ensure that its self-image and its public image are the same. Elements that are instrumental for the formation of the image include product quality, reliability, customer-orientation, customer service as well as social and ecological responsibility. Standards for customer relations should match standards for managing the people in the company.

The image of the company to its own employees is highly influenced by their sense of self-esteem and the extent to which there is a feeling of "we" rather than "they" when employees think about their company. Individual employees must be able to identify themselves as important players in the team. Expert knowledge, flexibility and credibility play key roles in relationships both inside and outside. Those who are meant to see and be influenced by the image include the owners, members, sponsors, neighbours, media and the public—in essence, all actual or potential stakeholders, who each have a different relationship to the organisation. The marketing function is normally responsible for the development and management of corporate identity, using methods such as public relations, sponsorships, promotion and even corporate social responsibility to create the right image. A positive corporate image is also important for human resource activities, particularly recruitment.

The development of a mission statement or set of guiding principles raises many questions, the answers to which necessarily differ, depending as they do on factors including the type of economic agent, its branch, size, legal status, ownership, goal concept and situation:

- Which values that have an influence on attitude and behaviour do the leaders hold?
- What kind of behaviour and which attitudes and approaches are accepted by the majority of employees?
- Who is aware of the economic entity and how do they form their opinion about it (i.e. its building, organisational structure, financials, products, campaigns etc.)?
- What symbols, stories, rituals, ideologies and artefacts have emerged and what do they say about the organisation?
- How large is the gap between what is claimed and the reality in the workplace? How strongly do managers and staff identify with the employer?
- What must be changed with regard to management style, career possibilities, information technology, customer service, compensation etc. in order to increase motivation and performance?

Fig. 5.5 Components of goal setting

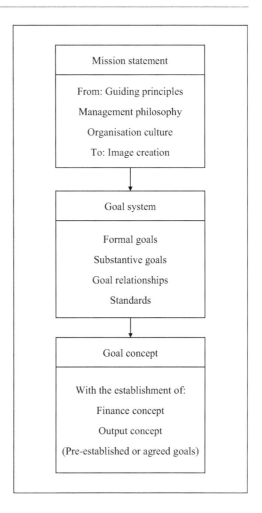

The path leads from the guiding principles to the clarification of the goals system (which goals should be pursued and how are they connected to one another?) to the establishment of the goal concept, which is then used as a basis for setting goals about how the factors of production are to be used.

This process is illustrated in Fig. 5.5.

5.2   Input Factors

5.2.1   Partial Systems

A factor of production is a good with which other tangible or intangible goods can be produced. The result of operations depends on the factors of production, specifically on their combination in terms of input, quality, flexibility and intensity. This

yield is influenced by legal and other issues such as regulations, uncertainty, expectations, capabilities, structures, processes, strategies and management styles.

Sometimes these influences are so intertwined with the factors that they become intrinsic to them, as occurs for instance with **information**, which is often considered to be a separate production factor. This perspective can be misleading because information in its various forms allows us to capture the state of the factors and the outcomes related to their use. The various factors and resources can be combined with the help of expertise and know-how. **Place and time** are not factors themselves, but they do represent dimensions of production factors.

In classical economics, production factors are usually separated into three categories—**labour, land, capital** (but sometimes only two—**labour and capital**, where capital is understood as real capital which includes land). A few economists identify technical progress, or technological knowledge, as a factor due to its use for the production of new and improved products and production processes. Systemic and ecological criteria, however, cannot be classified in this way.

It is methodologically unsound to identify capital as a derivative production factor next to the two original factors (labour and land), and the inclusion of land in capital when identifying only two groups is also unsatisfactory. From an economics standpoint, capital contains produced goods, e.g. manufactured tools, machines, buildings. Land and natural resources only count as capital when they enter into production processes, e.g. in agricultural activities; mining for coal, iron ore, natural gas and oil; as landfills or for construction. In short, land becomes a capital good only when utility of flora, fauna, minerals and bodies of water are being exploited. What then become relevant are the **returns resulting** from the combination of the factors of production **and their distribution** in the form of pay, rent and interest. A framework for factors based on the discipline of economics permits the analysis of production functions, the modelling and explanation of input-output relationships and the measuring of national income and net national product.

One problem with the traditional factor system is that it ignores **resources and effects that occur outside the market**. It leaves out land and natural resources like natural habitats, animal and plant species diversity, clean water and air in their functions as the natural necessities of life. On top of that, volunteer work and other unpaid work, such as that of a household primary caregiver, are not considered by this factor system because it includes only factors that have a defined cost associated with them. This narrow outlook is adequate only with regard to short-term economic interests; it hinders rather than promotes long-term ecologically and socially responsible development. It is therefore necessary to establish a universal system that includes all input factors.

Even the currently used **system of operational production factors** is unsatisfactory. It identifies labour, production resources and raw materials as basic factors and sets them up against a management factor that can be sub-divided into areas of leadership, planning, execution and supervision. Erich Gutenberg (1897–1984) developed this approach, which has since been taken over by many, even though its focus is the industrial production process and it ignores nature. It is a management studies counterpart to the view of classical economics: both are one-sided.

It is difficult to avoid the impression that these systems deal with only those factors of production that pay out. A universally applicable, realistic and consistent system for understanding production factors must be able to take into account **imponderable factors** and at least attempt to measure them and evaluate them in monetary terms. Employee motivation, the expandability of machines and heat or noise during manufacturing processes are examples of aspects of factors that are difficult to capture. Fortunately, mathematical, statistical and technical tools are available to help in the quantification and monetary evaluation of such qualitative characteristics of the factors of production.

5.2.2 A Universal Factor System

A system that is applicable to all economic entities has **seven factors of production**: personnel, capital, material, energy, services, legislation and the natural environment. Although it is not necessarily obvious when considering each factor individually, all are necessary for the production of the majority of goods and services. The degree to which each factor is involved in the production process will differ, and between factors there can be substitution and complementary relationships. How, when and where these factors are used is dependent upon the goal concept and the desired product, the production process, work conditions, the factor costs, quality and combination effect.

Figure 5.6 shows this universal factor system with the important sub-factors and interdependences.

5.2.3 Personnel

Personnel as a factor is not restricted to those working for money; the term also includes those doing voluntary and unpaid labour. It should be noted that the output of personnel is most relevant for analysis of this factor, rather than their input—although the relationship between the two is not unimportant. Personnel carry out two main types of task: making decisions and executing them. Both a top manager and a technician set goals and make decisions, and at the same time must implement them. Personnel sits at the top of our system of factors because it is both a **factor in itself** and **combiner of factors**. It connects the other factors with each other and is a factor which itself is combined with other factors.

Personnel consists of managers, specialists, semiskilled and unskilled workers, a classification based on their **activities** and there are obviously overlaps between the groups. We can also use other criteria to classify personnel, such as: type of compensation (wages or salary, commission), status (blue-collar, staff, civil servant, freelancer), type of employment (full-time, part-time, seasonal) or phase of education (apprentice, trainee, intern, working student).

The size of the tertiary sector in all economies has grown rapidly over the last thirty years, while at the same time the importance of services associated with the

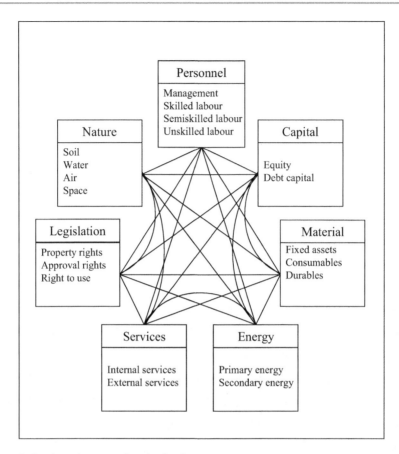

Fig. 5.6 A universal system of production factors

primary and secondary sectors of the economy has also greatly increased. The impact of these developments is that the personnel factor has become much more significant as a **determinant of costs** and as a **determinant of present and future performance**. Competition and globalisation have at the same time increased the pressure to increase productivity, meaning that the input:output relationship has changed and continues to do so—more output is now expected from the same input. The implication of this is that the quality of personnel has become central. Expert knowledge and intellectual, technical, communications, physical and psychological skills are in greater and greater demand.

5.2.4   Capital

Capital is essential in a non-barter economy. In the context of factors of production, capital does not mean the goods that have been produced, but **financial capital** (cash and banked funds), used for liquidity and investment in the form of equity and debt capital. This **monetary factor** includes financial resources and financial claims. On one side of the balance sheet of a company are equity and debt capital, and on the other side are tangible, intangible and financial assets (see Sect. 6.7.2 for more details).

Financial capital makes possible the purchase or the use of other production factors. Once capital reaches financial markets, it can then start to "perform" in the sense that it can generate income, just like the operational activities of a company. **Flows of goods and services** run in the opposite direction to **payment streams**. When a service is rendered or a product provided for no cost, there is no payment stream; similarly, when a payment is made without a direct connection to goods or services (as in the case of taxes), there is no flow in the opposite direction.

The legal rights of **capital providers** vary, depending on whether they are providing equity or debt capital, at least in the case of companies and households. When one thinks about capital, the main interest lies in the **sources of funds**, while when considering assets, it lies in the **use of resources** in the form of non-current tangible, intangible and financial assets (non-current assets), inventory, receivables and cash (current assets). Subtracting liabilities (debts, accounts payable) from total assets reveals the value of the equity: if liabilities are larger than assets, equity is negative.

5.2.5   Material

This factor of production covers **tangible assets**, including materials used in production. We can differentiate between different form of material, based on its use: fixed assets, durable goods, consumables and merchandise.

Fixed assets, often referred to in firms as capital goods, include: land, buildings, machinery, machine systems, production and commercial facilities. For public administrations, they include streets, dams, bridges, pipelines, water works, agricultural land and forests. Military assets are not normally included in official statistics.

Durable goods do not wear out quickly and are found in households, companies and public administrations. Examples are tools, vehicles, appliances, furniture, office and computer equipment.

While durables are used frequently, and generally over a long period of time, **consumables** can be only used once or just a few times. Examples are raw materials, auxiliary materials and operating materials as well as low value economic goods like office supplies, lubricants and packaging materials. Energy is excluded from this category, even though it is indeed a consumable, because its particular characteristics justify its identification as a factor of production in itself.

There are also semi-finished products and finished products, together referred to as **trade items**. They are often sold in the same state as which they were purchased—obvious examples of such goods are the products that are sold in shops.

The distinctions between the various kinds of assets are sometimes unclear and often depend upon legal considerations. The type of asset a good is classified to be can have repercussions for bookkeeping and accounting, and on tax bills (e.g. whether the value of an asset should be written off immediately or depreciated over a longer period).

5.2.6 Energy

An **intangible asset**, energy is the capacity to be active (in the physical sense); in essence it is stored work capacity. Energy sources are the materials and resources that lead to energy generation. Natural or **primary energy sources** include brown and black coal, mineral oil, natural gas, nuclear energy, biomass, geothermal energy, peat, water and wind energy, tidal energy and solar power. **Secondary energy sources** are developed through the conversion of primary energy sources in power plants, refineries and other facilities to useable forms such as hard coal, briquettes, gasoline, heating fuel, electricity, heat (steam and hot water) and compressed air.

The special features of energy as a factor of production are based on the **chemical and physical characteristics** of the form it takes. The ability to store it is limited or non-existent, and a delivery network is usually required to transport it. **Technical and legislative requirements** determine energy supply and demand. Network effects and company size are economic advantages in this sector, so there tends to be a development of natural monopolies of distribution for the types of energy that are transported over a network (electricity, gas and district heating), leading to a lack of direct competition.

5.2.7 Services

Services are one of the most frequently disregarded factors of production in previous models. They are an **intangible good** whose relevance for the combination of factors lies in intangible outputs. There are two forms of service: internal and external.

Internal services are provided by an economic entity itself. They are often closely linked to other factors, such as personnel, and it becomes difficult to separate them. In order to do so, it is helpful to ask the "make or buy" question (i.e. in-house provision or purchase from a third party): if a service activity can be outsourced, we can identify the service as being independent from other factors of production. Cleaning, repair, security and maintenance services that are run in-house can be included in the services factor of production. Work carried out for the senior management team, on the production line or behind the counter at a bank should be assigned to the personnel factor, internal transport of parts to the material factor. Making these distinctions is not simply an academic exercise, because doing so makes it easier to analyse processes, calculate costs and make decisions about outsourcing, and is also helpful for controllership (see Sect. 9.1.6).

External services come from third parties and are used as part of the combining of factors; external services are sometimes needed for the creation of internal services. Without them, production may be impossible, so it is surprising that external services have, until recently, been forgotten in factor systems. Examples of external services include consultancy, information, planning and auditing services, services for writing, press and printing, and other office-related services, manual services, exploration, research, development, education, financial and insurance-related services, travel agencies, hotels, transportation services, postal services and telecommunications. We should not forget that public administrations also provide services in the form of roads, footpaths, city squares, bridges, harbours, canals etc.

The service provider delivers paid-for or free services, not a tangible good. Among the issues associated with this factor are the complementary nature of services for other factors, the difficulties in explaining the value of the service, the quality of the service, its assessment and ensuring its delivery, the fact that a service is often provided and consumed simultaneously, the impossibility of storing services and (in some cases) their location-bound nature.

5.2.8   Legislation

Although both are **intangible factors of production**, we should differentiate between *legislation* and *services*. Legislation as a factor of production includes property rights and also approval and usage rights, but general rights such as the right to found a company or to use parking spaces are excluded, as these form part of the overall legal framework.

Property rights can be understood as the right to make decisions about objects. Owners or trustees in companies, associations, public authorities and courts exercise these rights, which are exercised carrying out activities related to purchasing, sales, job contracts, declarations of surety, proxy voting, shareholder meetings, land registration, donations, foundations, wills and testaments, expropriations etc. Legal rights may not necessarily correspond to actual rights—ownership is not the same as possession—so a third-party may be allowed to make use of property.

Approvals take many forms and are relevant for many areas of economic activity. Market entry may need authorisation, operating licences may be necessary for some activities, and processes, facilities, materials and people may require permits or licences. Getting approvals can represent a major bottleneck for factor combination. Typically (and theoretically) they cannot simply be bought and their granting is highly dependent upon legislation, regulations, legal interpretations and court decisions. Approvals generally depend on meeting certain obligations. Approvals influence decisions about location, for if an organisation cannot get the necessary approvals at a particular place or within a certain timeframe, or if the catalogue of obligations is found to be too extensive, or if the obligations are not as onerous elsewhere, the organisation may decide to move production to the location where requirements are perceived to be less onerous and the authorities more responsive and more efficient.

The granting of **rights of use** is equally important in factor combination. Rights of use encompass activities like searching for and mining natural resources, the use of public highways, the use of rental and lease property, the use of patents for technical innovations (patent law), the exploitation of works of art, literature, music and science (copyright) as well as the use and protection of trademarks.

Dealing with property rights, approvals and rights to use means working with various systems of rules and standards and leads to more or less complicated contracts and going through official application and approval processes. Because of the ever-increasing importance of this production factor, which is the result of growing juridification, the accompanying **transaction costs** are become more and more relevant to economic considerations. These costs arise from information gathering, applications, travel, preparing tenders, waiting time, preparatory work, negotiations, finalising and monitoring contracts, as well as from making sure that contractual obligations are met.

5.2.9   Nature

Nature refers to the natural basis of existence of **humans, animals and plants** and there is no factor combination that does not involve nature! Nevertheless, previous factor systems have ignored it despite its indispensability. **Earth, water, air and space** are directly or indirectly involved in the production process, from its beginning with the use of one or more factors of production to its end-product (development, manufacturing, storage, transport) and beyond (disposal, reuse, recycling).

Figure 5.7 shows the four areas and in more detail.

We can use earth to demonstrate which uses can result in negative external effects (Fig. 5.8) and show the associated external and operational costs (Fig. 5.9).

There exist not only negative external effects; positive external effects also exist, as when reforestation leads to improvements in air quality. Characteristic of **external effects** is that they occur outside the market, often without compensation and unnoticed—not least because causes and effects are often distant from each other in space and time. Even when a price has to be paid for making use of nature (e.g. waste disposal fees), this is essentially based on supply and demand. Producers and consumers are primarily interested in the price-performance ratio, and not in the overall relationship between the use of factors of production and pollution, with its impact on the balance of nature, health and quality of life. Only the internalisation of these environmental effects through rules and prohibitions, fees and incentives, will lead the responsible parties to take them into account when they are doing their cost calculations. Otherwise, those responsible for problems will be spared, but external costs will arise that nobody will pay specifically but which must

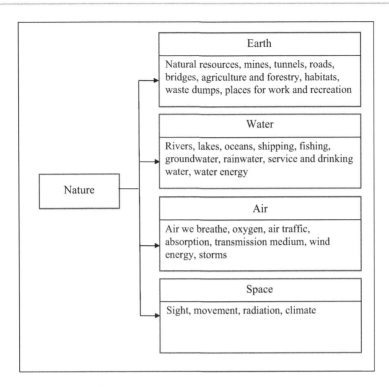

Fig. 5.7 The four areas of nature

be borne by all. Because of their seriousness, these negative external effects are at the forefront of developments in theory and practice.

These **(external) diseconomies** are shown in Figs. 5.10 and 5.11.

External diseconomies come during production, consumption and storage. Many negative or harmful joint products emerge during **production**: waste and hazardous materials as well as undesirable side-effects like humidity, dryness, cold, heat, smog, noise, gases, odours, sparks, disturbances, subsidence etc. These diseconomies can occur during regular production as the result of an accident or over a period of time. They can affect those involved in production and those not involved, as well as animals, plants and the environment in general; examples include work-related illness (silicosis, eczema, radiation damage etc.), noise pollution, soil contamination, contamination and climate change. These diseconomies mean more time, effort and money have had to be put into labour, health and environmental protection.

Diseconomies also occur during **consumption**—the use and consumption of goods and services, like driving a car, taking a flight, going on holiday, going to a concert or sports event. Consumption often means waste from packaging materials but can also be accompanied by other undesirable effects such as poor nutrition, sedentariness, stress and addiction—this is exemplified by the popular image of computer game players sitting for hours in front of their monitor, eating pizza and

Fig. 5.8 Negative effects of
use of the earth

Earth is...	Negative effects...
explored	groundwater contamination
removed	damage to biotope
dug up	ground subsidence
exhausted	groundwater contamination
excavated	soil erosion
cleared	damage to water reservoirs
terraced	soil erosion
relocated	damage to biotope
drained	-
channeled	groundwater level sinks
levelled	damage to natural cycles
sealed	groundwater level sinks
ploughed	-
harrowed	-
planted	-
drilled	-
fertilised	soil acidification
irrigated	-
grazed	-
dammed	damage to natural cycles
cultivated	damage to natural cycles
stored	groundwater contamination
accumulated	soil displacement
concentrated	damage to natural cycles
contaminated	damage to natural resources
decontaminated	waste of energy
cleaned	waste of energy
mined	fallow land
sieved	.
ventilated	.
.	.
.	.
.	.

being unable to stop playing. The reaction to such effects has also been the development of measures for health and environmental protection.

Storage also causes diseconomies. Places where goods are stored include the warehouses used in procurement, production and sales and distribution. Associated with warehouses, with public dumps and landfills are problems such as energy use and the dangerous nature of the materials stored or dumped. Long-term security and safety is important for storage spaces that hold waste—external diseconomies are just waiting to happen—building waste poses a long-term threat to the groundwater, for example, while nuclear waste must be safely stored for hundreds of years, a thought which does not inspire 100% confidence.

Many approaches to slowing down or stopping the emergence of external diseconomies are based on raising the cost of using nature as a factor of production. And what is true for nature also holds for the other factors of production in respect to their capacity to damage the environment through external diseconomies: they

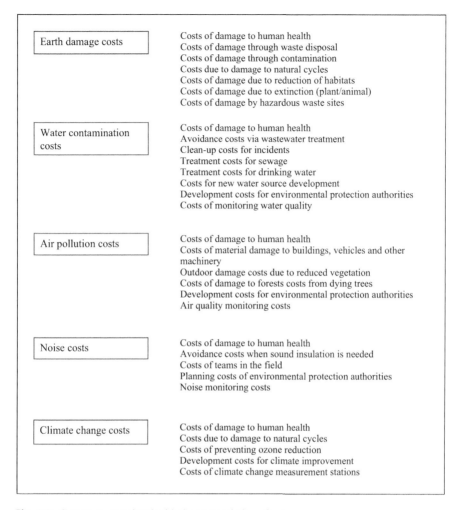

Fig. 5.9 Cost types associated with the appropriation of nature

are simply too cheap. It is unfortunately true that countries trying to go it alone to make the factors of production more expensive in order to protect the environment soon meet resistance in the form of international competition.

Fig. 5.10 Overview of
diseconomies

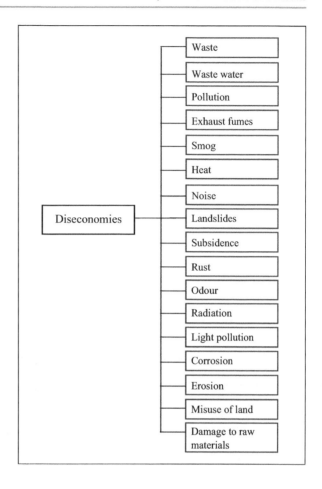

5.3   Factor Input

5.3.1   Factor Requirements

Prior to the input of the production factors it is necessary to establish the quantity of the factor required. The difficulty inherent in this sort of analysis can be exemplified by **personnel requirements,** which specify needs in terms of number of employees, the tasks they need to carry out and the required knowledge, skills and attributes, the number of hours they should work and so on. Needs analysis can be either input or output orientated, depending upon whether supply or demand is the starting point. In other words: what is the requirement for employees if the current production programme and methods are changed or reorganised? What happens if sales increase or decrease? Particularly tricky is predicting the requirements for knowledge-based tasks and other services. What amount of

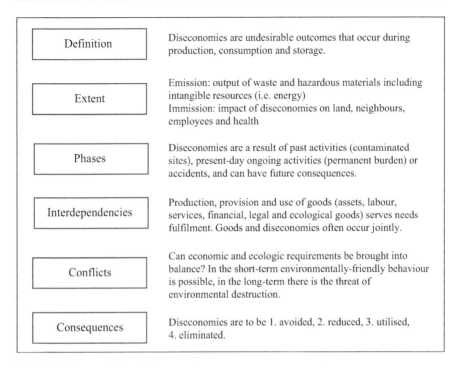

Definition	Diseconomies are undesirable outcomes that occur during production, consumption and storage.
Extent	Emission: output of waste and hazardous materials including intangible resources (i.e. energy) Immission: impact of diseconomies on land, neighbours, employees and health
Phases	Diseconomies are a result of past activities (contaminated sites), present-day ongoing activities (permanent burden) or accidents, and can have future consequences.
Interdependencies	Production, provision and use of goods (assets, labour, services, financial, legal and ecological goods) serves needs fulfilment. Goods and diseconomies often occur jointly.
Conflicts	Can economic and ecologic requirements be brought into balance? In the short-term environmentally-friendly behaviour is possible, in the long-term there is the threat of environmental destruction.
Consequences	Diseconomies are to be 1. avoided, 2. reduced, 3. utilised, 4. eliminated.

Fig. 5.11 Characteristics of diseconomies

personnel, what sort of qualifications are necessary for a growing architecture firm, a hotel, software house, insurance company, labour inspectorate or social assistance authority? In order to answer such questions, it is important to determine to what extent changes are due to operational matters or structural issues.

Short-term or long-term employee requirements (**target capacity**) first must be compared to the actual amount of personnel available (**actual capacity**) and the gap eliminated. This can be done within or between departments or divisions, or by getting resources from outside. A gap may develop because of increases or decreases in demand generally or seasonally, too much or little inventory, contract termination, cancellation, accidents, illness etc. Human resource management activities such as transfers, relocations and promotions may themselves lead to further requirements. It is not enough simply to know how many employees and what type of work force is required, because personnel requirements must also be **economically justifiable**. Generally, the needs for a factor depend on its contribution to meeting goals, and the personnel factor is only measurable when the output of the employees can be defined and compared with the costs of producing the output.

Organisations use various accounting procedures to capture costs, as discussed in Chap. 7, otherwise it is difficult to be precise about personnel requirements, and this is also true of the other production factors (except for capital). Capital structure is determined by the goals that have been set—this is the operative purpose, as outlined in a mission statement, for example—and by the intended size of the business. Based on this, a calculation is made about how much capital is necessary (capital requirements), how long it will be needed for (term) and from where it can be obtained (source). This issue can be approached from the opposite direction, when capital is already available and needs to be put to work. To ascertain **capital requirements,** it is necessary to differentiate between one-time capital needs, e.g. for a new investment, and continuous capital requirements for operative processes.

The question of **capital maturity** is answered by considering the commitment period for the relevant assets, or, coming from the other direction, looking at the capital investment and commitment period of alternative investment possibilities. A common guideline is that fixed assets should be financed using long-term capital. The higher the capitalisation ratio (the relationship between fixed and total assets), the larger the proportion of the long-term capital within total capital. Equity and long-term debt capital are the ideal choice for the long term financing of fixed assets, because with short-term debt capital financing of fixed assets, the length of the credit is shorter than the time need for their liquidation. In order to bridge this gap, credits must be extended and in extreme situations, revolving credit must be requested. The **coverage ratio** measures the coverage of fixed assets by long-term capital.

Unlike fixed assets, current assets can be financed through short-term debt capital, which can be measured by liquidity ratios. Three such ratios exist—the cash ratio, the quick ratio and the current ratio measure the relationship between short-term financial assets and short-term liabilities. They are described and discussed in Sect. 6.2.2.

Financial means must be available in the right quantity, at the right time and at the lowest cost—underfinancing and expensive capital should be avoided. The requirements for an optimal capital structure suggest that the return on equity can be increased by taking on debt capital to the point where the interest on it reaches the same level as the rate of return of total capital. This leveraging of increased debt on the return on equity is referred to as the **leverage effect**—the lower the ratio of equity capital to total capital, the higher the return on equity, the higher the risk and the lower the financial security.

The sources of capital depend on the legal status of the capital provider and the market chosen. A fundamental distinction is between **equity and debt financing**; equity capital is added in the form of shares, stocks and cooperative share and debt capital in the form of credits, loans and bonds. Equity financing occurs when associations increase fees and contributions or administrations collect taxes, when money is donated to an economic entity as well as when profits and surpluses are retained. Equity capital must cover debts owed, and can allow its owners voting rights and a right to distributed profits. Debt financing takes place through the credit markets.

A second fundamental distinction is between **internal and external financing**. External financing is when capital comes from financial or equity markets, although is some situations finance is arranged outside them, such as when an angel investor puts money into a company. The sources of internal financing exist in the non-financial market, i.e. the market where sales revenues are sought. Reserves, provisions and accruals can be built from sales revenues, and this frees up capital temporarily for financing the reorganising of asset structures and asset growth. Asset growth can otherwise be accomplished through a further type of internal financing—profit retention. The dues and membership fees of an association or union can be used to finance activities that are free of charge.

Tax considerations are important from the point of view of economic efficiency when it comes to choosing the type and source of finance. Economic efficiency can only be achieved within the existing legal and regulatory framework. However, other considerations need not be ignored, particularly ethics. Companies large and small always aim for tax efficiency, but this can lead to situations where companies like Amazon, Google and Microsoft pay very little tax despite generating billions in sales.

5.3.2   Factor Procurement

The recruiting of personnel, the raising of capital, purchasing of land, purchasing of machinery, acquisition of office equipment, raw and process materials, using postal services and public infrastructure, the obtaining of official approvals and the use of natural resources all involve the procurement of factors. Regardless of their characteristics, differences in the procurement of factors reside in the nature of **supply and demand** on the market. There are regulated or unregulated, domestic or foreign, competitive or monopolistic markets. Some are better organised than others, and some are more transparent with more available information than others. Technical, legal, geographic and time-related issues can also be important in this respect.

Those responsible for must look for **factor procurement alternatives** and answer questions like: Which types of factors are required, in which quantity and quality, where and when? Is the offer value for money? When making a decision about which factors are to be procured, one may be making a choice between similar (technical employees) and dissimilar factors (people or machines). A fundamental question is: make or buy? In other words, does it make sense for a firm to produce its own components or buy them? Should it hire permanent staff or get workers from an agency?

A second set of questions relates to the **procurement process**. In addition to determining the procurement objective and factor requirements, factor procurement itself must be planned and assessed. Important issues include procurement market research, planning (e.g. using models to find the optimal purchasing quantity), budgeting (finding the right combination of order size and order frequency to minimise procurement costs), procurement marketing, cooperation with third parties and the procurement of tenders. Procurement of the various factors involves supplier selection, the selection of applicants and contract negotiations, the checking of invoices and of the quantities and quality of what has been procured. The procurement process ends with the provision of factors for factor combination.

Economic efficiency and effectiveness in procurement also depend upon the **procurement organisation**. In addition to the questions of what is procured and how, the question of who does the procuring must be answered. Generally, procurement has centralised and decentralised components, i.e. people at headquarters and in the branch offices. The degree of centralisation depends on several factors, including how closely procurement is tied to production and distribution, whether specific areas of responsibility can be identified, whether common or individual interests should dominate, and whether economies of scale are more or less important than flexibility and responsiveness—the former calls for centralisation, the latter for decentralisation. In practice there tends to be a mixed form where central procurement specialists are responsible for basic contracts and the procurement of costly and/or infrequently used factors, while people located outside the main procurement department deal with the rest.

5.3.3 Factor Combination

Bringing factors together is factor combination. In the **broader sense** this occurs in all areas, functions and processes of economic entities. In the **narrower sense** factor combination is equivalent to the production of the goods and services which require the factors to actually be created. This definition also includes storage, transport, actual production completion, disposal and includes research and production-related administration. In an even narrower sense, factor combination refers to the main factors, i.e. humans and machines. Productivity is very frequently used as an indicator for factor combination, providing a quotient that is a quantity derived from input (e.g. number of employees) and output (e.g. total amount of steel produced) as shown in Eq. (5.1).

$$Productivity = \frac{Output\ quantity}{Input\ quantity} \tag{5.1}$$

Equation 5.1 Productivity

Which relationships exist between the quantities of production factors and produced products is captured in the **production functions** developed in production theory with its assumptions, models and conclusions. The areas investigated include the contribution of individual factors and homogeneity of factors, single and multiple stage production, forecasting with different levels of confidence, factors that can be substituted (or not), and limited and total analyses.

Cost functions assess and calculate factor costs. Because the quantity of factor input is dependent upon manufacturing capacity, cost functions reflect the dependency of cost on manufacturing capacity. The objective of cost theory is to supplement the quantity-based framework of production theory with a value-based framework. A straightforward example of this is the multiplication of the quantity produced by the sales price, where the result is the revenue. Cost functions are important for determining such information as minimal cost combination, which is the lowest cost factor input combination for a substitutional production function.

The analysis of cost determinants, cost drivers and cost trends is of practical relevance. Some **cost determinants, such as tax and employment laws and regulations relating to health and safety, opening hours or other issues relevant to specific factors,** cannot be influenced by an economic entity. Although the cost of factors may not be easy or even impossible to influence, it remains an action variable, as when large orders are subject to volume discounts. There are, of course, a number of influential cost determinants. Costs are especially dependent upon capacity (influenced by company size and production conditions), the volume of output (notably the production programme, order size and level of activity) and the qualities of the factors.

Figure 5.12 provides an overview of cost determinants.

Seeing costs as a piece of data that cannot be changed or as an action variable is quite fundamental. Indeed, cost determinants that cannot be influenced because they are set by law can be avoided by relocation abroad, for example. At the same time, past decisions about company size—an action variable—have such a long-term effect that the action variable is an item of data that cannot be influenced.

Among the most relevant issues related to **cost trends** are how costs are constructed (e.g. legal requirements), how the relationships between direct and overhead costs, and variable and fixed costs, develop, which cost reduction measures are promising, or where cost inertia exists (e.g. how quickly costs fall in the face of declining production). Closely related to cost trends are first, the types of production processes (e.g. batch manufacturing or assembly-line production) and central or decentral information processing, second, the production conditions in the workplace and third, how much value is added.

5.4   Types of Result

5.4.1   Causal Relationships

Analysis of economic efficiency and effectiveness is in essence the analysis of the effects of economic activities. Efforts are made to explain cause-effect relationships because a causal relationship means that *if… then* and functional dependencies exist, and these serve as a foundation for decision making. In management, the investigation of causal relationships is part of a **weak point analysis**. This involves a constant process of discovering and removing bottlenecks so that goals can be achieved. Erich Gutenberg referred to planning as a compensatory activity in which overall planning has to be orientated to that of the weakest areas. Companies' plans often aim to remove weak points, and of course, the removal of one is always an invitation to search for the next one—this is one of the basic points of Total Quality Management.

Fig. 5.12 Cost determinants

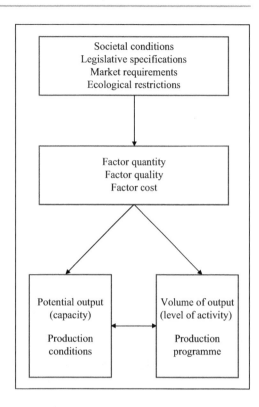

When customers, suppliers, users, employees or other stakeholders are dissatisfied, the causes need to be found. The immediate problem that has been identified should be viewed as a symptom and not a disease, and the root cause must be discovered.

Figure 5.13 includes a selection of the areas where investigation could begin.

One difficulty is that there is rarely a single cause, but usually a variety of contributing factors. No less complex is understanding effects, as the next section shows in its discussion of the three forms effects can take: output, outcome, impact.

5.4.2   Outputs

One result of factor combination is the output of tangible and intangible goods of all kinds. There is a continuum—a restaurant serves food and drink, which are tangible goods, but the act of cooking and serving dishes is a service, i.e. an intangible good. The books are the product of a printer, a practice session with a teacher the product of a driving school, advice and expertise the products of consultants, tax audits are the products of a tax office, regulations the products of ministries etc.

One most often concentrates on the **main outputs**, but these often necessarily involve **secondary outputs** in the form of goods and/or services. For instance, a

> **Management:** goal system, goal agreement and target setting, planning and control system, controllership, information management, management philosophy
>
> **Organisation:** organisational culture, span of control, division of responsibilities, space for decision making, business processes, optimal company size
>
> **Personnel:** human resources requirements, assessment and recruitment, allocation, (junior) staff development, job satisfaction and workplace environment, cost consciousness, incentives, knowledge and creativity
>
> **Financials:** budgets, liquidity planning and follow-up costs, finance, insurance, cost accounting, cost-benefit analysis
>
> **Production:** factor utility, capacity utilisation, turnover rate, optimal purchasing quantity, logistics and storage, production scheduling and control, quality assurance, maintenance, rationalisation, in and outsourcing.
>
> **Marketing:** corporate identity, product, price, distribution and communications politics, portfolio mix

Fig. 5.13 Potential sources of weaknesses

restaurant's secondary outputs include ambience, service, accessibility and parking spaces.

Adding together all outputs provides the **total output**. To speak in monetary terms, it includes not just the revenues generated by sales, but also what has been put in the warehouse, what has been produced for the firm's own use, as well as other operating earnings. Statements, and the resulting conclusions, about the efficiency and effectiveness of the production of outputs depend on several factors—which costs are allocated and how, which outputs are evaluated and how, and which costs are allocated to which outputs and how.

5.4.3 Outcomes

Analyses of efficiency and effectiveness are not unproblematic and complications arise when we think about input-output relationships in a wider context than the market. It is not straightforward to find answers to questions about outcomes: How large is the benefit for society and for the economy as a whole of the medications for influenza that have been sold? Was the cultural mission of the municipal theatre completed? Was the broadcaster able to communicate the desired social values?

Beyond this, it is important to remember that **diseconomies** can also be a result of factor combination. They are often neglected or hastily described as imponderable, but just as imponderable input factors must not be ignored, neither should imponderable effects. For example, transportation by car, train, boat or aeroplane always causes pollution. Even if transportation services can be provided at a low economic cost, the **emissions** for which they are responsible cause external costs that can tilt the balance in terms of overall—not just economic—efficiency and effectiveness.

5.4.4 Impacts

Building on the question about the benefit of medications, we need to ask questions like: How large is the benefit of the medicines on the health of the patient? Does their impact satisfy the general public?

External diseconomies are also relevant here. Emissions can be significant, as can **immissions** caused by waste, air pollution, residual heat, waste water, radioactive and other hazardous materials. If the external costs of the production and consumption of a good can be calculated, and if they are found to be significant, they can then be compared in economic efficiency and outcome-impact analyses with the operative costs, to which they can be added, so that an overall picture of costs and benefits emerges.

Figures 5.14 and 5.15 present what has been so far discussed in this chapter in a summary form and also point towards the next topic—measuring and valuing effects.

5.5   Measurement of Results

5.5.1 Indicators

The initial objective of casual analyses is to determine **what** should be measured and the follow-up question is **how** it should be measured. Attention needs to be paid to the types of effect an activity has, and then to which indicators should be used as quantitative targets. The choice of indicators must always follow a critical examination of the assumptions that underlie them and the desired goals.

Physical or technical indicators are often useful in economic efficiency and effectiveness analyses of *if. . . then* and *means:end* relationships. For instance: data about the quantity produced per employee or per hour says something about productivity, the yield of a particular field helps establish land output, the cost-revenue relationship makes it possible to draw conclusions about the success of a product, cost accounting of the value of production factors used in a period helps with the analysis of the return on capital invested.

It is more difficult with **qualitative characteristics**. Which indicators can be used to measure the workplace environment, for example? Are sick leave or the fluctuation rate relevant? Or can employee satisfaction be assessed by considering unpaid overtime, participation in company outings or works council elections?

Technically, product quality is a question of durability. Economically, product quality is measured by looking at the degree it is accepted by consumers or its anticipated profitable lifespan. These are **profit-oriented indicators; needs-**

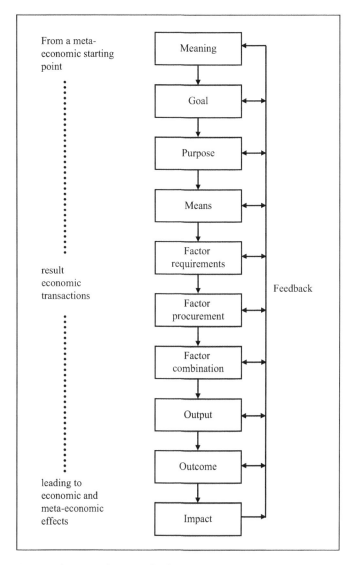

Fig. 5.14 Ten steps from meaning to realisation

economy indicators of product quality are, for example, the universal provision of goods or services and the equal treatment of clients.

Such considerations lead to making a distinction between **operational and social indicators** in an economic entity. To be more concrete: employment of a safety engineer incurs costs and this employee's work performance is measured by a reduction in work-place accidents and injuries, reduced accident-related costs as well as a reduction in disruptions in production and sick-leave costs incurred by the employer. In addition to these operative indicators there are also the social

Fig. 5.15 Measurement and valuation of effects

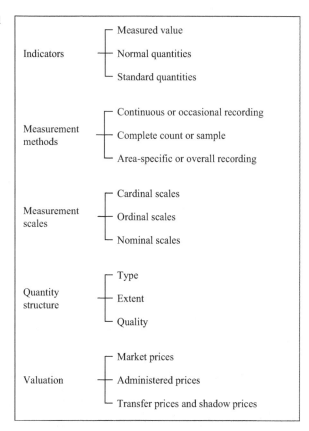

indicators which deal with the results of the accident prevention measures for those potentially affected (health, ability to work, health insurance, realised income) and third parties (dependents, hospitals, rehabilitation centres, unions as well as accident insurance and retirement insurance). These indicators allow the company to judge the success of the programme and its benefits.

Company success as captured in operative indicators can be seen as a contribution to the social product and the social benefits as a contribution to qualitative growth. It would therefore be reasonable to define operational and social indicators of an individual business entity as **institutional** and to speak of macroeconomics only when operational or social indicators are **aggregated**.

It is important to note that indicators can be used not only as tools for measurement but also as benchmarks (averages, trends), and standards (norms or targets).

5.5.2   Measurement Methods

The step after deciding **what** to measure is understanding **how** to measure. **Different measurement methods** must be implemented, depending upon what is to be assessed. Among the options are continuous or intermittent measuring, complete counts or samples. Tools used include observation, survey, experiments, instruments (software programmes, laboratory test equipment, measurement stations, scales, timers etc.) and meters.

To be acceptable, **a measurement method** must meet four criteria:

- objectivity, in order for it to be transparent,
- reliability, which is achieved when the same conditions always produce the same result,
- validity, i.e. the method measures what it is supposed to measure, and
- economic efficiency and effectiveness compared to other possibilities.

The last criterion is not easy to establish; a rule of thumb is that the more precise the measurement should be, the more expensive it is. Consideration therefore needs to be given to the degree of accuracy required.

5.5.3   Measurement Scales

Measurements need scales. **Cardinal scales** exist in two forms. The ratio scale—a classic example is a ruler—is best suited for economic analyses because it has a defined zero, can be used for measuring quantities and prices and is based on addition or subtraction. For example, the number of completed hours multiplied by the hourly pay results in total pay, or number of hours saved by a new method multiplied by hourly pay provides the time saved in monetary terms. An interval scale—e.g. the temperature scale—also has a defined zero and shows differences between two points. For example, the investment risk for one proposal is twice as high as that of another proposal, or employees are awarded scores of ten, nine and five points for their performance.

Ordinal scales can be used to indicate intensities, the size or strength of individual measures as quantitative characteristics in a ranked order. An example of such a scale is a hardness scale with hardness grades 0–30 for water or hardness levels from 1–10 for minerals. For example, a dichotomous ordinal scale allows for a choice to be made between sick and healthy, right and wrong. A non-dichotomous scale is used in marketing for example, where respondents are asked to say whether they completely agree, agree, disagree of completely disagree with a statement.

The measurement scales that are generally the least helpful are **nominal scales**, which can only determine if a given measurement belongs to one of several groups. For example, in software engineering a bug can be said to be caused by problem with a variable or with memory allocation.

5.5.4 Quantity Structure

Efforts to quantitatively summarise internal or external effects need a quantity structure, which is best explained using the example of cost accounting. Costs are established by multiplying the quantities of production factors used as inputs by their price. When the **volume component** of the costs is examined, it becomes clear that the quantities of factors needed for production are dependent upon the factors' characteristics.

The **provision and use of capacities** in the areas of personnel, capital, materials, energy, services, legislation and nature must relate to the size of contracts or production quantities, because they are usually a major factor in fixed costs. How can peak demand be covered or how can employee turnover be dealt with? Is internal adaptation possible or is contracting out or outsourcing necessary?

5.5.5 Valuation

A prerequisite of economic efficiency and effectiveness analyses are measurements of visitor numbers, exhibition space, staff, production units, storage space, work times, patients treated, permits issued, and so on and so forth. In conjunction with factor and product prices they allow statements about economic and business activities to be made.

Market prices develop though supply and demand in competition. Because there is by no means constant competition, market or price mechanisms can partially or completely fail, as when monopolies and monopoly prices exist. In this case, the degree of economic efficiency and effectiveness cannot be unambiguously calculated, but must be worked out with the help of assumptions. Industry and cost comparisons between regional and national monopolies are helpful in such circumstances.

Far too little attention is paid in price theory to **administered prices**. They are politically determined and implemented when market mechanisms lead to socially unwanted outcomes. Administered prices are determined and can be controlled by international and national parliaments and authorities, contracting partners in national industry-union negotiations, chambers and professional bodies, municipal councils and administrations. Administrative prices are found mainly in agriculture, water and waste water services, electricity, heating and gas, waste disposal, transportation (including trains, trams, buses, airports, inland and sea ports and navigable waters), broadcasting, post and telecommunications as well as health, culture and administration. When administrative prices play a significant role for a business entity, its economic efficiency and effectiveness can only be estimated.

Transfer prices are often used for internal analyses. They are used to value and coordinate internal services, and serve to connect interdependent units to overall goals. Transfer prices have a directive function and they make it possible to see the contribution of an organisational unit to overall success.

Sometimes there exists no price that can be used to carry out an analysis of the economic efficiency and effectiveness of volunteer work, unpaid services, further education and training, environmental protection measures and so on. In such cases **shadow prices** are used. Such fictive prices help establish the most optimal allocation of limited factors for given needs. Decisions about quantity are always closely related to decisions about price, as the quantity of a good determines its value, and price of a good determines the quantity.

5.6   Examples and Exercises

5.6.1   Factor Requirements: Personnel

Situation
Detlef Schulz is the manager of cleaning services at one of the largest hotels in Berlin. It has 1100 rooms on sixteen floors; 300 of the bedrooms are single rooms, 750 are double rooms and there are 50 suites. The hotel has three restaurants, two bars and ten meeting rooms. He has been asked to calculate how many cleaning staff are needed.

Solution
Detlef, an experienced manager, knows that he must do more than multiply the number of rooms by the expected productivity rate, so he proceeds as follows:

- He divides the building into areas that have similar requirements in terms of cleaning. His list has three groupings: bedrooms, lobby and meeting rooms, bars and restaurants.
- Next he works out how big is the area that needs to be cleaned and what must be cleaned (e.g. 200 sq.m. of carpet in the lobby, 20 sq.m of carpet in the single rooms, one bathroom per room etc.)
- He now identifies in more detail exactly what needs doing. In a bedroom, for example, the bed must be made (or changed if the guest checks out), the bathroom cleaned, the carpet vacuumed, the furniture dusted and so on.
- Knowing how long it should take for each task and the number of times the task must be performed on a daily or weekly basis, he is now in a position to calculate labour hours. If, for instance, the carpet in the lobby must be vacuumed three times a day, and it takes 20 minutes each time, he knows how many labour hours he needs for this activity. It takes 50 minutes to clean the meeting rooms on average, a total of 8 hours 20 minutes; since the contracts of the cleaners are for 8 hours per day, he knows that he will either need to employ a second person, part of whose responsibilities will include the meeting rooms, or pay a little overtime.
- With this information, he is now in a position to determine the cost of labour by multiplying the number of hours needed for a task by the gross pay of the person who carries it out.

He is also aware that finding cleaning staff is not easy. There is high fluctuation because the pay is poor and the hours are unsocial. A further complication is that hotel occupancy varies over the year between 80% and 100%. If he employs enough staff so that the busiest times of the year are covered, he will be in a situation where some staff are idle when the hotel is not so busy.

Detlef decides that he will employ enough permanent staff so that they can cover 70% occupancy. The flexibility he needs will come from a contract he will sign with a job agency that is in a position to provide staff at very short notice, which will help Detlef deal with peaks and troughs in the demand for cleaning services and also with the high fluctuation. To counteract the fluctuation he reaches an agreement with the hotel's General manager that the hotel will pay 10% more than the standard rate. Detlef hopes this will make the hotel a more attractive employer and reduce cleaning staff turnover.

5.6.2   Measuring Productivity

Situation

Matthias Barthel has to produce the monthly productivity report for the board of directors of a small manufacturing company. He opens the email he received with the following data:

Units produced	200,000
Labour hours	20,000
Machine hours	10,000
Cost of materials	70,000€
Cost of energy	30,000€
Average labour cost	30/h€
Average machine usage rate	20/h€

What can he calculate?

Solution

1.	Labour productivity = Output ÷ Labour hours = 200,000 ÷ 20,000 = 10 units/h
2.	Machine productivity = Output ÷ Machine hours = 200,000 ÷ 10,000 = 20 units/h
3.	Overall (multifactor) productivity = Output ÷ (Labour costs + Machine costs + Material costs + Energy costs) = 200,000 ÷ ((20,000 * 30€) + (10,000 * 20€) + 70,000€ + 30,000€) = 200,000 ÷ 900,000€ = 0.22 units per € spent

5.6.3   Root Cause Investigation

Situation
Anja Schwarz runs the delivery fleet of a soft drink manufacturer and has noticed that the fuel consumption of the new lorries she has just leased is below what she was expecting. She want to find out why.

Solution
She decides to do a root cause analysis on the basis that poor fuel consumption is a symptom of an underlying problem. She identifies the following possible reasons:

- Machinery
  - Underinflated types
  - Engine badly adjusted
- Materials
  - Wrong kind of oil used to lubricate
  - Wrong octane level petrol used
- People
  - Poor maintenance
  - Poor driving habits
- Methods
  - Driving too fast
  - Not using gears properly

After further investigation, she realises that the drivers did not realise that they needed to change gears less frequently than on the older lorries. This, of course, raises the question of why they did not know, so she continues her investigation and discovers that no training was offered. Naturally, she needs to find out why that was the case and it emerges that the human resource department, which is responsible for training, was missing some key resources. The HR manager takes over to understand why key resources were missing. . ..

The lesson here, reflects Anja, is that a symptom like poor fuel consumption can have deep-lying causes.

5.6.4   MyCompany Project

The cafe has now been in existence for 6 months and you are pleased with progress so far, indeed, you are even thinking of opening a second cafe.

Goals
The possibility of expansion has caused you to think again about the goals you have set for yourself. The first goal you had was simply to survive, but now other goals might be added. For example, what goals do you have for yourself? You had to borrow money from friends and family to start up—do they have any influence on

the goals you have? At the moment, you don't need to buy very much, what might some relevant goals for procurement be? You now employ some staff—what goals could you have in the area of personnel?

Generally—what are your formal goals and what are your substantive goals? What do your finance and solutions concepts look like?

If you could summarise what your business is all about in a mission statement, what would it say?

Factors of Production
The chapter describes a universal system of factors of production: personnel, capital, material, energy, services, the law and the natural environment.

Give an example for each of these factors that is relevant for your cafe. Does your business have any diseconomies? if so, which ones and what could you do about them?

You employ people to serve in the cafe. How can you decide how many you need, when you need them and how much it will all cost?

Causal Relationships
At the moment you are slightly concerned because a situation has arisen where some of your customers are unhappy because their coffee is too cold. You offer to put it in a microwave and—somewhat to your surprise—the customers agree to this. It happens too frequently for your liking, so you investigate. Where do you think the reasons might lie?

Indicators
The chapter discusses the importance of indicators. Which ones apply to your business? What could you measure in a cup of coffee? (Hint: there are at least four variables—see end of chapter.)

5.6.5 Self-Test Questions

- *What are the different goal types of economic entities?*
- *Describe the "magic triangle".*
- *Which goals dominate the goal system of public administrations?*
- *What are the components of a goal concept?*
- *What is the function of a mission statement and what aspects should be considered in its development?*
- *What sub-factors are included in the universal system of production factors?*
- *What are assets?*
- *What characterises internal services?*
- *Give examples of external services.*
- *What is meant by licensing?*
- *What costs can arise due to effects on nature and natural resources?*
- *What are external diseconomies?*

- *How can personnel requirements be determined?*
- *What is meant by coverage rate?*
- *What factors shape the organisation of procurement?*
- *What is the relationship described by the production function?*
- *What are outcome and impact in the context of an efficiency analysis?*
- *What are the different kinds of scale and when are they used?*
- *Why are administrative prices useful?*

Answer to cup of coffee question: you could measure the quantity, temperature, taste, aroma, time it took to prepare, cleanliness of the cup and saucer.

The Conceptual Basis

6

Attention!
Qui numerare incipit,
errare incipit.
Who begins to count,
starts to err.

Opening Vignette

Marcel and Max were sitting one pleasant Friday evening at a table in a beer garden. They had known each other for more than 10 years, having met as students of business administration in Mannheim. They had both ended up in Berlin, but neither had known that the other was also in the city. It was only a chance meeting at Potsdamer Platz that had brought them back in contact, and they had decided to meet up after work.

"Tell me more about your job, Max," said Marcel, taking a swig of his craft beer. "Well, as I told you the other day, I'm an accountant. I work for one of the Big Four, running around from client to client, auditing their accounts, and. . ."

He couldn't continue because Marcel interrupted him, "And helping them to minimise their taxes, no doubt!"

"We don't break the law!" replied Max slightly annoyed.

"Maybe not, but you try to find ways and means of reducing the tax burden of these companies," responded Marcel. "And if they don't pay enough tax, then that means they're not contributing to society! They might not break any laws, but they do everything they can to minimise what they pay to society. It reminds me of an old joke I heard—do you want to hear it?"

"Before you start telling jokes, Marcel, tell me more about your work for the government."

Marcel took another swallow of his beer before replying. "I work for the Federal Ministry of Food and Agriculture, I have to do with the advisory board on

© Springer International Publishing AG 2018
P. Eichhorn, I. Towers, *Principles of Management*, Springer Texts in Business and
Economics, https://doi.org/10.1007/978-3-319-70902-4_6

agricultural policy, food and consumer health protection, and in particular I work on food labelling."

"Not much happening there, though, is there?" asked Max with something of a smirk. "There's no traffic-light system on labels, is there?"

"Not yet," sighed Marcel, "but we're getting there, slowly but surely."

"What's the point of the system anyway?" said Max.

Marcel answered, "It's to let people know that if the label has a red light because of too much sugar, for example, they shouldn't eat that food very often. I personally would then say to the manufacturers, 'Look, you're selling lots and lots of food that's unhealthy, with too much fat, too much sugar, too many chemicals. People who eat a lot of your food get overweight very quickly, that's bad for them and it's bad for the health system, but you don't care because it doesn't cost you anything, this damage to people's health.'"

He took a breath so Max took the opportunity to get a word in. "At least you can measure exactly how much sugar there is in a litre of beer, but I suppose it's hard to measure how much the fact that people are overweight costs them and the economy."

Marcel nodded and said, "That's one of our problems. And it's one of your problems as an accountant too, I think."

"That's right, accounting isn't as clear cut as people think."

"I know!" Max almost shouted. "Now let me tell you my joke. Someone wanted to hire a new accountant and the interview consisted of only one question—what's two plus two? The first and second candidates said, 'Four.' The third candidate said, 'How many do you want it to be?' and got the job."

6.1 Measuring Quantities and Monetary Value

6.1.1 Operationalisation

We need numbers. Those of us who are not particularly mathematically inclined need not be afraid, though, because it is not necessary to be a mathematical genius to manage efficiently and effectively, but it *is* necessary to be able to deal with numbers. By allowing us to operationalise economic activities, they help us determine economic efficiency and effectiveness. Before any economic analyses are done, it is necessary to think about a basic question: which type of economic efficiency and effectiveness is the goal? As outlined in Chap. 4, the possibilities are needs or returns, self-interest or the common interest, individual or aggregate. Then we must consider whether the measurement categories are adequate for answering the particular question that is being investigated. There is the danger of only analysing that which can be captured in the numbers representing quantity and monetary value.

The former express input factors, factor combinations and combination effects in quantitative terms, for instance the number of employees, hourly wages, land areas, road distances, water consumption, noise reduction in decibels, manufacturing speed, rate of turnover, length of stay, output units etc. The advantage of these units lies in their **countability**. Of course, like can only be added to or subtracted from like—as the American saying has it, "You can't compare apples and oranges"; to put it more academically, one should not try to sum or subtract unrelated variables.

The disadvantage of these concrete categories is that they often only partly reflect the economic context as they are not able to easily express the scarcity and utility value of the goods. The degree of **scarcity** of a good is a result of growing needs for it and/or less of it being available. The **utility value** of a good is based on its importance in satisfying needs. Scarcity and utility value depend on circumstances of time and place, and on how the good can and does meet individual and collective needs.

By definition, units of quantity cannot say anything about the **unquantifiable**, i.e. abstract phenomena such as industrial safety, workplace health, flexibility of machines, favourability of a location, city image, commitment, well-being, and good corporate citizenship. Efforts are made to capture these elements by developing appropriate indicators, but even with this kind of quantification the difficulties mentioned above do not disappear and little or nothing is revealed about the economic situation.

Compared to most units of quantity, monetary units are much more able to capture the essence of economic efficiency. They provide a **common denominator** that can be used to compare economic characteristics and enables us to more easily analyse and make judgements about the economic context in which the economic agent is acting. Monetary units allow us to use both types of unit in the same calculation, such as when we compute cost efficiency as an expression of the relationship of output (unit of quantity) to factor costs (monetary unit).

Monetary units are not without their problems, a significant one being the **veil of money**. Money itself is a type of good, being a medium of exchange and a store of value and existing in the form of banknotes and coins as well as bank deposits. It is a legal means of payment for all the economic agents of an economy or monetary community and its value depends on the regard is it is generally held in. Behind money as a unit used in calculations is hidden a measure of value that varies, that is affected by subjective or objective influences and is constituted in relation to other goods. This becomes evident when there is a devaluation, meaning that the purchasing power of money is reduced, especially in comparison to foreign currencies. No clearer example of this can be found than the decline in the value of the pound against the euro and the dollar following the Brexit referendum. On 24 June 2016, the day of the referendum one pound was worth 1.23 € or \$1.47, and at the end of August 2017 one pound was worth 1.08 € or \$1.29. Developments like this have a serious effect on economies and firms, with British exports becoming cheaper and imports to the UK becoming more expensive due to the change in currency rates.

6.1.2 Nominal and Real Values

Differences between the nominal and real value of money lead to the **problem of the proper economic valuation** of input factors and the goods that are produced.

This is not the same issue as that of the difference between price and value. The perceived value of a good that is to be bought is generally higher than the price that must be paid for it, because otherwise there could be no exchange transaction of good in return for money. Economists speak of the buyer's and consumer's surplus. The former is the difference between what buyers receive for a good and the minimum they are willing to accept for it: it is the benefit a producer receives for selling a good on the market. The consumer's surplus is the difference between the total amount consumers are willing to pay for a good and what they actually do pay. At this point, other questions are also of interest, such as: How can fictitious profits be avoided? Are there any hidden reserves? Are any values are wrongly stated and by how much? Which value did a good possess at some point in the past? Is preservation of capital guaranteed?

The valuation is comparatively simple if both values are available and have been established objectively. The **nominal rate of interest** is determined by measuring profit against nominal capital (i.e. share capital). To establish the **effective rate of interest**, the dividend is measured against the market value of a share. The use of fluctuating market prices to evaluate the monetary worth of goods causes their value to fluctuate. Fixed prices are subject to the risk of growing discrepancies between nominal and real value, especially in times of high inflation, in long-term contracts or for export transactions with fluctuating exchange rates. **Indexing** is a method with which prices can be adjusted; nominal values are tied to the movement of a specific price index. An index can be developed for any given type of good or service, such as wages, raw materials, rent, tax and interest rates.

The principle of the **nominal preservation of capital** is applied to balance sheets. Using this principle, valuations are generally based on purchase cost or production cost. Market fluctuations in the value of money or tangible assets play no role, but price increases caused by inflation can lead to paper profits that are subject to taxation. Unlike nominal capital maintenance, the goal of the principle of the **effective preservation of capital** is to express the initial capital in monetary units that represent the equivalent purchasing power, and this is achieved with indexes, so the asset mentioned above might be shown as having a value of 110,000 €, this change being due to inflation.

The aim of applying the principle of the **preservation of assets** is to show the quantity of assets that exist behind their monetary value, rather than their monetary value itself. This is the case when, for example, there are the same number of assets in inventory at the end of a period as at the beginning. Absolute preservation of assets means that the goods consumed over a period during the production process are replaced in the same amount and quality by the proceeds of sales during that period. The relative (qualified) preservation of assets takes into account technological progress and economic growth (more usually growth in the industry). This concept was devised by Fritz Schmidt (1882–1950), who called it the principle of value consistency. Under this principle, goods are arranged in an organic balance sheet (organic in the sense of an enterprise as a part of the economic organism of a nation) in such a way that tangible assets are covered by equity and financial assets are covered by debt capital. A change in the monetary value on one side of the organic balance sheet is compensated for by value gains on the other side. In practice this means that inflation reduces the value of receivables, bank balances and cash on hand, but at the same time also the value of liabilities.

6.2 Outpayments and Receipts of Payment

6.2.1 Definitions and Types

Its use as a means of payment means that money comes into and goes out of economic agents. Legal means of payment are cash and deposits at banks, the latter also known as book money. There is an **outpayment** when money flows out and a **receipt of payment** when money flows in. Liquid funds flow in one direction or the other at cash registers or via accounts held at banks (including central banks). The difference between outpayments and receipts of payment results in either a positive or negative cash balance or account balance.

Starting with the opening balance of liquid funds, cash-based and bank deposit-based inflows and outflows are added and subtracted to reach the closing balance, as shown in Fig. 6.1.

Typical outpayments are cash payments, cash withdrawals and payments for everything from wages to donations to charities, from insurance premiums to income tax, from interest on loans to unemployment insurance. **Typical receipts of payment** are cash receipts, cash deposits, incomes from sales, tax refunds, donations etc. Various types of payment can be identified: recurring or one-time, regular or irregular, planned or completed, expected or unexpected, one-way or with something in return, fixed or variable, voluntary or involuntary, affecting or not affecting net income, affecting or not affecting assets.

Outpayments and receipts of payment can take place with or without any other economic agent being involved; an example of the former is when a company makes a payment to another company, and of the latter is when a company transfers money from one to another of its own accounts. **Payment streams** occur within firms, within a single national economy and between currency zones. The speed of the payment streams is relevant from the perspective of individual economic entities as well as at the level of the national and global economy; it depends on what structures exist for the movement of money and on payment arrangements.

Fig. 6.1 Calculating the closing balance

	Opening balance
+	Receipts of payment
-	Outpayments
=	Closing balance

Legal considerations, the structure of the banking industry, competition and payment habits all vary by region.

6.2.2 Liquidity Calculations

The survival of economic agents generally depends on payments. There are a few exceptions to the rule—the barter of goods or services or when goods and services are provided by one side with no expectation of payment by the other. Households, firms, associations and public administrations need to maintain the **ability to pay**, i.e. preserve liquidity, over their whole lifespan. If they are faced with an **inability to pay** (non-liquidity), they are threatened by bankruptcy, dissolution or liquidation, and individuals affected (whether as a member of a household, business owner or employee) can face social decline and poverty.

The ability to pay must be accompanied by the willingness to pay, but this in itself is not enough because the objective of economic agents is to protect liquidity in a way that is most economically efficient. In Chap. 5 we discussed the magic triangle of corporate policy that emphasised the interdependencies between the goals of profitability, liquidity and security. These three objectives are, in different ways, applicable to all economic agents. Liquidity planning—short and longer-term finance planning—is used to manage these three goals and involves predicting inflows, outflows and balances for a given period, which could be decades, years, months, weeks, days, even hours, minutes or seconds (as is the case for banks involved in high-speed trading). The planning of payment streams makes possible their management and supervision. **Optimal liquidity management** is achieved when the needed amount of funds is available at the right time for the necessary period and at the best possible conditions (e.g. interest rate and size of collateral in the case of loans). The implication of this is that funds not immediately required should be invested at favourable rates of interest, securely and should be accessible when needed. In the reverse case, liquid funds can be procured through payments from a bank (loans, credit lines, overdrafts) and/or higher receivables or by bringing forward receivables. Liquid funds are what connect all the parts of an economic entity; cash flows like blood through a body and is always in motion. For this reason, behaviour related to liquidity is dynamic and influenced by the past, and is based on financial calculations.

Various types of liquidity measures are available:

- the creation of a liquidity plan that is constantly monitored and changed as needed, bearing in mind the longer the period the plan covers, the greater the uncertainty and the higher the risks involved,
- permanent monitoring of monetary inflows and outflows,
- reduction of cycle times in production, in pre-production and post-production warehousing, in distribution (e.g. through the implementation of just-in-time manufacturing),
- a moratorium on new investments,

Fig. 6.2 Short-term
coverage ratios

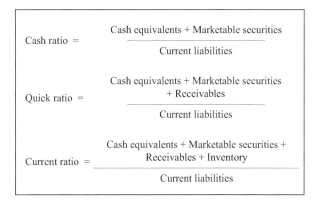

- reduction of the time allowed for payments to be made (e.g. by not waiting long to send out reminders, a tactic that is only possible with when a company has a sound market position),
- avoidance of liquidity peaks (e.g. by ensuring that not all moneys due are received over a very short period),
- ensuring that liquidity reserves are in place (but not too high),
- liquidating unnecessary business assets, and
- arranging credit relationships with banks (e.g. establishing a line of credit that can be used if the situation warrants it).

Calculations about future liquidity serve as planning tools whose value lies in the comparisons that are made between the actual state of liquidity and the planned state. Financial analyst use liquidity ratios to analyse companies' economic performance, but it should be noted that these ratios say nothing about the ability to pay (see Sect. 5.3.1). These ratios are calculated through comparison of assets and liabilities and measure a company's ability to meet its financial obligations; a more accurate term for them is **short-term coverage ratios**.

Three of the most common are shown in Fig. 6.2.

These balance sheet analysis ratios present information on the relationship between current assets and current liabilities, but since a company possesses both current and long-term assets, and current and long-term liabilities, they are not enough to capture the full extent of the relationship between a company's assets and liabilities. We therefore need other ratios to capture the relationships between long-term assets and liabilities and total assets and liabilities.

Examples of these are seen in Fig. 6.3. Long-term coverage ratios are an essential tool for understanding the state of a company's solvency and should be calculated on a constant basis.

Based on hard-won experience, a **golden rule of financing** has emerged over the years, according to which current assets should be financed by current liabilities, and long-term assets should be financed by long-term liabilities (some even argue that long-term assets should be financed by owners' equity). In other words, the life-

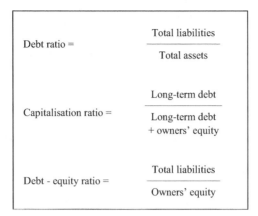

Fig. 6.3 Long-term coverage ratios

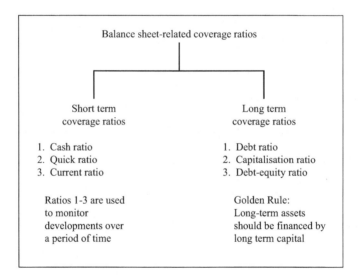

Fig. 6.4 Ratios and the golden rule

time use of the asset and the length of the financial commitment that permitted its acquisition should match. Figure 6.4 presents the golden rule.

All these ratios reflect the extent of coverage only at a specific point in time while the ability to pay depends on actual outflows and inflows over a period of time. According to Ludwig Mülhaupt (1912–1997), this makes necessary **cumulative cash-based liquidity planning** which analyses payment streams and forecasts how they will develop based on probabilities and taking the state of the economy and businesses into account. For example: liquidity planning should take into account the likelihood that a major customer might go bankrupt. The planning of the flows of funds is mainly done on a short-term basis and is based to a great extent on the financial transactions related to the flows of the goods and services that are procured as factors of production and that are sold in the course of the current financial year.

Managers involved in liquidity planning use **cash flow analysis**, in which past movements of financial resources serve as a foundation for future financial decisions, but using only this method is not adequate for safeguarding liquidity. Cash flow is calculated from line-items in financial statements, mainly the income statement. Cash flow statements have three sections:

1. Cash flows from operative activities. This is cash generated from day-to-day operations and the starting point is net income. Some adjustments need to be made to this to arrive calculate cash flows. These include:
   - Non-cash expenses are eliminated. Examples include depreciation and written-off debts.
   - Non-cash income is eliminated (e.g. write-ups, which is an increase to the book value of an asset).
   - Interest income is excluded because it is presented elsewhere in the cash flow statement.
2. Cash flow from investing activities. This section of the statement includes cash flows from activities other than those which are the company's main business activities, e.g. if a car manufacturer sells a factory, the cash flow would appear in this section of the statement, while cash from the sale of cars would appear in the operative activities section. The main components of cash flow from investing activities are:
   - outflows due to the purchase of investments and fixed assets, and
   - inflows of income from investments and the disposal of investments and fixed assets
3. Cash flow from financing activities. This section includes movements due to:
   - inflows after issuing share capital, and
   - outflows caused by the cost of finance (e.g. dividends and expense interest).

At the bottom of the cash flow statement is a number that shows the liquid funds that a company has at the end of the period and that enables predictions to be made about the company's future ability to make investments, pay off debts and distribute dividends. The result of estimating future cash flows and discounting them back to their present value is the discounted cash flow, an important figure that represents the current value of a listed corporation.

Figure 6.5 shows a simplified formula for calculating cash flows from operating activities.

Fig. 6.5 Cash flow
calculation

	Profit for the year
+	Depreciation / – Write-ups
+	Increase in / – Reduction of long term accruals
=	Gross cash flow
–	Taxes on profits
–	Distribution of profits
=	Net cash flow

6.2.3 Capital Budgeting

In contrast to liquidity planning, which analyses and manages inflows and outflows of financial resources in the interest of liquidity, capital budgeting is concerned with profitability and security, and establishing whether, and to which extent, an investment is worthwhile. Investment planning is carried out before the investment decision, and after the investment has been made, investment monitoring follows.

What an investment is—the **investment concept**—can be defined in narrower or broader terms, depending on the nature of the problem or objective of the analysis. In a **narrow** sense, an investment is considered as a transformation of money into tangible assets (e.g. the purchase of a vehicle), in the **broader** sense as payments for tangible and financial assets (e.g. an investment in shares) and in the **broadest** sense an investment is understood as a term that covers all outflows of financial resources for asset-creating and non-asset-creating use. Examples of the latter are the wage costs of the workers operating a machine and payments for inventories, insurance etc.

We can distinguish between individual investments and when when procured for a common purpose, multiple investments are part of a project, and these can then be combined into an investment programme. This makes it easier for managers and other interested parties to take all dimensions of the organisational context into account when analysing investments and making decisions.

Investments can be classified according to **investment types**. There are investments that are expected to generate a financial return on the capital employed, and there are investments that are not expected to generate a return due to the goals for which the investment is being made—these investments are financed by levies on the public (e.g. taxes) or private donations. We can also differentiate between investments in real or tangible assets and finance investments, and to this we can add investments in people, which can take the form of creating new jobs, employing staff and raising the levels of knowledge and skills. The purpose of the investment can also be categorised: reinvestment, investments to replace, maintain and renew (including major repairs) assets on one hand and investments in new or additional assets, investments in modernisation and rationalisation on the other. One-off investments can be distinguished from ongoing investments.

Three questions need to be asked when making investment decisions.

- Will the investment (e.g. a machine, another company, an equity interest, acquisition) be profitable?
- Which of the various available alternatives should be chosen?
- When should an existing investment be replaced?

 The quality of the investment appraisal plays a central role in making sure that the correct answers are found. The capital budgeting calculation must take into consideration the initial purchase price, incidental costs, associated monetary inflows and outflows, the lifespan of the asset and its residual value. The next step is to use this information to calculate the present value of the asset, using a realistic interest rate. It is often not easy to allocate to the asset all associated payments, nor is it straightforward to identify all possible risks. Changes in the labour market, technical progress, new legal restrictions, higher interest rates that affect financing arrangements and changes in consumer tastes are examples of risks that can influence the outcome of investment decisions.

There are in essence two **methods of capital budgeting**. Practitioners tend to prefer static methods that only take a single period into account; dynamic methods consider several periods. Static methods see all inflows and outflows of financial resources as having the same value, whereas dynamic methods are based on the concept of the time value of money, i.e. the concept that the value of future inflows and outflows is not the same as the value of identical amounts today. We discuss this further in Chap. 7.

6.3 Expenditures and Revenues

6.3.1 Definitions and Types

Expenditures and revenues can be understood as **purchases and sales in monetary terms**. In legal terms they are based on the obligation to pay for goods or services received and the right to payment for goods or services delivered. In the business world, expenditures and revenues are not the same as outpayments and receipts of payment because of the role that **credit transactions** play. Expenditures consist of outpayments, reductions in receivables and increases in debt, while revenues consist of receipts of payment, increases in receivables and reduction of debt. Only in the case of payment on delivery does expenditure match outpayment, and revenue match payments received—this is the case when we buy something form a shop and pay with cash, for instance. However, credit transactions are much more common in the business-to-business world and expenditures are incurred without a corresponding payment (e.g. purchases on credit) and revenues are generated without payment being received (e.g. sales on credit).

See Fig. 6.6 for an overview.

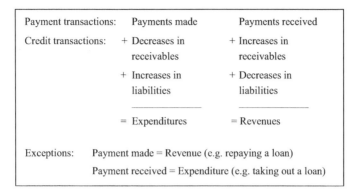

Fig. 6.6 Characteristics of expenditures and revenues

6.3.2   Finance Calculations

Finance calculations are prepared for payments made and received, expenditures and revenues, credit transactions, including liabilities and receivables related to tangible assets, and allowances from the transfer without payment of financial or tangible means. Finance calculations are different to liquidity and earnings calculations:

- Liquidity calculations are concerned with maintaining financial equilibrium over a short-term (usually up to a year) in a way that makes economic sense.
- The aim of earnings calculations is to ensure the success of capital investments, mainly by showing the inflows and outflows over the period that starts with the first payment received and ends with the last payment.

Dealing primarily with **finance requirements** and their **financing**, finance calculations' aim is to find the optimal capital structure, which is one that incorporates the optimal relationship of equity and debt capital, taking into account the three goals of liquidity, profitability and security. It will be remembered that security is concerned with protection against insolvency and the ability to keep business-related processes up and running over time.

Financing and capital budgeting analyses provide the foundations for **internal decisions** on:

- the proportion of equity to debt capital (cf. the discussion of the leverage effect in Chap. 5),
- the need for capital as business activities expand, and
- the possibilities of external and internal sources of financing.

The analyses are of no less interest to **external providers of capital** (shareholders, investment funds, credit institutions, pension funds, insurance companies) because they allow judgements to be made on earning capacity, creditworthiness, debt coverage and growth.

In most management literature, finance calculations generally focus on the capital need and the capital ratios of **profit-earning companies**, distinguishing between one-off and continuous capital needs. When determining capital requirements for the one-off procurement of an asset, the following expenditures may need to be taken into consideration:

- design, development and trials,
- market analyses,
- the initial costs of forming a company (legal fees, registration costs etc.),
- raw materials and bought-in parts (enough to meet minimum inventory levels, reserves of sufficient consumables to enable production to proceed without interruption),
- establishing organisational structures and building up relationships with suppliers and customers,
- wages and other forms of compensation,
- marketing, from setting up web-sites to package design and PR, and
- covering start-up losses.

The sum of all relevant expenditures represents the **one-off capital requirement.**

Continuous capital needs are calculated by multiplying daily expenditures on wages, materials, services etc. by the cycle time in days or the costs of the capital tied up in the production process. The forecast expenditures of one day are based on the planned operating rate and expenditures per output unit.

Managers use the cash conversion cycle as a tool to manage working capital, i.e. the financial resources an economic agent has on hand—see Fig. 6.7.

Traditional business management books typically ignore the finance requirements of any economic entity that is not a firm. The financial requirements of private households, non-profit old people's homes, hospitals, museums, public broadcasters, state and municipal administrations have much in common with those of companies, but each type of economic agent has aspects that are specific to it because particular requirements can have many origins: the promotion of health, the fair distribution of national wealth, human dignity, charity, sustainability, the ecological use of resources, social policies and so on.

Finance calculations have two main tasks: they must determine one-off and recurring finance requirements, and how they can best be covered. In this respect, it is helpful to split financial management activities into structural and procedural financing.

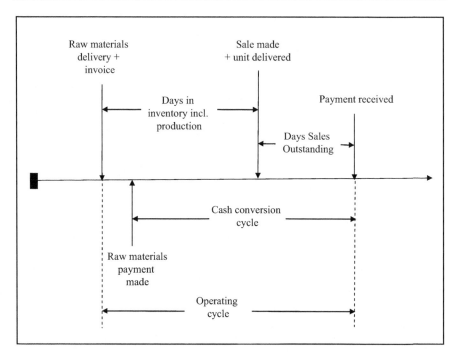

Fig. 6.7 Cash conversion cycle

Structural financing involves activities related to equity, debt and allowance financing. The first two areas are analysed intensively in traditional business management literature, but the third one is neglected. It is of importance when financing shortfalls are covered by finance allocations (e.g. from the government), investment contributions, capital grants, subsidies or other contributions from third parties to the acquisition of assets.

Procedural financing comes from sales revenues, income and tax contributions. Businesses focus mainly on managing turnover, because the existence of sales revenues that are not directly needed to make payments opens up decision-making possibilities in the areas of depreciation, rationalisation, accruals, financial restructuring and self-financing through retained profits. When companies debate how they should finance themselves, they can take into account all forms of income, including income subsidies and non-operational income. The same applies to households and other economic agents. Associations are either predominantly financed by from membership fees or social contributions from employers and employees. Public administrations mainly finance themselves through charges on the public, like taxes, fees and duties.

Figure 6.8 provides an overview of all forms of financing, not just those relevant for firms.

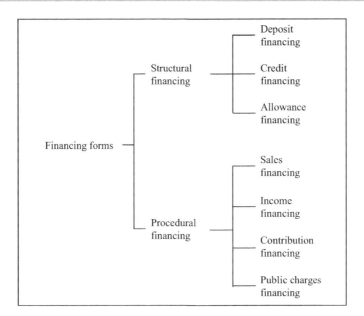

Fig. 6.8 General forms of financing

6.4 Expenses and Income

6.4.1 Definitions and Types

When expenditures and revenues are related to one accounting period, they become—in accounting terms—expenses and income. They then form the basis of the earnings calculations used to determine performance during that accounting period.

It is important to identify the various type of income that can flow into a company and the various types of expenses that flow out. The income that is received in exchange for goods sold or services rendered as part of the organisation's primary business activities is sales revenue or operating income. Operating expenses are incurred to purchase the goods and services that are needed to produce the organisation's main output. There is generally a close relationship between operating income and expenses in profit-earning companies, but this may not be the case for other types of economic agent that provide services without charging for them (e.g. non-profits).

There are several ways in which we can categorise expenses and income that occur in a given period. The first of these is based on how they are categorised from an accounting point of view:

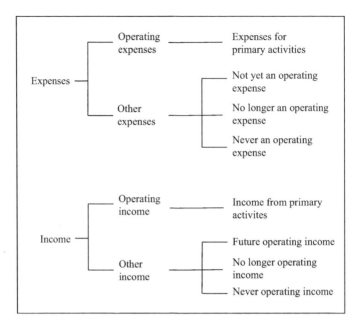

Fig. 6.9 Types of expenses and income

- Future operating expense: when a company buys parts from suppliers for later use. These parts are assets.
- No longer an operating expense: payment for goods that were used in a previous period. This is a reduction of liabilities.
- Never an operating expense: taking money out of cash for private use.
- Future operating income: payment in advance by customers. This is an asset.
- No longer operating income: customers pays debt for goods/service received in previous period. This is a reduction in receivables and increase in bank.
- Never operating income: adding more owner's equity.

Figure 6.9 summarises this.

Companies and other organisations make a **breakdown** to be in a position to measure earnings over a given period. A distinction is made between operating expenses and income and other types of expenses and income, which are called neutral expenses and income in the German-speaking world, while in the Anglo-Saxon world they fall into the general category of non-operating expenses and income. This is the basis of our second categorisation.

There are four categories of non-operating expenses:

- non-operating (i.e. expenses for activities other than the company's primary business activity),
- accounting period-unrelated (e.g. additional tax charges),

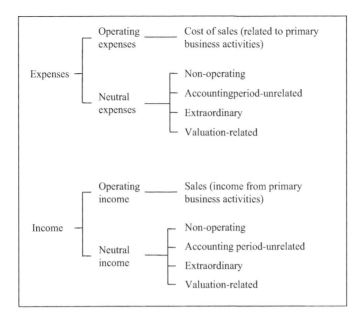

Fig. 6.10 Categories of expenses and income

- extraordinary (e.g. fire damages), and
- valuation-related (e.g. special depreciation due to fiscal regulations).

Non-operating income can be categorised similarly:

- non-operating (e.g. profits from equity investments),
- accounting period-unrelated (e.g. tax refunds),
- extraordinary (e.g. sale of fixed assets above net book value), and
- valuation-related (e.g. valuation of capitalised company-produced assets).

Figure 6.10 provides an overview of these categories.

Differentiating between operating and non-operating income is not always straightforward. For example, if an airline states it is making an operating loss, this would normally be taken to mean that that it is losing money in its primary activity of flying people from A to B. It can compensate the operating loss either completely or in part by selling services (e.g. on-board articles, servicing aircraft of other companies, catering and through foreign currency earnings) and by disposing of assets. But where does the border lie between core and non-core business, i.e. between the results of operating and non-operating activities? With single-product firms the border is much easier to identify.

Expenses and income are not necessarily expenditures and revenues in the same period, so a differentiation can be made according to whether or not expenditures and revenues are connected to the operating result, as Fig. 6.11 shows.

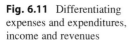
Fig. 6.11 Differentiating expenses and expenditures, income and revenues

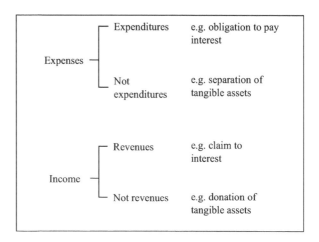

6.4.2   Earnings Calculations

The types of expenses and income described in the previous section are used for earnings calculations which produce the income statement (often referred to as a profit-and-loss statement), the operating income statement and the non-operating income statement. The results of these statements change depending on how inflows and outflows of financial resources are classified.

The **income statement** contains all the expenses and income of an accounting period and is one of the three core financial statements that all companies use as a basis for financial management; the others are the balance sheet and statement of cashflows. Joint-stock companies must put their financial figures into context by adding notes and managers' comments about the line items in the financial statements. It is expected that they mention risks and significant developments that have influenced or may affect the company. There will be an analysis of the company and its performance, discussion of its fields of activity, and a look to the future. Bell Canada's 2016 annual report is typical; the management's discussion and analysis section is over 80 pages in length, while the financial statements themselves take up only six pages.

Two forms of income statement exist: total cost format and cost of sales format. In the former, all income items (sales revenues, capitalised company-produced additions to plant and equipment, and other operating income) and all expenses are grouped together, while the latter presents sales revenues and the costs of production, distribution and general administration. Most US companies, for instance, prefer the latter and this raises an important point: the format chosen for income statements depends on accounting standards, national legislation, company tradition and policies, and what stakeholders expect. Deutsche Telekom, as a German company, must provide its financial statements in a form that conforms to German GAAP (Generally Accepted Accounting Principles). In the case of the income statement, they use the total cost method, which takes as a starting point total operating performance of the period (sales ± changes in inventories) and then subtracts the relevant costs. Deutsche Telekom changed to this form of presenting their income statement in January 2016, having previously used the cost of sales format.

Both formats are depicted in Fig. 6.12. They meet the requirements of Article 275 of the German Commercial Code (Handelsgesetzbuch—HGB).

No matter which format is used, the end result will be the same, as the example in Fig. 6.13 shows.

The size of expenses and income depends on the valuation of assets (influenced by depreciation, stocks of raw material etc.) and rating of liabilities (e.g. accrued remaining amounts). The balance on an income statement represents an **annual surplus or deficit**, often referred to as **net income**. The surplus is used to build up earnings reserves or to cover an annual deficit from the previous period. If a surplus or a deficit carried forward from the previous period is included, the result is a **net surplus** (a balance sheet profit) that could, for example, be distributed, or a **net deficit** (a balance sheet loss).

Shown in Fig. 6.14, which is based on the multiple-step format of the income statement, is where the annual surplus or deficit come from and how they are dealt with. *Other income* refers to income over and above sales revenues, e.g. income from equity investments and interest income. Similarly, *other expenses* include items such as labour costs, depreciation, interest expenses and taxes.

With increasing internationalisation and the need to compare the performance of firms, the published financial results of joint-stock companies nearly always show the following indicators of performance:

- EBIT—earnings before interest and taxes, and
- EBITDA—earnings before interest, taxes, depreciation and amortisation.

They are used because they eliminate the effects of capital structures and the effect that different national tax regimes have on profits. EBIT is also known as the **operating profit** or **operating income**; it is however not an official GAAP financial measure so should be interpreted carefully.

As Fig. 6.15 shows, EBITDA is a narrower measure of company performance than EBIT. EBIT indicates a company's earning power, while EBITDA is a cash flow value that indicates the fiscal claim of shareholders and the possible financing of replacement investments.

One of most popular measure for comparing the performance of listed companies is the price/earnings (P/E) ratio as shown in Eq. (6.1).

$$P/E \ Ratio = \frac{(Market \ price \ per \ share)}{(Earnings \ per \ share)} \qquad (6.1)$$

Equation 6.1 P/E Ratio

Total Cost Format	Cost of Sales Format
1. Sales revenues	1. Sales revenues
2. Increase or decrease of finished goods and work in progress	
3. Other company-produced additions to plant and equipment	
4. Other operating income	
5. Material expenses a) Expenses for raw materials and supplies b) Expenses for procured goods and services	2. Production costs for the outputs realized in order to generate the sales revenues
6. Labour expenses a) Salaries and wages b) Social levies and expenses for pension schemes and for support	3. Gross result from sales 4. Distribution costs
7. Depreciation a) On intangible assets and tangible assets as well as capitalized expenses for start-up and extension of business operations b) On current assets, as long as the depreciation exceeds the common depreciation in the limited company	5. General administration costs 6. Other operating income

8. (7.) Other operating expenses

9. (8.) Income from equity investments

10. (9.) Income from other shares and loans

11. (10.) Other interest and similar income

12. (11.) Depreciation on finance assets

13. (12.) Interest and similar expenses

14. (13.) Result from ordinary business activities

15. (14.) Extraordinary income

16. (15.) Extraordinary expenses

17. (16.) Extraordinary result

18. (17.) Taxes on revenue and income

19. (18.) Other taxes

20. (19.) Profit for the year / loss for the year

Fig. 6.12 Structure of income statements

Total Cost Format	Cost of Sales Format

Total operating performance 12
  i.e. Sales revenues   9
  ± Changes in
    inventory   3
− Production expenses   8
 	
= Net income   4
	Sales revenues 9
	− Expenses 5
	  i.e. Production expenses 8
	  ± Changes in inventory 3
	
	= Net income 4

Fig. 6.13 Two income statement formats

```
   Sales revenues
+  Other income
−  Materials expenses
−  Other expenses
_____
=  Annual surplus / deficit
+  Surplus carried forward / − deficit carried
                              forward
+  Transfer from reserves
−  Allocation to reserves
_____
=  Net surplus / deficit
```

Fig. 6.14 From annual surplus to net surplus

For example, a share price of 80 € and a profit of 10 € per share results in a P/E ratio of 8. Financial analysts use the P/E ratio to judge how a company's performance has changed over a given period and also to compare the value of companies with one another. The average P/E ratio varies strongly between individual industries.

Company valuations are required when the firm is affected by an acquisition, a merger, dissolution, an expropriation and or when it needs to be restructured. Valuations are also needed for analyses of creditworthiness and may sometimes be required by tax authorities. It soon becomes evident when performing an evaluation that book values as seen in the balance sheet do not reflect the overall worth of a concern, so other tools are needed.

Fig. 6.15 EBIT and
EBITDA calculation

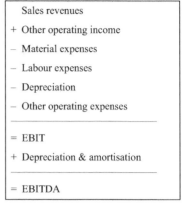

Sales revenues

+ Other operating income

− Material expenses

− Labour expenses

− Depreciation

− Other operating expenses

─────────────────────

= EBIT

+ Depreciation & amortisation

─────────────────────

= EBITDA

The **net asset value method** is based on the assumption that a solvent company could sell off its assets and pay its liabilities. The valuer works on the basis that she is trying to construct an identical company and calculates the reproduction or reconstruction cost value for the necessary working assets, taking only the items that can be included in the balance sheet and valuing them at market value. The **earning capacity value method** is based on profits. Using past returns (often the average of the last 5 years) a value is calculated, with certain assumptions about company lifespan and the typical rate of interest. Both approaches are combined in the **average value method**, where the company's estimated value is half of the value of its net assets plus half of the value of its earning capacity. A fourth method is the **market value approach**, which uses the sale of comparable companies as a basis of calculation. Of course, it may be difficult to find comparable companies when trying to put a value on a large and complex one.

Other values may be taken into consideration during negotiations for the sale of a company. The **liquidation value** of assets represents what they can be sold for when the seller is under duress—the assets have to be sold quickly so are not exposed to potential buyers for a long enough period. The **going concern value** of a company is the value of a company as an operating venture and includes goodwill.

The **operating income statement** shows the earning power of the core business. Transactions that affect this statement need to be charged to the appropriate accounting period, using **accruals**. Accruals are adjustments for revenues that have been earned or for expenditures that have been incurred but have not yet been recorded in the accounts. For example, the supplier of household water used staff and resources to provide water in December. However, the meters are only read in January, so the company needs to show that it earned incomes in December, even though it only received payment in January—operating income needs to be charged to the correct accounting periods. The operating result is the bottom line of a statement of operating income statement, as it captures a company's performance in a single accounting period that is one of the many accounting periods that make up the lifetime of the company.

Even though the **statement of non-operating income** is viewed by some people simply as a 'nice to have', it very often performs an important function because it permits analysts to see the extent to which non-core activities contribute to a company's overall financial performance. Income from financial activities (e.g. buying and selling shares or bonds), for example, can contribute considerably to the overall performance of an industrial company and in certain circumstances make up for disappointing results in the core business.

6.5   Costs and Outputs

6.5.1   Terms and Types

Costs and revenues are usually paired with each other in everyday language, reflecting a monetary relationship. Two German authors are well known in their own country for their pioneering work on the definitions of these two concepts. Following Eugen Schmalenbach's (1873–1955) **value-based definition**, costs are understood as the value of the resources that are consumed to produce an output and revenues measure the value of the outputs produced in monetary terms. At the heart of this definition is the understanding that factors of production are employed, used, transformed or consumed and combined in the process of producing the (tangible or intangible) good. Both what goes into the transformation process and what emerges is measured in monetary terms. The values that are given to the inputs depend on the accounting purpose and can be stated in nominal or real terms, they can be historic or predictive, orientated to monitoring or planning, and intended for an internal or external audience.

Schmalenbach's definition leads to ambiguity, so Helmut Koch (1919–2015) tried to bring clarity with his **payment-based definition**. He treats costs as payments for the factors of production that are employed in operational processes and, correspondingly, sales revenues are payments received for goods sold. However, even though valuation problems are rarely an issue, the value-based definition has proved to be more useful in practice because it makes it possible to align valuations with the various accounting purposes and thereby differentiate between them. In addition, the terms *operating expenses* and *operating income* essentially cover Schmalenbach's understanding of costs and revenues. In the medium term *costs* become identical with *expenditures*, and *revenues* with *income*, while over the longer term *costs* become *outpayments* and *revenues* become *receipts of payment*.

This view however leads to a new and complex problem. No matter how we define *costs* and *outputs*, we always express them in terms of money and only with reference to the economic agent involved. A significant consequence and weakness of this is that the only costs which are included in income and other financial statements of the economic agent are its own costs: demands placed on third parties

Fig. 6.16 Categories of costs
and outputs

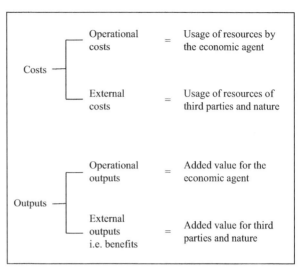

and nature (earth, water, air and space) are ignored. More equitable would be a
division of costs into operational and external. Viewed this way, costs represent in
general the values of the inputs necessary to produce tangible and intangible goods.
Operational costs are carried by the economic subject and reflect the values of the
factors of production that have been consumed to produce the output.

To simply treat operational costs as the counterpart of sales revenues
(as understood in both the value-based and payment-based definitions) is insufficient, because the outputs of many economic agents are not intended for sale
(thereby generating sales revenues), nor are they measured in monetary terms.
Voluntary work, religious activities, domestic work, basic research, administrative
acts by the state, internal and external national security, unused capacity, the
implied warranty offered by public authorities and jurisprudence are examples of
this. Just like the products and services of commercial organisations, they are the
outputs of operational activities and can be measured both qualitatively and
quantitively. They represent value added to their inputs, measured in monetary or
non-monetary ways (such as appreciation). We therefore propose a **division of
outputs**: in a narrower sense, outputs as tangible and intangible goods produced
through operational activities, and in a broader sense, outputs that generate positive
external effects or benefits, such as better education, health or security, improved
infrastructure and increased quality of life.

Figure 6.16 shows this categorisation of costs and outputs. Internal cost accounting is concerned with operational costs and outputs, whereas external cost-benefit-
analyses deal with what happens externally.

We now look at operational costs in more depth. Depending on which factors of
production are employed, different **cost types** arise, such as personnel costs, costs
of capital, material costs including depreciation, costs for maintenance and repairs,
costs for energy, costs for services and rights of third parties and environmental

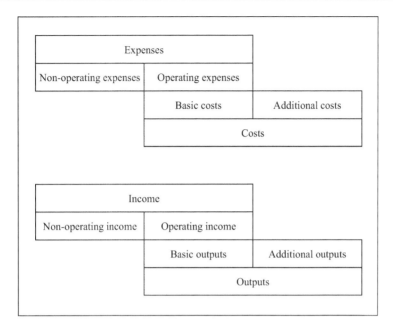

Fig. 6.17 Categories of costs and outputs

costs. (We are not concerned here with resources that can be used for no charge, of which nature is often one of the most important ones.) **Basic costs** are the expenses that are necessary for operations. In contrast, **additional costs** do not represent expenses, but rather lost income as they are the opportunity costs that a firm gives up when using its factors of production; for example, a company could rent or sell its property rather than using it for the production of goods and services. These costs are not recorded in any financial report.

Different **output types** can also be identified. The operational output of a company comprises sales revenues (from the sale of products, i.e. output for the market), the increase in stocks of finished goods and work-in-progress (i.e. output for stock) and internal outputs (e.g. machines or vehicles produced by the company for its own use, which are valued at the cost of production). Gains from equity investments are not outputs for an industrial company, but non-operating (neutral) income. Free-of-charge goods and services however are output; they contribute to reaching substantive goals. Outputs produced to generate operating income are **basic outputs. Additional outputs** have no corresponding income and are therefore not included in the income statement; an example of this is a product that is given away. Free-of-charge goods and services are always by definition additional outputs.

Eugen Schmalenbach's schema (Fig. 6.17) shows the various categories.

How can we measure efficiency? Efficiency is an expression of the relationship between output and input, so when we want to measure economic efficiency, we must calculate the **ratio of costs to outputs.** It is necessary to be specific when defining the numerator and denominator; we can measure per unit, per product type or programme, per workplace, department or area of production and/or over a specific period. Denominator and numerator can be expressed in terms of quantity, of value or by a mixed approach. A quantity ratio provides information on the productivity (technical efficiency) of the processes involved in the production of goods and services. Since costs are always expressed in monetary units, using quantity as a denominator tells us the quantity of the factor of production that was used. The relationship of quantity-based outputs to costs is cost efficiency. The reverse relationship, e.g. sales to number of employees, provides information about the revenues generated per unit of that specific factor of production.

Many ratios are used to measure economic efficiency. Two of the most significant are **planned and actual costs** and **planned and actual outputs**. Figure 6.18 shows some of the more common ratios used by managers.

6.5.2   Cost Accounting

The tasks of cost accounting are generally stated to be: (i) **cost planning** to aid decision making about what should be done in the future, (ii) the **cost management** of current activities and (iii) **cost monitoring** (German: *Kostkontrolle*) which continuously reviews actual costs against planned costs and identifies measures that should be taken when there is a discrepancy. Since costs always stand in relation to outputs, cost accounting of necessity involves **output planning**, **output management** and **output monitoring**. The distinction between cost accounting and management accounting is not a clearly defined one in English as the definitions of each of them are somewhat imprecise. For us, management accounting is the generation of accounting information to facilitate decision making by managers, and cost accounting provides information specifically about costs. Cost accounting can therefore be viewed as a subset of management accounting.

Questions to which cost accounting provides answers include: How much do actual costs deviate from planned costs? Are the causes of differences to be found in planning activities or in the production process? Make or buy—does it more economic sense for a company to produce itself some or all of goods and services it needs for its own operations, or should they be bought in? Which option is the most cost-effective: purchase, rent or lease? How do cost changes affect the range of products and services offered? What effects do changes in the capacity utilisation rate of assets have on cost structures (e.g. in terms of fixed and variable costs, total and marginal costs)? What is the optimal size of a company from a costs point of view? What is the relationship between job lot size and costs? What is the lowest price for an individual product? Which cost increases are to be expected when external costs are included (i.e. when social and ecological costs are internalised rather than externalised)?

The information needed for future decisions and analysis of past and present decisions is obtained by collecting and recording costs, and then by allocating them. One must identify which costs occur (cost types, e.g. staff, energy), where they

$$\text{Max !} \ \frac{\text{Outputs}}{\text{Costs}} \qquad\qquad \text{Min !} \ \frac{\text{Costs}}{\text{Outputs}}$$

$$\frac{\text{Actual output}}{\text{Planned output}} \cdot x \ 100 \geq 100\% \qquad \frac{\text{Actual costs}}{\text{Planned costs}} \cdot x \ 100 \leq 100\%$$

Quantity-based approach:

$$\text{Productivity} \quad = \quad \frac{\text{Output quantity}}{\text{Factor input quantity}}$$

Value-based approach:

$$\text{Profitability} \quad = \quad \frac{\text{Total costs}}{\text{Sales revenues}} \cdot x \ 100$$

Mixed approaches:

$$\text{Cost efficiency} \quad = \quad \frac{\text{Output volume}}{\text{Costs}}$$

$$\text{Factor output} \quad = \quad \frac{\text{Sales revenues}}{\text{Number of personnel}}$$

$$\text{Staff performance} \quad = \quad \frac{\text{Number of meals}}{\text{Number of kitchen}}$$

$$\text{Productivity of transport company} \quad = \quad \frac{\text{Passenger-km (paid)}}{\text{Number of personnel}}$$

$$\text{Various (in percentages)} \qquad \frac{\text{Personnel costs}}{\text{Total costs}} \cdot x \ 100$$

$$\frac{\text{Costs of administrative staff}}{\text{Personnel costs}} \cdot x \ 100$$

$$\frac{\text{Costs of energy}}{\text{Total costs}} \cdot x \ 100$$

$$\text{Staff turnover} \quad = \quad \frac{\text{Replaced leavers}}{\text{Average number of}} \cdot x \ 100$$

$$\text{Disposal rate} \quad = \quad \frac{\text{Disposal costs}}{\text{Costs of production}} \cdot x \ 100$$

$$\text{Waste rate} \quad = \quad \frac{\text{Waste volume}}{\text{Product volume}} \cdot x \ 100$$

$$\text{Packaging ratio} \quad = \quad \frac{\text{Packaging weight}}{\text{Sales weight}} \cdot x \ 100$$

$$\text{Water efficiency} \quad = \quad \frac{\text{Water volume}}{\text{Product quantity}} \cdot x \ 100$$

$$\text{Level of activity} \quad = \quad \frac{\text{Actual output}}{\text{Planned output}} \cdot x \ 100$$

$$\text{Capacity utilisation} \quad = \quad \frac{\text{Actual output}}{\text{Attainable output}} \cdot x \ 100$$

Fig. 6.18 Examples of financial ratios

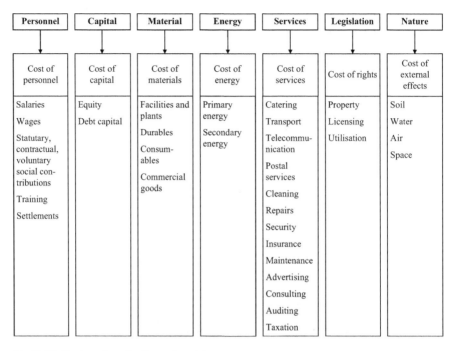

Fig. 6.19 Factors of production and cost types

occur (cost centres) and for what (cost units, which are the units of service or products for which costs can be ascertained—the appropriate cost unit depends on the industry and what is being measured, e.g. passenger km. (transport companies), chair (furniture manufacturer)). Cost accounting then consists of **cost type, cost centre and cost unit accounting**. The first two generate the overhead allocation sheet, while the latter involves calculating the costs of goods sold or to be sold.

Various ways of categorising cost types exist. In Fig. 6.19 we show a scheme based on the factors of production (see Sect. 5.2.2).

A **uniform system of accounts** is a list of accounts which is used to record financial and operating transactions (including costs). In some countries, including Germany, systems of accounts for a particular industry are determined by an outside body. In Germany, the Bundesverband der deutschen Industrie (BDI, Federation of Geman Industry) has established such systems for industrial companies. They provide a framework that can be adapted to better meet individual requirements; each company develops its own unified system which includes the accounts necessary to capture the costs associated with the various cost types, as illustrated in Fig. 6.20, which shows a typical uniform system of accounts as seen in practice.

We can also classify cost types based on operational activity, cost allocation, origin and cost behaviour pattern as illustrated in Fig. 6.21.

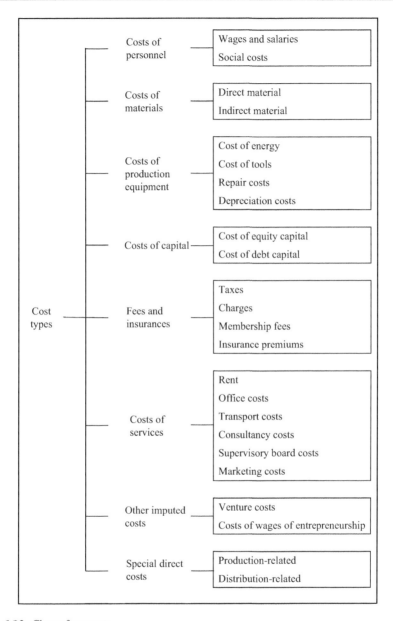

Fig. 6.20 Chart of accounts

The goal of a **cost centre plan** is to make it possible to assign costs to a particular department which is then made responsible for the costs. This makes it easier to manage costs because their sources are easier to identify, thus avoiding confusion. Individual cost centres can be grouped on the basis of the organisation's activities, allowing for bigger picture of the origin of costs to merge. Operational

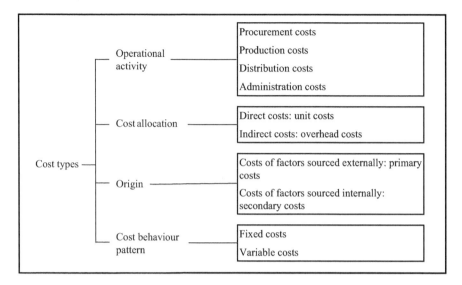

Fig. 6.21 Further categories of cost types

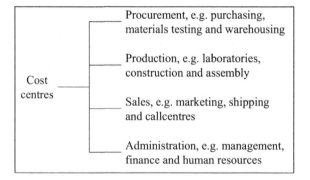

Fig. 6.22 Cost centres

functions serve as a basic structure, with relevant departments being defined as cost centres, as shown in Fig. 6.22.

Cost centre accounting allocates costs that have been recorded according to cost type to cost centres. Since cost centres are more or less closely connected to cost units, they are allocated to *final cost centres* for the output produced for customers, and to *preliminary cost centres* for preliminary inputs like purchased materials and services from other firms. Final cost centres can be divided further into *primary cost centres* for the actual operational output, the costs of which are directly allocated to the cost units (i.e. to their products or services) through cost unit accounting, and into *secondary cost centres*. Primary cost centres record costs, such as those of operating resources, that accrue constantly, and secondary cost

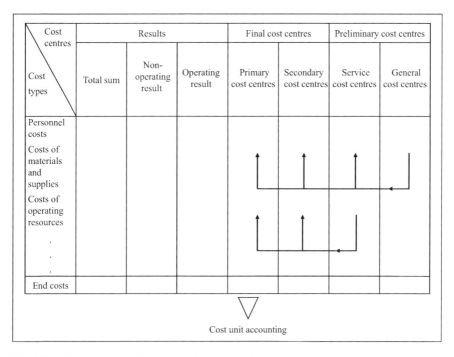

Cost centres / Cost types	Results			Final cost centres		Preliminary cost centres	
	Total sum	Non-operating result	Operating result	Primary cost centres	Secondary cost centres	Service cost centres	General cost centres
Personnel costs							
Costs of materials and supplies							
Costs of operating resources							
.							
.							
.							
End costs							

Cost unit accounting

Fig. 6.23 Basic structure of an overhead allocation sheet

centres record non-operating costs that should be allocated to other areas. Preliminary cost centres comprise (i) *service cost centres* that do not transfer costs directly to the cost units, but rather to one or more final cost centres on the basis of what was actually done (e.g. number of hours worked or kilometres driven), and (ii) *general cost centres* whose output is used by other cost centres; they are therefore actually *overhead cost centres*. With the help of allocation formulas, the costs are initially allocated to the general cost centres and then via service cost centres to the final cost centres according to the step-ladder method. The primary cost centres create the link to cost unit accounting.

Figure 6.23 shows the structure and method of cost allocation, with the arrows indicating the flow of allocated costs.

The task of **cost unit accounting** is to allocate the costs incurred by the production of goods and services to the output according to the principle of causation, i.e. costs are allocated on the basis of where they originated. Cost units come into existence either because of external orders (from customers or distributors) or internal orders (for internally produced outputs that can be capitalised like plant and equipment, or in-house goods and services like repairs and other activities that form general overhead and which cannot be capitalised). The costs extracted from the overhead allocation sheet serve to calculate the production costs and cost price per unit or order: this process is referred to as **unit-of-output costing** (other terms are *output cost accounting*, *product cost accounting*, *cost price accounting* or simply *costing*). The cost price is (or expressed differently, the prime costs are) the lower price limit (i.e. the break-even price) and creates the basis for the quotation price or, in more general terms, the pricing policy. Costing is based on the assumption that operations have been recorded (e.g. in terms of number of units or hours). When the sales revenues per product unit or cost unit are known, unit-of-output costing can be extended to generate a unit-of-output profit statement.

Two main forms of costing methods exist, with the one chosen depending on the type of production process: output costing and job order costing. Output costing is common when there is mass production of uniform products without changes in stock (single-stage output costing, e.g. power generation) and with changes in stock (double- or multi-stage output costing, e.g. manufacture of cement). It involves taking total costs, or the costs incurred in individual areas (production costs on the one hand, administration and distribution costs on the other hand) over a given period and dividing this sum by the number of products produced or sold during the same period, as shown in Eq. (6.2).

$$Unit\ costs = \frac{Costs}{Output} \tag{6.2}$$

Equation 6.2 Unit costs

Continuous batch production is used for products that are similar in nature (it can be found in breweries or brickworks, for example), whose costs are in a more or less fixed relation with each other. The relation of the costs of the different cost units for an identical number of units produced is expressed through an equivalence coefficient (leading to single, double or multi-staged **equivalence coefficient costing**). An equivalence coefficient of 1 for product A and 1.2 for product B means that 120% of the costs for A are incurred when product B is produced.

A further type of output costing is **joint-product costing**. This procedure is used when a production process unavoidably creates more than one kind of product. For example, the joint products of refineries are gas, petrol, oil and tar, and the joint products of university clinics are medical research, teaching and medical services. Since costing according to the principle of causation for individual joint products is not possible, it is necessary to either:

- apply averages by subtracting the sales revenues of the by-products (minus additional costs from further processing) from the total costs of the joint production and then dividing the residual costs by the volume of the main product (the residual value-method), or
- not differentiate into main and by-products, but instead to estimate equivalence coefficients that can be used to allocate costs to the joint products (the distribution method). In practice, this is similar to the calculation of equivalence coefficients, with the difference that equivalence coefficients measure the sources of costs in batch production, whereas they measure cost carrying capacity in joint product costing.

Fig. 6.24 Cost estimate
sheet for goods

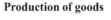

Production of goods
Direct material costs
+ Material overhead costs

= Material costs
Direct labour costs
+ Production overheads
+ Special direct production costs

= Manufacturing costs
Material costs
+ Manufacturing costs

= Production costs
+ Administration overhead costs
+ Distribution overhead costs
+ Special direct distribution costs

= Prime costs

Job order costing is principally employed in job (one-off) and mass production where outputs are the result of multi-stage processes with various causes of costs and continuous changes in stock. Unlike output costing, job order costing always differentiates between direct and overhead costs. Direct costs are allocated straight to cost units, whereas overhead costs are distributed on the basis of ratios which are established by, and are therefore an output of, cost centre accounting. There are two common methods; the choice is dependent on the quantities involved and the job itself. The first method—**summary job order costing**—involves relating total direct costs to total overhead costs and then calculating a costing rate. This simple technique assumes that there is a constant relationship between direct and overhead costs in all cost units, which is often not the case. **Elective job order costing** is the second method. Here, overhead cost types are grouped, with the proviso that they must be closely related to a particular type of direct cost. Once this has been done, costs can be calculated and allocated as fairly as possible using the principle of causation.

Cost estimate sheets have been developed for this sophisticated method and are in widespread use. Figures 6.24 and 6.25 provide examples for manufacturing and services.

Figure 6.26 provides an overview of the costing methods described above.

Unit-of-output costing is followed by **cost unit period accounting**. Based on accruals accounting, its task is to determine the total costs incurred in an accounting

Production of services	
	Direct costs of personnel
+	Direct material costs
+	Direct imputed costs
+	Directly chargeable services

=	Costs of producing service
+	Charge for costs of building (as % of costs of producing service)
+	Charge for other overheads (as % of costs of producing service)

=	Prime costs
+	Charge for executive functions (as % of prime costs)

=	Total costs

Fig. 6.25 Cost estimate sheet for services

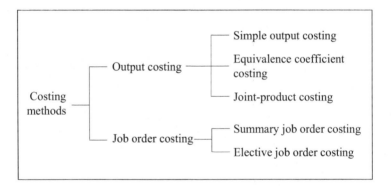

Fig. 6.26 Costing methods

period, with the costs being grouped according to type of output. While costs per unit are captured in unit-of-output costing (as its name implies), costs that arise over the given period are recorded for cost unit period accounting. If operating income from the company's goods and services is included, the cost unit period accounting statement becomes a **statement of operating result**, produced on a weekly, monthly or annual basis. The statement balance—the operating result—shows how well the company is performing in terms of its business purpose since it does not include expenses or income from non-operating activities. The operating

Basic outputs	-	Basic costs	=	Operating profit/loss
+		+		+
Additional outputs	-	Additional costs	=	Additional profit/loss
-----------------------		--------------------		--------------------------
(Total) Outputs	-	(Total) Costs	=	(Total) Operating profit/loss

Fig. 6.27 Components of an operating statement

result includes income and expenses of core (basic) activities; these are calculated by financial accounting. In addition, it includes outputs and costs from additional activities; these are calculated by internal cost accounting. Figure 6.27 shows the components of an operating statement.

Two **costing systems** can be identified, with the differentiating factors being time and scope. We can identify three costings based on the different periods to which cost accounting is being applied:

- **actual costing** is used when costs have incurred in the past (actual costs = actual quantities used × actual prices),
- **normal costing** for costs incurred in the past that are calculated with average quantities and prices (normal costs), and
- **standard costing** estimates future costs with the attendant uncertainties, and allocates them to cost centres and cost units. The actual costs are recorded on a regular basis. If the costs cannot be captured directly (e.g. depreciation), a pro rata figure is used. Average actual costs then become normal costs, a process which means that large cost fluctuations do not distort costing activities. Unlike actual and normal costs, standard costs include estimates of future factor consumption (standard costs = planned quantity × planned price for the planned level of activity).

Cost monitoring in order to eliminate inefficiency involves the comparison of actual costs with target costs which, unlike standard costs, are based on actual activities (target costs = planned quantities × planned price for the actual level of activity). Cost variances are determined and their causes are analysed. The difference between standard costs and target costs reflects a variance in the level of activity.

There are two costings with different scopes: **full costing** which records all costs and allocates them to the appropriate cost unit(s), and **marginal costing** which only assigns a part of the costs to the cost units. It can be argued that full costing does not adequately capture cost causation, since fixed costs and overheads are also allocated to outputs. This is done on the basis of pre-defined rules, which means that the costs to produce a product or service depend on which rules are applied. As a result, wrong decisions may be taken for the short term when knowledge of variable or direct costs is essential. Full costing's assignment of fixed costs to outputs means that costs per unit are high when few units are produced, and that costs sink as more

Fig. 6.28 Combinations of costing systems

Scope / Period	Full costing	Marginal costing
Actual costing	✓	✓
Normal costing	✓	✓
Standard costing	✓	✓

units are produced. This information is only of limited use for the calculation of product prices, and in such a situation marginal costing is helpful because it is based on the principle of cost-causation. Instead of dealing with averages and the principle of cost carrying capacity as does full costing, marginal costing means that only a part of incurred costs is passed on to the cost unit.

With marginal costing based on variable costs (direct costing method), only the variable costs—direct costs and overheads—are allocated, since they change with the level of activity. Marginal costing on the basis of relative direct costs, as devised by Paul Riebel (1918–2001), assumes that all costs can be direct costs, depending on the chosen base. An appropriate hierarchy of bases permits any cost to be recorded as a direct cost and to be assigned to cost units.

A combination of both costing systems results in the six options shown in Fig. 6.28, all of which can be found in practice. It is by no means the case that marginal costing is replacing full costing, because total costs (with the inclusion of fixed costs and overheads) are still relevant. The type of costing that should be used depends on the business purpose, objectives and the decision to be made.

Marginal costing can be used to produce statements of operating result, commonly known as operating statements, through the inclusion of sales revenues. These are essentially short-term income statements for the production and provision of goods and services. In full costing, all costs are assigned to the cost units and the operating result equals sales revenues minus these total costs. In marginal costing the resulting balances are contribution margins for covering costs which have not yet been allocated to cost units. **Contribution costing** with variable costs and relative direct costs is another possibility, depending on the type of marginal costing. In practice, contribution costing can be done by actual costing or standard costing.

These differences are shown in Fig. 6.29. For business entities with a high share of fixed costs in the total costs (e.g. labour-intensive companies or public administrations) it is recommended that instead of applying a single contribution margin to cover all fixed costs, these should be split up and several contribution margins used in costing. The starting point of multi-stage contribution costing is the sales revenues of a product, from which are subtracted the variable costs per product (contribution margin I), the fixed costs of the product (contribution margin II), the fixed costs of the product group (contribution margin III), the fixed costs of the unit responsible for the product, such as a department or an office (contribution margin IV) etc.

Full costing	Marginal costing	
	Direct costing method	Relative direct cost method
Sales revenues - Total costs = Operating result	Sales revenues - Variable costs * = Contribution margin - Fixed costs = Operating result * including (variable) direct costs and variable overhead costs (e.g. variable production overhead costs)	Sales revenues - Direct costs = Contribution margin - Overhead costs = Operating result

Fig. 6.29 Methods of calculating the operating result

The constant increase of overhead costs in industrial as well as service companies, together with a greater customer orientation, a higher number of product versions and increasing complexity in production have raised awareness of internal performance processes and cost structures. Since contribution costing treats the major share of overhead costs as unchangeable on a short-term basis, the goal remains of determining relevant process costs in order to optimise planning and monitoring systems, procurement processes, automatisation, digitalisation, just-in-time deliveries and other value adding processes. Processes are the base of **activity based costing**, which is a form of full costing; they are the cost units. The preferred field of application is overhead costs, for the method is not as suitable for the areas of a manufacturing company that are directly involved in production. Of special interest are the triggers of processes—the cost drivers. These are the activities in cost centres that are carried out following a quantifiable stimulus (e.g. number of orders) and can be understood as sub-processes. The costs per element of a sub-process are established and the sub-processes clustered to form an overarching process (e.g. the complete process of procurement) that may span more than one cost centre. The costs of the process are then assigned to cost units (or products) based on utilisation.

The customer orientation in highly competitive buyer markets has also led to **target costing**, a method that originated in Japan. Unlike the more common costings, which take supply-led costs and prices as their basis, here the emphasis is on demand-oriented pricing and cost calculation. The starting point is the probable target price for a company's product as determined by market research. This price is what can be reached on the market, and from it is subtracted the profit margin (e.g. a 12% return on sales). The result of this calculation is the allowable costs for the market, and these mark the long-term minimum selling price. They are then compared to the mostly higher current costs (drifting costs, standard costs) in the company with its current (and possible future) technological processes, and the target costs are derived from this comparison. Since the allowable costs are often not immediately attainable, a value is determined for the target costs which lies between the allowable costs and the drifting costs. Depending on the intensity of competition and corporate strategy, the goal is to reduce the target costs to the height of allowable costs through cost reduction measures. In essence, target costs form a moving target.

6.6 External Costs and Benefits

6.6.1 Terms and Types

The total costs of operational activities (factor procurement, production and distribution of goods and services) are regularly higher than the operational costs: the difference is made up of external costs, i.e. those that are generated outside the company. These are the social and ecological costs that represent the negative externalities caused by the operational activities. Two types of negative externalities can be distinguished: buyers' surplus and diseconomies.

Buyers' surplus is the amount of money that an economic agent is willing to pay for a factor compared to its market price because it values the benefit of the factor as being worth more than its market price. If the factor could realise a higher price if used for a different purpose, its supplier is missing out on the difference in the two prices. Whereas such a factor rent is linked to market activities and can be quantified, **diseconomies**—damage to the natural world and to people—are found outside the market. It is not easy to capture these negative externalities and even their causes cannot easily be determined since there is rarely a single one. In addition, there are the problems in measuring the size of negative externalities and even larger problems in coming up with a valuation.

The counterparts of external costs are external benefits which are the result of operational outputs and can be divided into consumers' surplus and general social benefits.

The **consumers' surplus** is the amount of money that a consumer would be willing to pay over and above the market price before giving up on the purchase of a product, i.e. deciding not to buy it. The consumer values the utility of a product more than the purchase price, or in other words, the producer offers a benefit that exceeds the market price. The difference between the two is influenced by various factors, for instance how dependent on this good the consumer is, or demand elasticity (i.e. the extent to which demand for a good changes as the price or income changes).

Positive externalities, where third parties and nature benefit from operating activities, are a **general social benefit**. They represent the counterpart to external diseconomies. Among the third parties that can profit from operating activities are, for example, neighbours, the local economy, the community, the state, the national economy through jobs, income, research, education and advanced training and so on. As with diseconomies, it is not straightforward to identify the causes of general social benefit or to put a value to it.

6.6.2 Benefit Calculations

Benefit calculations go beyond the earnings calculations of a company as shown in its income statement; they show the social and ecological effects of operational activities. Originally developed for large national projects such as dams, waterways, highways, bridges, defence facilities and weaponry, their intention was and still is to determine if, and to what extent, commercially unprofitable investments deliver a positive net benefit. What is the optimal size of such projects and which is the best alternative? There are three types of analysis that help in this respect: the cost-benefit analysis, the cost-effectiveness analysis and the utility-value analysis. The starting point for all three analyses is a goal defined in terms of operational benefits (e.g. the improvement of the municipal traffic situation) and its sub-goals (e.g. flow volume, speed, traffic safety, noise pollution, air pollution and the safeguarding of urban planning priorities).

The purpose of a **cost-benefit analysis** is to measure all costs (i.e. operating costs and external costs) and all benefits (i.e. revenues and external benefits) and compare them with each other. Costs can include: the willingness to pay in order to prevent negative impacts (usually captured in a survey of those impacted); extra costs for those affected; damages; secondary effects (losses due to a reduction in business activity caused by the project in question or due to a reduction in the value of assets that are indirectly affected); opportunity costs. Regarding benefits, an effort is made to determine: the willingness to pay for goods and services that are not provided in return for payment; cost savings; damages that will be prevented; secondary effects (e.g. increases in the value of assets that are indirectly affected); shadow prices (values assigned to resources, goods or services for which there is no market price). In the best case of being able to express all costs and benefits in monetary terms, we obtain the cost-benefit difference or the cost-benefit ratio. Costs and benefits generally occur at different points in time, so the capital value method is used to determine values.

Figures 6.30 and 6.31 summarise the valuation methods.

If the benefits of the project under analysis cannot be measured in monetary terms, a different method is required. The **cost-effectiveness analysis** develops scales of effectiveness for the benefits on the basis of a system of goals, where each goal is given its own weighting. The costs continue to be determined in monetary

| Survey method |
| Used to assess the willingness to pay to avoid negative external effects (e.g. shadows caused by a new building) |

| Additional costs |
| Higher costs for third parties, also for customers, due to operational activities or lack thereof. |

| Damages incurred |
| Risks linked to the production and use of products – can cause injury and damage, and therefore incur costs |

| Secondary effects |
| Changes in the market (e.g. reduction in rents) affect value of other assets (e.g. nearby apartment buildings) |

| Opportunity costs |
| Benefits that will not be received because the necessary resources are being used for another purpose |

Fig. 6.30 Valuation methods for external costs

units. For example: the costs of a research project might be viewed in relation to indicators of success. In this case, success could be expressed in terms of knowledge gains, follow-up research, citation frequency and patents. Since the goals often have different dimensions, the only measures that can be excluded from the group of possible measures are those that are worse than others as far as meeting targets is concerned.

The consolidation of goals that have different dimensions into a consolidated goal—utility value—is the task of a **utility-value analysis**. It is based on measuring of individual goals, just as with the cost effectiveness analysis. According to Christof Zangemeister (1972), the starting point of a utility value analysis is to develop a hierarchy of goals. There is a main goal, and under it and supporting it are other goals (sub-goals) that are weighted in two ways—their relationship to the goal at the next level up in the goal hierarchy (node-weighting), and their relationship to

Survey method

Used to assess the willingness to pay to receive positive external
effects (e.g. construction of noise protection embankment)

Cost savings

Costs saved for third parties, but also for customers, due to
operational activities or lack thereof.

Damages prevented

Improved quality assurance, warranties and traffic safety lead
to fewer injuries and less material damage, thereby reducing
costs.

Secondary effects

Changes in the market (e.g. higher property prices or
business revenues) lead to gains in the asset values of other
goods (e.g. neighbouring properties).

Shadow prices

Fictitious prices are employed for goods and services that do
not reach the customer (e.g. the price for entry into a park).

Fig. 6.31 Valuation methods for external benefits

the overall goal (tier weighting). The total for both weightings is 100. The effects on these goals of the measures being (potentially) taken are measured with the help of indicators. In the next step, alternatives are compared with each other with regard to their ability to meet goals and given a score which is then multiplied by the weightings and added to the utility value. For example, production processes can be classified according to their capital value, their technical characteristics and external effects. Each of these parameters can be divided further into other criteria. Taken together, the weighting, goal-related performance and an adequate scale result in utility values that are used to rank the alternatives.

Common to all three types of analyses is that they judge the economic efficiency of projects from an economics point of view. Consequently, categories drawn from economics are the most widely used—examples of this are: aggregated input and output volumes, factor and product prices, income, assets, and willingness to pay.

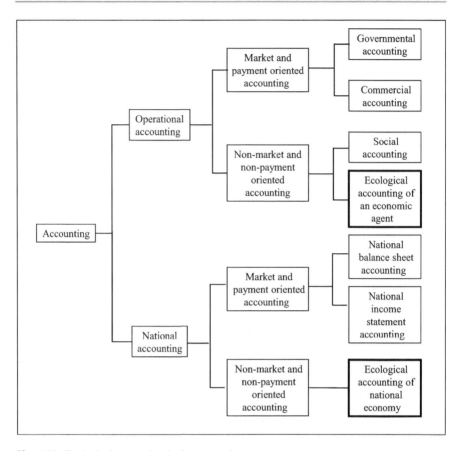

Fig. 6.32 Ecological accounting in the accounting system

Even though their methods are similar, the benefit calculations of companies and other economic agents have specific features. **Operational benefit calculations** allocate external costs and benefits to the company responsible and do not include individual or combined benefit calculations of affected third parties. External costs and benefits are those which have not already been considered by commercial accounting. Operational benefit calculations supplement commercial calculations; by no means do they replace them. Operational benefit calculations not only reflect the economic context, but also social, political, cultural, health-related and ecological effects of both a positive and negative nature. The present stage of research identifies two types of operational benefit calculations: society-related and ecology-related.

In order to show their position more clearly, Fig. 6.32 presents them in relationship to other types of accounting.

Different types of accounting in companies are shown in Fig. 6.33.

Social accounting, also known as socio-economic accounting, can be carried out on a narrow or broad basis. **Socio-economic accounting in the narrower sense**

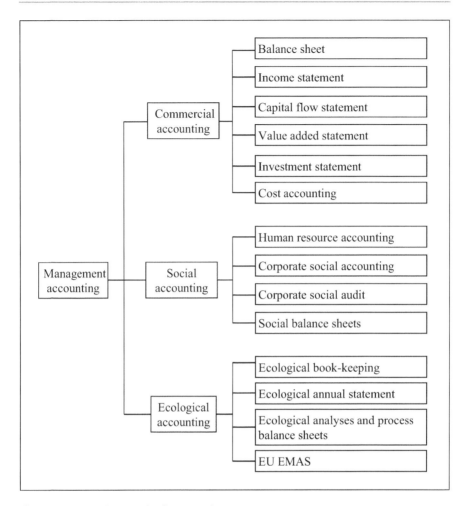

Fig. 6.33 Types of accounting in companies

is concerned with determining the value of the regular workforce for the company. **Human resource accounting** is concerned with assessing the workforce's future contributions to performance. This is achieved by assessing the expected increases or decreases in the value of the human capital. That is determined by hiring new employees and training staff on the one hand (increasing value); a reduction in the number of employees, harmful influences as well as knowledge becoming obsolete on the other hand (decreasing value). These changes in value are captured in special statements (as described in Sect. 6.8) and show up in asset and flow accounts. Human capital represents a kind of social claim of the company against its staff. The opposite is human liabilities or social liabilities that result when a company has neglected to invest in the performance potential of its employees. In view of the size and continued growth of the tertiary sector with its labour-intensive service

Goodwill model	by Roger H. Hermanson

Ratio comparison between company profitability and industry profitability and capitalising the difference

Adjusted discount future wages model	by Roger H. Hermanson

Discounting future personnel costs using an efficiency ratio based on the difference between company profitability and industry profitability

Opportunity cost model	by James Hekimian and Curtis H. Jones

Determining the value of difficult to replace workers through an internal bidding system

Future earnings model	by Baruch Lev and Aba Schwartz

Discounting the expected income of employee groups weighted according to the probability of staying with the company

Reward valuation model	by Eric Flamholtz

Value of the services the employee is expected to provide taking into account positions(s), performance level and duration of employment. The revenues are attributed to factors of production and the individual's contribution determined

Cost value model	by RG Barry Corp

Recording individual and system costs for knowledge and ability of employees with weighting for size of flows and quantities

Behavioural variables model	by Rensis Likert

Human capital as the result of the impact of different types of variable

Fig. 6.34 Human resource accounting

companies, personnel is becoming ever more significant as a factor of production, so the maintenance and improvement of competence levels—i.e. making the most of employees' potential—is crucial. Traditional financial statements are unsatisfactory in this area; the income statement only mentions labour as an expense, and it only shows up in the balance sheet in the context of the provision for pensions.

Seven well-known approaches to human resource accounting are shown in Fig. 6.34.

Socio-economic accounting in the broader sense compares positive and negative external effects, taking into account employees (the internal environment of the company) and the external environment, in the form of stakeholders (customers, general public, municipalities, the state) and areas such as research, waste disposal and nature. Among the better known approaches are **corporate social accounting** and the **corporate social audit**, both of which go beyond the reporting of the performance potential of the employees in financial terms to include the external effects on society of corporate activities outside the market. Corporate social accounting is concerned with the quantitative recording and valuation of the ways in which the company affects the (non-commercial) environment; it is only recently that these have started to be quantified and expressed in monetary terms. A corporate social audit involves the development of standards for social accounting, ideally by external experts in order to increase their credibility and objectivity. A basis for the standards can be the specifications of the European Union and national regulatory bodies (such as the German Institute for Standardisation (DIN)). In order to increase the value of the statement, and in particular to show the timing and size of the external effects, variables that measure flows and quantities should be used.

Most of the approaches to social accounting developed by companies and associations in Germany do not come close to the approaches described in the last paragraph. Indeed, some of them are not just unsuitable but also misleading, and do not really justify being called social accounting statements—external benefits (such as job safety, education and advanced training, time savings) and external costs (such as contaminated land, educational deficits, health risks, air pollution) are not contrasted.

Ecological accounting deals with the outcomes and impacts of operational activities on natural resources, energy resources, the climate, animal and plant protection as well as health. One method is **ecological bookkeeping** as developed by Ruedi Müller-Wenk (born 1934). Its focus is on capturing quantitatively and then weighting positive and harmful effects on the physical environment. It looks at the relationships between manufactured products and the associated consumption of materials and energy, waste products, wasted heat and water, disruption, noise, soot, other emissions as well as relief through further deliveries. This is all (only!) recorded in terms of volume, and each type of effect is given an equivalence coefficient. Multiplying the volumes by the equivalence coefficients (which provide a relative scale for negative and positive ecological effects), allows the calculation and comparison of individual outputs. The equivalence coefficients are determined on the basis of ecological scarcity. The rate of scarcity of an emission represents the critical rate, beyond which an ecologically inacceptable effect is reached. *Cumulative scarcity* illustrates the foreseeable depletion of the resource as goods are consumed. One goal is that the state should determine and adjust equivalence coefficients. This method endeavours to make the different external effects comparable on the basis of a single dimension, but this concept does not go further than providing a quantitative mapping.

Matthias Schellhorn (born 1962) proposed a way of integrating an **annual ecological statement** into traditional end-of-year financial statements. He regards the natural environment as a supplier of inputs and as a medium that absorbs wastes. The utilisation of these external assets has to be accounted for, but this cannot be achieved by stating the environmental protection costs that the company must carry. Instead, the environmental pollution caused by the company should be determined and expressed in monetary units. The utilisation of the environment can be determined by using quantities that have already been captured internally (e.g. the costs of soil pollution through the use of land for mining coal), and by taking external costs caused by the utilisation of resources (e.g. air pollution by carbon dioxide, sulphur dioxide, nitrogen dioxide and particles). Important characteristics and assumptions of this model are: pollutants spread evenly, allowing emission values to be weighted with critical immission values; only national emissions can be recorded; the quantities of pollutants emitted are over the period of 1 year; cumulative effects and synergistic effects are ignored. Weighting coefficients provides a common denominator for detrimental effects on health and damage to materials and plants. Values provided by national environmental agencies form the basis for the costs of polluted air per ton of pollutant. Schellhorn's model extends the traditional income statement by including the costs of industrial land utilisation and the external environmental costs of air pollution and, as an offsetting accounting entry, a corresponding liability toward third parties is recorded in the traditional balance sheet.

Next we present several accounting methods that we categorise as ecological analyses and process balance sheets because they are concerned with more specific problems. **ABC environment analyses** are based on a more qualitative valuation method that rates its objects against each other in order to record and prevent environmental pollution. A company is assessed in ecological terms on whether it meets the requirements of environmental law, and to which extent. Further considerations are the extent to which it complies with societal demands, pollutes the environment through its activities and operational mishaps; makes public internalised environmental costs; pollutes the environment through the pre-production of input factors. The ABC classification is as follows:

A. Environmental laws are ignored, the company is facing criticism, critical thresholds are being exceeded: there is a great need for action.
B. There is a degree of concern, a medium risk exists, harm to health is possible: the need for action is not so urgent.
C. No environmental pollution: no need for action.

An **event pollution analysis** examines the environmental effects of events (fairs, sport events etc.) by recording the pollution caused by the event organiser and by visitors (energy and water consumption, emission of pollutants, noise pollution, amount of waste, land use, changes to the landscape or cityscape).

An example was provided by CeBIT, the largest computer fair in the world. In the late 1990s there were typically around 700,000 visitors a year who produced 69 tons of rubbish daily during the 8 days of the fair, and 455,000 bottles and cans had to be removed from the site. Twelve gigawatt hours of electricity were used by the exhibitors and suppliers, and travel to the event was responsible for 700 million kilowatt hours (one kilowatt hour is typically needed for each kilometre travelled). In order to supply each visitor with brochures, 31,000 trees were chopped down and 380,000 cubic metres of water were polluted (equivalent to the annual consumption of a small town of 7000 inhabitants).

An **eco-efficiency analysis** (developed and used by BASF) sets the total operating costs of alternative projects, processes or products against the possible or actual pollution they might or do cause. Standardised total operating costs (that the customer has to pay) are set against standardised environmental pollution (expressed in weighted points scores and calculated according to ISO 14040 and 140044). A graph of these data-points is produced, where the higher the costs and the higher the pollution, the lower the score, so a project with a high level of eco-efficiency will be found in the upper right quadrant. For example, the environmental pollution caused by the process of dying indigo is shown in five categories. The input side (representing 50% of the total) measures energy (25%) and raw material consumption (25%), while the factors measured on the output side (50% of the total) are the unintended outcomes of risks (10%), toxic waste (20%) and emissions (20%). The latter are divided into water emissions (35%), waste (15%) and air emissions (50%). Air pollution is then further subdivided based on its potential for different kinds of harmful outcomes: greenhouse gases (50%), damage to the ozone layer (20%), producing photochemical ozone (20%) and outputs that contribute to acidic rain (10%).

The investigation and assessment of the environmental benefits and issues of products is the goal of **product line analysis** (also referred to as life cycle analysis and life cycle assessment). It records external effects, from the extraction of raw materials to the consumption of products and their disposal, including transport, storage and production. This tool is used for individual case analyses and also for general analyses in which ecological aspects take priority, although social and economic aspects are not ignored. The data basis is often poor and there is a wide range of valuation methods, so the results of these analyses cannot often be directly compared with each other. Such an analysis could, for example, be carried out on ways in which milk can be packaged for home consumption: reusable bottles, milk cartons or milk bags (made of plastic). The total consumption of raw materials, water and energy would be analysed, as well as transportation requirements, air pollution and the amount of waste.

The aim of an **environmental risk analysis** is to detect potential dangers for the environment and ensure that companies are not affected. Depending on the situation, an environmental risk analysis may be needed when forecasting the consequences of technical progress or carrying out a credit-worthiness check (needed because banks examine the ecological risk factors of collateral, e.g. the possibility of contaminated soil on land). Other occasions where such an analysis is necessary include building up an eco-fund (an investment portfolio containing the shares of environmentally friendly companies), producing an eco-rating by ranking companies according to their ecological performance—environmental risks faced by a supplier can be business risks for the buyer. An environmental risk analysis is used mainly by bank credit officers and financial analysts.

A materials balance and an energy balance are ecological accounting statements which focus on transformation processes. The roots of this kind of ecological accounting lie in science and technology rather than business. These **process statements** are prepared by and for individual companies, and for the economy as a whole. Process statements use physical units as the starting point of valuations; they are not statements of stocks at a particular point in time but are statements of flows over a period. Materials and energy inputs are set against outputs, which should be equal in size because they represent transformed materials and energy (following the first law of thermodynamics) and the "consumption" of materials and energy is measured. The aim is to find alternatives (savings, substitutions) for manufacturing processes and for the use of materials (including a better utilisation of waste by recycling) that reduce the burden on nature. One of the main goals of these statements is to inform the public about environmental protection measures by showing what is taken from the environment and what is put back into it.

Common to all types of **ecological accounting** is that they all have their own standards and methods of recording and judging effects on the environment. Uniform, coherent and generally accepted standards and regulations do not exist at either the national or international level. Consequently, the results of the analyses vary, which then increases the amount of criticism against ecological accounting. It is true that the problems are complex. One of many other issues, for example, is the unresolved problem of environmental pollution by substances whose harmful effects only become known at a later point in time. Asbestos, chlorofluorocarbons (CFCs) and several wood preservatives were introduced as environmentally friendly substances and were only later found to be harmful to health. In conventional commercial accounting, problems of valuation are circumvented because legal guidelines (e.g. the historic cost principle) and accounting frameworks exist (e.g. GAAP—Generally Accepted Accounting Principles). Why should it not be possible to establish similar kinds of principles for ecological accounting?

The European Union tried to find an answer when it established the **Eco-Management and Audit Scheme** (EMAS) in 1993, the goal of which is for all kinds of organisation to evaluate and report on their environmental performance, and then, of course, to improve it. The core elements of EMAS are:

- Performance—actions are taken to achieve and evaluate environmental policy targets.
- Credibility—third-party, independent, auditors verify the information provided.
- Transparency—the public is provided with information about environmental performance of organisations.

The key indicators are energy efficiency, material efficiency, water, waste, biodiversity and emissions. The environmental statement required by EMAS must include:

- a clear description of the company and its activities,
- the environmental policy and a brief description of the organisation's environmental management system,
- a description of all the significant direct and indirect environmental aspects which result in significant environmental impacts,
- a description of the environmental objectives and targets, and
- summary of the data available on the performance of the organisation against its environmental objectives and targets, including core indicators.

ISO 14001 is the main standard in a family of standards developed by the International Organisation for Standards for organisations' use in designing and implementing environmental management policies and procedures. EMAS and ISO 14001 share the same objective, but EMAS goes further by requiring that the auditor be independent and that employees be actively involved, for example. Another standard for reporting is provided by the **Global Reporting Initiative** (GRI) whose guidelines for sustainability reporting are used internationally by over 7500 organisations of all types. The guidelines include indicators on economic, social, environmental and governance performance.

If the division between social and ecological accounting is abandoned, and if all positive and negative effects are summarised, the result is **outcome-impact** or **effects statements** that take into account the themes discussed above. Outcomes and impacts are the external effects of inputs and outputs that are not recorded by commercial accounting. For firms, these represent side-effects, but for other kinds of organisation (e.g. non-government organisations and charities) they are the primary objective. Outcomes and impacts take the form of buyers' and consumers' surpluses when they occur in relation to market processes. Outcomes and impacts beyond the market consist of beneficial and harmful effects on the social environment, and factors which help or damage the natural environment. **Outcome-impact statements** do not provide any evidence of money spent on health and safety measures, social services, the promotion of research, culture and sport, tax payments, the protection of animals, plants and nature—all of which are recorded and calculated by commercial accounting. However, what these statements do show—in monetary units whenever possible—are the attributable positive and negative external effects (whether caused directly or not) on employees, customers, suppliers, shareholders, stakeholders, the general public and nature.

By taking elements from standard commercial bookkeeping—double-entry, debits and credits—and elements from the approaches discussed above, it is possible to develop two new forms of statement: the **outcome-impact operating result statement** and the **outcome-impact balance sheet**. The former records the external benefits and costs incurred within a specific period (e.g. 1 year), whereas the latter shows the potential positive and negative effects—or those that have been foregone—on the internal and external environment on the date of the balance sheet. In this way information is obtained about a company's contribution towards the improvement of the environment (in the negative case: deterioration of the environment); this is over and above its results in the market (sales, costs, profit, profitability).

Ultimately of interest is a company's **overall performance** (market, social and ecological) with respect to means and ends (efficiency) and to planned and actual use of factors of production (effectiveness). Social success in this context is the value added to society and state. A company is acting efficiently in the sense of the maximum principle if the greatest possible positive outcome and impact is achieved for the given production and use of a given product, as shown in Eq. (6.3).

$$\text{Max!} \ \frac{Positive \ outcome + Impact}{Production + Product} \tag{6.3}$$

Equation 6.3 Maximum principle and positive outcome and impact

According to the minimum principle, firms are efficient when the lowest possible negative outcome and impact is realised for the given production and use of a given product. Equation (6.4) illustrates this.

$$\text{Min!} \ \frac{Negative \ outcome + Impact}{Production + Product} \tag{6.4}$$

Equation 6.4 Minimum principle and negative outcome and impact

If outcome and impact are given, business results can be derived in a similar manner, as Eqs. (6.5) and (6.6) show.

$$\text{Max!} \ \frac{Profit}{Outcome + Impact} \tag{6.5}$$

Equation 6.5 Maximum principle and business results

$$\text{Min!} \ \frac{Loss}{Outcome + Impact} \tag{6.6}$$

Equation 6.6 Minimum principle and business results

When analysing effectiveness, the extent to which a target was achieved is assessed, as can be seen in Eq. (6.7).

$$Activity \ level = \frac{Actual \ output}{Target \ output} \times 100 \tag{6.7}$$

Equation 6.7 Activity level

In respect to overall performance, as Eq. (6.8) shows, a company is efficient if the actual outcome and impact are as close as possible to the desired result for the production and use of a given product.

$$Effectiveness = \frac{Actual\ result}{Target\ result} \times 100 \qquad (6.8)$$

Equation 6.8 Effectiveness

The desired outcome and impact are derived from national specifications and/or self-determined standards. It is possible that a high degree of effectiveness is accompanied by an extremely costly production and product. Overall performance is highly relevant in this regard. Conventional accounting contributes towards determining this by reflecting market success.

Figure 6.35 shows how an **outcome-impact result statement** measures social and ecological success.

6.7   Assets and Capital

6.7.1   Terms and Types

The concepts that we have considered so far have in common that they are concerned with flows over a period of time, measured in terms of quantity and expressed as financial values. The sizes of flows need to be complemented by balance sheet items. Taking the form of statements of assets at a particular point in time (reporting date), balance sheets serve as starting points for the allocation to the correct period of processes and results (e.g. profitability). The starting point is the opening balance, which is adjusted as additions and disposals occur during the period, giving the quantity of items available at the end of the period. For example, the positive or negative development of liquid cash reserves is shown by comparing the opening cash balance with the closing cash balance. So in general, the **result for a period** can be determined not only by measuring flows but also by the **comparison of asset levels**.

The assets of an economic agent are comprised of all its tangible and financial assets. Examples of **tangible assets** are land, buildings, machines, inventories, furniture, works of art, equipment and tools; **financial assets** include investments, shares, receivables, patents, licenses, and cash. It is normally the case that there exists a legal relationship between the assets and the economic agent. One relationship is ownership, and a second one is possession, which means having control over an asset.

Many questions need to be addressed concerning assets: What is its value? How is it to be valued as part of hidden reserves? How are assets treated from a tax point of view? What quantity of operationally necessary assets and free assets does the

External costs	External benefits

I.   Factor rent
     (Buyers' surplus)
     for personnel
       capital
       material
       energy
       services
       legislation
       nature
 	
     negative consumers'
     surplus
	I. Consumers' surplus
	
	     for product A
	       product B
	       product C
	       product D
	       product E
	
	     positive factor rent
	     (positive buyers' surplus)

II. Disadvantages
 	
     for workers
       customers
       suppliers
       shareholders
       stakeholders
       general public
	II. Advantages
	
	     for workers
	       customers
	       suppliers
	       shareholders
	       stakeholders
	       general public

III. Harmful effects
 	
     for earth
       water
       air
       space
	III. Relief from harmful effects
	
	     for earth
	       water
	       air
	       space

IV. External net benefits
     (balance)
	IV. External net costs
	     (balance)

Fig. 6.35 Outcome-impact result statement

economic agent have? Which purposes do the assets serve? What is the optimal asset structure? How long is the commitment period of assets? How long does it take to transform them into money? What relationships exist between assets and capital?

Tangible assets and financial assets represent **net assets,** determined by subtracting debt from **gross assets**. In the German speaking world, reference is made to the *active* and *passive* sides of a balance sheet, and we will follow that terminology here. Assets form the active side of the balance sheet; capital—without which there could be no assets—is on the passive (liabilities) side. Seen from the perspective of the capital, the passive side shows the origin of funds and the active side the use of funds. When assets are being reported in a balance sheet, there is now a common global practice in which assets are divided first into fixed and current assets, and then further categorised according to the period of commitment. Liabilities are reported differently. They are categorised based on capital rights, i.e. there is equity and debt capital. **Equity** is the difference between assets and debt capital, and is therefore identical with **net worth**, which is another term for net assets.

Fixed assets are composed of tangible assets (e.g. properties, buildings, machines and tools), intangible assets (e.g. patents and licenses) and financial assets (e.g. equity interests, shares and long-term receivables from loans). **Current assets** consist of inventories (e.g. raw materials and consumables, semi-finished and finished goods, commodities), receivables, securities (of short-termed nature) and liquid assets (e.g. bank balances and cash on hand).

The active side of the balance sheet includes objects that are assets, the passive side of the balance sheet is more abstract, listing the capital and the rights to capital of the owners and creditors.

Equity capital can originate from shareholders, owners, members of a cooperative, donors or entrepreneurs; it can be self-financed through retained profits or surpluses; in associations it can come from membership fees, or in the case of professional bodies and social insurance from contributions, and in public administrations from the taxpayer. The equity capital of incorporated firms can have several sources: share capital or nominal capital, retained income, capital reserves, any provisions which are no longer required (through overvaluation of liabilities), profits carried forward and profit. Changes in equity of joint-stock companies can be the result of raising or reducing capital, while contributions and withdrawals have similar effects in partnerships, as well as generally of profits and losses. Equity also accrues from the undervaluation of assets in the form of hidden reserves.

Debt capital is comprised of the resources provided to an economic agent by third parties, mostly in the form of bank, supplier and customer credits (the latter through advance payments), bonds (federal, state and municipal bonds, covered bonds, industrial bonds, convertible, option and income bonds) and loans from individuals, companies and public programmes. A differentiation is made between short-term credit (in some circumstances short term means 3 months, in others 12 months), medium-term credits (depending on circumstances up to 5 years) and long-term credits (above 5 years).

6.7.2   Commercial Balance Sheets

The most common statement that summarises the situation of an economic agent is the commercial balance sheet, i.e. the annual balance sheet which is drawn up in Germany according to commercial law, which is different from the tax balance sheet which follows tax law. (It is important to distinguish between this type of balance sheet and the balance of trade which is calculated for the national economy

Active side (Assets)	Passive side (Liabilities)

A: Fixed assets
    I.   Intangible assets
    II.   Tangible assets
    III.   Financial assets
 	
B. Current assets
    I.   Inventories
    II.   Receivables and other
           assets
    III.   Marketable securities
    IV.   Cash on hand/
           Bank deposits
 	
C. Accrued and deferred items
	A: Equity
	    I. Subscribed capital
	    II. Capital reserves
	    III. Retained income
	    IV. Profit carried forward/
	           Loss carried forward
	    V. Annual surplus/
	           Annual deficit
	
	B. Provisions
	
	C. Liabilities
	
	D. Accrued and deferred items

Fig. 6.36 Structure of balance sheet

and whose active side shows the export of goods and passive side the import of goods from and to a country over a given time period).

A balance sheet issued as one of the annual statements of German companies is shown in Fig. 6.36. The structure is defined by Para. 266 of the German Commercial Code (Handelsgesetzbuch—HGB).

The optimum amounts of assets and capital depend on priorities (formal or substantive goals, growth targets), the business purpose (offering services, manufacturing goods, trading goods etc.), the composition of the factors of production (personnel, capital, materials and/or energy intense), the development of demand and stage of the market (introduction, expansion, maturity and stagnation), technical progress (invention and innovation processes, diffusion of innovations) and financial conditions (expectations, terms, costs, restrictions, tax burdens). These **diverse factors** emphasise that there is not just one single asset and capital statement, but that balance sheets depend on estimates and valuations. Consequently, there is no single correct answer to questions such as: Should the vehicle be bought, leased or rented? How high should the minimum reserves be? What percentage of total capital should equity? The annual balance sheets of companies must meet legal requirements and follow bookkeeping and accounting principles for the purposes of taxation, transparency, uniformity and comparability. Apart from management and staff, parties interested in balance sheets are shareholders and creditors, tax offices, financial analysts, trade unions and associations, the media and the public.

A balance sheet is a statement of position, i.e. it shows the state of an economic agent at a particular moment. The difference between two statements of position can be found in a **flow balance sheet** which covers the period in question. It is also

Simple form	
Use of funds	Origin of funds
Increase in assets	Decrease in assets
Decrease in liabilities	Increase in liabilities
Loss (balance)	Profit (balance)

Extended form	
Use of funds	Origin of funds
A. Decrease in equity	A. Increase in equity
I. Distribution of profits	I. Capital increase
II. Capital withdrawals	II. Transfer to reserves
III. Balance sheet loss	III. Balance sheet profit
B. Increase in investments	B. Decrease in investments
I. Tangible assets	
II. Intangible assets	
C. Increase in working capital	C. Decrease in working capital
I. Inventories	
II. Receivables	
D. Debt servicing	D. Increase in debt
E. Increase in liquid funds	E. Decrease in liquid funds

Fig. 6.37 Flow balance sheet

known as a **capital-flow statement**, because it shows how line items (positions) have changed over a period by setting the use of funds against their origin. Changes in line items will either be a profit or loss, so the flow balance sheet shows which changes in which line items contributed to success.

Figure 6.37 shows a basic and an extended flow balance sheet.

Apart from the annual balance sheets, joint-stock companies often also issue quarterly balance sheets, and there are various types of commercial **special-purpose balance sheets**. Examples of these are the balance sheet produced when a company is founded, when it is reorganised or when subject to takeover or merger. Balance sheets are usually also necessary when there is a legal dispute, or when the company is being made insolvent or put back on its feet.

6.8   External Assets and Liabilities

6.8.1   Terms and Types

In this section statements of positions at a given point in time—i.e. balance sheets—are treated similarly to calculations of benefits over given periods of time. They follow the logic of double-entry bookkeeping with its T-accounts, profit and loss accounts, and asset and liability accounts. *External* refers to the effects of business operations outside the market and beyond payment transactions. External assets and liabilities arise when operating activities add value to or remove value from the assets of third parties through mechanisms that are outside the marketplace. The discussion of benefit calculations showed that external costs and benefits occurring in a single period or over several periods can be captured in statements of the size of flows which can be transformed to statements of the size of positions. As with capital budgeting calculations, this is done by using the capital value method to calculate the present value of an investment. An external snapshot of the **human assets** of a company records the performance potential of employees at a specific point in time. This social balance sheet is a representation of the knowledge, skills and competencies of the executives and skilled labour of a company that could be used in the future to improve its performance and competitiveness—this is like having a reservoir. Neglecting to provide sufficient training, for example, can lead to the level of the reservoir sinking and possibly to the reservoir drying completely out. **Human liabilities** can also arise if safety regulations are missing or faulty and through other dangers that have not been removed.

Positive and negative external effects can be established when the external environments of companies or other economic agents is considered. These effects are not the result of market activities, as market transactions, compensation and tax payments are already recorded by commercial accounting. When society and nature are considered, additional types of external assets and liabilities can be identified. Operating activities can create common assets and common liabilities, and natural assets and natural liabilities. **Common assets** are the values created by the company which the general public receives free of charge. This value may be a more pleasant townscape, improved access to goods and services, the successful integration of apprentices or an increase in urban attractiveness—a newspaper publisher's added value, for example, is freedom of the press and diversity of opinions. Expressed in balance sheet terms, they are social receivables for the company, owed by the public. **Common liabilities**, e.g. works traffic, smells and noise, are detrimental to the general community and may be classed as social liabilities. Similarly, both positive and negative ecological effects exist. Those that either maintain or increase

nature assets (e.g. environmentally-friendly recycling, disposal, recultivation of waste land and reforestation), while the reduction of natural resources through consumption creates **nature liabilities**.

6.8.2 External Balance Sheets

Because of the special difficulties of recording and valuing the many and varied external effects and discounting them individually to a cutoff date in order to prepare a balance sheet, an alternative would be to develop separate balance sheets for employees, society and nature. We take a different approach. The central ideas of a uniform external balance sheet are an **integrative approach** that combines insights from the humanities, science, social and business studies, and a **holistic approach** that does not view the effects in isolation but considers how they interact over the long term. The interconnections of effects can be captured in an effects balance sheet that presents outcomes and impacts at a specific point in time.

The **outcome-impact balance sheet** complements the outcome-impact result statement, which depicts benefits and harm that occurred over a period. The outcome-impact balance sheet shows the potential and obligations an economic agent has in terms of its internal and external environment. It does not show its market situation or provide information relevant for tax purposes, for these are dealt with by commercial accounting.

Figure 6.38 shows an outcome-impact balance sheet.

External assets	External liabilities
I. Human assets (= value of performance potential of staff as developed by company; potential improved performance of staff is an external receivable for the company)	I. Human liabilities (= value of unused performance potential of staff; unused potential is an external debt owed to staff)
II. Common assets (= same concept applied to social groups and general public)	II. Common liabilities (= same concept applied to social groups and general public)
III. Nature assets (= same concept applied to earth, water, air and space)	III. Nature liabilities (= same concept applied to earth, water, air and space)
IV. Net external costs (Balance)	IV. Net external benefits (Balance)

Fig. 6.38 Outcome-impact balance sheet

6.9   Examples and Exercises

6.9.1   Calculating the Closing Balance

Situation

The Yildiz family operates a small corner shop in one of the trendier areas of Stuttgart. On Monday morning Hasan Yildiz, the son of the owners, checked the bank balance of the account they used on a day-to-day basis—he was happy to see that it was 7525.00 €. It is possible to pay by cash or debit card in the shop. It was a fairly busy day, during which they sold:

	€
Beer	750.00
Other drinks	100.00
Cigarettes	250.00
Snacks	120.00
Newspapers and magazines	60.00
Bicycle hire	80.00

Mr Yildiz went to the wholesaler and bought some supplies, paying 350.00 € by debit card. At the end of the day he deposited all the cash that the shop had taken in that day. What was the closing balance?

Solution

We start with the opening balance, and receipts of payment and subtract outpayment to calculate the opening balance.

	€
Opening balance	7525.00
+	
Receipts of payment	1360.00
−	
Outpayments	350.00
=	
Closing balance	8535.00

6.9.2   Financial Ratios

Situation

Monique Desautels owns a company—Great Sounds—that manufactures hi-fi equipment. She is an excellent designer, but as she herself admits, is not the comfortable with financing and book-keeping. Her accountant has prepared a balance sheet for her, but she cannot really interpret it so has asked for your help. She is particularly concerned about her liquidity, because she knows that many companies fail because they run out of cash.

She gives you the balance sheet, which was prepared in the format used in the US because many of her investors live there—what would you tell her?

Great Sounds Balance Sheet 31 December 2017 (all figures in Euros).

Assets		Liabilities	
Current assets		Current liabilities	
Cash	3500	Accounts payable	90,900
Petty cash	200	Wages payable	8500
Temporary investments	10,000	Interest payable	4400
Accounts receivable	40,500	Taxes payable	7200
Inventory	81,000		
Supplies	3800		
Total current assets	139,000	Total current liabilities	111,000
Investments	36,000	Long-term liabilities	
		Mortgage	220,000
Non-current assets		Long-term loan	200,000
Land	12,000	Total long-term liabilities	420,000
Buildings	286,000		
Equipment	201,000	Total liabilities	531,000
Non-current assets	499,000		
Intangible assets		Owners' equity	
Patents	135,000	Common stock	300,000
Trade names	200,000	Retained earnings	178,000
Total intangible assets	335,000	Total Owners' equity	478,000
Total assets	1,009,000	Total liab. & Owners' equity	1,009,000

Solution

As Monique already knows, liquidity is critical to survival. You apply the short-term coverage ratios to the figures she has supplied.

$$Cash\ ratio = \frac{Cash\ equivalents + Marketable\ securities}{Current\ liabilities}$$

$$= \frac{(3500\ € + 200\ €) + 10,000}{111,000\ €} = 0.12$$

$$Quick\ ratio = \frac{Cash\ equivalents + Marketable\ securities + Receivables}{Current\ liabilities}$$

$$= \frac{(3500\ € + 200\ €) + 10,000\ € + 40,500\ €}{111,000\ €} = 0.48$$

$$\begin{aligned} Current\ ratio &= \frac{\begin{array}{c} Cash\ equivalents + Marketable\ securities \\ + Receivables + Inventory \end{array}}{Current\ liabilities} \\ &= \frac{(3500\ € + 200\ €) + 10,000\ € + 40,500\ € + 81,000\ €}{111,000\ €} = 1.21 \end{aligned}$$

Monique naturally wants to know what are the implications of a cash ratio of 0.12, a quick ratio of 0.48 and a current ratio of 1.21.

The current ratio looks relatively good—it means that Monique's company has more than one euro in current assets for every euro of current liabilities. It is important to compare Monique's current ratio with that of other companies in the same industry and to carefully monitor trends in its development.

The quick ratio result of 0.48 is, of course, lower than the current ratio as it does not include inventory. Most companies hope to have a quick ratio of around 1, so Monique should start thinking about managing her liquidity. She owes more than twice as much to her suppliers than her customers owe to her, and she also has a relatively high level of inventory.

A cash ratio of 0.12 is a cause for concern, because it means that Monique has very low cash reserves. Industry comparisons are important, because in some industries operate with higher liabilities and lower cash reserves. Too high a cash ratio could also be a sign that the company is not using its cash efficiently.

Long-term coverage ratios are also very useful tools, so you also apply them.

$$Debt\ ratio = \frac{Total\ liabilities}{Total\ assets} = \frac{531,000\ €}{1,009,000\ €} = 0.52$$

$$\begin{aligned} Capitalisation\ ratio &= \frac{Long-term\ debt}{Long-term\ debt + Owners'equity} \\ &= \frac{420,000\ €}{420,000\ € + 478,000\ €} = 0.46 \end{aligned}$$

$$Debt-equity\ ratio = \frac{Total\ liabilities}{Owners'\ equity} = \frac{531,000\ €}{478,000\ €} = 1.11$$

Monique asks you what a debt ratio of 0.52, a capitalisation ratio of 0.46 and a debt-equity ratio of 1.11 all mean.

The debt ratio says something about a company's leverage—the higher it is, the more leveraged the company. In Monique's case, the debt ratio indicates that the company is not too highly leveraged, which is positive in that the higher the leverage, the higher the risk. At the same time, however, historical and industry comparisons must be made. In industries with volatile cash flows, a debt ratio of even 0.25 might be seen as too high.

The capitalisation ratio is also helpful to see how leveraged a company is. In capital intensive industries, which require large investments, capitalisation ratios will tend to be higher. A significant issue for Monique is whether the cashflows of her company are adequate for servicing the debt.

A high debt-equity ratio usually indicates that a company has been financing its growth mainly through debt. This ratio is important for lenders, because the higher the ratio, the more risky the loan. Monique's company's ratio shows that she has been fairly conservative in financing the company's growth.

The Golden Rule is that long-term assets should be financed by long-term debt. Monique's company has 499,000 € of long-term assets and 420,000 € of long-term liabilities, so she is not breaking this rule.

6.9.3   Estimating Costs

Situation
Erwin von der Grün is a chemist with a major multinational firm. He is also a keen triathlete and in his spare time he has been developing an energy bar that should help athletes to improve their performance if they consume it during a triathlon or marathon. He has finally decided to leave his job and set up a company to sell and market the product.

He has decided that the most effective way to distribute it would be through the internet and so he is planning to set up a sales and promotion web site called TaktiFit.com. He will produce the bars himself and outsource the development of the web site. How can he best estimate his costs?

Solution
He should use a cost estimate sheet for goods.

Production of goods		Comments
	Direct material costs	His direct material costs will be those of the ingredients for his bars, plus the wrappers.
+	Material overhead costs	

=	Material costs	
	Direct labour costs	Direct labour costs will be the gross wages of any staff he hires to produce the bars.
+	Production overheads	Production overheads can include maintenance, testing and health certification costs.
+	Special direct production costs	

=	Manufacturing costs	
	Material costs	Erwin may need to hire someone to run his office. He is going to selling online, so his distribution costs will be quite high. Special distribution costs would be incurred if he takes a stand at a triathlon event.
+	Manufacturing costs	

=	Production costs	
+	Administration overhead costs	
+	Distribution overhead costs	
+	Special direct distribution costs	

=	Prime costs	

6.9.4   Calculating the Return on Investment of Volunteers

Situation

Fatima Al-Sharif runs CommonSense, an organisation that provides support to young people in difficult situations and which uses many volunteers. It has 4 full-time staff, part of whose time is spent on coordinating volunteer activities. She is thinking about applying to the European Union to get a grant. She is aware that the EU will want to know about the value for money they would be getting for their money, so Fatima wants to come up with some monetary values for what her organisation achieves. She decides to start with their volunteer programme.

Solution

Quantifying the benefits that CommonSense brings is difficult. The first steps must include having a very clear idea of the costs of the volunteers to the organisation, which in the case of CommonSense look like this for the 12 months to 30 September 2017:

Staff costs (33% of their time @ 60,000 €/year, including benefits)	20,000 €
Marketing activities for finding volunteers	10,000 €
Training	5000 €
Rewarding volunteers (awards, meals)	1000 €
Software (Better Impact volunteer management software suite)	1500 €
Website (used for coordination)	1000 €
Office overhead (15% of overall budget to cover use of facilities)	25,000 €
Total	63,500 €

The second step is to calculate the value of the time the volunteers contributed. Fatima's data show they have on average 60 volunteers who contribute 100 h/year, a total of 6000 h. The challenge is to convert this into a monetary value. Fatima finds the website of the Corporation for National and Community Service, where she finds that the estimated value of volunteer time in the US is \$24.14/h. She can't find a figure for Germany, so she decides to assume a value of 25 €/h.

She can now calculate the volunteer wage value: 25 € × 6000 = 150,000 €. She can now calculate Return on Investment: (150,000 € − 63,500 €) ÷ 63,500 € = 1.36 €. She concludes that every 1 € invested in the volunteer programme, 1.36 € worth of work is done.

Fatima decides to go further and starts to calculate the benefits that their work brings. She looks at her data and finds, for example:

Category	Savings	Value
Unemployment—CommonSense was able to help 15 young people to avoid unemployment for 2 months each. She estimates that they would otherwise have received social benefits from the state.	Social benefits are approximately 900 €/month	27,000 €

(continued)

Psychiatric help—she concludes that the organisation's counselling service was able to keep 5 clients to keep out of psychiatric hospitals. Typical length of stay per patient is 1 month.	One month of psychiatric care in a hospital costs approximately 5000 €/month	25,000 €

Fatima is now in a position to prepare statements that express in monetary terms the benefits of what her organisation does.

6.9.5 MyCompany Project

One of your main concerns as the owner of a coffee shop is liquidity, and managing this while at the same time bearing in mind profitability and security. You must have a realistic understanding of the financial needs of your business and you will need to have a complete set of financial records.

- Investigate the available software solutions for financial planning. Look at the differences between them and decide which one you would choose.

Costs
Use a cost estimate sheet such as those in Figs. 6.24 and 6.25 to identify the costs you will incur.

- What are the cost types?
- How can you estimate what your actual costs will be?

These are operational costs, but as the chapter suggests, they are only a part of the whole story, because you will also be incurring external costs.

- Which external costs will you incur? Will you have to pay them or will society as a whole?

Revenues
You will have to decide how people will pay for your products.

- What methods would you choose apart from cash?
- What procedures would you follow so you could handle cash safely?

Your revenues come from your operational outputs.

- Is your cafe responsible for any external benefits?

Overall

- Which financial ratios are helpful in a cafe? (See Fig. 6.18 for some ideas.)
- Go the website of Starbucks and look at their financial statements. Is there anything you could learn from them in this respect?
- What would your outcome-impact result look like?

6.9.6   Self-Test Questions

- *Why is it important to operationalise?*
- *What payment streams exist?*
- *What does the golden financing rule say?*
- *How is cash flow calculated?*
- *What are the general forms of financing and what do each of them compromise?*
- *How is a performance split conducted?*
- *How are income statements structured?*
- *What is the structure of a balance sheet?*
- *What is the goal of creating a cost centre plan?*
- *What is the task of cost unit accounting?*
- *What is an operating statement?*
- *What is the difference between the direct costing-method and the method of relative direct costs?*
- *What is the goal of the cost-benefit analysis?*
- *How can the benefits of a project be analysed if it cannot be measured in monetary terms?*
- *Which accounting branches are part of the systematic arrangement of management accounting?*
- *What is the eco-efficiency analysis?*
- *What are the contents of outcome-impact-result statements?*
- *What is a flow statement?*
- *What is included in an outcome-impact-balance sheet?*
- *What are external assets and liabilities?*
- *Distinguish between expenditures and expenses.*
- *What is the difference between revenues and income?*

Calculating Economic Efficiency

7

The most certain of certain things is doubt.
Bertolt Brecht (1898–1956)

Opening Vignette

Judith and Tim Pollmer were exhausted. They had spent the whole day going from one car showroom to the next, taking test drives, discussing technical details in minute details with a lot of salespeople, all of whom had tried hard to get them to sign their names on the dotted line. The married couple had steadfastly refuse to do so despite the willingness of some of the salespeople to give them a 'special deal'.

Judith pushed aside the pile of brochures on the kitchen table as they sat down to drink a reenergising cup of coffee. "Right," she said, "it's time to make up our minds. What do you think?' Ninety minutes later they had narrowed the choice down to two models—an Audi A4 and a Toyota Prius.

"It's obvious," said Tim, "it's got to be the Audi. I feel so good when I sit in the driving seat, it handles so well, and. . .." He was interrupted by his wife.

"You can forget that. The Prius is much better for the environment!"

"But the handling is not so good, it feels soft when you turn into a corner," replied Tim.

The discussion continued for another 20 min, then Judith smiled. "We'll make a decision like we do at work when we buy a new machine for the factory. What we need is a spreadsheet!"

She started her laptop, opened Excel and spoke as she typed. "OK, we need two columns, one for each car. We have the purchase price, we need to estimate the maintenance costs, insurance, fuel costs. What else?"

"We got a better offer for a loan from Toyota than from Audi," Tim remarked. "And I think the Audi will last longer."

© Springer International Publishing AG 2018
P. Eichhorn, I. Towers, *Principles of Management*, Springer Texts in Business and Economics, https://doi.org/10.1007/978-3-319-70902-4_7

"The Toyota probably has a higher resale value. So, let me just work out the depreciation." Judith entered the figure, pressed Enter and smiled when she saw the result.

"The Prius is going to cost us 2500 € less over the next 4 years. The choice is obvious."

"Wait a minute," Tim responded in an aggrieved tone of voice. "That's typical of you accountants, you reduce everything to numbers! What about the pleasure of driving the car? What about the impression the car makes on people?"

The smile left Judith's face. "The spreadsheet gives us the result, no arguing about it. Is it worth 2500 € to you to look cool and feel good when you're stuck in a traffic jam?"

"Yes, it is!" replied Tim heatedly. "You need to find a better way of calculating what we should buy that just doesn't rely on numbers, but on things you can't put numbers to."

"You may have a point," Judith replied, knowing the decision had now been made. "But then, the Prius would have won by even more because driving an environmentally-friendly car is good for society as a whole and I will feel good knowing I'm doing something to help. So if we could put that in our calculation, the decision would be even more obvious than it is now."

7.1   Ratio Calculations

7.1.1   Ratio Analysis

In order to calculate, figures are necessary. Indicators make it possible to represent activities, tasks, events, behaviours, procedures, goals, interrelationships etc. and this makes their planning, control and monitoring easier. Indicators of particular interest in this respect are those that reveal information on the **status and development of operations**. (In addition, economic entities require data on industries, markets, industrial sectors and regions, the national and global economy, legislation, population, education, technology and much more, but that is beyond the scope of this book.)

Ratios are helpful for operational purposes, and there are three types (Fig. 7.1 provides examples):

- classification figures, which show the relative size of parts of a whole,
- relationship figures, which are used to show significant relationships between two numbers, and
- indexes, which show changes over time (often 1 year) of a given measure, expressed as a percentage.

Normally ratios are not used in isolation but as part of a **ratio system**, whose aim is to offer a complete overview of the relationships within business activities. In such a system, the ratios are arranged in a hierarchy, and one central ratio is calculated on the basis of other ratios that have been fed into it, as illustrated in Fig. 7.2. The classic

Classification figure:
$$\text{Proportion of labour costs compared to total costs} = \frac{\text{Personnel costs}}{\text{Total costs}}$$

Relationship figure:
$$\text{Sales per member of staff} = \frac{\text{Sales revenues}}{\text{Number of staff}}$$

Index:
$$\text{Index on rent income 2017 in percent} = \frac{\text{Income from rent in 2017}}{\text{Income from rent in 2016}} \times 100$$

Fig. 7.1 Examples of ratios

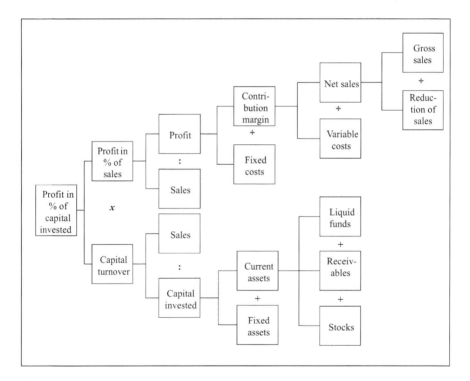

Fig. 7.2 RoI ratio system

model has Return on Investment (RoI) as the central ratio and was devised as early as 1919 by Du Pont de Nemours and Company.

Operational figures are used particularly for the purposes of comparison. By **comparing targets and results**, lessons can be drawn about the processes in question and how they might be better managed in the future. Internal **process comparisons** reveal advantages and disadvantages, information that is needed, for example, to decide which type of production is best for a product. **Comparisons over time** provide information on annual, quarterly, seasonal, monthly, weekly and daily developments.

Inter-company comparisons compare the ratios of one company with those of another; it is essential that the ratios be actually comparable (e.g. the companies should be in the same industry, or of the same structure or size). Several companies will often be compared to determine averages and individual rankings. These comparisons are, in essence, **benchmarking**, a favoured method of business consultants, which measures aspects of one company against other companies. This structured comparison starts with quantifying performances of the 'host' company and identifying differences to the best in class inside and outside the industry. The company should learn from best practices, adapt and then implement them.

All kinds of ratio analysis are done by economic entities—balance sheet, performance, cost, liquidity, employees, customer, market and demand—because ratios translate complicated situations into numbers that are somewhat easier to understand and use. The value of indicators should not be overstated, however, because details and quality can (and often do) suffer during the translation process, so it is wise to have a questioning attitude towards **simplification through the reduction of complexity**. Knowing the origin of the figures used in the ratios is essential.

7.1.2 Indicator Method

Indicators (in a narrow sense) are measurements that allow conclusions to be drawn (e.g. progress towards meeting a target) on the basis of certain hypotheses. Indicators form a **type of replacement value** in those areas where measuring and rating are either difficult or too expensive. Technical progress is recorded by productivity statistics, where it is assumed that the result is useful and marketable. The number of listeners to a radio news programme says something about how widely it was received, but nothing about the accuracy of the reporting. A low rate of staff turnover is sometimes interpreted as being due to high job satisfaction, but it can be heavily influenced by the local labour market. Permitted noise levels are based on what is generally acceptable, but can mean health risks for some individuals.

When using indicators, assumptions must be made explicit and closely examined because they directly affect the value of the information the indicators provide. Many are the **information sources** that can be used: internal and external analyses, reports, programmes, statistics, accounting statements, information systems, publications, official announcements, public tenders, laws and directives, development plans and other official documents. Indeed, there is so much information and data available that it is sometimes difficult to know where to start and when to stop. This is particularly true with big data; it will be interesting to observe the extent to which algorithms will help managers to make sense of all the data to which they have access.

7.2   Static Methods for Capital Budgeting

7.2.1   Cost Comparison Calculation

The difference between static and dynamic methods is that the former ignore the time value of money, and so they are highly popular in practice because of their simplicity.

Cost comparison methods are used mainly when analysing replacement and rationalisation investments, where the main criterion is cost saving. The decision as to which alternative to choose is based on the comparison of the costs of existing equipment with the costs of the equipment that is to be procured. Two types of procedures exist. The **total cost comparison method** employs average costs per unit of time (e.g. 1 year) and assumes that both alternatives (i.e. the old and the new systems) are equal in terms of quantity and quality of output. Equal output quantities are not considered by the **unit cost comparison method** which divides the total costs of each alternative by its output (expressed as a quantity), and identifies the best alternative as being the one with the lowest unit costs. One problem with this approach is that it does not take into account a possible reduction in capacity.

These cost comparison methods have been criticised for several reasons: the production oriented focus of their decision making, changeable cost determinants are not taken into consideration, outputs are assumed to have the same standard of quality and revenues are ignored.

7.2.2   Profit Comparison Calculation

This approach is used most when analysing investments whose purpose is expansion. Current profit is compared with the profit expected after the expansion has been completed. Since the calculation is only applicable for single-period decisions, average values are chosen for operational life spans which are longer than a single period and the presumption is made that these values are valid for all periods. Unlike cost comparison calculation, revenues are included. The expansion alternative to be chosen is the one that realises the highest average annual profit. If the outputs of the expansion alternatives are expected to be equal, a **profit comparison per period** and a **profit comparison per output unit** can be carried out. Both methods lead to the same result.

The possibility of inaccurate forecasts is an issue with profit comparison methods because a comparison is being made between potential profits and profits already achieved. Furthermore, the assumption is made that revenues can be allocated to individual investments, which is extremely difficult but can be done by comparing the total revenues and total costs of the firm, but it should be noted that the method does not say anything about the return on capital invested. When looking at investment decisions from a commercial point of view, relative profit levels (the return on capital invested) are of greater interest than absolute profit levels.

7.2.3 Profitability Calculation

Profitability calculations represent an improved form of the profit comparison method. Starting with the result of the profit comparison calculation, the average annual return on capital invested in an investment object can be determined. This **return on investment** is calculated by dividing the profit earned in a period by the capital invested. The profitability method is used to analyse single period investments; average values are applied in the case of multiple periods. The method is suitable for rating property, as properties tend to be more or less unique, so finding comparisons is difficult.

   In order to use this method, it must be possible to match revenues to operational and capital costs, and then allocate the difference between them to the equity and/or debt capital invested. It is necessary to assign an interest rate to equity capital or debt capital, depending of course on whether the investment is financed by equity or debt. The opportunity costs for the loss of profits on an alternative investment must also be added to the costs. Otherwise, this method has the same issues as other static calculations.

7.2.4 Payback Calculation

The payback calculation deals with the question of how long it will take to recover the costs of an investment, or in other words, how long will it be before the outflows (payments) for an investment are covered by the surplus of inflows. The method is also known as the capital recovery method, and payoff, payback or payout method. Capital recovery for replacement and rationalisation investments is determined by annual cost savings, and for expansion investments by annual surpluses, as seen in Eqs. (7.1) and (7.2).

$$Payback\ period\ (years) = \frac{Capital\ invested}{Annual\ cost\ savings} \qquad (7.1)$$

Equation 7.1 Payback time of replacement or rationalisation investment

$$Payback\ period\ (years) = \frac{Capital\ invested}{Annual\ surpluses} \qquad (7.2)$$

Equation 7.2 Payback time of expansion investment

The payback period is the time span within which the investment can be amortised; in other words, when the receipts of payment (normally the revenues) have covered the purchasing outpayments and the current outpayments. The payback calculation aims particularly at satisfying the need of investors for security. If—according to the investors' risk assessment—the length of the payoff period with which the investor would be comfortable is longer than the actual payoff period, the investment is judged favourably. The payback calculation uses average values if it can be assumed that surpluses will be constant over the whole economic life span of the investment (**average calculation**). If different payback flows occur, the payback period must be calculated by a cumulative method. This is done by adding the various effective annual payback flows until they equal the amount of capital invested (**cumulative or total calculation**).

Unlike the previous methods which are linked to the firm's goals, the payback calculation reveals the investment risk; however, time is emphasised more than the type of investment. The longer the payback period, the more uncertain is the recovery of the capital invested. The remaining useful life of the investment and the development of profit after its amortisation are not considered by this approach and nothing is learned about the profitability of the investment.

7.2.5 Equivalence Coefficient Calculation

An equivalence coefficient is an indicator that establishes a relationship between individual production factors or products. It is most often used to establish cost relationships. The goal is to **divide pooled costs among the individual outputs to which they are linked;** if it is not possible to clearly determine the cause of the costs, they can be allocated in a way that seems the most appropriate. The precondition for using this method is that the outputs should be similar—but not identical. For example: suppose a paper-mill produces different kinds of paper. The production process is identical, but the volume of consumables used in their production is different. Equivalence coefficients make it possible to compare the costs involved in the production of each type of paper—one that has high consumables usage is given (say) a coefficient of 1.5 while one with lower materials usage costs has a coefficient of 0.8. The costs associated with running the production process can then be allocated accordingly.

This method is not without problems. Even with closely related outputs it is not always possible to identify a reference value that allows a clear division of costs. A single reference value, normally assumed by the equivalence coefficient calculation, is rarely sufficient. The lack of separation between fixed and variable costs is a problem with this method because of the implicit assumption that fixed costs can be allocated. The equivalence coefficient calculation is only suitable for allocating variable costs on a fair basis. It is focused on what can be quantitatively measured and is thus production-oriented and one-dimensional.

7.2.6   Break-Even Calculation

This method is concerned with determining the critical output volume at which the sales revenues cover the total costs. It should be noted that, unlike in pricing theory, the goal is not to determine the optimal profit. The **assumptions** of break-even calculations are: a single-product firm, production equals sales (in other words, there is no inventory), output volume is the sole determinant of costs, a linear relationship of variable costs to output volume, no stepped fixed costs (i.e. costs initially remain constant despite fluctuations in the operating level, but jump when production capacity is expanded) and the sales price remains the same, regardless of production quantities.

It is obvious that the information value of the break-even analysis is restricted by these assumptions. When managers do this in reality though, the necessity of being a single-product firm is not significant and inventories are basically ignored. It is imagined that costs can easily be split into fixed and variable, and that stepped fixed costs and volume discounts can be ignored. In spite of these restrictions the straightforwardness of this calculation method and its easy employment and application are commendable—see Eq. (7.3).

$$Break - even\ point = \frac{Fixed\ costs}{Price - Variable\ costs} \qquad (7.3)$$

Equation 7.3 Break-even point

7.2.7   Value Added Calculation

This method establishes how high are the added value or the increase in value that an economic entity produces over a certain time period (as a rule 1 year). The value added calculation can be done by taking either a production approach or a use approach, as illustrated in Figs. 7.3 and 7.4.

Ultimately, the value added calculation is no more than a reordering of the income statement, but the calculation creates transparency. It illustrates the total output and allocates the operational expenses to the recipients of net value added. If

Fig. 7.3 Value added
calculation—production
approach

Sales
±   Changes in inventories
±   Other company-produced additions to plant and equipment
±   Other operational returns (including financial returns, but excluding returns form valuations and liquidations)
=   Total output
-   Materials expenses (including bought-in goods and services)
-   Depreciation on tangible and financial assets
-   Other operational expenses
=   Value added

Fig. 7.4 Value added
calculation—use approach

Income from employment (wages, salaries, social security and pension expenses)
+   Income from debt capital (interest)
+   Income from equity capital (distributed profits and retained earnings)
+   Community income (taxes on income and profit)
=   Value added

comparable companies show different degrees of net value added, then the reasons are likely to be found in the area of production, usually the degree of automation and labour intensity—outsourcing and insourcing are often considered as options at this point.

7.3   Dynamic Methods for Capital Budgeting

7.3.1   Present Value Method

Static methods' single-period analyses with their calculations that use only average values are inadequate when longer time periods are concerned. Dynamic calculations include interest, so they are able to deal with the fact that receipts of payment and outpayments can and often do occur at different points in time during the total economic life of an investment object. Dynamic calculations are based on the principle of the time value of money, i.e. that the value of 1 euro in 5 years is not the same as the value of 1 euro today and vice-versa. They are oriented towards capital whereas static calculations are more concerned with production and related costs.

The point of the present value (also known as present discounted value) method is to determine current value, which is the difference between receipts of payment and outpayments once they are discounted to the beginning of the investment at a given interest rate. In other words: all receipts of payment and outpayments are related to the start of the investment, and differences caused by the fact that the timings of flows vary are removed by discounting. An investment is desirable in absolute terms when its present value is greater than or equal to zero (**problem of profitability**). If there are several investment alternatives, then the alternative with the highest present value is the most favourable one in relative terms (**problem of choice**). An old facility is replaced by a new one as soon as the present value of the new facility exceeds the present value of the old one (**problem of replacement**).

The basic formula for calculating the present value (PV) is straightforward, as Eq. (7.4) shows. C is the sum that must be discounted, n is the number of compounding periods and i is the interest rate per compounding period.

$$PV = \frac{C}{(1+i)^n} \qquad (7.4)$$

Equation 7.4 Present value

From a mathematical point of view, the present value method is not demanding, but from a business point of view this is not the case. The problems already start with the definition of the investment object: should the labour costs of the driver, for example, be included when deciding whether or not to purchase a vehicle? They continue with the estimating and allocation of receipts of payment and outpayments to the investment object: what returns can be expected from a fork-lift truck? They end with the determination of the discount rate and the economic life. Since the result of the calculation depends considerably on the interest rate, its determination is of significant importance. The **actual interest rate** can be decided on the basis of the medium-term costs of (debt) capital, the average return of companies in the same industry, the marginal return (i.e. the increase of profitability from an additional injection of capital) or a minimum return that the company itself establishes. The higher the interest rate, the lower the present value if payments are made that are greater than the concurrent payments received. The calculation becomes more complicated when interest rates vary over time.

7.3.2   Future Value Method

The future value of an investment is determined by establishing the difference between all the related flows of its economic life. An investment is profitable when the future value is greater than zero, where future value is the amount of money that an investor can take out at the end of the economic life of the investment while still being in a position to make any payments related to the investment—taking into account the interest rate that was previously determined—because the revenues generated by the investment cover these outflows. The future value method differs from the present value method not only by having a different reference date; it is also distinctive in that a **specific interest rate is determined for each period** of the capital investment, which means that the future value is not the same as the accumulated capital value. When comparing alternatives, the investment object with the highest future value is preferred. The time to replace an old asset is reached when its future value is lower than that of a new one.

The basic formula for calculating the future value (FV) of a sum of money is straightforward, as Eq. (7.5) shows. C is the present value, n is the number of compounding periods and i is the interest rate per compounding period.

$$FV = C(1+i)^n \qquad (7.5)$$

Equation 7.5 Future value

A problem not faced by the present value method is forecasting the varying interest rates of future periods, so the additional informational value of this method has to be weighed against the costs of being in a position to provide reasonable forecasts.

7.3.3   Internal Rate of Return Method

In a manner of speaking, the internal rate of return method represents the inverse of the present value method, because no interest rate is set for the payments—the discount rate of interest is itself what is being calculated. The **effective internal rate of return** that is being sought is one that sets the present value of all cash flows to zero. This method answers three basic questions about an investment as follows:

- An investment is profitable if its internal rate of return is greater than the target interest rate (e.g. the interest earned by a comparable investment on the capital market).
- The investment with the highest internal rate of return is considered the best.
- It is time to replace an old asset when its internal rate of return is lower than that of a new asset.

The internal rate of return method is based on the assumption that surpluses generated by the investment can be invested at the appropriate internal rate of return, bearing in mind that there will be differences in the size and timing of the receipts of payment and outpayments of the investments to be compared. This reinvestment premise is also valid for the present value and future value methods, as well as for the annuity method. However, in this method the reinvestment premise is more realistic because it is assumed that the reinvestment of inpayment surpluses always occurs at the calculated interest rate which themselves should correspond to the capital costs of the investor.

7.3.4 Annuity Method

This method, sometimes known as the equivalent annual cost method, is a variant of the present value method. Its basis is a calculation of the cost per year of the investment over its lifetime, providing equally sized annual values. As a first step, positive and negative cashflows are discounted and their present values calculated. Then the present value is divided by the present value annuity factor, giving the discounted annual cost of the investment over its lifetime. For instance, this method allows a choice to be made between two machines, each with a different investment cost, expected lifetime and annual maintenance costs—each has a different equivalent annual cost.

An investment is profitable in absolute terms when the positive cashflow annuity is greater than the negative cashflow annuity. If several investment alternatives exist, the one with the highest surplus annuity (i.e. with the greatest difference between positive and negative cashflow annuities) is preferable. In other words, the best choice has the lowest equivalent annual cost (EAC); when the EAC of an old investment is greater than that of a replacement, it is time to replace it.

As with the previous described dynamic methods, the annuity method is based on the following assumptions:

- There are no fluctuations in interest rates over the economic life of an asset.
- A perfect capital market exists in which interest rates are the same for loans and deposits.
- There are no restrictions on credit.

The annuity method yields the same results as the present value method about the profitability of an investment (all things being equal), so is used if easier to calculate.

7.4   Optimisation Methods

7.4.1 Differential Calculus

Optimisation calculations are instruments whose aim is to help determine the best possible solutions in a complex decision-making situation. As a rule, they are characterised by one or more target functions and a number of restricting factors that place limitations on the target. The objective is to find that combination of factors that produces the best result, which is either a maximum or minimum value of the target function (e.g. the maximum profit, lowest cost, lowest quantity of materials used or highest quantity produced).

Fundamental to these types of calculation is differential calculus. In its simplest form, it has a **single variable** and the function to be optimised is then derived according to this variable and the result is set to zero. If the function to be optimised depends on **several variables**, the function is derived according to each variable and the resulting expression set to zero.

Using differential calculus as a method means assuming that the optimisation problem can be presented as a calculus problem with quantitative criteria, which is clearly not the case when decisions need to be made about qualitative goals. In addition, the use of differential calculus as a tool is based on future expectations being reduced to a single-value, which does not do justice to the complexities of economic life.

7.4.2   Linear Programming

This method is suitable for optimisation purposes if both the target function to be maximised (minimised) and the accompanying variables can be formulated as **linear equations**. Linear programming is helpful in the case of simple models of production, inventory, transportation, distribution and financial planning. It enables optimisation calculations with several restrictions to be carried out in a relative straightforward manner but, as with differential calculus, this method has limited applicability because it is a purely quantitative model that ignores qualitative aspects.

7.4.3   Vector Analysis

Vector analysis can also be employed for optimisation purposes because it enables large amounts of data to be processed in a well-structured way. Unlike the other optimisation calculations, vector analyses use complex equation systems of vectors and matrixes to produce a **simultaneous solution**. An example for the application of the vector calculation is internal service output allocation. The goal of a vector analysis in this case would be to capture all intra-plant relationships in terms of outputs between individual cost centres. The exchange of outputs between cost centres is described in a system of linear equations in which the quantities of outputs exchanged are known but the cost rates are unknown. The number of equations is equal to the number of cost centres that are included in the calculation. The output of a vector analysis applied to this problem is a determination of the costs of the internal outputs taking into consideration exchanges of outputs between the cost centres.

7.4.4   Risk Analysis

Risk analysis is a core component of capital planning, where it is used to establish the risk profile of the present value of the result of the capital budgeting calculations, or put more simply, to determine the risk profile of an investment. The statistical basis of the analysis is **estimated subjective probability distributions** of what is being calculated, i.e. of the receipts of payment and outpayments and economic life of an asset. In this way, uncertainties regarding these elements are considered. The result of the risk analysis is a probability distribution that permits the risks connected to the realisation of the investment to be estimated. The risk analysis can then be used in the selection of the investment opportunity, as it shows which one has the highest expected value.

Expected value is not so unproblematic, however. On the one hand, risk neutrality is assumed; on the other, expected value can strictly speaking only be a decision criterion when an experiment to determine possible values is repeatedly carried out. For example, when a component supplier regularly orders raw materials to manufacture the parts for its main customer, the managers of the supplier must consider the risks of carrying on procurement as usual versus the risks involved with finding and using a new source of supply. Risk neutrality describes the attitude of a decision-maker who disregards the probability distribution and always prefers an alternative with a higher expected value to an alternative with a lower expected value, even if the former carries greater risks.

7.5   Forecast Analyses

7.5.1   Time-Series Analysis

Whereas static, dynamic and optimisation methods use mathematical tools, forecast calculations are mainly based on statistics. Forecasts are predictions of future developments that are based on observations and analysis; they are based on intellect and rationality and so are not wild guesses. The starting point is analysis of the past, where trends are identified and conclusions drawn.

In a time-series analysis the values a variable has taken are indexed in time order as a series of data points. Whereas qualitative forecasts are verbal, quantitative forecasts work with indexes, using a single value. With the **simple average method**, the premise is that all the past values included have the same weighting, so this method is only suitable if a low fluctuation of the dependent variable and a stable mean value can be assumed (for example, consumption rates of soft drinks have been constant for the past 3 years). The **weighted average method** argues that the more recent the data, the more relevant they are for forecasting, so they are given a higher weighting than older values. The influence of more recent data on the forecast is greater in this method than in the simple average method. An extension of this is the **moving average method**, in which the oldest values are replaced by the most recent on a continuous basis. The advantage is that forecast values more quickly reflect new developments. Related to the moving average method is **exponential smoothing**, where the analyst chooses a value to weight the values in time series. In this method, past values are not equally weighted; the relative weight of a value decreases with its increasing age.

These four methods described in this section neglect the possibility of a trend developing over time, i.e. they assume that demand is a function of time. A consequence of this is that when there is a growth or decline in the values of a variable due to what appears to be a trend (e.g. a particular kind of food becomes popular), the forecast values of the variable as used in the forecast calculation are either above or below its most recent actual values. It is precisely for this reason that **trend extrapolation** is helpful. It develops a function to establish the relationship between the variable and time, and it can then be used to extrapolate. The function is derived from past values using one of several available function types, depending on the basis of the fluctuation (e.g. linear or cyclical).

7.5.2   Regression Analysis

Regression analysis is based on the assumption that a causal connection (correlation) exists between a dependent variable and one or more independent variables, thereby enabling forecasts to be made of how the development of the dependent variable. A **simple regression analysis** explains the dependent variable through a single independent variable. Compared to the time-series analysis, the single regression is advantageous because the connection between time and the variable to be explained is abandoned in favour of a more specific statistical causal relationship (e.g. the weather and the number of umbrellas sold). This does not imply that a real causal relationship exists between a dependent and independent variable—correlation is not necessarily causation. A **double regression analysis** deals with one dependent and two independent variables, whereas a **multiple regression analysis** is employed to determine dependencies between more than two variables.

As with all forecast analyses, forecasting on the basis of single and multiple regressions is useful only if the relationships that existed in the past between independent and dependent variables also exist in the future. They are therefore predicated on stable environmental conditions.

7.6   Examples and Exercises

7.6.1   Forecasting Sales: Simple Linear Regression

Situation

Kindy, a chain of children's clothes shops is doing very well; its market share is increasing and this is related to the number of shops in the chain. Sarah, the vice-president of sales development and her team want to be able to forecast sales for sites where they are thinking of opening a shop and realise that size of the shop is a highly important factor. Her team puts together some information:

Shop	Area (sq. m.)	Annual sales (€ millions)
1	157	5291
2	148	5577
3	260	9581
4	520	13,585
5	121	4862
6	204	8008
7	121	5291
8	102	3861
9	297	7865
10	139	4147
11	483	15,301
12	427	10,868
13	539	16,874
14	279	5863

Solution

Using simple linear regression as a tool, Sarah's team enters this information into Excel to produce a scatter diagram with sales and area as the axes. The graph—see Fig. 7.5—also has a line of best fit which shows how well the regression equation fits the data. It will be noticed that there are a couple of outliers.

The software produces the regression equation shown here, where Yi is the forecast for shop i and Xi is the area of the shop:

$$Yi = -22.7867 + 35.1953 \, Xi$$

They can now use this equation to predict sales of shops of different sizes, as shown in the following table:

Candidate shop	Area (sq. m.)	Forecast annual sales (€ millions)
A	255	8952
B	610	21,446
C	555	19,511
D	520	18,279

Of course, size is only one factor when deciding on store location. The general surroundings, local competition and many more other issues play a role. Sarah and her team at least know what kind of sales figures they can expect simply based on the area.

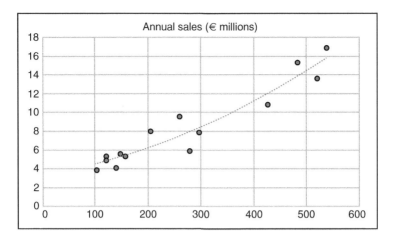

Fig. 7.5 Linear regression forecast

7.6.2 Forecasting Sales: Moving Average Method

Situation

Nils Britze works for a Hannover based producer of bottled non-alcoholic drinks, where he is the product manager for iced coffee and iced tea. The firm, H96 Drinks, has been in existence for 4 years and one of Nils' tasks is to forecast sales. He always has a few problems with this because the drinks for which he is responsible are seasonal products. The iced coffee product has been on the market for 2 years now and Nils has just received the latest sales figures, shown in the following table.

2016		2017	
Month	Sales (1000s of bottles)	Month	Sales (1000s of bottles)
January	34	January	36
February	42	February	43
March	38	March	43
April	46	April	50
May	50	May	54
June	55	June	59
July	62	July	64
August	66	August	70
September	50	September	52
October	48	October	50
November	40	November	42
December	39	December	41

It is his first day back at work in January 2018 and Nils has to produce a forecast for iced coffee sales for 2017. How can he approach this problem?

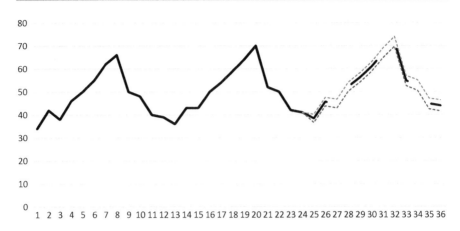

Fig. 7.6 Moving average forecast

Solution

Nils is aware of the several times-series forecasting methods—simple average method, weighted average method, moving average method and exponential smoothing, and decides to use the moving average method, given the seasonal nature of the product. He decides to use Microsoft Excel's built-in forecasting tool to forecast sales for 2018. He tells the software to use a seasonality of 12 months and it produces the following chart—the y-axis shows sales (thousands of bottles) and the x-axis is month number. Months 1–24 represent 2016 and 2017; months 25 and up are the months of 2018 (Fig. 7.6).

The thick dotted line represents the forecast sales; Excel has recognised the seasonality. The lighter dotted lines are the upper and lower confidence limits, i.e. they represent the maximum and minimum values of the forecast with a 95% confidence interval, which means that sales in 2017 will lie between these values nineteen times out of twenty.

Nils recognises that a forecast is only as good as the historical data that is entered and also realises that any number of external or internal events could make the forecast worthless   a competitor may reduce prices, the price of coffee beans could increase sharply, or even that there is a trend away from caffeinated drinks. He will of course need to do a risk analysis and plan appropriate measures.

7.6.3 Time Value of Money

Situation

Deborah has just joined one of the Big Four auditing firms and is training to be an accountant. On her first day, she has been sent to audit a medium size company and her supervisor has asked her to test the client's accounting software to ensure it is producing the correct answers. The supervisor selects two transactions at random and asks Deborah to verify the numbers that the client is using in its accounts:

- The Chief Financial Officer has just invested 10,000,000 € in a fund with a maturity of 5 years offering a promising semi-annual return of 2%. What is the amount available when the fund matures?

and

- The company will need a sum of 50,000 € in 3 years to pay for the chairwoman's retirement party. How much does the company have to deposit today into an account earning 6% annually in order to have this sum?

As she works on these two problems, Deborah thinks about the question her neighbour asked her. Harry has just bought a lottery ticket and won 100,000 €. He wants to finance the future study of his newly born daughter and invests this money in a fund with a maturity of 18 years offering a return of 4%; the interest is compounded semi-annually. What is the amount available on the 18th birthday of his daughter? Will it be enough to pay for her education?

Solution
Deborah understands that all three problems are related to the time value of value of money.

The Chief Financial Officer's is interested in the future value of his investment, where the relevant formula is:

$$FV = C\,(1+i)^n$$

Here, $C = 10,000,000$ €, $i = 0.02$, and $n = 10$ (because the interest is compounded semi-annually). The formula looks like this:

$$FV = 10,000,000 \text{ €} \,(1+0.02)^{10} = 12,189,944.20 \text{ €}$$

The issue of having enough money for the party is related to present value, where the formula is:

$$PV = \frac{C}{(1+i)^n}$$

Here, $C = 50,000$ €, $i = 0.06$, and $n = 3$, giving:

$$PV = \frac{50,000 \text{ €}}{(1+0.06)^3} = 41,980.96 \text{ €}$$

Deborah checks her results against what the company's software said and finds that they are the same: the CFO's investment of 10,000,000 € will be worth 12,189,944.20 € in 5 years, and the company will need to invest 41,980.96 € today to have 50,000 € for a retirement party in 3 years' time.

Her neighbour's problem is also about future value, and the formula looks like this:

$$FV = 100,000 \text{ €} \, (1 + 0.02)^{36} = 203,988.73 \text{ €}$$

Harry will be happy to learn that his winnings of 100,000 € will be worth more than twice as much in 18 years, thinks Deborah. But she also realises that tuition fees could be even higher in 18 years.

7.6.4   MyCompany Project

Business in the café continues to go well. Customers are satisfied, the workers are happy and revenues are coming in. You are in fact so busy that you decide to buy a bigger espresso machine. The one you have now is purely manual; the serious barista working for you really likes it, but it is too slow and labour intensive. After looking over what's available on the market, you are left with a choice between a Vasari 2S made by La Pavoni or a Grindmaster-Cecilware ESP2-220V Venezia II. Both are semi-automatic continuous brewing machines.

- There are several calculations that can be used for capital budgeting—cost comparison, profitability, payback etc. Which one would you choose and why? Find the relevant information on the internet and work out which machine you would buy.

You will probably need to go to the bank to get a loan to buy the machine, and you expect the bank manager will want to know about how you are managing the café. It strikes you that it would be ideal if you could show her some ratios, such as sales per member of staff.

- Which other ratios would be useful to you as you manage the café?

The bank manager will probably be particularly interested in your justification for the purpose. You know intuitively that you will be selling more cups of coffee in the next year, but you will need to show this in black and white and so decide to prepare a forecast.

- Which forecasting method would you use? What might affect your actual sales in the next year? Make a list
- What measures would you have ready to react to the items on your list (such as a new Starbucks opens up two doors away or coffee prices rise dramatically)?

7.6.5 Self-Test Questions

– *What is a ratio system and what does it include?*
– *Why are ratios so popular?*
– *How are the characteristics of static calculations? And dynamic calculations?*
– *Describe how the profit comparison method works.*
– *What is the prerequisite for the use of profitability calculations?*
– *What conclusions can be drawn from payback calculations?*
– *What conclusions can be drawn from a break-even calculation?*
– *What are the two ways of calculating added value?*
– *What is meant by capital value and what are the problems of the capital value method?*
– *What is the assumption behind the interest rate method?*
– *How is the profitability of an investment calculated with the annuity method?*
– *How can the vector analysis be applied in operational business activities?*
– *What is a risk analysis used for?*
– *How does the moving average method work?*
– *What is the advantage of regression analysis compared to time-series analysis?*

Economic Efficiency in Practice

8

> *The rational thing about man is the insights that he has.*
> *The irrational thing about man is that he does not act*
> *according to them.*
>
> Friedrich Dürrenmatt (1921–1990)

Opening Vignette

Isabelle Borduas and Kjell Hansen, her marketing manager, were discussing the new campaign that they were planning for Better Fashion Now!, the company Isabelle had founded 4 years previously. At the time, she had chosen the name to emphasise the label's style and quality, but, truth be told, over the last year she had become increasingly disenchanted with the industry. As she had told Kjell several times, she no longer felt that it was ethical to ask people to buy something, wear it a few times and then replace with something new. "We need to think differently," she had said in a meeting, "and we need a fresh approach."

The new approach was, even if she said so herself, innovative. Her idea was to buy used leather, preferably from developing countries, and use it to produce leather jackets. The jackets could then be bought or leased. If a customer bought a jacket, Better Fashion Now! would buy it back from the customer, take the jacket apart and use the leather to make a new jacket. "Each jacket will be unique!" she explained, "And nothing will go to waste. It's a perfect example of the circular economy."

Kjell put down his cup of organic coffee and spoke. "So, as we agreed, we'll do a trial run first here in Berlin. We have some great posters that we'll be putting up around town, the social media marketing plan is complete and ready to go, we've got a stand at Bread and Butter next year, we're placing a few advertisements in magazines. . ."

© Springer International Publishing AG 2018   243
P. Eichhorn, I. Towers, *Principles of Management*, Springer Texts in Business and
Economics, https://doi.org/10.1007/978-3-319-70902-4_8

He was interrupted by Isabelle. "Ok, very good, but. . . and it's a big but—all this costs money! How do you know all this marketing is going to work? How will you be able to say it's effective?"

"You remember we tested the posters and the messages with focus groups and got very positive feedback. It will be fine," Kjell said soothingly.

"You know what they used to say? They used to say, 'We know half of our advertising budget is effective, but we don't know which half!'"

"That was a long time ago, that was in the days of Mad Men. We're much more advanced now, we can do real time monitoring of what's happening online, and we can directly link people's responses to a marketing message to their actions."

"Well, OK," replied Isabelle somewhat grudgingly. "One thing I do know, though, is that we have a great slogan!"

"Oh yes," Kjell exclaimed. "I'm proud of it! Look, you can see it here." He reached into his portfolio case and pulled out a poster. "Better Fashion Now! Making fashion better", it said.

8.1 Procurement

8.1.1 Buy or Rent?

"Buy or rent?" is one of the fundamental questions to be answered during the procurement process. Normally, the payment streams connected with the alternatives that are under consideration are calculated and their respective present values determined and compared; all things being equal, the alternative with the highest present value is chosen. Factors that have an **effect on the result** of this calculation are correct estimates of operating lives, depreciation rates, rent or lease payments, and the cost of the capital if the purchase is to be self-financed or financed by a loan. In common usage, renting implies a short-term arrangement, while leasing implies a longer-term arrangement (e.g. renting a car vs. leasing a car). In some leases, the asset will (or can) become the property of the person who was leasing it. Under certain conditions there may be tax advantages if the asset is leased.

The method of depreciation is highly significant and there are various methods, generally based on the passage of time or on use, e.g. the straight-line depreciation, declining balance and units-of-production methods. Depreciation can be deducted from income for tax purposes and each country has its own rules about what can be depreciated, over which period of time and at which rates. For this reason, companies report their income before depreciation and amortisation in order to allow comparisons to be made; see Chap. 6 for more on EBITDA.

8.1.2 Economic Order Quantity

The economic order quantity represents that quantity at which the total purchasing costs (e.g. of the annual demand for a particular item) are minimised. Purchasing costs are composed of direct purchase costs (volume multiplied by purchase price), indirect purchase costs (ordering costs—the fixed-costs for each order, e.g. communication and transport) and holding costs (e.g. costs of warehousing, insurance and interest). With an increasing order size, the number of actual orders declines, meaning that total ordering costs fall, but holding costs rise. The basic model for determining the economic order quantity is shown in Eq. (8.1), where *EOQ* is the economic order quantity in units, *D* is the annual demand in units, *S* is ordering costs and *H* is the holding cost per unit.

$$EOQ = \sqrt{\frac{2DS}{H}}$$ (8.1)

Equation 8.1 Economic order quantity

This calculation has some **simplifying assumptions**: a known and stable demand, a stable price, no limitations in terms of warehousing and financing, a constant level of fixed order costs, steady holding and interest costs as well as the possibility of replenishing stock directly after the consumption of the last unit, so that no minimum stock quantity is held. This basic model is only of limited use because these assumptions are not particularly realistic. A decision not to maintain minimum inventory levels should only be considered if the future is certain and the suppliers extremely reliable. The model excludes partial deliveries as well as deliberate or accidental loss and spoilage. It also ignores how purchase prices can vary according to the order quantity. Should any of the assumptions not hold, the result is a considerable increase in planning and calculation work.

8.1.3 Degree of Centralisation

Procurement can be centralised or decentralised; the choice between the two depends on which is the more economically efficient. The answer could be very easily found if the goal were simply to minimise costs. It is necessary to go beyond that and recognise that economic efficiency depends on the relationship between the benefits the procurement processes provide to an economic entity and what they cost. With centralised purchasing, purchasing processes pass through one purchasing organisation. When purchasing is decentralised—geographically or organisationally—multiple purchasing organisations exist. **Advantages of centralisation** are: economies of scale (ordering costs are spread over a larger order volume, resulting in volume discounts); uniform planning, controlling and monitoring; less complex production through the use of standardised material; lower levels of stock, meaning less capital is tied-up due to demand planning; more procurement specialists. Exaggerated centralisation, however, also leads to **disadvantages**: higher coordination costs; communication and cooperation efforts resulting from longer lines of authority; slow reaction times due to longer information channels when urgency is needed; increased transport costs if warehousing is also centralised. The advantages and disadvantages of centralisation are mirrored by the disadvantages and advantages of decentralisation, so the latter need not be discussed here.

It is necessary to determine the pros and cons of the various possible degrees of centralisation in the form of benefits and costs in order to be able to calculate them using a static or dynamic method. If it is not possible or feasible to quantify and put a value on the advantages and disadvantages, **partial centralisation** can be a good solution. It involves having a central coordinating unit that, for instance, develops outline agreements for purchasing, puts out tenders and negotiates for particularly large or important purchases, while the decentralised purchasing units are responsible for less valuable purchases and must follow standards that have been set centrally.

Special Note Economic efficiency in procurement means having low-cost input factors of the right quality, in the right number, in the right place, at the right time. Adding ecological criteria results in **environmentally aware procurement** because suppliers have to deal with ecological issues, which can include such matters as pollutants, economic life, labelling requirements, environmental liability, environmentally friendly disposal as well as suppliers' take-back obligations. Conditions can be attached to just-in-time deliveries and the transport of hazardous goods in order to avoid negative external effects.

8.2   Transport

8.2.1   Optimal Location

Location choice plays an important role in enabling economically efficient transport because it allows journeys to be carried out cost-effectively. A simple location model with which the transport costs can be minimised is based on the following assumptions: all sites within a given area represent potential locations; transport costs are directly proportional to distance and not related to the type of goods to be transported; a straight line is used to measure distances.

These simplifications make it easier to calculate costs but do not correspond to reality. The assumption of that all sites represent possible locations is problematic; local regulations and restrictions, and the characteristics of goods often affect costs (e.g. transporting dangerous goods is more expensive than transporting clothes). Transport capacity (e.g. the size of load a lorry can transport) should also be included in deliberations. The consideration of such specific features is fundamentally possible, but requires complex models.

8.2.2   Minimisation of Transport Costs

Once the location has been selected, attention must be given to the minimisation of transport costs which essentially involves thinking about two questions. Firstly, single routes, for example the delivery of goods from a central warehouse to individual customers (**travelling salesman problem**), and secondly, a larger number of routes and the allocation of individual delivery points to routes that are driven simultaneously (**vehicle routing problem**). It would be theoretically possible to include all the tour routes and determine the lowest cost solution, but since many delivery points could be allocated to multiple routes, a complete enumeration of possibilities is likely to uneconomic in terms of justifying the investment in time needed. In practice, heuristic methods are preferred as they provide solutions that are satisficing ("good enough").

In one method of travelling path optimisation—**the strategy of the next neighbour**—the point that is chosen as the next stop is the one which is closest. The method is simple to carry out, but its results are moderate because the degree of freedom shrinks as the end of the route approaches, meaning the most unfavourable paths have to be chosen. Other methods of optimisation exist, but their specialised nature means they are beyond the scope of this book.

Special Note   Transport should be organised in a way which is—all at the same time if possible—cost-effective, safe, fast and punctual. It should also be convenient and should ensure nothing gets lost. Over and above these characteristics, **environmentally aware transport** pays attention to energy consumption and traffic pollution, to the external effects of transportation on earth, water, air and climate caused by corrosive, flammable and toxic materials, and to nuisances and threats to humans, animals and plants. These thoughts are behind the development of **green logistics**, where the concern is to measure and minimise ecological outcomes and impacts.

8.3   Inventory Management

8.3.1   ABC Analysis

Economically efficient inventory management is achieved in essence by ensuring that storage demand is determined as exactly as possible. Anything tangible may be stored—raw materials and consumables, replacement parts, semi-manufactured goods, intermediate and finished goods as well as components (in industrial companies), items for resale (e.g. in supermarkets). Since there can be so many different types and kinds of materials, they must be categorised according to their importance, which usually depends on their value. In an ABC analysis, **A items** are very important for the organisation, **B items** are still important, while **C items** are the least important. There are several breakdowns, and one of the most common ones is:

- A items—around 10% of items or 80% of total value
- B items—around 20% of items or 15% of total value
- C items—around 70% of items or 5% of total value

By dividing stocks into three groups in this way, it becomes possible to calculate economic efficiency. When planning the requirements for A items, a computer-controlled assessment of demand is carried out using bills of materials and a component-usage list. Due to the high value of the goods and the related high capital tie-up costs, emphasis is placed on accuracy. C items, however, are managed on the basis of their rate of consumption, which is done by studying past consumption figures and determining future requirements by using analytical time-series methods (as discussed in the previous chapter). This comparatively low level of accuracy is acceptable because of the relative lack of importance of C items; to achieve a higher degree of accuracy would not be efficient as it would take too long and cost too much and the extra accuracy would not be helpful. With B items, the aim is to have a level of accuracy between those of A items and C items.

8.3.2 XYZ Analysis

An XYZ analysis is structured similarly to an ABC analysis. In an XYZ analysis, the goods are categorised on the basis of forecast accuracy, which is relevant for the whole procurement process. The consumption of **X items** is relatively stable and is subject to only occasional fluctuations, which allows a high forecast accuracy. **Y items** allow a middling level of forecast accuracy; their consumption generally follows a pattern, but trends (in both directions) or seasonal fluctuations can occur. If consumption is irregular, forecasts become inaccurate; goods like this are **Z items**.

This analysis is also a precondition for being able to operate in an economically efficient way. If relatively stable consumption over time can be assumed, then relatively unchanging quantities can be procured at regular intervals. The trigger for ordering X items is then normally a fixed date. Z items, on the other hand, are ordered only if they are immediately required, which means a demand-related trigger. The start of procurement actions for Y items—the forecast for which is only of limited accuracy—is in many cases when inventory falls below a fixed critical value.

8.3.3 Sampling Analysis

The recording of inventory is mostly done physically, by counting, measuring or weighing, depending on the type of stock. If the relation between effort and purpose is disproportionate, i.e. if it would take too long or require too many people, then inventory quantities are determined by estimation or calculation, in other words, through a sampling analysis. The value of inventory is found in balance sheets, so the commercial laws of most countries specify when sampling is an approved way of recording inventory levels and how it should be carried out. For example, Article 241 Para. 1 of the German Commercial Code states that inventory can be recorded on the basis of sampling.

Stocktaking based on sampling is dependent on the level of information. Objects that are similar in type and price can be grouped together. A preliminary value, derived from the results of a previous full count (i.e. when every item was counted), can be calculated for each grouping. A differentiated approach is possible, where items with a high preliminary value are subject to a full count, while sampling is used for groupings of lower value to check the preliminary values.

Special Note As a rule, the aim of inventory models is to reach an optimal solution that takes into account the timing of stock replenishment, stock usage and the quantities involved. The models deal with factors like the costs of inventories (e.g. capital tie-up costs, insurance premiums), costs of storage space, warehouse administration and handling inventory items (e.g. reception, storage, relocation and release of stocks, ventilation, mixing, processing, preparing, screening, counting and packing). **Ecologically aware warehousing** considers in addition the external effects related to the warehousing of everything from parts to industrial waste, using the opportunity cost approach to focus in particular on land use and disposal site use. Further external effects that can be taken into account are the energy consumption of refrigerated warehouses and air conditioning, as well as any potential risks to nature and people from warehouse fires, toxic leaks from disposal sites and underground storage facilities, and radiation from nuclear waste (each ton of processed uranium fuel rods produces 600,000 tons of radioactive waste).

8.4 Manufacturing

8.4.1 Make or Buy?

This is a core question that can be asked about almost every single economic activity. The **history of economic life** shows that the answer to the question has varied at different points in time and in different locations. In-house production dominated the domestic economy of the ancient world and is nowadays found widely in developing countries. This form of production is favoured by some big firms and conglomerates and of course by people who like "do-it-yourself". An interesting recent development is the maker movement, where individuals manufacture products (on a small scale, of course) using new technologies (e.g. 3D printers). The plans are usually open source, meaning that anyone can make the products using documentation provided by the original creator.

In recent years there has been a move towards using third parties, as the growth in outsourcing and contracting out demonstrates. Business entities do this to benefit from division of labour, specialisation, technical progress, increased flexibility, the ability to focus on their core competencies and, last but not least, lower costs.

The following issues must be considered: external production generates variable costs which depend on the quantities purchased from the external supplier. Internal production also generates variable costs, but in addition it generates fixed costs. The fixed costs associated with employees and the assets needed for operations are considerable and significant, because capacity (people or assets) can only be reduced more slowly than the speed at which production levels decline. This leads to **cost stickiness**—costs that are resistant to change because of contractual agreements (e.g. commitments to buy a given amount to benefit from volume discounts) or technical characteristics.

Apart from the substitution of fixed costs by variable costs when changing from internal to external production, it is important to note that specialised suppliers can offer cheaper prices due to their **economies of scale**—as long as several companies outsource the same particular tasks. With external production and **just-in-time deliveries** manufacturing companies can largely dispense with warehousing. One consequence is that dependence upon the supplier increases, also bringing with it an increase in **transaction costs** for information, coordination, contracts and control as well as rising **transport costs** for outsourced production.

8.4.2 Optimal Lot Size

Lot size, *batch size* or *production lot* express the number of production units that can be worked on successively without retooling a machine. The optimal lot size is reached by minimising production costs, i.e. set-up costs on the one hand, and storage costs and interest charges on the other. Set-up costs result from a batch changeover and fixed ancillary costs are the set-up costs incurred for each reconfiguration of a machine and therefore for every individual production lot. The fewer the reconfigurations and the larger the production lots, the smaller the fixed ancillary costs per unit produced. On the other hand, storage costs and interest charges increase, the latter being due to capital being tied up in the resources. In order to determine the optimal lot size, the logic of the model of the economic order quantity is transferred to the area of production. A basic model is based on the following **premises**: continuous outward stock movement; no limitations in terms of warehousing, production and financing; a steady level of production, holding and interest costs; reconfiguration costs being unaffected by the order size (playing the same role as fixed order costs in the model of economic order quantity).

From a practical point of view, these premises are of only limited help since restrictions always apply to warehousing and financing. The assumption that the size of production lots is unlimited is also unrealistic. For practical purposes, an optimisation with constraints is of greater value, but although more sophisticated models are closer to reality, the efforts involved in their use become disproportionate and cast doubt on the economic efficiency of the procedure.

8.4.3 Capacity Utilisation

Capacity is the output potential of an entity, be it a firm, a municipal authority, a single machine or an individual worker. The ratio of actual output to design capacity gives the capacity utilisation rate as seen in Eq. (8.2).

$$Capacity\ utilisation\ rate = \frac{Actual\ output}{Design\ capacity} \times 100 \qquad (8.2)$$

Equation 8.2 Capacity utilisation rate

The design capacity is the possible output; it is the maximum performance given any relevant technical or personnel limitations. Working for too long at the design capacity can lead to higher costs, because this can result in a larger volume of rejects, faulty products and complaints, increased conflicts and unplanned down time. The design capacity is in any case only achievable for a short duration of time. Instead of producing the maximum output, it is preferable to produce at a rate that can be sustained over the long term, which is the effective or optimal capacity. The capacity utilisation ratio is the ratio between used and usable capacity, shown in Eq. (8.3).

$$Capacity\ ratio = \frac{Capacity\ used}{Design\ capacity} \times 100 \qquad (8.3)$$

Equation 8.3 Capacity utilisation ratio

The optimal operating level is often viewed as a cost-effective operating level; in other words, it is reached by aiming for minimal costs for a given output, defined in terms of quantity and quality.

The **cost structure** of a company is determined by its fixed and variable costs. **Fixed costs** are independent of the activity level. The provision of capacity brings with itself considerable fixed costs for staff, capital and material, so capacity must match objectives. Fixed costs are incurred for the potential output and do not change, no matter what the actual utilisation of capacities might be. Used capacity costs are the costs that result from the capacity that is actually being utilised; idle capacity costs represent the difference between fixed costs and used capacity costs. Capacity is being utilised optimally when fixed costs and used capacity costs are identical. For example, even the simple provision of vehicles for the fire brigade can bring about an optimal capacity utilisation in regards to the operational objective of safety. When these vehicles are actually employed for fire-fighting, their idle capacity costs are replaced by used capacity costs.

Variable costs depend on the operating level. The relation between the two can be proportional (costs change in relation to the operating level), progressive (costs increase proportionally more than does the operating level), degressive (costs rise with the operating level in absolute terms, but not to the same degree) or regressive (costs sink in absolute terms in spite of rising operating levels).

It is possible that a firm has no other option but to move away from having costs at the optimal level, such as when it is temporarily overextended in terms of production, but not to an extent that can justify an investment in new capacities. In this case, different **possibilities of adaptation** to different operating levels are possible. Open to adjustment are one or more of the following: the quantities produced (overall or particular items), the capacity utilisation rate (intensity) and the hours of operation (time).

Industry 4.0 refers to the growing links between automation and data exchange in production processes. Machines are being provided with ever more computing power and the ability to communicate with other machines, leading to the development of the **internet of things**. These developments are going to make production cheaper, but raise a question: who or what will produce? Will it be people or machines and software?

Special Note Economically efficient production is very often linked to cost-cutting measures, such as substituting one input with another, searching for alternative production processes and less vertical integration. Layoffs of workers are not uncommon in this regard, and these have social costs that are borne by the state, the community and the laid-off workers and their families. **Environmentally aware manufacturing** goes further by ensuring that the resources employed are environmentally sound and that production processes are low in negative by-products and high in recycling potential, with internal and external processes being part of closed systems that contribute to the circular economy as illustrated in Fig. 8.1.

Disposal is closely connected with the production process. It involves the recovery, the recycling and the disposal of waste and other negative by-products from products such as vehicles, furniture, computers and clothing. A waste disposal market, with private and public companies (recycling companies, waste transport companies, incineration plants, sewage treatment plants, second-hand shops etc.), has grown up alongside the sales market. **Environmentally sound disposal** emphasises a waste management that is at all stages, from collection to recycling and disposal, safe and secure for the environment and for people, from collection to recycling and disposal. Figure 8.2 shows options for the recovery and recycling of waste.

8.5   Administration

8.5.1   Rationalisation

Administration is **an operational function, being office work in the service of other functions** (procurement, transport, warehousing, production, human resource management, marketing and so on). Of necessity, administration involves the factors of production. Administration is made visible by the clerical activities necessary to administer something—managing files, making assessments, documenting, archiving, gathering statistics and financial data, and much more. At the point where the goal of administrative activities is not just to provide services—i.e. be a means to an end—but is to be the end itself, operational administration turns into operational management, which has its own goals and decisions to be made; property management is not identical with property administration (Chap. 9 discusses management).

Administrative services in a company are hard to measure and it is difficult to allocate them to individual tasks, areas, divisions or products. From the point of

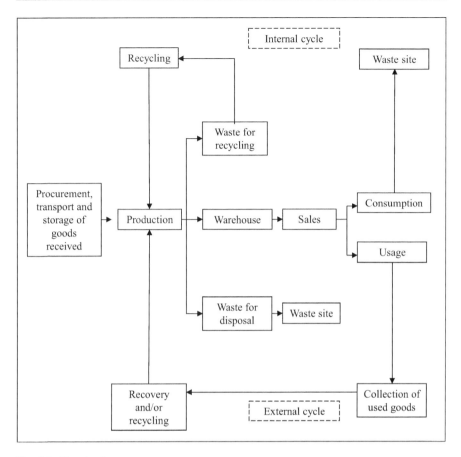

Fig. 8.1 The circular economy

view of costs and economic efficiency, the costs of administrative services represent overhead costs. Unlike overheads that are related to production, **administrative overheads** are mostly fixed as undifferentiated sums—the difficulties just mentioned make this the best solution from an accounting point of view. However, attention is being increasingly paid to the size of these overheads, leading to the introduction of measures to reduce costs further and/or increase output further: this is no more or less than the rationalisation of administrative work.

Overhead-value analysis records and evaluates the costs and benefits of administrative services in a systematic process that examines how fit the services are for the purposes they are intended to serve. In practice, a project team is established, made up of senior management and consultants, and it tries to determine where costs can be saved. Crucial questions are: Who provides which administrative service to whom and why? Can the recipient of the services wholly or partially do without them? Are there more cost-effective alternatives like redesigning processes to be more efficient or even outsourcing? This analysis frequently leads to recommendations to reduce costs by eliminating unnecessary services.

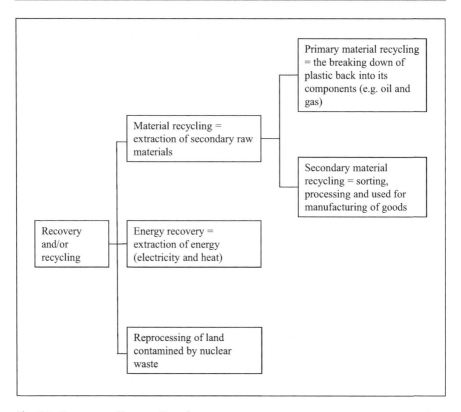

Fig. 8.2 Recovery and/or recycling of waste

Zero-based budgeting (ZBB) is a rolling process that begins with the selection of the functional areas to which it is to be applied. Once chosen, the activities in the functional area are analysed, the first time in depth, subsequently on a rolling basis, to determine needs and costs. This method, originally conceived for the administrative departments of companies concerned about high sales, general and administrative (SG&A) costs, aims to redirect resources from less important to more important activities. Traditionally, the budgets of administrative units for the next financial year are based on the previous year's budget—employees often make an extra effort to make sure that they have used up all the budget that was allocated to them before the end of the year, being afraid that the following year's budget will be reduced if not everything has been spent. Under ZBB the starting point is zero—all activities have to be justified, and activities are ranked by priority; the probable costs for the services to be provided must of course be known. The individual administrative units and their activities are gradually, based on priority, included into the overall budget until its limit is reached. The advantage of ZBB is that it prevents uncontrolled increases in administrative costs. As experience shows, however, administrative units develop a certain momentum of their own once they have been established, and their fixed costs cannot be reduced overnight. A further problem is that zero-based budgeting does not take sufficiently into account the benefits of synergies between the individual units but instead only considers the performance levels of individual administrative units in isolation.

8.5.2 Communication

The physiocrats—a group of eighteenth century French economists—were of the opinion that productivity only existed in agriculture and forestry. Industrialisation in the nineteenth century put an end to this view, and to this day this ratio of input to output is generally still only used in connection with the production of goods. In fact, the **greatest advances in productivity** are now to be found in the administrative activities of economic entities in all sectors, and particularly in the service industries. The key concept here is communication. Administrative work can be done more efficiently and effectively by taking advantages of the possibilities that technology offers. Accurate and comprehensive information can now be acquired rapidly and securely, processed, assessed and disseminated; if well implemented and integrated into processes, all this means that administrative work can be done more efficiently and effectively. The flow of information moves much more quickly, and distance is no longer a barrier to communication within the company, and between the organisation and its environment. The global availability of data and the establishment of service providers in all parts of the world have led many organisations to outsource administrative activities, allowing them to focus on their core competencies. Human relations departments alone provide examples of what can be outsourced: recruiting, payroll, and training, for example. One of the first areas of activity that is outsourced is often the one that provides the infrastructure that makes the outsourcing of administrative activities possible—information systems. A comparison of administrative work before and after the development and use of modern communications technology shows a clear increase in economic efficiency. This trend is going to continue as more and more algorithms are introduced into administrative processes. Many expect that algorithms will have the capability of performing many of the tasks that today are carried out by humans, meaning that there will be huge changes in the ways economic entities work.

Special Note Administration, as so far discussed in this chapter, is a function within a company that carries out office work related to management functions (planning, organisation and supervision), operational functions (administration of procurement, warehousing, research facilities, marketing etc.) or the use of factors of production (human resources and finance administration, accounting, facility management). **Environmentally aware administration** can improve the environment in offices in many ways. Environmentally friendly electronic equipment can be used (printers which emit fewer pollutants and are quieter, monitors and computers that save energy), office material reused (refilling laser printer toner cartridges), recycled paper used (manufactured from waste paper using up to 90% less water compared to normal paper), the number of documents printed reduced, electronic waste reduced (as a result of take-back obligations and recycling) and so on.

8.6   Marketing

8.6.1   Optimal Marketing Mix

The optimal marketing mix is the right combination of the four marketing instruments (the four Ps—product, price, place (distribution) and promotion) at a given point in time. When making the relevant decisions, it is firstly necessary to achieve the most cost-effective relationship between **information value and the transaction costs** of obtaining, processing, assessing and disseminating the information. The remaining budget is then distributed among the marketing instruments in order to reach an **optimal allocation**. A prerequisite of an optimal mix is that there must be substitutability of the components, at least within certain limits, since a search for realistic new combinations would otherwise not be possible. Theoretically, a marketing budget could be divided up in such a way that the marginal benefits of the individual instruments are balanced (see Chap. 2). Even if this model is too theoretical for practical purposes, this way of thinking can help decision makers to make an economic whole out of individual parts.

8.6.2   Evaluating Advertising Effectiveness

A vital issue in marketing is trying to understand how worthwhile advertising is, given what it costs. Quantitative goals include turnover, market share and profit, while qualitative goals include awareness and attitude. One example of the evaluation of **quantitative advertising goals** is to use experimental methods to find the number of orders that were influenced by an advertisement. A further possibility is regression analysis; the dependent and independent variable refer in the static approach to a single period, in the dynamic approach to several periods (see Sects. 7.2 and 7.3). An example for the dependent variable is units sold, for the independent variable advertising expense. There is the danger that a causality is assumed that in reality does not exist in such a form; sales are not exclusively dependent on advertising, i.e. on the promotion policy, but on all the marketing instruments—correlation does not imply causation. Because of this difficulty, the measuring of **qualitative advertisement goals** may be preferred. Recall, recognition and attitude can all be measured in order to determine the extent to which goals have been achieved. However, problems also arise here. Memory may only be loosely connected with purchase acts. For instance, humorous advertising can produce a high degree of awareness without resulting in higher sales. There is a similar issue with measuring attitudes—even if the customer has a positive predisposition towards a product, it does not necessarily result in a purchase.

Special Note
Marketing tries to activate and satisfy the needs of existing and potential customers. **Environmentally aware marketing**, often called green marketing, has additional tasks. It emphasises that having environmentally compatible production and products helps generate sales. Marketing instruments are chosen that support the

environmental goals of resource preservation, reduction of pollution and non-harmful waste disposal. **Green marketing** is also used to promote indirect product advantages (e.g. campaigns to promote travelling by tram can refer to their low energy consumption as well as their time saving advantages compared to cars) and so influence the attitude to the environment of those being addressed.

The four marketing instruments can reflect the producer's attitude and behaviour towards the environment. **Product policy** guidelines might mandate that the company offers environmentally friendly goods in each market in which it is active—a processed food company would also offer organic food products, car manufacturers would also offer electric vehicles, and so on. **Price policy** can consider price differentiation and delivery conditions based on environmental issues, while core to **distribution** can be an environmentally sound choice of location, regional suppliers, regional sales and reusable packaging. Finally, **communication policy** can place importance on showing environmental guidelines and publishing environmental reports and environmental balance sheets. The employment of marketing instruments in this way and the resulting marketing mix enable companies to differentiate themselves from their competitors. Doing so should in our opinion be a *sine qua non* not only for individual business entities but also for the entire economy.

8.7   Examples and Exercises

8.7.1   ABC Analysis

Situation
Gartengrün AG manufactures lawn mowers and various gardening tools. A variety of different materials are used in the production process.

The company would like to use an ABC analysis to classify the various materials used and to find indications for efficient material management and order quantity planning. The following material list has been produced:

No.	Annual consumption (units)	Price per unit (€)
1	120	280.00
2	15,000	1.70
3	1000	2.70
4	4000	1.80
5	600	5.80
6	30,000	0.08
7	18,000	0.05
8	20,000	0.08
9	500	8.50
10	100	23.00

In carrying out the ABC analysis it can be assumed that the A items are worth 70% of the total value, B items 18% and C items 12%.

Solution

No.	Annual consumption (units)	Price per unit (€)	Annual consumption (€)	Share of value (%)	Share of quantity (%)
1	120	280.00	33,600	40.0	0.1
2	15,000	1.70	25,500	30.4	16.8
3	1000	2.70	2700	3.2	1.1
4	4000	1.80	7200	8.6	4.5
5	600	5.80	3480	4.1	0.7
6	30,000	0.08	2400	2.9	33.5
7	18,000	0.05	900	1.1	20.2
8	20,000	0.08	1600	1.9	22.4
9	500	8.50	4250	5.1	0.6
10	100	23.00	2300	2.7	0.1
	$\sum = 89,320$		$\sum = 83,930$	100	100

Class	Number of items	Percentage of total units (%)	Percentage of total value (%)
A	2 (No. 1 + 2)	20	70.4
B	3 (No. 4 + 9 + 5)	30	17.8
C	5 (No. 3 + 6 + 7 + 8 + 10)	50	11.8
Total	10	100	100

The results of the ABC analysis indicate that most effort should be put into managing items 1 and 2, which represent 70% of total value. A rule of thumb is that the percentage of time that is spent on optimisation of inventory management should be the same as the percentage of total value that the class represents. In this case, the managers should spend 70% of the time they are spending on this activity on these two items. By the same token, they should only spend around one-tenth of their time on the Class C items.

8.7.2   Make or Buy?

Situation

Pascale and Geneviève have decided to open a muffin shop; muffins have become trendy and that want to get into the market quickly. They are in the process of writing their business plan and must make a fundamental decision—buy or make? Should they bake the muffins themselves on their own premises or outsource their production to a local bakery?

If they buy the products in, they will need some special containers that will keep the muffins fresh. The containers only last for 1 year and would cost 500 € per year.

The muffins from the bakery will cost 0.80 € each. If they make the muffins themselves they will need a small kitchen, which with all the necessary equipment, will cost 10,000 €, and each muffin will cost them 0.20 € to make. They expect to sell 20,000 muffins per year.

Should they make or buy?

Solution

The most straightforward way to find the answer is to determine the total costs using the following formula, where TC = total costs, FC = fixed costs, VC = variable costs and Q = quantity.

$$TC = FC + (VC \times Q)$$

The total costs of outsourcing production are shown in the next equation:

$$500 \text{ €} + (0.80 \text{ €} \times 20{,}000) = 16{,}500 \text{ €}$$

Inhouse production has the following costs:

$$10{,}000 \text{ €} + (0.20 \text{ €} \times 20{,}000) = 14{,}000 \text{ €}$$

It clearly makes sense for them to produce the muffins themselves. Numbers are, however, not the only consideration in such decisions. If outsourcing were cheaper, Pascale and Geneviève would have needed to ask themselves if their shop would be as popular if they did not make their own muffins. The answer to that question is probably 'No', so they would need to a wider view before reaching a decision.

The following equation allows the point of indifference to be found, i.e. the quantity where the costs of inhouse and outsourced production are the same.

$$FC_{Buy} + \left(VC_{Buy} \times Q\right) = FC_{Make} + (VC_{Make} \times Q)$$

This gives

$$500 \text{ €} + (0.80 \text{ €} \times Q) = 10{,}000 \text{ €} + (0.20 \text{ €} \times Q)$$

$$Q = 15{,}833 \text{ €}$$

8.7.3   Economic Order Quantity

Situation

Mein Haus und Garten is a large regional supplier of building and garden materials to the trade and hobbyists. Among the items it sells is topsoil, used for borders and beds. For each of the past 3 years it has sold an average of 1500 tonnes and demand is fairly constant over the year. Edyta Mirnik, the new procurement manager has been reviewing procurement policies and found that there was little planning, so she has decided to improve this area. She estimates that the cost of placing an order is 30 €, and that the holding costs are 20% of the purchase price, which is 50 € per tonne. What is the economic order quantity?

Solution
Using the formula presented earlier in the chapter, where D is the annual demand in units, S is ordering costs and H is the holding cost per unit,

$$EOQ = \sqrt{\frac{2DS}{H}}$$

We find

$$EOQ = \sqrt{\frac{2 \times 1500 \times 30}{0.2 \times 50}} = 94.868$$

Edyta should therefore order 95 tonnes per order.

One of her goals is to reduce holding costs by 50%. What difference would this make?

$$EOQ = \sqrt{\frac{2 \times 1500 \times 30}{0.1 \times 50}} = 134.164$$

If she can order 135 tonnes each time, she may be in a better position to get a volume discount.

8.7.4   Evaluating Marketing

Situation
Hampton Mayhew, a small private bank sent out 5000 letters to potential clients. The letters were printed on expensive paper and had been designed to give the impression of stability, reliability and understated competence. Included with each letter was a small high-quality pocket calculator. The letters were sent to people all over Europe with a net worth of over 5 million euros. The total cost of this campaign was 350,000 € (including the letters and follow up calls and visits). Alex Kendall, the director of marketing, has been provided with the following summary of the results, 1 month after the campaign ended:

- 150 people indicated that they would like to see a bank representative. 30 of them opened an account
- 180 people provided their contact details and indicated they would like to be contacted again within the next year

- 90 people indicated that they wanted further written details. Follow-up calls and/or visits were made to them, and 15 of them opened an account.

What should Alex say to the board when asked about the campaign?

Solution
At first glance, the fact that only 45 people have so far opened an account, when a grand total of 5000 potential customers were contacted, seems disappointing—it means there was a conversion rate of 45 ÷ 5000, i.e. less than 1%. The campaign cost 350,000 €, so the cost of acquiring each new customer was 350,000 € ÷ 45, i.e. 7777 €.

Alex is not particularly concerned. He will first argue that the lifetime profit that the bank makes from each customer will be much more than 7777 €. Second, he will make the point that the money the new customers put in the bank is a useful source of capital that the bank can use for its own investments. Third, he will emphasise that the decision-making process regarding which bank to use is a much longer one that the decision-making process about which refrigerator to buy and that he therefore expects at least 30 of the 180 potential customers who wanted to be contacted later to open an account. This argument is based on the ratio of people who opened accounts after a follow-up call or visit. The cost of acquiring each new customer would then be 350,000 € ÷ 75, i.e. 4667 €.

Despite his confidence, though, he would not be surprised if he were told to achieve the same results more cheaply next time.

8.7.5 MyCompany Project

Your café has been going so well that you will be able to open a second branch, located some 5 km from the other one. The new café is 50% bigger than the other one, and you plan to expand the range of food on offer. You will be hiring a manager for the new café. Now that your will be selling more coffee, you are giving some thought to procurement and inventory management.

- How would you organise procurement? Will you do the procurement for both branches, or will you let the new branch manager do her own procurement? What are the arguments for and against each alternative?
- How will you check the quantities you have in your storeroom? Would you count each milk carton to make sure that you have the quantity of milk you expect to have? How often would you check the number of coffee cups you have?

A significant decision needs to be made about the food offering in the new branch. You are expanding the menu, and need to think about whether you and your employees are going to prepare the food, or whether you are going to buy from one of the many outside companies that can provide vegan food.

- How would you approach this problem? What criteria will you consider when deciding what to do?

As the owner of cafes serving vegan and organic food and drinks, you feel that there is an expectation that you do your part for the natural environment. You have read about the circular economy and find the concept very interesting.

- What can you and your cafes do to become part of the circular economy? Why would you take these actions?

The final issue on your mind is your marketing budget. Your marketing has so far been low key, but now you intend to spend more. You expect that you will do online and social media marketing.

- How will you know if you are getting value for money from your marketing budget?

8.7.6   Self-Test Questions

- *What influences the decision to buy or rent?*
- *What are the underlying assumptions of the basic model of economic order quantity?*
- *What are the advantages and disadvantages of a low degree of centralisation of procurement?*
- *What does a simple model of optimal location consist of?*
- *What are A items, B items and C items?*
- *What aspects must be considered in environmentally aware warehousing?*
- *What is meant by cost lag?*
- *On what assumptions is the basic model of the optimal lot size based and to what extent are they problematic?*
- *What is the level of activity?*
- *Which factors determine cost structure?*
- *What recycling and recovery alternatives exist for industrial waste?*
- *What are administrative overheads?*
- *How is the method of zero-based budgeting carried out?*

Managerial Methods

9

The difference between a manager and a leader: A manager does all things right. A leader does the right things.

Opening Vignette

Michelle Johnson and Howard Dawson were not in a very good mood. They had just come back from the bank where the manager had told them in a rather direct way that they needed to decide on a strategy and not just react to whatever was happening.

"He was rude! Very rude!" complained Howard, running his hand through his luxuriant beard. "Just because I've never heard of a BCG matrix doesn't mean that I'm bad at running our business."

"We have been successful," Michelle threw in, "but things haven't been going that well recently, though, have they?"

Howard and Michelle had started a bicycle company 5 years ago. Keen cyclists living in Berlin, they had noticed that there was as big demand there for fixies—bicycle with a single, fixed gear—as that was in Hoxteth, a trendy area in London where they used to live, and not as many producers, so they had started producing this kind of bike themselves. Things had gone so well that they had quickly expanded their range. They had added mountain bikes to their offering and they now also produced skateboards and scooters. Their share of the skateboard market was very small, however, even though Michelle put a lot of time, money and effort into the development and marketing of their products. The same was unfortunately true of the mountain bike market. On the other hand, they had a good share of the scooter market, which was growing an amazing 25% per year, and they had just under 20% of the Berlin fixie market.

"I'm afraid the fixie market isn't growing at all," said Howard, admiring his new tattoo.

© Springer International Publishing AG 2018
P. Eichhorn, I. Towers, *Principles of Management*, Springer Texts in Business and Economics, https://doi.org/10.1007/978-3-319-70902-4_9

"But the scooter market is growing very fast and we have as big a market share there as we do of the fixie market, even if the overall market for scooters is small right now;" Michelle smiled. "We could do something there."

"So... should we get out of the skateboard market?" asked Howard.

Michelle reluctantly said, "Yes, I think we probably should. We'll put more money into the scooters. And we should keep spending on the fixies at about the same level, because there'll always be hipsters who want one."

"Why are you looking at me like that?" asked Howard as he turned on his Apple notebook.

"No reason," said Michelle innocently.

One week later they were back talking to the bank manager and told him what they were considering.

"Excellent," he said, "you've just done a BCG portfolio analysis and produced a matrix."

"What?" cried Michelle and Howard simultaneously.

9.1   Management

9.1.1   Approaches to Management

There is no escape from the principles of economic efficiency and effectiveness. They are applicable to all economic agents: households, enterprises, associations and administrations. The managers of these economic entities are ultimately those who are responsible for identifying inefficiency and ineffectiveness and for turning things around. Depending on the economic agent, the leadership role is taken by individuals and/or governing bodies. In colloquial speech, we talk of heads of the household, chairs (many organisations use this gender-neutral term instead of chairmen and chairwomen) of foundations, managing directors, directors, presidents, spokespersons, chief officers, chancellors, ministers, rectors, heads of administration departments, and so on. They all have in common that they stand at the top of an institution, either alone, or together with one or more colleagues on a board. From the point of view of the discipline of business administration, management is a decision-making factor; it is part of the personnel factor of production, and it combines production factors to work towards chosen goals. This involves setting targets, making decisions, implementing actions and monitoring; in a nutshell, **management consists of setting targets and implementation**. In a narrow sense, management is related to employees and staff (people management) and in a broader sense to institutions (business management, top management, managing a department, plant management, managing an office). It is interesting to note that the distinction between management and leadership is not made to the same extent in Germany as in the English-speaking world.

Most research into management has focussed on the management of firms because of their size, complexity, the amounts of money involved and the importance of good management in a competitive environment. A fundamental question

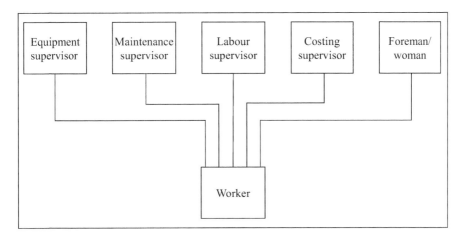

Fig. 9.1 Functional system

is: What should top managers do? Its answer requires identifying the areas, problems and issues managers (should) deal with, and how they (should) deal with them. There are a number of approaches to management, each with a different focus.

The first approaches that gained worldwide attention were those of the American engineer Frederick Winslow Taylor (1856–1915), who is regarded as the founder of Scientific Management, and of the French engineer Henri Fayol (1841–1925) with his studies on the organisation of firms and administrations. Both focus on the organisation of responsibilities, more specifically on systems of competences and of authority, as well as on the organisation of hierarchies. Taylor proposed the **functional system** (Fig. 9.1) that is characterised by direct supervision of workers with multiple lines of authority based on the principle of the shortest distance. Fayol's proposal was for a **hierarchical system** (Fig. 9.2). In this system, managers higher up ensure that instructions are given in a coordinated way to subordinates through the principle of unity of command—there is a single line of authority. Both approaches can be found in management as it is practised today (Fig. 9.3), with the functional structure dominating because it makes it easier to define competences and responsibilities; one reason for this is that each employee has a single supervisor.

The management structures of modern corporations and administrations are very complex. Many of them include supporting staff units (such as HRM and legal departments) which exist to provide support to line managers and have only limited direct authority. In order to make a large organisation manageable by top managers, it is necessary to group the departments and business units in the organisation in a meaningful way. This can be done on the basis of type of customer, geography, product or function. As mentioned above, the functional structure dominates in organisations because of the unity of command. Matrix organisations go against this principle, because they combine product organisational structures with functional structures so that individual employees can have two (sometimes even more) supervisors.

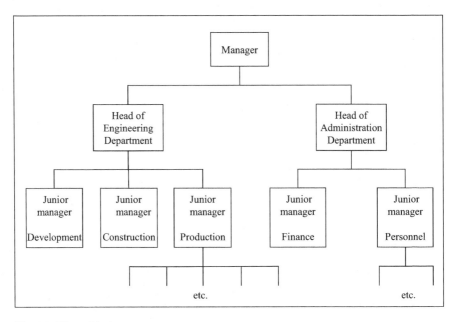

Fig. 9.2 Hierarchical system

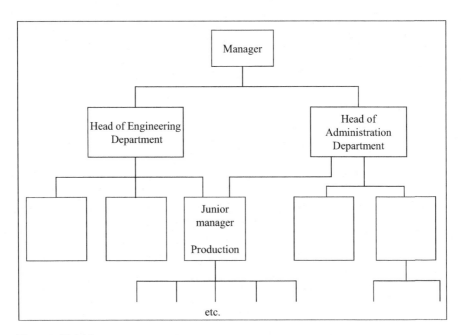

Fig. 9.3 Hybrid system

It is interesting to look at two classic management approaches developed in Germany because they are still highly relevant for corporate policy. One is by Curt Sandig (1901–1981), the other by Konrad Mellerowicz (1891–1984).

According to Sandig, managing a company has two aspects: **business policy and management policy**. For him, business policy consists of generating ideas, setting goals, making fundamental and routine decisions, and taking on responsibility. He argues that the goals of firms are to maintain and increase their economic power. The search for profit and security should take place as a dialectical process between "pushing forward" and "holding back". All the fundamental decisions that have to be made are related to the establishment phase of a firm's life (in particular the purpose of a company, choice of location, size, funding, legal form, recruiting and structuring the management team, organisational structure, getting on to the market). The routine decisions made within this framework are about issues such as personnel policies, purchasing policies, sales policies and financial policies. Decisions have to be made and the people making them are accountable for them to the law, shareholders, creditors, employees other stakeholders and their own conscience. In contrast, management policy is mainly responsible for the implementation of ideas, for developing plans, for organising—in essence, for turning decisions into reality.

Sandig's approach has the advantages that it allows the interdependencies of corporate policy decisions to be identified and that it provides systematic help to managers with the classification of complex leadership problems. However, it does not present concrete solutions regarding which goals to set, how to optimise decisions and how to choose the best alternative for implementation.

Konrad Mellerowicz' approach also developed out of applied business management studies but it emphasises applicability in real business life, and his aim was to establish academically sound rules to improve decision-making. The management of a company involves two tasks; the first is **corporate policy making**, which is taking fundamental decisions that affect the entire company. The second task is creating the conditions for management, or in other words, for the **implementation** of corporate policy via basic management functions: organisation, information, planning, coordination and supervision. Corporate policy consists of bringing together three kinds of sub-policies:

- function-related sub-policies, dealing with areas such as sales, production, purchasing, inventory management, personnel and finance,
- non-function-related sub-policies in such areas as costs, prices, balance sheet, profit, maintenance of asset value, dividends, tax and marketing, and
- sub-policies related to the whole enterprise, like company policy.

A theory is needed to develop decision-making rules that are universally valid. Such a theory can only be established by going beyond descriptions, even if they are the result of hard won experience; it is necessary to turn assertions that have been empirically derived and verified into laws, and then combine them on the basis of logic. However, the Mellerowicz approach is only partially based on such a theoretical foundation (for example, his use of cost and price theory as a theoretical basis for an entire corporate policy), so that its practical value is limited.

More recent theoretically oriented fundamental approaches have tried to correct this shortcoming. Again, two that have been given a positive reception in academia and in practice will be outlined here. One was published by Hans Ulrich (1919–1997), the other by Peter Ulrich (born 1948) and Edgar Fluri (born 1947).

Ulrich's approach is based on systems theory. A firm is viewed as a system of circuits and corporate policy represents the upper circuit. It must be based on the values of senior management and the state of the environment and the firm. The tasks of corporate policy are to make fundamental long-term decisions, to establish capabilities and corporate strategies, to implement and supervise operational measures, to adapt to developments in the environment and to generally define what the firm offers on the market. Decision criteria for corporate policies are: validity for many different management situations, materiality (not being concerned with details), validity for the long-term, comprehensiveness (by taking into consideration capabilities and strategies), truth, feasibility, consistency and clarity. In short: decisions should be coordinated and unequivocal. Corporate policy provides the mid-level circuit—planning—and the low-level circuit—arrange-ment—with three documents. A mission statement is a short document that captures the fundamental goals and principles of a company. A company concept explains what the business is going to do, how it will do it, and how all this will be financed. It may include statements of the social values of the company. The third document is a management concept, in which the goals and principles to be used in running the company are described. All circuits are connected by information gathered from monitoring and control activities so that deviations from planned targets can be identified and improvements be made.

This approach characterises corporate policy as the shaping of circuits. Corpo-rate policy is a process of problem solving, which requires certain structures, instruments and information. Hans Ulrich's approach has a strong theoretical base, and can at the same time be used in practice. However, it does not sufficiently deal with conflicts of interest, how groups are formed and goals are set.

Peter Ulrich and Edgar Fluri do consider these issues. They argue that **corporate policy is derived from corporate philosophy** and emerges from the debates about values, interests and goals between those inside the firm and those on the outside who are in some way affected by it. Three internal stakeholders—owners, manage-ment and employees—and five external stakeholders—providers of debt capital, suppliers, customers, competitors, the state and society—can be identified. Power relationships between stakeholders and the value systems of the dominant groups determine how the process of setting the corporate policy runs and where it ends. Setting corporate policy therefore involves conflict management and consensus building. The nature of the decision-making role of management emerges from this process, as do the way a company behaves in the market, its approach to ecology and, in the case of a firm that does business internationally, its approach to development issues. The norms that develop are naturally also influenced by the current state and future developments of the company and its environment; coupled with the relevant data, these become part of corporate planning. Corporate planning and monitoring, the process of organising, management and management development then provide the basis for the implementation of corporate policy.

This approach emphasises the balancing of interests between the firm and what is expected and required from it with regards to the social and ecological environment. Depending as it does on power relationships, the outcome is uncertain. If a balance cannot be struck, the company may become marginal and exit the market. The nature of these processes means that there must be a regulatory framework for corporate policy that concerns itself with the exertion of power and conflicts.

Special Note Spurred on by the German business community, a government commission developed the **German Corporate Governance Code** in an attempt to regulate conflicts of interest and to clearly define responsibilities within companies. German companies have a dual board management system—the Management Board is responsible for managing the company and the Supervisory Board appoints, advises and supervises the Management Board. Some statements from the latest version of the Code (June 2017) illustrate its themes:

3.5 Good corporate governance requires an open dialogue between the Management Board and Supervisory Board as well as between the members of these individual Boards. Comprehensive observance of confidentiality is of paramount importance in this regard.

3.8 The members of the Management Board and Supervisory Board comply with the rules of proper corporate management. If they violate the duty of due care and diligence of a prudent and conscientious manager or Supervisory Board member, they will be held liable to the corporation for damages. [...]

4.1.1 The Management Board assumes full responsibility for managing the company in the best interests of the company, meaning that it considers the needs of the shareholders, the employees and other stakeholders, with the objective of sustainable value creation.

The management approach developed in the following sections is based on an understanding that politics is a force that shapes everything. In the past, **politics** was always understood as being related to states, cities, churches and other forms of community. For Aristoteles (384–322 BCE), politics deals with the organisation of communities and their constitution. For Aurelius Augustinus (354–430), it is the management of change, for Niccolo Machiavelli (1469–1527) seizing and using power, while for Max Weber (1864–1920) politics is the struggle for power or influencing how power is distributed. From these various understandings it is possible to draw some conclusions about the role politics has and the form it takes in institutions, be they companies or other kind of economic entity, such as public administrations.

Politics has three aspects. First, it has a functional dimension—**policy**—that sets goals and solves problems. Second, it has an institutional (formal, systemic) dimension—**polity**—which revolves around the organisation of politics and its rules and regulations. The third dimension is process-related and is **politics** in a narrow sense, dealing with asserting interests and with conflicts.

The following sections show the role politics—in all its forms—plays in firms, analysing corporate policy as an example. This management approach with its orientation to politics can also be applied *mutatis mutandis* to other economic agents. It is based on reaching a desired state, and can therefore be called a **goal-based management approach**. The goals that are set determine the management system, the management process and the challenges posed to management competences.

9.1.2 Management Goals

The most important goals of a company are those of the corporate policy; from this are derived all other goals. The system of different goals can be shown in a matrix that combines production factors and operational functions (Fig. 9.4).

Additional **goal areas** are created when factors or functions are combined with products. When looking at individual products or groups of products it is useful to know, for example, the proportion of total costs represented by individual production factors, or which process steps are involved in the manufacturing of a good. It is possible to create a **goal cube** by adding to the goal matrix the organisational

Factors \ Functions	Procurement	Transport	Inventory management	Manufacturing	Administration	Marketing
Personnel	recruiting goals	mobility goals	personnel capacities goals	labour costs goals	overhead costs goals	communication goals
Capital	financing goals	payment transactions goals	tied-up capital goals	capital turnover goals	liquidity goals	pricing goals
Material	material quality goals	transport efficiency goals	warehouse capacity goals	manufacturing productivity goals	control costs goals	product quality goals
Energy	energy reduction goals	energy safety goals	energy reserve goals	energy peak load goals	energy mix goals	energy consumption goals
Services	service procurement goals	on-time goals	service call goals	make or buy goals	insourcing & outsourcing goals	customer service goals
Legislation	patent acquisition goals	risk reduction goals	patent length goals	rights management goals	brand protection goals	sale of rights goals
Nature	resource conservation goals	environmental protection goals	waste site provision goals	recycling goals	safety of waste disposal goals	PR for nature protection goals

Fig. 9.4 Goal matrix with factors and functions

units (divisions, departments, profit centres, cost centres, etc.) responsible for setting and achieving goals.

One of the main problems of corporate policy is to devise a goal system (see Sect. 5.1.2) from the different kinds of goals (see Sect. 5.1.1) while taking into consideration the relationship between them. Such a goal system needs to serve as a guide for concrete goal concepts (see Sect. 5.1.3) and at the same time it must be aligned with the business principles (see Sect. 5.1.4). The process for the **formation of goals** can only succeed when it is both top down and bottom up, which means that managers from all levels must be involved. This ensures that the individuals involved identify with the goals and this then motivates them. When formulating goals, the members of the top-management bodies (e.g. a German management board) and also the members of the supervisory bodies (e.g. a German supervisory board) emphasise **corporate goals** in particular, e.g. the survival of the company, profitability, product and service quality, high innovation rate, public image, company growth, turnover and market share, power and influence on the market, satisfying customers, social responsibility, being environmentally friendly. Everyone in the organisation has goals related to their situation and area of responsibility; the lower down in their hierarchy one goes, the narrower and more specific the goals.

It is however necessary to go beyond goal systems; standards need to be established and finally **goals defined and agreed**—if goals are not set, they cannot be reached. When the goals that are non-economic in nature are being set, there are no numbers that can be used for measuring, so alternative indicators need to be found (see Sect. 5.5.1), different measurement methods need to be applied (see Sect. 5.5.2) and different measurement scales need to be used (see Sect. 5.5.3). If it is not possible to set a specific goal, a **target range** must be identified, with upper and lower limits.

Implementation goals are often neglected even though they are essential to the achievement of overall goals. There are two different kinds; in one of them an assignment is delegated, in the other directives are issued. In **management by objective**s, when an **assignment is delegated**, methods are not specified and the employee is free to choose her own approach, which requires firstly the ability to think independently and holistically, and secondly knowledge of the methods and resources that might be used. In contrast **management by directive** does not leave the employee with any scope for making decisions or room for manoeuvre. Interim goals are given which must be met in order to achieve the overall target. The instructions can be made on a case-by-case basis or exist for general use. According to the substitution law of organisation of Erich Gutenberg (1897–1984), taking decisions on a case-by-case basis should be replaced by the introduction of general rules—if possible—as this promotes simplification and standardisation, i.e. less bureaucracy. This approach is mainly appropriate for recurring routine work, but it should not be inferred that it applies only when there are large amounts of work involved, as general rules can even be found for isolated cases that will (hopefully) never occur—this is the foundation of disaster management.

9.1.3 Management System

A management system comprises all the rules that apply to the management tasks in an organisation, including those of top management, the group that is in charge of these activities. Like every system it exists through its elements and their combination. The starting point is a goal system with formal and substantive goals that are formalised in financial and performance concepts, all underpinning an orientation that derives from the leadership philosophy, organisational culture and a unique corporate identity (see Chap. 5).

Figure 9.5 shows the most important elements of the management system; they develop from management goals—in firms, these are the corporate goals—and affect all other areas related to management—the management process, management competences and controlling.

Management tasks can be divided into four categories:

- making decisions related to company foundation, survival, expansion, modernisation and management,
- establishing and implementing corporate goals, determining the orientation and goal system,

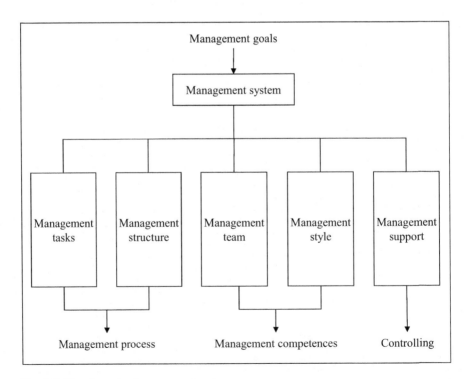

Fig. 9.5 The elements of management systems

- making decisions about the production programme, the deployment of human, financial, organisational and other resources, and quality assurance, and
- carrying out all vital ongoing tasks of management.

Management tasks are primarily concerned with organising and directing. Personal and political interests, power and business logic influence the way in which tasks are interpreted and carried out, as do general conditions that cannot be influenced by managers.

Management tasks can differ, depending on the **management structure**, which describes how the management team is organised, i.e. which responsibilities are assigned and how they are assigned. Many factors play a role in this: the industry in which the firm operates, the firm's size, structure, culture, ownership structure, corporate governance system (either a single tier board system, as in the United Kingdom, United States and Japan, or the German two-tier board system with a management board and a supervisory board), legal form and right of co-determination.

A further consideration is the management culture, i.e. whether senior managers work more as autocrats or as team players. Thought must also be given to the **span of control**, which describes how many direct reports a manager has, and to the extent to which responsibilities are combined or split up, and centralised or decentralised.

Management teams take many forms. In firms, they are made up of the members of the board of directors and the middle managers and supervisors who are to be found lower down the hierarchy in all areas of activity. Executives are employees with entrepreneurial responsibilities, for they have a significant influence on corporate policy and possess considerable scope for decision-making. Because of the nature of their tasks, executives also represent interests (those of the shareholders) that can be diametrically opposed to those of the rest of the employees. In Germany, the term 'executive' (*leitender Angestellte*) is a legal concept, bringing with it certain rights and obligations that are laid out in various laws. The human resource departments of larger companies often establish career development and training programmes for managers, paying special attention to those junior managers who are seen as representing the next generation of senior managers—these efforts are usually referred to as **talent management**.

Management style stands for the ways in which managers get their subordinates to do what they want them to do. There is a continuum of styles, from authoritarian to participatory, and the aim is always to motivate subordinates to perform. The goal is to find **an** ideal management style; there is not **one** ideal style, because needs vary according to time, place and situation—the task in hand and people involved influence the management style that should be used. A company dealing with research and development with creative personnel will be more successful if a participatory or cooperative leadership style is used, whereas a company that is specialised in the disposal of waste that contains asbestos or is radioactive needs, for safety reasons, to be managed in a more authoritarian way. In critical situations, such as a fire, the person in charge needs to act swiftly and in an unbureaucratic way, which implies a more authoritarian style. It is important to be aware that subordinates have different needs. Some prefer to be told clearly what they should be doing, in which case an authoritarian management style makes sense, while others perform better if they feel they can participate in decision making. Managers need, then, to take into account the situation and the needs of their employees when deciding on the appropriate management style.

Management styles are influenced by organisational culture and also by national culture. Geert Hofstede (born 1928) developed a series of dimensions on which cultures can be measured. One of them is power distance; in cultures with a high power distance (e.g. Guatemala and Poland), employees do not expect to have much input into decisions, so the typical management style is authoritarian. On the other hand, low power distance cultures such as Sweden and the UK produce expectations of participatory management styles.

Incentives are related to the management style; they are sometimes used to achieve feelings of group belonging and to influence the working atmosphere. Similarly, the delegation of certain tasks and responsibilities can also serve as incentives, as can opportunities for training and promotion. Last but not least, compensation can be an incentive; often forgotten is that pay is not the only motivator for some people, so rewards should match their wishes.

Finally, a management system needs **management support**—this is mainly provided by information and communication technology. The information system has to gather data and turn it into information, supplying it in a user-friendly way (the right time, the right form, the right quantity and the right place) so managers can make well-founded decisions. **Information and communication technology**—hardware, software and complementary services—has led to huge improvements in productivity.

9.1.4 Management Process

The management process forms a control loop that makes it possible to track the different phases of the management tasks that are being carried out in management structures. Courses of action can be broken down into a sequence of steps starting with **problem analysis** (which often becomes an analysis of weak spots), followed by the **development of solutions**, which consists of information gathering, identifying alternatives, and then using impact analyses to evaluate them. This is followed by **decision making**, i.e. choosing the best alternative, **operational planning,** which involves either establishing a project programme for the chosen alternative or its inclusion in existing programmes, with the necessary detailed budgeting, **implementation**, and finally by **evaluation** using the performance indicators that were established earlier in the process. The process itself should also be evaluated, of course.

Figure 9.6 shows these steps and the questions that should be asked in the course of this process.

Feedback links these steps to a control loop. If the above six steps—there are many more in reality—are simplified by merging the first four into a single planning phase, by viewing implementation as an execution phase, by viewing the evaluation

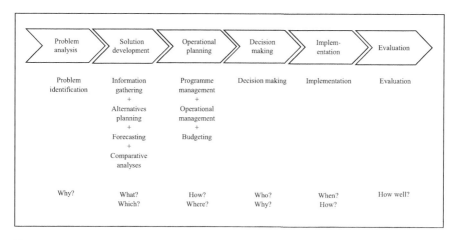

Fig. 9.6 Process steps of management

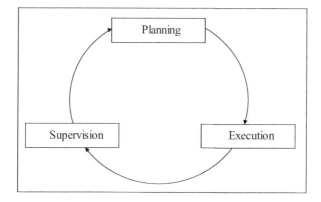

Fig. 9.7 Management process as activity circuit

phase as a supervision phase, and if the outcomes are then linked with the planning phase, the management process takes the form of an activity circuit.

Figure 9.7 presents the **primary circuit**; around each of these phases are three sub-phases, forming **secondary circuits**.

The **planning phase** itself needs to be planned, as numerous approaches to planning exist. Is planning to take place centrally or decentrally, bottom up or top down, as general planning or detailed planning? Is it to be based on sampling or should information be gathered from a full survey? Is planning to be done in-house or entrusted to a third party? The planning phase involves the generation of plans for everything that is affected, and it should include a review of the planning method. At the end of the planning phase—or often during it—a formal decision is taken by management to approve the plan and release it for implementation.

The implementation or **execution phase** also involves three steps. Fundamental questions (should) have already been answered during operational planning, such as which production factors need to be combined, when, where and how. Having been planned, the execution phase needs to be implemented and monitored. The liquidity plan is an example of a tool that can be used in this phase, because it takes the budget that was developed during the planning phase and transforms the budgeted revenues and expenditures into payment flows that can be applied to financial execution.

Similar considerations apply to the **supervision phase** which can also be divided in at least three parts. The activities involved in comparing planned and actual results must themselves also be planned, implemented and supervised. Feedback derived from the analysis of differences and their causes helps to improve planning for the next project.

Figure 9.8 shows the correlations. It needs to be borne in mind that what is shown by no means only happens in neat sequences, but that phases can run in parallel.

Details of the management process from the point of view of controllership are dealt with later in this chapter. At this point, the impression is to be avoided that management tasks can only be accomplished through these technocratic circuits. The assertion of interests and the playing out of conflicts in a political sense are also part of the management process. Individuals with different abilities, competences and levels of performance play a role in all phases. They differ in their attitude towards the company as well as in ambition or use of power. **Decision making** is often a difficult undertaking, associated with insecurity, uncertainty and unknowns, not immune to departmental egotism, manipulation and insider relationships. Frequently it is not just one single decision—even if it has been made formally and is a

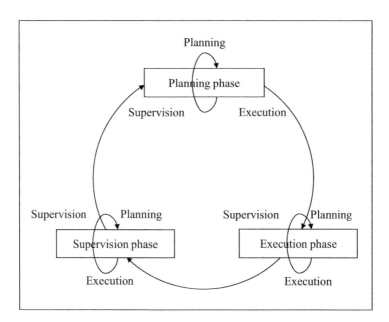

Fig. 9.8 Primary and secondary circuits in the management process

big decision—that creates new facts in the shorter or longer term, but rather a series
of directives, approvals and decisions that are limited in their individual scope, but
which cumulatively move the organisation in a particular direction.

9.1.5 Management Competence

Management competence is the result of acting responsibly, which means being
guided by ethical and legal norms, being committed to the job and to the entire
company, and being accountable. It is built on professional competence, which
includes specialist knowledge and the ability to apply it, competence in methods,
systemic competence, which means acting in a holistic, interdisciplinary and
intercultural manner, and social competence.

Which of these various competences is of particular importance in comparison
to the others depends on the characteristics of the business entity: its size, goals,
location, culture and so on. It is generally safe to say that no firm can survive if its
managers have neither professional nor social competences. The former means
that work activities are organised correctly and the latter leads to the involvement
of others. The tendency to overestimate their own capabilities and unnecessary
ruthlessness are frequently observed when a manager's social competence is
limited.

The capabilities of managers must include knowledge and skills. **General
knowledge** is the knowledge that is acquired through general education.
Specialised knowledge is classified according to the different disciplines—it is
the knowledge of doctors, bankers, librarians, chemists, forest wardens, craftsmen,
engineers, nurses, and so on. **Management knowledge** is interdisciplinary. General
knowledge is the basis on which specialist and management knowledge are built.
General and management knowledge present relatively few communication
problems, as the vocabulary used is in common usage, but this is not the case
with specialised knowledge. "Nerds" are therefore not executive material if they
can only express themselves in their specialised language. In other words: a
scientist who knows only about splicing DNA and has no knowledge of the labour
market, co-determination, capital markets, budgeting, balance sheets or other
elements of management knowledge is hardly likely to be chosen to become a senior
executive even in a pharmaceutical company.

As Fig. 9.9 shows, the boundaries between the different kinds of knowledge are
not cast in stone.

Knowledge on its own is insufficient in the real world; it must be complemented
by skills. Gaining knowledge requires skills, as does applying knowledge; the skill
of applying knowledge to practice is **know-how**. Often, only three types of skills
are identified: technical, social and conceptual. However, this is too broad a
categorisation, so we identify five sets of skills: intellectual, communication,
technocratic, physical and psychological skills.

We place knowledge in the centre of Fig. 9.10 to show clearly that skills are
grouped around knowledge, and that it is skills that produce external effects.

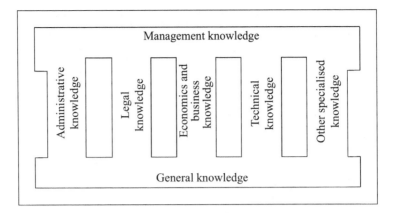

Fig. 9.9 Kinds of knowledge

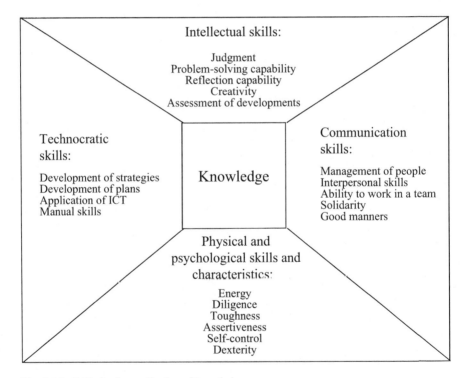

Fig. 9.10 Skills for the application of knowledge

Knowledge and skills come from aptitude and learning, but where management competences come from is less important than that they actually exist at a high enough level. Their existence is obviously an important factor in decisions made in human resource management—the performance and potential performance of an individual play an important role in selection processes, for example. Employees, in turn, need to work on weak areas. They may be informed about these in a performance evaluation, or they can take do a self-evaluation of their performance and motivation levels. They may ask themselves if their knowledge and skills (all four types) are at the level they could or should be, and if not, what can be done to remedy this. Being capable and motivated also means being willing to be led.

Competence and responsibility do not have just a personal dimension, for there are also functional and institutional dimensions. The former refers to the **area of responsibility** within which the manager makes decisions, and the latter to the **positioning** of the job in the organisation, i.e. where the job sits. Good management seeks to align individual, tasks and position. Everyone benefits if it is possible to match the goals of the individual manager or employee with the goals of management and the company. Achieving this is not easy and depends on management style, incentives and deterrents.

There have been numerous attempts to create simple and uniform **rules about management styles**. However, they are all ultimately bound to fail because everyone is different, with age, gender, ethnicity, language, national culture, personal traits and characteristics all influencing their personality and behaviours. No less heterogeneous are the tasks in a firm in its environment of market, society, state and nature. Even the positioning of managers and employees—both in the organisational structure and geographically—is not simple because the company can be organised in a centralised or decentralised way, based on functions or on markets. On top of this come job classification and remuneration with its fixed and variable elements. Given such diversity, it is really only possible to establish broad principles for a management style, dealing with broader questions like the situations in which being participative or authoritarian is appropriate. Companies that are active internationally face particular challenges for which they need managers who have intercultural skills.

Special Note The German company Siemens AG was founded in 1847. Today, it has over 350,000 employees and its revenues in 2016 were 79.64 billion €. Its path in recent years has not always been smooth, for it has been involved in numerous cases of bribery and price fixing which have led to hefty fines. The company decided to do something to change a corporate culture that made such behaviour possible. It built up its compliance organisation whose remit is to stop misconduct and one of its methods was to produce and distribute the company's Business Conduct Guidelines. The following extracts are from the latest version of the guidelines (January 2009) include:

A.2 Mutual Respect, Honesty and Integrity

We respect the personal dignity, privacy, and personal rights of every individual. We work together with individuals of various ethnic backgrounds, cultures, religions, ages, disabilities, races, sexual identity, world view and gender. Consistent with our corporate principles and with the employment laws of numerous countries in which we work, we do not tolerate discrimination against anyone on the basis of any of these characteristics or harassment or offensive behaviour, whether sexual or otherwise personal [. . .].

A.4. Management, Responsibility and Supervision

The culture of integrity and compliance in an organization starts at the top. All managers must fulfil their duties of organization and supervision. All managers bear responsibility for all employees entrusted to them. All managers must earn respect by exemplary personal behaviour, performance, openness, and social competence. This means, among other things, that each manager must emphasize the importance of ethical conduct and compliance, make them regular topics of everyday business and promote them through personal leadership and training. Each manager must also set clear, ambitious and realistic goals and lead by example [. . .].

F.1. Environment and Technical Safety

Protecting the environment and conserving natural resources are high priorities for our Company. Through management leadership and employee commitment, Siemens strives to conduct its operations in a manner that is safe for the environment and continually improves environmental performance. A worldwide environmental management system has been implemented by Siemens to ensure observation of the law and sets high standards for this purpose. Beginning at the product development stage, environmentally compatible design, technical safety and health protection are fixed as targets.

All employees must contribute to these goals through their own behaviour.

9.1.6 Controllership

It is a truism that management systems cannot get by without information and communication technologies, but other, older, forms of support continue to be vital. These include analytical, statistical and evaluation-based methods and tools such as company and process benchmarking, cost accounting and investment appraisal, balance sheet and asset analysis. The use in German of the term *Controlling* for these activities started in the 1970s but the function (called **controllership** in English, although some firms today use *controlling*) has existed in US companies for over 100 years, and those carrying it out are **controllers** (sometimes **comptrollers**).

Controllership focuses on the procurement, analysis and distribution of information relevant to decisions that need to be made; such information is needed when management is faced with complex tasks in difficult situations requiring a lot of time and effort to coordinate. This is particularly the case in large and medium-sized companies where many employees work together on the basis of the division of labour. Executives in small companies tend to perform controllership tasks themselves, as they represent the preparatory work for the decisions the executives themselves need to take. **Strategic controllership** is concerned with fundamental goals and far-reaching decisions, and **operational controllership** deals with sub-goals and ongoing operational and tactical decisions. Top management are responsible for strategic controllership because the decisions involved concern the continuing existence of the organisation, its actual and potential performance, its structure, future directions and characteristics as an employer.

Controllers in their function as information managers have to monitor objectives and plans, to identify deviations and their causes and advise on course corrections. They carry out their activities for the factors of production, for functions and to some extent for projects and processes. It is common to set up first controllership "islands" that look at narrow topics, and that are later brought together to form a comprehensive controllership system.

External and internal **sources of information** are used to meet the demand for information. Among external sources are research reports and market analyses by consulting firms, government statistics, reports by industry associations, legislation and legal decisions, government declarations and party programmes. Internal information comes from analysis of all the different budgets, accounting reports, financial analyses and various performance data that a company has.

There is some discussion about where controllership as a function and the employees assigned to the activity should sit in the organisation structure. On the assumption that the goal of controllership is to provide management support, controllers should have access to the decision-makers but not be decision-makers themselves. Controllers can be found in line functions as part of the chain of command as well as in staff functions, where they are independent of the line organisation. When there is more than one controller, they are either integrated in a single controllership department which interfaces with the rest of the organisation, or they are placed in decentralised specialised organisational units (e.g. in profit centres).

Controllership is a complement to the management process, not a substitute for it. Planning, execution and supervision remain the basic tools of managers; the results of controllers' activities are a form of counter-check to what the managers are doing. If the management process is understood as a **circuit**, controllership represents a **dialogue** with its individual phases, forcing management to deal with additional favourable—or unfavourable—data and facts prior to taking decisions. In this respect, controllers are managers' economic long-term opponents who are aiming to reach their own goals.

Figure 9.11 illustrates the role of controllership.

The following sections deal with the correlations indicated by the three bold arrows. **Controllership serves to provide planning, execution and supervision with the sound basis a successful corporate policy needs**.

9.2 Planning

9.2.1 Strategies

Planning is the theoretical anticipation of future events. It is a deliberate and systematic activity, not an improvised one, carried out within the framework of analyses of economic efficiency and effectiveness. Business entities plan in order to

Fig. 9.11 Controllership in
the management process

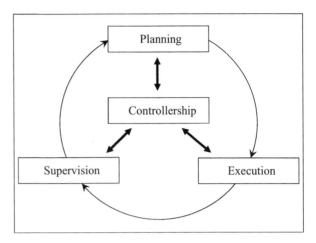

achieve stability, which leads to longevity, and flexibility, which leads to adaptability; they then have a solid base on which to build. Together with setting goals,
establishing a strategy is the most important task of planning. The term *strategy* was
originally used by the military. In his main work, "On War", Carl von Clausewitz
(1780–1831) defines strategy as being about winning a war, and he considers tactics
as being about winning a battle. Based on this differentiation, we can then say that
strategic planning, strategic management and strategic behaviour are concerned
with fundamental issues and the long term.

A company's strategic direction usually follows one of three kinds of **basic
strategy** (see Fig. 9.12). A firm using the cost leadership strategy seeks to gain a
considerable cost advantage compared to competitors, and this requires large
outputs and a lean cost structure. The differentiation strategy aims at positioning
products favourably against competing offers with respect to quality, design, image
and service. The niche strategy is defined by a concentration on the demands of one
market segment, and is of particular interest for small companies.

Firms need a conceptual framework that allows managers to choose strategies
for future growth. Four types of strategy have emerged (see Fig. 9.13):

- the market penetration strategy involves trying to increase the market share of
  existing products on existing markets,
- the market development strategy means that existing products are sold in new
  markets, while
- selling new products in existing markets is the basis of the product development
  strategy, and
- diversification involves offering new products in new markets.

These strategy types are often combined in practice.

Little research has been done about the strategies of non-profit organisations or types
of business entity other than firms. The research that has been done on how they see
future developments suggests that the medium and short term dominate. Operational

Fig. 9.12 Basic strategies

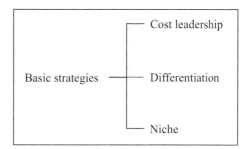

Fig. 9.13 Growth strategies

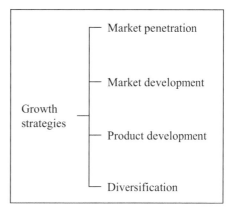

considerations determine actions: uncertainty about income, payments that need to be made in the near future, the fixed bureaucracy and the election cycle are uppermost in thoughts of private households, associations, professional chambers and church, municipal, state and government administrations.

Strategic planning starts with an assessment of the **current position**, with the goal of identifying the opportunities and threats in the environment of the company and its own strengths and weaknesses. The **company environment** is more than just the markets where sales are made and goods and services are bought; it includes society, the state and natural environment. Society—the local population and the general public—is aware of what organisations do, through opinion leaders, parties, the media and academia, and either accepts or criticises it. The state is not just the national government, but also the European Union, regional and municipal governments; all play a significant role through the legal frameworks they create, and their economic policies. The prevailing political climate plays a role that should not be underestimated. The natural environment is also significant; it is affected through the location choices made about organisational activities and it is the source of raw materials and the recipient of waste materials and pollutants.

A **PESTLE analysis** is a tool for examining these external factors:

- Political factors, e.g. government regulations, tax policies, political stability, trade regulations
- Economic factors, e.g. economic growth, exchange rate, inflation, interest rates
- Socio-cultural factors, e.g. demographics, education levels, attitudes, trends
- Technological factors, e.g. state of technology, infrastructure
- Legal factors, e.g. laws related to intellectual property and employment
- Environmental factors, e.g. the ecological effect of a coal-mine.

The external environment is one starting point for strategic considerations because, while it cannot be influenced by management, it provides many possibilities for companies—as long as they have the right strategy. The other starting point is an **internal assessment.** Managers have a much higher degree of control over what happens inside the company and are able to adapt and make changes. Tools for an internal assessment have been discussed in previous chapters.

The controllership department has the responsibility of supplying the information on these external and internal factors which must be taken into account when deciding on a strategy. A number of tools are available of which the best known is the **SWOT analysis** (strengths-weaknesses-opportunities-threats—see Fig. 9.14) which should ideally use quantitative data to identify and prioritise challenges. Those responsible for strategic planning evaluate the state of affairs, using as a starting point the degree of success of the various programmes and products, processes and structures, always compared to the resources used. The outcomes

Fig. 9.14 SWOT analysis

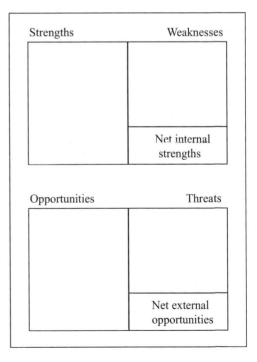

of the planning process will include a variety of elements, e.g. some parts of a firm may be expanded, others cut back, or there could be a total restructuring, all of these options will of course be reflected in the appropriate budgets. The elements need to be prioritised and then integrated into an overall strategy.

The **strengths** of a company can include an attractive portfolio of products and services, stable market share and turnover, a strong brand, a knowledgeable workforce, a high standard of research and development, good labour relations, modern fixed assets, sufficient capital for expansion. A company can show **weaknesses** in these same areas. Other weaknesses can include poor marketing and sales, group structure, an insufficient use of synergies, executives playing it safe, below average profitability, a large percentage of the turnover coming from very few customers. The opposite of these weaknesses are of course strengths.

Opportunities for a firm may be changes in consumer behaviour, the removal of restrictions in world trade, structural reform in a market that is relevant for the firm (for instance, healthcare deregulation), improvement of infrastructure and logistics, the development of new markets (for instance, online services), shakeouts in the market and a large well-qualified labour force. **Threats** include intensified competition, innovative competitors, increased cost pressure, shortage of capital, abolition of public subsidies, declining prices for products, bureaucratic restraints (for example, long-winded approval procedures), new legal bans or requirements, media criticism, risk of law suits.

An **opportunity analysis** is used to determine where a company might find success. The strengths of the company are compared to those of the most important competitors and the critical success factors of the market. The analysis focuses on how the factors can be managed in order to be more successful. Customer surveys are a useful tool for this kind of analysis, as they can provide information about which problems customers would like to see solved.

A **portfolio analysis** is a collaborative effort between strategy development and controllership. The usual method is to construct a matrix as seen in Fig. 9.15, which shows the Boston Consulting Group model. The position to which products and services are allocated should be based on numbers, of course. This analysis is used

Fig. 9.15 Portfolio analysis matrix

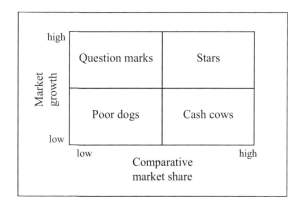

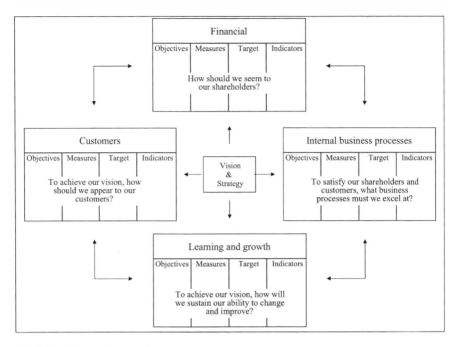

Fig. 9.16 Balanced scorecard

to help decide where resources should be put so the company can take advantage of its competitive advantages.

A **value chain analysis** investigates the creation of value in each process step and relates this to costs and potential for differentiation; suggestions for rationalisation, insourcing and outsourcing may be the result.

Inter-company and intra-company comparisons are very valuable—provided that access to facts and data is possible. Comparisons can be made in many areas, including products, processes, financial ratios, marketing campaigns and so on. The aim is to find out whether a company is above or below average in the given area. In the special case of **benchmarking** the aim to identify the best in class and then copy and adapt what the best company does.

A popular tool is Robert S. Kaplan (b. 1940) and David P. Norton's (b. 1941) **Balanced Scorecard (BSC)** which tries to overcome the common focus on finance-oriented business ratios by establishing a balanced mix of monetary and non-monetary information in a scorecard that maps the critical success factors to four perspectives: financial, customers, internal business processes, and learning and growth [Fig. 9.16—based on Kaplan and Norton (1996)]. The company vision and strategic targets are the starting point. The latter are quantified and goals for each company division are set top-down, after which the next step is taking action. The manager responsible for any given task is given a target expressed as a percentage; typical examples are a reduction in personnel costs, increase in sales to a particular customer, the speeding up internal business processes and raising employee potential by means of further training.

The Balanced Scorecard can also be applied to non-profit enterprises by expanding the financial perspective to include substantive goals, by adding stakeholders to the customers section, by paying more attention to services in the business process section and by viewing the qualification and motivation of the full-time, part-time and voluntary staff as the main factor for increasing performance potential in the learning and growth section.

The **scenario planning technique** is used for generating alternatives of what the future may look like. Usually the outcome of a series of workshop, various possibilities for the future are established and ways of dealing with best case, unchanged and worst case situations are developed.

9.2.2 Operational Planning

Operational planning is usually done for a period of 1–5 years; it can be understood as the element between strategic planning and short-term planning (that mostly deals with time spans of under 1 year). It involves the generation of plans that use quantitative data, and ideally also monetary units, for the medium term. Operational plans are developed for **goals** (e.g. profit and loss, reorganisation, redundancies, acquisitions, liquidation), **institutions** (e.g. group, branch, profit centre, department), **factors** (e.g. financing, staff positions, material plan), **functions** (e.g. sales, production, purchasing, waste disposal, research) and **processes** (e.g. work scheduling, inspections).

Operational plans serve to make strategies real in two respects, for they have **an informational** and an **instrumental** role. They contribute information to strategy development and once the strategy is established they implement it. In this respect, they fulfil. Where operational planning is used **to support the development of strategies**, the controller checks if and to what extent the plans are aligned to the potential strategic focus of the company as a whole. The controller must watch for possible departmental self-interest, isolated planning approaches, over-optimistic expectations, and planning and calculation mistakes. Controllers themselves are not infallible so they must be particularly vigilant about their own efforts when themselves developing operational plans. Unlike strategic controllership, operational controllership's goal is to ensure that operational plans are appropriate for the organisation's **strategy implementation**.

As discussed in Chap. 7, a number of different **controllership tools** are deployed during operational planning processes; these are methods used to collect, structure, analyse, store and forward information.

Earnings planning using financial ratios provides a good example of the role controllers can play. The starting point is how the business developed over the

Years	2016		2017					2018	2019
Ratios	plan	actual	plan	actual				plan	plan
				I.	II.	III.	IV.		
Sales revenues									
Other income									
Operating expenses									
Annual surplus									
Return on sales									
Return on equity									
Cash flow									
Free cash flow									
Investment ratio									
Sales productivity									

Return on sales $= \dfrac{\text{Annual surplus}}{\text{Sales revenues}} \cdot 100$ Investment ratio $= \dfrac{\text{Investments}}{\text{Sales revenues}} \cdot 100$

Return on equity $= \dfrac{\text{Annual surplus}}{\text{Equity}} \cdot 100$ Sales productivity $= \dfrac{\text{Sales revenues}}{\text{Employees}}$

Cash flow $=$ Annual surplus + Depreciation

Free cash flow $=$ Cash flow − Investments

Fig. 9.17 Earnings planning

previous period, then the planned results of the current year are compared to the actual quarterly results. This then provides a basis for planning future results, as illustrated in Fig. 9.17, which also shows some key financial ratios.

The various fields contain forecast values which are developed from the desired strategy; they are based on certain assumptions and depend on the firm's activities and market expectations. Income growth can be achieved by concentrating on the core business, by building up secondary businesses or diversification, which may require investment in new assets, in expansion or in replacement investments—these affect the investment ratio. Rationalisation and economies of scale and scope can contribute to lower expenses, while increased marketing and sales efforts may lead to better operating results, as may innovation goals such as that new products should bring about a 10% increase in turnover every year. Financial ratios sometimes conceal quality improvements of products that are the result of employee training, or improvements in factor combination which have a positive effect on productivity.

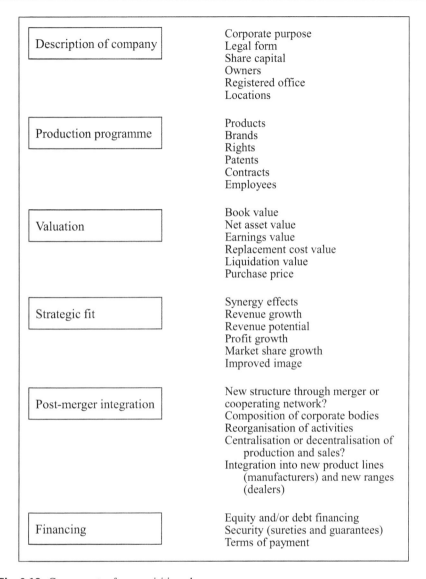

Description of company	Corporate purpose Legal form Share capital Owners Registered office Locations
Production programme	Products Brands Rights Patents Contracts Employees
Valuation	Book value Net asset value Earnings value Replacement cost value Liquidation value Purchase price
Strategic fit	Synergy effects Revenue growth Revenue potential Profit growth Market share growth Improved image
Post-merger integration	New structure through merger or cooperating network? Composition of corporate bodies Reorganisation of activities Centralisation or decentralisation of production and sales? Integration into new product lines (manufacturers) and new ranges (dealers)
Financing	Equity and/or debt financing Security (sureties and guarantees) Terms of payment

Fig. 9.18 Components of an acquisition plan

An **acquisition project** is a second example of where operational planning is carried out. The work could be done by a business development staff unit or by a team of controllers before the plan is submitted to top management board.

Figure 9.18 shows the information included in an acquisition plan.

9.2.3 Budgeting

Strategic and operational plans are usually implemented via budgets. Budgets are short-term (up to one year) plans that require a certain level of commitment; the amounts in them are tied to specific purposes. Budgeting, i.e. the process of **creating a budget**, is usually part of operational controllership. In the narrow sense, budgeting ends with the **approval of the budget** and **the passing of budget responsibility** to the appropriate departments or individuals. In a broader sense, the activity of budgeting also includes the **implementation and supervision of a budget**, including the analysis of variances as well as any necessary **budget modifications**.

Budgets can be classified according to a number of characteristics. Classifying by **purpose** enables us to identify purchasing, production, research and development, sales, personnel and project budgets, etc.; using **volume** as a criterion means a distinction can be made between overall and partial budgets, global and detail budgets, group, company, department and branch budgets; the **period of validity** allows a differentiation between weekly, monthly, quarterly and yearly budgets, while the **value dimension** distinguishes between expenditure, cost, contribution margin and turnover budgets. Examples of budgets that one would find in a company are the yearly budget for the public relations department, the quarterly budget for sales revenues and the monthly budget for a production cost centre.

When working out a budget, care should be taken that the figures correspond with those that have been decided at a higher level and that individual budgets, although managed in isolation, are coordinated with each other. This is made possible by a **budget system** that brings together individual budgets (such as those of business units, subsidiaries, profit centre employees, domestic and foreign investments) into a single comprehensive budget. In groups of affiliated companies, a multi-level structure is used, where the units at the base (e.g. subsidiary limited companies) belong to a division or intermediate holding, which in turn represent investments that the holding at the top of the hierarchy of companies has made.

When each company has its own budget, as is generally the case, the budget system of such a multi-level group looks like that shown in Fig. 9.19 [where *AG* means Aktiengesellschaft (stock company, i.e. one that issues shares) and *GmbH* means Gesellschaft mit beschränkter Haftung (limited liability company)].

The short-term focus of the financial framework (up to a year) means that budgets are the most important operational control tool between and within group companies—this is of course true for all kinds of companies, from the smallest and newest to the largest and oldest. It is of vital importance that budgets are linked with responsibilities for resources and results, as well as with incentives and sanctions. **Budget execution** requires first of all that the budget be guaranteed, secondly that there is a degree of flexibility in how and when budgetary resources are used, third, that there is an immediate reaction to positive and negative changes regarding the budget, and finally that success is rewarded in the form of bonuses.

Budgeting can really only start after difficult and complex decisions have been made about goals and strategies, and after other requirements and expectations have

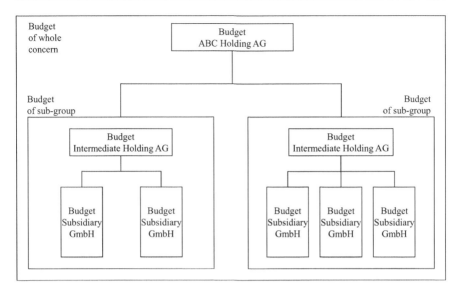

Fig. 9.19 Budget system of a multi-level concern

been made laid out. Sometimes departments struggle to get benchmark figures for operational resources and market potential, and occasionally estimates (e.g. sales of a new product) must be tested in pilot projects before releasing to the wider market. At the same time budgets can and should play a role in the balancing of interests within a company, the motivating of executives and employees, encouraging economic efficiency, opening up possibilities for more effective controllership activities. In general budgets are vital to a company's survival.

9.3 Execution

9.3.1 Organisational Structure

Execution follows planning in the management process. It is more than merely realising intentions; it is the goal oriented implementation of concrete concepts within a framework that is essentially set by the organisational structure, personnel and finances. Behind all this lie a huge number of individual discussions, decisions and actions that take place in the different parts of the business entity, such as implementing change in business divisions, making use of properties, deploying technology, arguments between top managers, talent management, going public, taking steps to assure liquidity and so on.

The importance of the organisational structure in turning plans into reality cannot be overstated, because it allows the institutionalisation of relationships between the production factors. One of the first to identify the essential elements of organisational structures was Erich Kosiol (1899–1990). The starting point is **task**

analysis, which examines what is actually happening in the organisation—what kind of work is being done? Mental and/or physical? Giving instructions or executing them? The analysis also looks at tangible and intangible assets and financial resources. Tasks are broken down into their individual elements and their interdependencies are established, always taking into consideration the time and space required to carry out the tasks.

After the tasks that have been deconstructed by task analysis, **task synthesis** combines the task elements on the basis of the division of labour into jobs. A decision has to be made as to whether or not machines or people will carry out the jobs, which naturally requires a great deal of thought. If people are to do the jobs, a job description is prepared, which is not linked to individuals but describes the tasks associated with the job. The compensation for the job must be established and then someone has to be recruited and selected. Recruitment involves finding qualified candidates and selection processes use various kinds of test to ensure that the chosen candidate has the competences and skills needed to perform the tasks.

The **competences and responsibilities** of the person who holds the job are defined; these include the authority to make decisions, to give instructions, to commit someone to something, to dispose of something or to pass on information. In public administrations superiors have the right to take over a task from someone else if they think it is necessary; they also have the right to supervise, to overturn decisions that have been made by superior authorities, the right to be heard, to make suggestions, to consent, to approve, to coordinate and to sanction. There are also attendant obligations, such as to give instructions, to comply, to inform, to report, to supervise, to consent, to obtain permission, to desist, to perform, to coordinate, to account for past actions.

Three different **degrees of participation** are to be found in coordination processes: communication (notification, briefing), consulting, and co-decision making (agreement, approval). This can be done in oral or written form.

The relation of the positions among each other depends not only on the distribution of competences and responsibilities but also on the design of the organisational structure. **Concentrating positions** is the pooling of those positions that closely cooperate while completing a task. The **creation of departments** provides a horizontal relationship between cooperating organisational areas and the **creation of management units** creates a vertical relationship. In this context, the span of control needs to be taken into consideration since it defines the number of subordinated people or organisational units.

The **line and staff unit organisation** must be designed. As discussed in Sect. 9.1.1, the principles of Henri Fayol require a hierarchical structure with a single line of authority, in which an employee receives direction from a single superior. In Taylor's system one position is subordinated to two or more positions and unity of command is replaced by the principle of the shortest distance. The staff unit organisation, which in most cases exists as an add-on to the line system, is defined by staff units, i.e. organisational units without the authority to give instructions but which have advisory, planning, preparatory and supporting roles. Figure 9.20 shows a typical organisational structure with two staff departments (HR and Legal) and four line departments.

Fig. 9.20 Organisational
structure

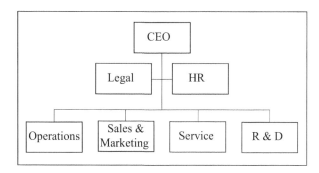

Committees of various types are established to coordinate activities and to avoid the need for constant reorganisation whenever there are new tasks and projects. Also known as working groups, advisory boards, project groups or commissions, they enable long-term cooperation between staff that are normally located in different areas and can be created for permanent tasks or specific reasons. Typical examples are a project group for the advertising campaign of a company, a committee of an industry association that is preparing a report on a particular issue, or the examination board of a Chamber of Commerce and Industry. Very rarely do they have job positions permanently attached to them, but resources will be made available to them to enable them to complete their tasks.

Centralisation and decentralisation must be distinguished from concentration of positions, which relates to functional relationships. Here the issue is about where organisational units should be physically located. The frame of reference can be a building (e.g. the accounting department should be on the fourth floor next to the financial department; the head of sales should have a corner office) or a region, country, continent or planet (the marketing department should be at headquarters in Berlin, but manufacturing should be done in China, while the software programmers should be in India).

The **organisation of top management** is a difficult issue for which there is no single solution. Participation in the decision-making process and the distribution of power are key concerns. Autocratic management is found when one person makes decisions alone, while in the case of directorial management one person decides and other members of the management team are collectively responsible—in some cases they have veto rights. Under the collegial principle several people make decisions together.

As noted above, the role of the controllership function is to support management, so it must examine the organisational structure to see if it will allow corporate objectives to be met and if it is fit for the future. The higher up in the organisation sit the people with whom the controller must deal, the more difficult the job. Controllers should involve top management in their activities; however, restructuring processes often fail because of top executives, especially those who are negatively affected by the analyses and recommendations of the controllers. The German company Bertelsmann, a large media and publishing company, for instance, has found an innovative solution to prevent blocking by individual executives. According to the rules of procedure of the management board, the head controller—although not a member—has the right to report to the management board, so she can submit suggestions to the top management and, at the same time, remain uninvolved in possible conflicts at that level.

When looking for tools that can be used for the controllership of the organisational structure, controllers have essentially to rely on insights from around the world about the optimal size of a firm, spans of control, lean management, organisational development, the benefits and problems of matrix organisational structures, profit centre concepts, and other relevant topics. In short, they have to determine what best practice is.

9.3.2 Process Management

The organisational process structure is concerned with the organisation of operational activities and as such is the companion to the organisational structure. This division into processes and structure is helpful for didactic and analytical purposes, but is limited in that structure determines processes and vice versa. At the same time, it is indeed possible to analyse individual work processes and their elements in a given organisational process structure.

Similar to task analysis, **process analysis** investigates how processes are carried out, their subject matter, the resources used, use of space and time, and their interrelationships. One popular approach is to establish the present state of business or production processes, to identify weak points and measurement criteria, to develop goals and propose a concept (business or production process analysis). Activity based costing (see Sect. 6.5.2) is carried out in parallel, this being a cost analysis of the present and proposed processes which includes identifying the main and supporting processes, cost types and cost drivers.

Whereas process analysis focuses on deconstructing processes, **process synthesis** aims at the grouping of individual process elements. Viewed at the level of personnel: process synthesis (distribution of work) allocates process steps to individual positions (division of labour) and their holders (allocation of work). Temporal process synthesis (pooling of work) tries to establish the sequence of process steps (order of operation), the intervals (coordination of timing), the work to be done during time periods (coordination of rhythm) and the adjustment of the timing of process steps (coordination of rest periods). Local process synthesis (design of work spaces) allocates process steps to specific workplaces and workstations, linking their equipment to the process steps.

The organisational process structure has the responsibility of enabling the synchronisation of process steps with the **exchange of information**. The flow of information takes place through official process channels, but also informally, as when colleagues share a table in the cafeteria or smokers stand together outside in the rain. A management information system supports preparing for decision making (controllership), regular or ad hoc reporting and the monitoring of progress.

Processes have to be reviewed with the aim of establishing if there should be **general or case-to-case** rules and regulations. General regulation means that there is a single, binding way of doing things, which can be achieved through means like procedural rules, instructions from supervisor, guidelines, timetables and schedules, and flow charts. General regulation can turn processes into routines, but the danger is that they deal with things in a mechanical way. Gutenberg's substitution law of organisation (see Sect. 1.2) states that case-by-case decision making should, if possible, be replaced by general regulation, but this law has limited applicability because special activities may not be carried out optimally if a general regulation is followed that ignores important specifics.

Process controllership consists of activities like examining procurement transactions, transport routes, work processes, product development, production processes, distribution channels, product life cycles and coming up with suggestions for improvement. These might aim at lowering costs, increasing productivity, securing and raising quality and increasing turnover. The most important methods include process comparison, competitive analysis, innovation circles, quality management measures such as training on processes and quality management manuals, as well as the sophisticated use of information technology.

Product controllership and **production controllership** are related to process controllership—all three support managers by providing targeted information for decisions that have to be made. They focus on the issues related to the coordination of those involved in processes, products and production. Questions that come up in this context include: Where can synergies be made and redundancies eliminated? How can deviations from plan be forecast better? Can processes be improved by insourcing or outsourcing? How can capacities be better used?

9.3.3 Human Resource Management

It is a commonplace that institutions exist through people, but there is more than a kern of truth in that saying. In today's knowledge society, where services generate three times more of the gross national product than manufacturing, the success of a company or government department or hospital depends ever more on skills and competencies of executives and employees. Executives make the central decisions, establish principles and goals, and make plans, but they depend on having skilful employees to implement all this and deal with customers, suppliers and other stakeholders. Human resource management therefore has a key—but sometimes underappreciated—role. Its main areas of responsibility include recruitment, selection, evaluation, training and development, and compensation. Its goals can be summarised as having the right people, in the right number, in the right place, at the right time.

Human resource (HR) policy and personnel development form the basis, on top of which come HR administration and personnel management. **HR policy** establishes the principles and must be aligned with the strategy of the business entity. **Personnel development** is mainly concerned with management development. It offers training, coaching and specially chosen job placements, and assesses

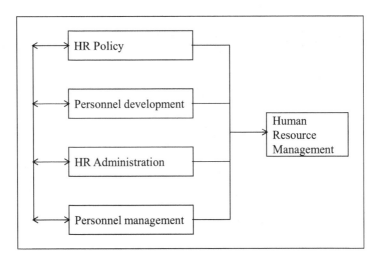

Fig. 9.21 Components of human resource management

performance and potential. **HR administration** is an administrative function whose tasks include the organisation of recruitment, looking after individual personnel files, producing statistics, dealing with the payroll, recording absences and holidays and much more. **Personnel management** is concerned with operational aspects. It involves personnel planning, where future needs are identified in terms of numbers and types of employee, job planning, job evaluation (for remuneration purposes). It also involves manpower planning which allocates employees to their positions (in offices, vehicles, on shop floors, at machines, as field sales force and abroad). Other responsibilities include identifying personnel costs and the performance evaluation process.

Although all four areas are heavily interconnected, they are shown separately in Fig. 9.21 to make clear that together they constitute Human Resource Management.

The process of filling vacancies starts with **recruitment**. During this process, HR managers need to decide whether to use internal sources of candidates (the in-house solution) or external sources—'buying-in' through private and government agencies, advertisements (online or offline) or job applications. This is followed by the **selection** of the most qualified individual. Typical questions at this stage are: Which selection tests are appropriate? Should an external assessment centre be used? Who should carry out interviews? Are probationary periods appropriate for top managers and which criteria for success should then apply?

Hiring is not only a formal act but creates a new situation for the new hire and for the existing employees. The onboarding process is the way in which new employees are introduced to their new employer, its culture and history, to their job, workplace and their colleagues. These first experiences can have long-lasting effects.

Managing and **developing** employees involves two parties—the supervisor and the employee, each of whom has a responsibility to the other. The superior is normally well advised to set goals and incentives, and supervise performance in ways that integrate and motivate employees. Only then can they identify with their supervisor and company and (hopefully) become top performers.

Career planning is a task whose importance is often underestimated. Often referred to as talent management, it is a critical success factor in organisations given the shortage of well-qualified employees in all areas of an organisation. Positions offering the chance to learn and opportunities for promotion are a significant part of successful HR management. Individuals want to boost their career options and good companies provide training and other ways of building up competences and skills.

Compensation is a significant topic. It should not be assumed however that money is the main motivating factor. Theories of motivation, such as that Frederik Herzberg (1923–2000) suggest that factors like challenging work, recognition and a feeling of achievement motivate, while pay and fringe benefits are hygiene factors which do not motivate in themselves, but can cause dissatisfaction. There are of course groups where maximising income appears to have the highest priority—many heads of global corporations, especially those in the financial sector, appear to use the amount of compensation as a measure of their individual worldwide ranking.

Pay can be divided into two categories: guaranteed pay and variable pay. The former is the fixed amount that the employee receives on a regular basis and the latter is pay that depends on one or more factors, which can include performance, time worked and results achieved. The two types can of course be combined. The level of pay has several influences—there may be legal requirements (e.g. a minimum wage), and agreements with unions include rates of pay. Variable pay can take the form of bonusses and incentives, which can be monetary rewards or (options on) shares in the company. **Non-monetary incentives** can be important for motivation—status symbols (e.g. a good parking spot) and awards (employee of the month) are examples.

Voluntary **benefits** are provided by companies for economic, ethical and/or socially motivated reasons; a precondition is usually that the company is making a profit. Examples are extra cash and non-cash benefits and services such as above-scale holiday pay and Christmas allowances, employee pension schemes that go beyond legal requirements, support for commuting, subsidised cafeterias, company childcare and sports facilities. Such benefits increase the attractiveness of the employer and contribute to a positive employer brand, which reflects how present and potential employees view the company as a place to work.

Human resource management is supported by **personnel controllership** that ensures that corporate policy goals being met, especially those that are relevant to personnel. Among the items the personnel controller checks are the extent to which HR administration, personnel development and management are meeting their goals, how analyses of demand and personnel procurement activities can be improved, and the strengths and weaknesses in personnel deployment (e.g. in shift operations, the use of resource pool employees and teleworkers, absenteeism or higher than usual employee turnover). Controllers also look at the extent to which employee complaints are justified and harm the culture of the organisation and what can and should be done about them. They analyse which indicators do not stand up to

$$\text{Personnel ratio} \quad = \quad \frac{\text{Personnel costs}}{\text{Total costs}}$$

$$\text{Labour productivity} = \frac{\text{Output}}{\text{Employees}}$$

$$\text{Labour utilisation} \quad = \quad \frac{\text{Standard employees}}{\text{Actual employees}} \cdot 100$$

The number of standard employees is based on labour agreements

$$\text{Illness ratio} \quad = \quad \frac{\text{Sick hours}}{\text{Working hours}} \cdot 100$$

$$\text{Staff turnover} \quad = \quad \frac{\text{Employees leaving}}{\text{Employees}} \cdot 100$$

$$\text{Labour utilisation productivity} = \frac{\text{Actual working hours}}{\text{Paid working hours}} \cdot 100$$

Fig. 9.22 Indicators in personnel controllership

internal or inter-company comparisons and only score below average—the first step is to establish ways in which the current situation can quickly be brought up to target, and the second step is to look for the root causes of the problems and fix them.

The indicators shown in Fig. 9.22 are typical examples of those used in personnel controllership.

9.3.4 Financial Management

The way in which a financial plan is implemented always reveals how the management of financial resources contributes to optimal financial management. Decided on at the end of the planning phase, the financial plan is the basis for expenditures and revenues as well as for investments and their financing. Financial plans can be made for short or long periods, from months to years. The shorter the period, the narrower the scope for decision-making and the more limited the room for manoeuvre. Short-term financial plans (up to a year) are also called liquidity plans because they focus on the management of financial inflows and outflows. Medium-term and long-term financial plans are more concerned with the management of expenditures and revenues related to investments. A **timeline** can be produced on which are shown the timings of recurring money and credit transactions, such as payments of salaries and wages, advance payments, rent payments, debt servicing and tax payments on the one side and on the other sales revenues, revenues from rents, credit notes and credits for accrued interest. Certain kinds of transactions allow for more flexibility in that neither the timing nor the amount are fixed, depending on any agreement, of course. How much and when to invest, lend money, dispose of assets, borrow and sometimes repay are decisions made at the discretion of the company.

Financial management means in essence taking decisions on the use of financial means to realise plans, and as such is bound by what the budget permits. Within the limits of the budget, it must always take into consideration the formal goal triad: liquidity, profitability and security. In the case of decentralised business entities like global corporations, a decision has to be made about whether they are managed as a system of divisions by one **central financial department** or by means of a concept similar to that of profit centres, i.e. **independent financial management** is permitted. The trend in recent years has been towards the division of power and of labour. Plans are drawn up centrally—with input from the periphery—and managed at the local level.

The relationship between **financial management** with its responsibilities for the planning, execution and monitoring of finance activities and **financial controllership** can take different forms in companies. In most cases financial controllership is organised as a relatively independent part of financial management, offering critical and constructive supporting services but not making any financial decisions. Two other approaches are less common. In the first, financial controllership is seen as being the core of financial management, in which case financial controllership exerts a kind of preventative control on financial transactions. The other approach makes a distinction by classifying financial management as a line activity and financial controllership as a staff unit that either reports to the management board or directly to the chief financial officer.

In general, the activities assigned to financial controllership are primarily concerned with the goal-oriented and future-oriented **management of liquidity** while taking into consideration any factors that are relevant for the organisation's outputs. A further important activity is **investment and financial analysis** because these produce benchmarks that are used during the financial decision-making process. Performing the tasks of controllership requires constant communication with relevant departments, but since all areas of a company are affected by financial issues, financial controllership runs the risk of lacking focus. It should therefore focus on cash management, asset management and debt management, paying particular attention to the risks involved in reaching corporate goals. This implies that meeting goals set for balance sheet financial ratios (e.g. working capital ratio, current ratio and others discussed in Sect. 6.6.2) is of less interest. Such historic data do serve as a basis for planning, but current information is needed for decisions in the domain of financial management.

Figure 9.23 shows some vital questions and aspects of financial controllership.

Cash Management

- Are the various business accounts linked and conciliated regarding the withdrawal and the investment of short-term funds?
- Is cash management achieving favourable debit and credit interest rates?
- Are managers provided with relevant external data (accounts, interest rates, foreign exchange rates, money market forecasts) and internal information (invoices, contract terms, tax and social security payments?)
- Are maturity analyses and forecast statements made for liquidity planning?
- Are rebates and discounts regularly monitored and adjusted?
- Do managers use currency netting to offset currency exchange costs?

Asset Management

$$\text{Asset turnover rate} \quad = \quad \frac{\text{Revenues}}{\text{Capital invested}}$$

Asset turnover is vital to return on capital employed (see also Section 7.1.1). The goal is to reduce debt equity to an optimum necessary to secure business operations, which – with the same turnover – increases asset turnover and therefore the return on total capital employed.

The capital invested is the sum of fixed and current assets. The goal is to have just those that are necessary. Should receivables be sold to a factor or more favourable payment terms agreed with customers? Can inventory be reduced by reducing waiting and storage times with the help of more detailed sales planning and control procedures or just-in-time deliveries? Are all fixed and financial assets required for operations or profitability?

Return on investment = Return on sales · Asset turnover

$$\text{Return on sales} \quad = \quad \frac{\text{Profit}}{\text{Sales}} \cdot 100$$

Debt Management

This is not so much about the optimal capital structure for a given investment programme, rather the debt-equity ratio and the leverage effect with its impact on return on equity as the debt-equity ratio increases (see Section 5.3.1).

Liabilities and the possibility of restructuring with more favourable credit conditions should be examined – payment obligations and bonds, generally categorised by maturity date (≤ 1 year, 1-5 years and > 5 years), pension obligations and foreign currency liabilities. Although the amount and maturity are not clearly defined, provisions are also included.

Debt restructuring can be affected by creditors and their behaviour, the state of the economy and interest rates, company strategy and bargaining power.

Fig. 9.23 Aspects of financial controllership

9.4 Supervision

9.4.1 Checking

Planning activities set the target, the activities involved in execution determine the actual state—supervision involves comparing them. Supervision, the third phase of the management process, has two dimensions: checking[1] by those involved which

---

[1]The German word *Kontrolle* is difficult to translate. There is no single English word that can always be used as an equivalent; depending on the context one might use check, control, screening, supervision, verification etc.

is to a certain extent dependent, and independent auditing. 'Dependent' and 'independent' have a double meaning in this context, referring firstly to the degree of autonomy, and secondly to the relationship to the process steps. Concerning the latter, checks are dependent on processes and auditing is independent. While there is some overlap, this distinction is increasingly accepted. Checking, as the term is used today, means to look at something twice, think about something twice or recalculate something—and make comparisons, which can be done for just about everything: incidents, data, objects, size, facts, processes, and so on.

The objects and characteristics of **checking** activities can be grouped in various ways:

- Timing in relation to what is being checked: prior (preventive checks), accompanying and after.
- Object: production factors—checks on staff, capital, material and so on.
- Functions—checks on purchasing, transport, stock, production, disposal and sales.
- Intensity—formal (e.g. compliance) and material (e.g. economic efficiency).
- Level—global (e.g. trends) and detailed (e.g. liquidity).
- Accuracy—accurate (e.g. electric power consumption) and approximate (e.g. sales) are distinguished.
- Extent—complete (e.g. valuation of an entire businesses) and partial (e.g. stock); full (e.g. in cases of embezzlement) and sampling (e.g. stock-taking).
- Relationship—direct (e.g. working hours) and indirect (e.g. consistency); centralised (e.g. in a holding) and decentralised controls.
- Choice—voluntary (e.g. creditworthiness) and involuntary (e.g. supervision).
- Notice—planned (e.g. monthly turnover) and unannounced (e.g. cash balance).
- Activity—coordination or recording.
- Objective—legality, correctness, economic efficiency and effectiveness.
- Accomplishment—task completion, target, performance, product, quality, output, outcome and impact.

Timing is a criterion that itself has a whole range of possibilities which include:

- Term—short-term (e.g. accounts), monthly (e.g. stocks), 1-year (e.g. issuing of invoices), ongoing (e.g. investments) and long-term controls (e.g. growth).
- Periodicity—irregular (e.g. giving a loan) and regular (e.g. number of staff sick); continuous (e.g. working hours) and occasional.
- Recurrence—one-time (e.g. acceptance of construction work) and ongoing (e.g. payment documents).
- Sequence—step-by-step (e.g., process steps) and simultaneous (e.g. laboratory test).

Ultimately, most checks are concerned with structure, processes, resources and results. They look for deviations, sources of error and weak spots in order to eliminate them or at least to reduce their effect. The **costs of checking** are an important consideration, because they need to be lower than the savings they generate (e.g. as a result of process improvements) or they must lead to benefits that are greater. Costs are influenced by how the checks are organised, the methods used, their extent and their frequency.

Entrepreneurial activities are activities that are checked, so checks are ubiquitous and crucial, as they help the organisation in its pursuit of strategic goals as discussed in Sect. 9.1.2. The checks on these goals require the use of two methods: monitoring and reporting. The basic question is: are goals being met? Senior management must be informed about deviations and their causes, corrective measures initiated and, if necessary, plans revised.

Checking can be done successfully if these **six principles** are followed:

- The separation of functions is the most important principle.
- Staff members must be given the authority to carry out checks.
- Checks must be targeted and objective, and try to avoid provoking resistance.
- Staff who are subject to checks need to be heard.
- Reports should be succinct and to the point.
- The costs of checking must be compared and contrasted to its benefits.

Monitoring the goal system means permanently keeping an eye on crucial business indicators and processes in order to detect unexpected developments as early as possible. Crucial business indicators and processes are those which significantly influence the overall goals, such as decreasing turnover and increasing costs, delivery failure and business interruptions (because of fire, other accidents, strikes) but also bad investments and the need to pay back taxes. To give an example: a large construction project carries risks that can only be made managed though exhaustive checking. Does cost planning for the work of the tradesmen employed match the invoices issued? Are due dates, quantities and the agreed quality being kept to at the construction site? Where, when and why are additional claims arising and for how much? Are the estimated follow-up costs and follow-up investments accurate, or will they increase? Will additional costs become apparent when the building is handed over? Can warranty claims be secured?

Senior management needs to be informed—at least given the highlights—about the answers to such questions. Furthermore, company departments must also be informed about issues that concern them so that they can take appropriate actions. **Reporting** to the management board needs to be concise. Indicators reduce complexity; comparative figures show relative changes; scales show levels of achievement; bar and pie charts make reading easier, as do graphs and other forms of illustration. The reports very frequently use the metaphor of a traffic light, where a green light means things are progressing as planned, yellow indicates that there is a deviation of (for example) 10% from what was planned and that actions need to be taken. A red light shows that there are large deviations which call for urgent counter measures.

If checking becomes a routine activity, it can lose its effect. Counterchecks, i.e. checking the checks, is carried out as part of **controllership** and can prevent this happening. Questions are asked about the checking that is being carried out to discover if, and to which extent, it is contributing to the achievement of goals.

9.4.2 Auditing

Auditing—or verification—is mostly carried out by people independent from the activities and processes being audited. Internal audits, year-end audits carried out by chartered accountants and the supervision of the management board of a German company by its supervisory board are typical examples. Other examples are the special audits that are carried out when limited liability companies are started, merge and change their legal structure; tax, embezzlement and insolvency audits; environmental impact assessments; audits by regulatory and legal agencies.

The people carrying out the **auditing tasks** produce written statements and audit reports that generally come to conclusions on the correctness of records and valuations and the legality of activities. In contrast, questions of economic efficiency and effectiveness are rarely dealt with, because they lie more in the domain of non-accountant consultants, although auditing and consulting sometimes form part of a whole package that large international firms of accountants can offer to their clients.

An **internal audit** is an example of an internal verification process. Staff members, acting on behalf of top management, independently audit internal processes, in particular those related to financing, business accounting and information technology, but organisational structures and other areas of operation can also be investigated. The main tasks of internal audits are the critical analysis and evaluation of directives, processes, and internal control and reporting systems. Internal auditors also verify the effectiveness of measures taken to prevent the loss of assets. Internal audits mainly have a preventative effect because internal auditors' work consists primarily of looking at documents. The effects of internal audits partly overlap with those of controllership, but controllership places less emphasis on the past and more on the future, but it does use the results of internal audits as an input.

Year-end auditing is the most exhaustive and most developed external verification. It examines the financial statements of companies listed on the stock market (but also private ones) for accuracy; only rarely are findings made about economic efficiency and effectiveness. It is therefore not surprising that auditing emphasises standards and techniques, the latter divided into audit planning, methods and procedures. In contrast, **audits of economic efficiency** focus on the characteristics of the principle of economic efficiency (as outlined in previous chapters), goals, the combination of factors of production; non-financial aspects may be mentioned and recorded in social or ecological balance sheets.

The high degree of **complexity in auditing** becomes apparent when looking at the example of the same multi-level corporation seen in Sect. 9.2.3. The auditing process takes a similar form to the budget process; it is adapted to the group structure and complies with commercial law, while at the same time it must take

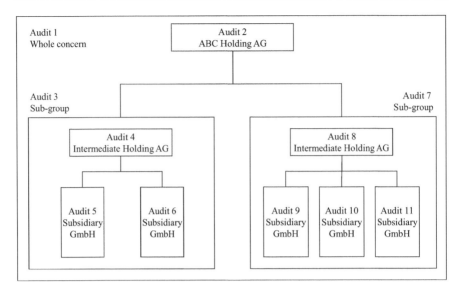

Fig. 9.24 Year-end auditing in a multi-level concern

into consideration the principles defined by the professional bodies of chartered accountants. The audit includes:

1. the management report and the consolidated accounts (group balance sheet, group income statement and group annexe) for the whole concern,
2. the management report and annual financial statements (balance sheet, income statement and annexe) of the parent company of the group,
3. the group management report and the consolidated accounts of each subgroup,
4. the management report and annual financial statements of each intermediate holding, and
5. the management report and annual financial statements of each affiliated company.

The group structure shown in Fig. 9.24 means 11 audits and audit reports.

The audit reports of the **whole concern** and the **sub–groups** reflect the management reports of the management board of the group's parent company and the intermediate holdings. They include key data such as profit for the year, equity capital, balance sheet totals and liquid funds including bonds as well as, in a summarised form, information on business purpose, lines of businesses, turnover, number of employees, possible risks concerning orders and profitability of the group companies. The auditors comment on all of this. The audit reports for the whole concern and for the sub-groups include evaluations of other statements and documents related to the group, the internal control system, and the consolidation basis. The reports judge if the consolidated financial statements were prepared for all the various management boards in the concern according to the appropriate standards. The paramount goal is to determine if there have been any changes in the bases used for valuation that might have an impact on the balance sheet elements and profitability of the whole concern and sub-groups.

The audit reports for the **individual subsidiary companies** follow a similar pattern. First of all, they contain the key data that have been submitted by management, and information on the development of business along with an assessment by the external auditor. The annual audit deals with the firm's book-keeping, the annual financial statements as signed-off by top management and the company management report. Attention is also paid to internal control systems for invoicing, fixed assets, receivables and liabilities, provisions, sales revenues and personnel expenses.

The audit reports finish after a brief description of size and content of the audit with an **auditor's statement** to the effect that the annual financial statements are accurate and complete in their representation of the financial and assets situation and the profitability of the company—assuming that no reasons have been found not to make such a statement.

The management reports, balance sheets and income statements that were submitted by the management board and managements of the different companies appear as **annexes in the audit reports** and are usually produced by financial management together with financial controllership management.

In two-tier governance systems, the **supervisory board** representing the owners reviews the management report and the annual financial statement that was audited by the external auditor. The sequence of monitoring and reporting that is followed in the checking process is turned round here: first, the management board reports on the situation of the company and submits the annual financial statement plus annex, which are then reviewed by the external auditor who summarises the results of the review in an audit report. This report is then submitted to the supervisory board for review. The supervisory board in turn reports in writing on the results of its review and of that of the annual auditor to the annual general meeting. Thus, a chain of **reporting** and **monitoring** is created, whose rhythm is different to that of checking processes. In the case of the latter, monitoring and reporting is a permanent and continuous process, the external statutory audit of accounting (i.e. the annual financial statements and management report) follows a one-year cycle. The two patterns are as follows:

Checking: Monitoring $\rightarrow$ Reporting
Auditing: Reporting $\rightarrow$ Monitoring

The verification activities of the supervisory board go by far beyond annual external audits for they include the auditing of plans, developments, construction projects, company founding, mergers, liquidations, personnel matters, and so on. Methods used include information gathering, producing statements, making decisions, approving, and appointing and dismissing senior managers. A comparison of planned and actual results is usually made and possible reactions to the strategies employed by the firm are also discussed. The preparation of such validation activities is done by strategic controllership, which provides its results to the management board which then integrates them in its submissions to the supervisory board.

9.4.3 Feedback

Feedback is the final element in the management process and closes the circuit. Feedback between supervision and planning turns the process into a control loop. When deviations exist between planned and actual results—this applies to goals as well as the strategic and operational measures that were decided on—the causes must be discovered. Are there internal or external reasons? Could advantage have been taken of them or could they have been avoided if they had been detected earlier? To whom or what are business successes owed? Who or what is responsible for poor decisions?

The **analysis and evaluation of deviations and their causes** provide inputs into planning activities. Two basic cases can be identified. In one case, the actual situation is data that cannot be changed—only new plans can achieve anything: this is feedback. In the other case, the actual situation to be analysed still allows for immediate corrections, without going through a planning phase: this is feedforward. Positive feedback indicates that the management process is optimal, while negative feedback shows a need for better plans and decisions. Systems theory, in particular the theory of system dynamics, models feedback mathematically. Applied cybernetics takes up this interactive system and tries to develop control loops that control themselves.

Due to the very high degree of complexity of business entities, economic efficiency and effectiveness can in practice only be optimised in small sub-systems, where results will in any case not be ideal. Theory is important but practical experience is indispensable for developing and implementing a holistic approach to the principle of economic efficiency and effectiveness.

9.5   Examples and Exercises

9.5.1   Microsoft's Mission Statements

Mission statements are supposed to capture what a business entity is all about. They play a significant role when strategies are being decided and are part of the framework within which employees act on a daily basis.

Situation
Microsoft's first mission statement said the company's mission was to put "a computer on every desk and in every home." This was seen by Microsoft executives to be too limiting. Under its then CEO, Steve Ballmer, the mission statement of Microsoft in 2013 became "to create a family of devices and services for individuals and businesses that empower people around the globe at home, at work and on the go, for the activities they value most."[2]

---

[2]https://www.microsoft.com/investor/reports/ar13/shareholder-letter/index.html, accessed 17.09.2017.

This change reflected the growing importance of the connectivity and the accompanying growth in the use of mobile devices. The statements shows that Microsoft wanted to be both the business and the consumer market, and produce both software and hardware and software, but not just software in the form of programs, but also in the form of services like cloud computing. The danger of such a mission statement is that it might mean that the company is trying to do everything for everybody.

Solution

Microsoft now says on its website, "Our mission is to empower every person and every organization on the planet to achieve more."[3] In June 2015 new CEO Satya Nadella sent an email to all employees which went into details about what this means in practice.

The 1500 word long mail says, "We must always ground our mission in both the world in which we live and the future we strive to create. Today, we live in a mobile-first, cloud-first world, and the transformation we are driving across our businesses is designed to enable Microsoft and our customers to thrive in this world."[4]

He describes the relationship between mission and strategy by stating:

"We will realize our mission and strategy by investing in three interconnected and bold ambitions.

1. Reinvent productivity and business processes
2. Build the intelligent cloud platform
3. Create more personal computing"

Activity

Look for other mission statements. What is the difference between a good and bad mission statement? Do as many German companies have them as American companies?

9.5.2 The Balanced Scorecard

The Balanced Scorecard is a system that business entities of all kinds can use for their strategic planning and management.

---

[3]https://www.microsoft.com/en-us/about, accessed 17.09.2017.

[4]The mail was obtained by a journalist. https://www.geekwire.com/2015/exclusive-satya-nadella-reveals-microsofts-new-mission-statement-sees-more-tough-choices-ahead/, accessed 17.09.2017.

Situation

The council of a medium size town in the north-west of England is facing some challenges. The central government has been cutting back funding, yet the demands on the services that the council provides have been growing. There were concerns that the objectives of the council were not being adequately communicated to staff, so that there was confusion in the minds of many employees about how their activities related to the council's overall goals.

Solution

Given the challenges they were facing, the mayor and chief executive decided that the Balanced Scorecard would be a very useful tool to align strategy with the activities of the employees, providing indicators that could be used to track progress. They put together a small team to prepare the implementation of the Balanced Scorecard.

The team decided that its priority was to identify the objectives of each of the perspectives. The results of their deliberations are found in the following table.

Perspective	Objective	Measure
Learning and growth	Improve quality of staff	Provide training so that staff possess the required knowledge, skills and competences
	Improve staff motivation	More and better communication Change compensation plan
Internal business processes	Improve technology capabilities	Invest in more up-to-date software and infrastructure
	Improve service delivery	Carry out a thorough review of all relevant processes and take action based on the results Expand quality management department
	Get local residents more involved	Establish some committees with members drawn from the council and the public Improve web site and become more active in social media
Financial	Reduce costs	Carry out an internal audit Introduce zero-based budgeting
	Improve financial management	Make costs more visible through improved reporting system Hire additional person for finance department
Customer	Improve programme outcomes	Outcome of improved business processes

The establishment of the objectives and measures means that it will a relatively straightforward process to develop the appropriate targets and indicators. Once this has been done, what is important will become clearer to each staff member, as will the reasons why it is important. The staff members will know what their targets are, and these could be linked to their compensation.

9.5.3 SWOT Analysis and Strategy

The great majority of business entities use a SWOT analysis as a basic tool for the development of strategy.

Situation

Fröse Musik GmbH is a typical example of a medium-size German company. It was formed 20 years ago and makes parts for hi-fi speakers. Most of its customers are small to medium-size European and North American companies who sell their speakers to hi-fi enthusiasts. The typical prices of the speakers that use Fröse Musik's parts are 750–5000 €.

Axel Fröse, the founder is about to retire and will be replaced by his daughter. What should her strategy be?

Solution

Ulla Fröse, having just completed an MBA, knows that a SWOT analysis, done using the various tools at her disposal and shown in the following table, is the best starting point.

Strengths	Weaknesses
Excellent quality	Too much stock
Innovative R&D	Cash flow could be better
Costs are under control	Sales have declined by 10% over the last 2 years
	Occasional delays in production meaning deliveries are late
Opportunities	**Threats**
Similar technology used in other types of consumer products, e.g. TVs and laptops	Market for high-end audio has shrunk by 15% over the last 2 years
	Chinese competitors with similar products

The company obviously faces some difficult short-term and long-term problems. Ulla decides that her priority must be to fix the cash flow problem, after which production processes should be analysed and improved. She is mainly concerned, though, by the fact that the decline in the market for high-end audio is declining and that this is affecting the sales of Fröse Musik's components. This situation is made worse by the entry into the market of Chinese competitors.

She thinks about the four growth strategies. She rejects the idea of introducing new products to their existing market (product development) because the market is in overall decline and she does not immediately intend to offer new products on a new market (diversification), not least because cash flow issues mean that there is not enough money to invest in new development, even though the R&D department is very good.

She could try to increase market share among high-end speaker manufacturers (market penetration), but the decline in the market implies that any gains will be limited, particularly given the existence of the Chinese competition. The most promising strategic option is market development—Fröse Musik can sell its existing products to TV manufacturers and to the producers of any other technology that has speakers. If this is successful, Müller Musik could take advantage of its R&D capabilities to develop new products for this new market.

9.5.4 Portfolio Analysis and Strategy

A firm that is involved in more than one market needs to manage the range of goods and services it offers in order to achieve the optimum allocation of resources. A Boston Consulting Group matrix is a useful tool for this.

Situation
A manufacturer of soft drinks sells three types of product: cola drinks, fruit juices and bottled water. Its senior managers need to know where to invest the company's resources.

Solution
David Connolly, one of the assistants to the CEO performs an analysis of the product portfolio using a BCG matrix. All figures in the following table are millions of euros.

	Cola drinks	Fruit juices	Bottled water
Sales last year	350	50	200
Sales this year	325	52	280
Sales next year (forecast)	295	53	350
Market size last year	900	800	500
Market size this year	910	820	750
Market size next year (forecast)	920	820	950

David then produces the following table based on the forecasts for next year and market growth since last year.

	Market share (%)	Market growth (%)
Cola	32	2
Fruit juices	6	2.5
Bottled water	36	47

These data are used to produce the following matrix (Fig. 9.25).

Based on this matrix, David predicts that senior management will probably decide to invest heavily in bottled water and avoid investing too much in cola drinks, where the goal would be to maintain the competitive position. The fruit juice business is not in good condition—it would not be suprising to David if senior management decided to abandon that market.

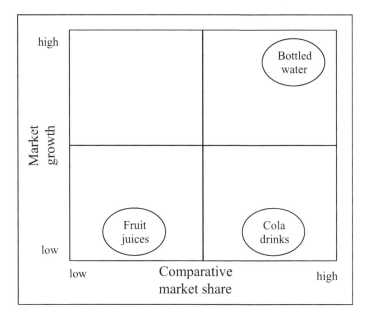

Fig. 9.25   BCG matrix

9.5.5   MyCompany Project

As mentioned in the previous chapter, you are going to open a second cafe and need a manager. You are going to place advertisements on several web sites and also inform the local Job Centre.

- What are you looking for in a cafe manager? What skills, competences and abilities will they need? What knowledge? What kind of experience do they need to have? Would you look for someone with a degree?

You are surprised, but happy, to receive over 30 applications, so you now need to think about the selections process.

- What questions would you ask in an interview? Assuming that you are looking for someone who is good at scheduling staff, how would you test for this during the selection process? After all, if you simply ask, "Are you good at scheduling?" every candidate will say, "Yes, of course."
- Would you involve anyone else in the selection process? What are the reasons for your answer?

You start thinking during the interview process about questions you would ask yourself.

- What skills and knowledge does the owner and manager of a chain of cafes need?

The new employee will of course need to be paid.

- You will need to pay the legal minimum wage, of course, but will that be enough? Will you offer a bonus, and if so, based on which criteria?

Since you expect the good candidates to ask you about the business, and since you realise it is an important activity that should in any case be carried out on a regular basis, you want to prepare a SWOT-analysis.

- How would you find out the strengths and weaknesses of your business?
- Which opportunities and threats do you see in the outside environment?

9.5.6 Self-Test Questions

– *What advantage does a hybrid system have over purely functional and hierarchical systems?*
– *What are the core ideas of Peter Ulrich and Edgar Fluri?*
– *Describe a goal matrix.*
– *What are the elements of management systems?*
– *What different kinds of knowledge exist and how do they relate to management?*
– *Why do many business entities use a Balanced Scorecard ?*
– *Describe the budget system of a multi-level concern,*
– *What is the connection between organisational structure and organisational process structure?*
– *What different types of controllership can be distinguished and which principles are essential for its success?*
– *What are the main responsibilities of human resource management?*
– *What are the elements of the management process?*

Glossary English—German

Ability to learn	Lernfähigkeit
Ability to pay	Zahlungsfähigkeit
Accompanying condition	Neben-/Rahmenbedingung
Account	Konto
Accountability	Rechenschaftslegung
Accounting	Rechnungslegung
Accounting period result	Periodenerfolg
Accounting system	Rechnungswesen
Accruals	Rechnungsabgrenzungsposten
Accruals accounting	Periodenrechnung
Accruals	Rückstellungen
Activity based accounting	Prozesskostenrechnung
Activity based costing	Prozesskostenrechnung
Actual assets	Reinvermögen
Actual capacity	Ist-Kapazität
Actual costing	Istkostenrechnung
Actual costs	Ist-Kosten
Actual output	Ist-Leistung
Additional expenses	Mehraufwendungen
Additional outputs	Zusatzleistungen
Additional costs	Zusatzkosten
Administration	Verwaltung
Administrative fee	Verwaltungsgebühr
Administrative goal	Verwaltungsziel
Administrativeoverheads	Verwaltungsgemeinkosten
Advance delivery	Vorleistung
Advance payment	Vorauszahlung
Advertising	Werbung
Aggregate economy	Gesamtwirtschaftlichkeit
Aim	Ziel
Allocated costs	Umlagekosten
Allocation formula	Umlageschlüssel
Allocation formula	Umlageschlüssel

(continued)

© Springer International Publishing AG 2018

P. Eichhorn, I. Towers, *Principles of Management*, Springer Texts in Business and Economics, https://doi.org/10.1007/978-3-319-70902-4

Allocation of work	Arbeitsbesetzung
Allowable costs	erlaubte/zugebilligte Kosten
Allowance	Zuwendung
Allowance financing	Zuschussfinanzierung
Allowance	Zuschuss
Analysis of ends	Finanzanalyse
Analysis of potential	Potenzialanalyse
Annual auditor	Abschlussprüfer
Annual financial statement	Jahresabschluss
Annual profit	Jahresüberschuss
Annuitymethod	Annuitätenmethode
Applied science	angewandte Wissenschaft
Approval procedure	Genehmigungsverfahren
Approval right	Zulassungsrecht
Arithmetical category	Rechenkategorie
Asking price	Angebotspreis
Assertion	Aussage
Assessment of current position/ situation	Bestandsaufnahme
Asset account	Bestandskonto
Asset turnover	Kapitalumschlag
Asset-effective	vermögenswirksam
Assets	Vermögen
Assignment period	Überlassungsdauer
Association	Verein/Vereinigung
Assumption	Annahme
Audit	Bestandsaufnahme, Prüfung
Audit report	Prüfungsbericht
Audit/auditors' certificate	Bestätigungsvermerk
Autonomous work	selbständige Arbeit
Auxiliary function	Nebenfunktion
Average	Mittelwert
Balance	Saldo
Balance sheet	Bilanz
Balance sheet date	Bilanzstichtag
Balance sheet loss	Bilanzverlust
Balance sheet profit	Bilanzgewinn
Balance sheet	Bestandsrechnung
Bank deposit	Bankguthaben
Barter economy	Tauschwirtschaft
Base stock inventory	eiserner Bestand
Basic costs	Grundkosten
Basic outputs	Grundleistungen
Basic research	Basisforschung
Benefit	Nutzen

(continued)

Benefit calculation	Nutzenrechnung
Book money	Buchgeld
Book value	Buchwert
Bookkeeping	Buchhaltung
Branch	Niederlassung
Break-even calculation	Gewinnschwellenrechnung
Budget costs	Plankosten
Budget implementation	Budgetvollzug
Budgetary requirement	Deckungserfordernis
Building authority	Bauamt
Bureaucratic restraint	Bürokratiehemmnis
Business accounting	betriebliches Rechnungswesen
Business administration	Betriebswirtschaftslehre
Business management policy	Betriebswirtschaftspolitik
Buyer, purchaser	Abnehmer/Käufer
Buyers' surplus	Beschaffungsrente
Buying, purchasing	Einkauf
By-product	Nebenprodukt
Calculation method	Rechenverfahren
Cameralistic accounting	kameralistisches Rechnungswesen
Capacity utilisation	Kapazitätsauslastung
Capacity utilisation rate	Beschäftigungsgrad
Capital acquirer	Kapitalnehmer
Capital assets	Kapitalvermögen
Capital budgeting	Investitionsrechnung
Capital coverage	Kapitaldeckung
Capital good	Investitionsgut
Capital maturity	Kapitalfristigkeit
Capital needs	Kapitalbedarf
Capital provider	Kapitalgeber
Capital requirements	Kapitalbedarf
Capital requirements calculation	Kapitalbedarfsrechnung
Capital reserve	Kapitalrücklage
Capital seeker	Kapitalnehmer
Capital turnover	Kapitalumschlag
Capital value	Kapitalwert
Capital value method	Kapitalwertmethode
Capital-flow statement	Kapitalflussrechnung
Capitalisable company-produced outputs	aktivierbare Eigenleistungen
Capitalisation ratio	Anlagenintensität
Career planning	Karriereplanung
Cash	Bargeld
Cash on hand	Kassenbestand

(continued)

Cash value	Barwert
Catchment area	Einzugsgebiet
Causal analysis	Kausalanalyse
Causal relationship	Kausalnexus
Cause-effect relationship	Ursache-Wirkungs-Zusammenhang
Cautionary principle	Vorsorgeprinzip
Certified public accountant	Wirtschaftsprüfer
Chairman	Vorsitzender
Chart of accounts	Kontenplan
Chartered public accountant	Wirtschaftsprüfer
Check	Kontrolle
Choice of location	Standortwahl
Circular economy	Kreislaufwirtschaft
Classification figure	Gliederungszahl
Cognition of facts	Tatsachenerkenntnis
Cognitive interest	Erkenntnisinteresse
Cognitive method	Erkenntnismethode
Cognitive process	Erkenntnisfortschritt
Colloquial language	Umgangssprache
Commercial accounting	kaufmännisches Rechnungswesen
Commercial balance sheet	Handelsbilanz
Commercial law	Handelsrecht
Commitment period	Bindungsdauer
Commodities	Güter, Verbrauchsgüter
Common assets	Gemeinvermögen
Common liabilities	Gemeinschulden
Common/public welfare	Gemeinwohl
Community of states	Staatsverbund
Company valuation	Unternehmensbewertung
Comparison of time	Zeitvergleich
Compensation	Belohnung, Entschädigung, Vergütung
Competitiveness	Wettbewerbsfähigkeit
Compliance	Ordnungsmäßigkeit
Composition	Zusammensetzung
Conscientious	gewissenhaft
Consideration, counter-performance	Gegenleistung
Consumables	Verbrauchsgüter
Consumer goods	Verbrauchsgüter
Consumers' surplus	Absatz-/Konsumentenrente
Consumption	Konsum
Consumption of resources	Faktorverzehr
Contribution	Beitrag
Contribution costing	Deckungsbeitragsrechnung
Contribution margin	Deckungsbeitrag

(continued)

Control	Steuerung
Control circuit	Regelkreis
Controllership	Controlling
Cooperation principle	Kooperationsprinzip
Cooperative	Genossenschaft
Coordination of rest periods	Ruhezeitenabstimmung
Coordination of rhythm	Rhythmenabstimmung
Coordination of timing	Taktabstimmung
Core business	Kerngeschäft
Corporate policy/strategy	Unternehmenspolitik, Unternehmungspolitik
Cost absorption capacity	Kostentragfähigkeit
Cost account(ing)	Kostenrechnung
Cost accounting system, costing system	Kostenrechnungssystem
Cost allocation	Kostenverrechnung
Cost apportionment to cost centres	Betriebsabrechnung
Cost carrying capacity	Kostentragfähigkeit
Cost centre	Kostenstelle
Cost centre accounting	Kostenstellenrechnung
Cost check/monitoring	Kostenkontrolle
Cost comparison calculation	Kostenvergleichsrechnung
Cost determinant	Kosteneinflussgröße
Cost effective kostengünstig	wirtschaftlich
Cost effectiveness analysis	Kostenwirksamkeitsanalyse
Cost efficiency	Kostenwirtschaftlichkeit
Costing	Kostenrechnung
Costing system	Kostenrechnungssystem
Cost leadership	Kostenführerschaft
Cost of materials	Materialaufwand
Cost of sales method	Umsatzkostenverfahren
Cost planning	Kostenplanung
Cost price accounting	Selbstkostenrechnung
Cost rate	Kostensatz
Cost saving	Kostenersparnis
Cost steering	Kostensteuerung
Cost stickiness	Kostenremanenz
Cost trend	Kostenverlauf
Cost type accounting Cost covering price	Kostenartenrechnung kostendeckender Preis
Cost types	Kostenarten
Cost unit	Kostenträger
Cost unit accounting	Kostenträgerrechnung
Cost unit period accounting	Kostenträgerzeitrechnung
Cost unit rate	Kostensatz

(continued)

Cost variance	Kostenabweichung
Cost-benefit analysis	Nutzen-Kosten-Analyse
Cost-effective	kostengünstig
Costing method	Kalkulationsverfahren
Costs of rendering	Erstellungskosten
Countability	Zählbarkeit
Course of coverage	Deckungsverlauf
Coverage ratio	Deckungsgrad
Coverage of individual needs	Eigenbedarfsdeckung
Coverage of needs of others	Fremdbedarfsdeckung
Craft business	Handwerksbetrieb
Creation of added value	Mehrwertschöpfung
Credit standing	Bonität
Credit standing investigation	Kreditwürdigkeitsprüfung
Credit transaction	Kreditvorgang
Creditor	Gläubiger
Criterion of identity	Auswahlkriterium
Cross-entry	Gegenbuchung
Cultural economics	Kulturökonomie
Cultural management	Kulturmanagement
Current assets	Umlaufvermögen
Customer	Kunde
Customer orientation	Kundenorientierung
Customer retention	Kundenbindung
Customer sourcing	Kundenakquisition
Damages incurred	Schadensverursachung
Damages prevented	Schadensverhinderung
Debt financing	Fremdfinanzierung
Debt capital	Fremdkapital
Debtor	Schuldner
Decision	Entscheidung
Decision making	Willensbildung
Deficit	Fehlbetrag
Defined goal/target	Zielvorgabe
Delivery	Lieferung
Deployment	Einsatz
Deployment of means	Mitteleinsatz
Deposits	Einlagen
Depreciation	Abschreibung
Design of work spaces	Raumgestaltung
Differential calculus	Differentialrechnung
Diligence	Sorgfalt
Dimension	Größenordnung
Direct costs	Einzelkosten
Discovery	Entdeckung

(continued)

Diseconomies (external)	Ungüter
Disposal rate	Entsorgungsquote
Dissolution (e.g. Of a partnership)	Auseinandersetzung
Distribution channel	Vertriebsweg
Distribution of profits	Gewinnausschüttung
Distribution of work	Arbeitsverteilung
Division of labour	Arbeitsteilung
Divisional organisation	Spartenorganisation
Domestic unit	Hauswirtschaft
Donation	Spende
Double-entry book keeping	doppelte kaufmännische Buchführung
Drifting costs	gängige Kosten
Driver	Treiber
Durables, durable goods	Gebrauchsgüter
During the fiscal year	unterjährig
Duty roster	Dienstplan
Earning capacity value	Ertragswert
Earning capacity value method	Ertragswertverfahren
Earning power	Ertragskraft
Earnings calculation	Erfolgsrechnung
Eco-efficiencyanalysis	Ökoeffizienzanalyse
Ecological book keeping	ökologische Buchhaltung
Economic	wirtschaftlich, kostengünstig
Economic constitution	Wirtschaftsverfassung
Economic efficiency	Wirtschaftlichkeit
Economic entity	Wirtschaftseinheit
Economic life	Nutzungsdauer
Economic pedagogics	Wirtschaftspädagogik
Economic power	Wirtschaftskraft
Economic sciences	Wirtschafswissenschaften
Economic subject	Wirtschaftssubjekt
Economic system	Wirtschaftssystem
Economic unit	Betriebswirtschaft, Einzelwirtschaft
Economically justifiable	wirtschaftlich vertretbar
Economics	Volkswirtschaftslehre
Economies of social care	Sozialökonomie
Economy of common interest	Gemeinwirtschaftlichkeit
Economy of needs	Bedarfswirtschaftlichkeit
Economy of returns	Erwerbswirtschaftlichkeit
Economy of self-interest	Eigenwirtschaftlichkeit
Education(al) economics	Bildungsökonomie
Educational management	Bildungsmanagement
Effect-impact statement	Wirkungsrechnung
Effective	effektiv, wirksam, zielbezogen, zielführend

(continued)

Effectiveness	Wirksamkeit
Efficiency	Zweckmäßigkeit
Efficiency analysis	Wirkungsanalyse
Efficient	effizient, zweckmäßig
Empiricism	Empirie
Employee	Arbeitnehmer
Employee pension scheme	betriebliche Altersversorgung
Employee	Mitarbeiter
Employer	Arbeitgeber
Employment	Beschäftigung
End costs	Endkosten
Ending balance	Endbestand
Endowment	Zustiftung
Energy balance	Energiebilanz
Enterprise	Unternehmen, Unternehmung
Entrepreneur	Unternehmer
Environment of a company	Unternehmensumfeld
Environmental accounting	umweltbezogenes Rechnungswesen
Environmental commodities	Umweltgüter
Environmental costs	Umweltkosten
Environmental economics	Umweltökonomie
Environmental expert	Umweltgutachter
Environmental liability	Umwelthaftung
Environmental management	Umweltmanagement
Environmental order	Umweltordnung
Environmental riskanalysis	Umweltrisikoanalyse
Environmental statement	Umwelterklärung
Equity	Eigenkapital
Equity financing	Eigenfinanzierung
Equivalence coefficient	Äquivalenzziffer
Equivalence coefficient calculation	Äquivalenzziffernrechnung
Evaluating science	wertende Wissenschaft
Evaluation of advertising effectiveness	Werbeerfolgskontrolle
Event pollution analysis	Eventbelastungsanalyse
Exchange value	Tauschwert
Executive	Führungskraft
Executive personnel	Führungskräfte
Expansion investment	Erweiterungsinvestition
Expenditure	Ausgabe
Expense	Aufwand, Aufwendung
Experienced reality	erfahrene Wirklichkeit
Explanation	Erklärung
External assets	externe Aktiva

(continued)

External benefits	externe Nutzen
External costs	externe Kosten
External financing	Außenfinanzierung
External liabilities	externe Passiva
External net benefit	externer Nettonutzen
External net damage	externer Nettoschaden
External trade	Außenhandel
Extraordinary expense	außerordentlicher Aufwand
Extraordinary income	außerordentlicher Ertrag
Factor cost	Faktorkosten
Factor input	Faktoreinsatz
Factor output	Faktorerlös
Factor requirements	Faktorbedarf
Feedback	Rückkopplung
Fictitious profit	Scheingewinn
Finalcost centre	Endkostenstelle
Final product	Endprodukt
Finance calculation	Finanzrechnung
Finance concept	Finanzkonzept
Finance requirement	Finanzbedarf
Financial accounting	Finanzbuchhaltung
Financial assets	Finanzvermögen
Financial assets	Geldvermögen
Financial coverage	Deckungsmittel
Financial equilibrium	finanzielles Gleichgewicht
Financial goal	Finanzziel
Financial planning	Finanzdisposition/-planung
Financial powers	Finanzkraft
Financial sphere	Finanzsphäre
Financier	Kapitalgeber
Financing	Finanzierung
Financing calculation	Finanzierungsrechnung
Financing rule	Finanzierungsregel
Firm	Unternehmen, Unternehmung
Fiscal charges	öffentliche Abgaben
Fixed assets	Anlagegüter/-vermögen, Sachanlagen
Fixed costs	Fixkosten
Flat fee	pauschales Entgelt
Flow balance sheet	Bewegungsbilanz
Flow of goods and services	Leistungsstrom
Flow production	Sortenfertigung
Flow unit	Stromgröße
Flow variable	Stromgröße
Forecast calculation	Prognoserechnung
Forecast costs	Plankosten

(continued)

Formal goal	Formalziel
Formation of goals/targets	Zielbildung
Formative relation	Gestaltungszusammenhang
Foundation	Stiftung
Foundation company	Stiftungsunternehmen
Founding investment	Gründungsinvestition
Free disposable means	freie Spitze
Free of charge	unentgeltlich
Freelance work	freiberufliche Tätigkeit
Fringe benefit	betriebliche Sozialleistung
Fulfilment of needs	Bedarfsdeckung
Full costing	Vollkostenrechnung
Functional research	Zweckforschung
Future valuemethod	Endwertmethode
Generalcost centre	Allgemeine Kostenstelle
General financial coverage	allgemeine Deckungsmittel
General knowledge	Allgemeinwissen
General meeting	Generalversammlung
General meeting	Hauptversammlung
General public	Allgemeinheit
German commercial code	Handelsgesetzbuch (HGB)
Goal	Ziel
Goal agreement	Zielvereinbarung
Goal ofcost coverage	Kostendeckungsziel
Goal relationship	Zielbeziehung
Goal setting	Zielsetzung
Goal concept	Zielkonzept
Goal orientation	Zielorientierung/-vorschrift
Goal system	Zielsystem
Going concern value	Teilwert
Governance	Steuerung
Governmental accounting	kameralistisches Rechnungswesen
Grant	Zuschuss
Gross assets	Bruttovermögen
Group structure	Konzernarchitektur
Groups policy	konzernpolitisch
Growth of wealth	Wohlstandsmehrung
Growth target	Wachstumsziel
Harmful effects	Belastungen
Health economics	Gesundheitsökonomie
Health safety	Gesundheitsschutz
Healthcare management	Gesundheitsmanagement
Hidden reserve	stille Reserve
Household	Haushalt(ung)
Human assets	Humanvermögen

(continued)

Human capital accounting	Humanvermögensrechnung
Human liabilities	Humanschulden
Human resource management	Personalführung/-steuerung/-wirtschaft
Human resource policy	Personalpolitik
Hypothesis	Hypothese
Ideal purpose	ideeller Zweck
Idle capacity costs	Leerkosten
Illness ratio	Krankenquote
Impact	Einwirkung
Impact research	Wirkungsforschung
Implication	Implikation
Imputed/implicit costs	kalkulatorische Kosten
Incentive	Leistungsanreiz
Incidentals, incidental costs	Nebenkosten
Income	Einkommen, Einkünfte, Ertrag
Income statement	Erfolgskonto/-rechnung
Increase in value	Wertzuwachs
Indexes	Indexzahlen
Indexing	Indexierung
Individual economy	Einzelwirtschaftlichkeit
Industrial espionage	Industriespionage
Inflows of liquid funds	Zahlungsmittelzugänge
Influencing factor	Einflussfaktor
Inheritance	Erbschaft
In-house goods and services	innerbetriebliche Leistungen
Initial costs	Gründungskosten
Initial investment	Anfangsinvestition
Initial product	Vorprodukt
Input	Einsatz, Faktoreinsatz
Inside of a company	Unternehmensinnere
Insolvency	Insolvenz
Inspection plan	Prüfplan
Institutional principle	Institutionalprinzip
Instrument of control	Lenkungsinstrument
Insurance	Versicherung
Intangible asset value	immaterielles Vermögenswert
Inter-company comparison	Betriebsvergleich
Interest	Verzinsung
Interest charges	Zinskosten
Interest on invested capital	Eigenkapitalzinsen
Interest rate	Zinsfuß
Interfirm comparison	zwischenbetrieblicher Vergleich
Interim product	Zwischenprodukt
Intermediate axiom	mittleres Axiom
Intermediate holding	Zwischenholding

(continued)

Intermediate input	Vorleistung
Internal audit	Innenrevision
Internal cost accounting	Betriebsbuchhaltung
Internal costs	betriebliche Kosten
Internal financing	Innenfinanzierung
Internal rate of returnmethod	interne Zinsfußmethode
Intrafirm comparison	innerbetrieblicher Vergleich
Inventory	Vorrat
Inventory management	Lagerhaltung
Investive wages	Investivlohn
Investment decision	Investitionsentscheidung
Investment monitoring activity	Investitionskontrolle
Investment planning activity	Investitionsplanung
Investment ratio	Investitionsquote
Job advertisement	Stellenausschreibung
Job formation	Stellenbildung
Job order costing	Zuschlagskalkulation
Job production	Einzelfertigung
Jobvaluation	Stellenbewertung
Joint product	Kuppelprodukt
Joint production	Kuppelproduktion
Joint production costing	Kuppelkalkulation
Joint-stock company	Kapitalgesellschaft
Junior management planning	Nachwuchsplanung
Knowledge	Kenntnis, Wissen
Land registry office	Grundbuchamt
Law suit	Gerichtsverfahren
Lawfulness	Rechtmäßigkeit
Leadership knowledge	Führungswissen
Leadership philosophy	Führungsphilosophie
Leadership policy	Führungspolitik
Leadership	Führung
Learning process	Lernprozess
Legal ban	gesetzliches Gebot
Legal form	Rechtsform
Legal imperative	gesetzliches Verbot
Level of activity	Beschäftigungsgrad
Level of familiarity	Bekanntheitsgrad
Level of performance	Leistungspotenzial
Leverage effect	Hebelwirkung
Liabilities	Schulden, Verbindlichkeiten
Liability reserves	Rückstellungen
Life cycle analysis	Lebensweganalyse/-zyklusanalyse
Lifespan	Laufzeit
Limited company	Gesellschaft mit beschränkter Haftung

(continued)

Line-and-staff system	Stabliniensystem
Liquid fund balance	Zahlungsmittelbestand
Liquidation value	Liquidationswert
Liquidity calculation	Liquiditätsrechnung
Liquidity plan	Liquiditätsplan
Liquidity planning	Liquiditätsplanung
Listed company/corporation	Börsenunternehmen
Local economy	örtliche Wirtschaft
Loss for the year	Jahresfehlbetrag
Lot size	Losgröße
Lower price limit	Preisuntergrenze
Maintenance investment	Erhaltungsinvestition
Management accounting	Unternehmensrechnung
Management	Führung
Management board	Vorstand
Management by instruction	Führung durch Weisung
Management competence	Führungskompetenz
Management development	Führungskräfteentwicklung, Personalentwicklung
Management goal	Führungsziel
Management of a company	Unternehmungsführung
Management of financial resources	Mittelbewirtschaftung
Management process	Führungsprozess
Management style	Führungsstil
Managementsupport	Führungsunterstützung
Management system	Führungssystem
Management unit	Instanz
Manager	Führungskraft
Manager-entrepreneur	Manager-Unternehmer
Managing an order	Auftragsführung
Manpower planning	Personaleinsatzplanung
Manufacturing	Fertigung
Manufacturing costs	Fertigungskosten
Manufacturing output	Ausbringungsmenge
Marginal costing	Teilkostenrechnung
Marginal costs	Grenzkosten
Marginal utility	Grenznutzen
Market economy	Marktwirtschaft
Market penetration	Marktdurchdringung
Market value	Marktwert
Marketing mix	Absatzmix
Matching of maturities	Fristenkongruenz
Materials	Werkstoffe
Materials balance	Stoffbilanz
Materials management	Lagerhaltung

(continued)

Mean value	Mittelwert
Means-end relationship	Zweck-Mittel-Beziehung
Measurement of operation	Wirkungserfassung
Membership fee	Mitgliedsbeitrag
Merchandise	Handelswaren
Merger	Verschmelzung
Metaeconomic	außerwirtschaftlich
Method of discovery	Entdeckungsmethode
Mission statement	Leitbild
Mode of thinking	Forschungsperspektive
Modelling	Modellbildung
Monetary capital	Geldkapital
Monetary holding	Geldbestand
Money-based economy	Geldwirtschaft
Monitoring, supervision	Überwachung
Motivation	Leistungsbereitschaft
Moving target	flexibles Ziel
Multiple-line system	Mehrliniensystem
Multiplicity of methods	Methodenvielfalt
Municipal enterprise	kommunales Unternehmen
Municipal special-purpose association	kommunaler Zweckverband
Mutual insurance association	Versicherungsverein auf Gegenseitigkeit
National accounting	volkswirtschaftliche Gesamtrechnung, volkswirtschaftliches Rechnungswesen
National balance sheet	volkswirtschaftliche Vermögensrechnung
National economy	Volkswirtschaft
Natural sciences	Naturwissenschaften
Nature assets	Naturvermögen
Nature liabilities	Naturschulden
Necessary business assets	betriebsnotwendiges Vermögen
Need	Bedarf, Bedürfnis
Needcreation	Bedarfsweckung
Needs control	Bedarfslenkung
Net asset value	Substanzwert
Net assets	Nettovermögen
Net damage	Nettoschaden
Net income of a given period	Periodenerfolg
Nichestrategy	Schwerpunktstrategie
Non-asset-effective	vermögensunwirksam
Non-competition obligation	Wettbewerbsverbot
Non-economic	nichtwirtschaftlich
Non-operating expense	betriebsfremder Aufwand, neutraler Aufwand
Non-operating income	betriebsfremder Ertrag, neutraler Ertrag
Non-operatingincome statement	neutrale Erfolgsrechnung

(continued)

Non-operational	außerbetrieblich
Non-profit organisation	Nonprofit-Organisation
Normal costing	Normalkostenrechnung
Notification	Mitteilung
Nursing home	Pflegeheim
Object of cognition	Erkenntnisobjekt
Object of experience	Erfahrungsgegenstand
Objective/purpose	Zweck
Office technology	Bürotechnik
One-off payment	einmalige Zahlung
Opening balance	Anfangsbestand
Operating benefit calculation	betriebliche Nutzenrechnung
Operating costs	betriebliche Kosten, Betriebskosten
Operating expense	Aufwandsausgabe, Betriebsaufwand, Zweckaufwand
Operating income	Betriebsertrag, Ertragseinnahme, Zweckertrag
Operatingincome statement	Betriebserfolgsrechnung
Operating life	Nutzungsdauer
Operating profit/loss	Betriebserfolg
Operating resources	Betriebsmittel
Operating result	Betriebsergebnis, Betriebserfolg
Operating statement	Betriebsergebnisrechnung
Operational	betrieblich
Operational indicator	Betriebsindikator
Operational planning	Fachplanung
Operational planning	Umsetzungsplanung
Operational sales	Umsatzprozess
Operative	operativ
Opportunity costs	Alternativ-/Opportunitätskosten
Optimum welfare	Wohlfahrtsoptimum
Order quantity	Bestellmenge
Order situation	Auftragslage
Organisational culture	Organisationskultur
Organisational structure	Aufbauorganisation
Outcome	Auswirkung
Outcome-impact-balance sheet	Wirkungsbestandsrechnung
Outcome-impact-result statement	Wirkungsergebnisrechnung
Outcome-impact statement	Wirkungsrechnung
Outflows of liquid funds	Zahlungsmittelabgänge
Outlay costs	Anderskosten
Outpayment	Auszahlung
Output check	Leistungskontrolle
Output concept	Leistungskonzept
Output costing	Divisionskalkulation
Output planning	Leistungsplanung

(continued)

Output steering	Leistungssteuerung
Output types	Leistungsarten
Output, performance	Leistung
Overall economy	Gesamtwirtschaft
Overhead allocation sheet	Betriebsabrechnungsbogen
Overhead costs	Gemeinkosten
Overhead-value analysis	Gemeinkostenwertanalyse
Overindebtedness	Überschuldung
Owner-entrepreneur	Eigentümer-Unternehmer
Ownership	Eigentum
Pair of concepts	Begriffspaar
Partial market entity	Teilmarktbetrieb
Partial target	Teilziel
Participation	Mitwirkung
Partnership	Personengesellschaft
Payback calculation	Amortisationsrechnung
Payment flow/stream	Zahlungsstrom
Payment-based	pagatorisch
Perception	Wahrnehmung
Performance appraisal	Leistungsbeurteilung
Performance bonus	Leistungszulage
Performance breakdown	Erfolgsspaltung
Performance capacity	Leistungsfähigkeit
Performance centre	Ergebniseinheit, Leistungszentrum
Performance control	Erfolgskontrolle
Performance goal	Leistungsziel
Performance sphere	Leistungssphäre
Performance split	Erfolgsspaltung
Period of validity	Geltungsdauer
Permanent assets	Anlagevermögen
Personnel development	Personalentwicklung
Personnel	Personal
Planned economy	Planwirtschaft
Planning	Planung
Planning calculation	Planungsrechnung
Policy goal	politisches Ziel
Policy of economic order	Ordnungspolitik
Policy of economic process	Prozesspolitik
Political-investment question	investitionspolitische Frage
Polluter principle	Verursacherprinzip
Pooling of work	Arbeitsvereinigung
Potential capabilities	Leistungspotenzial
Precaution	Vorsorge
Predicted costs	Plankosten
Prediction	Prognose

(continued)

Preliminarycost centre	Vorkostenstelle
Premise	Prämisse
Present value	Gegenwartswert
Preservation of assets	Substanzerhaltung
Preservation of capital	Kapitalerhaltung
Preservation target	Erhaltungsziel
Price-earnings ratio	Kurs-Gewinn-Verhältnis
Primary cost centre	Hauptkostenstelle
Primary effect	Hauptwirkung
Primary product	Hauptprodukt
Prime costs	Selbstkosten
Principal function	Hauptfunktion
Principle for action	Handlungsprinzip
Principle of aggregation	Aggregationsprinzip
Principle of alimentation	Alimentationsprinzip
Principle of common burden	Gemeinlastprinzip
Principle of competition	Konkurrenzprinzip
Principle of equivalence	Äquivalenzprinzip
Principle of maximum result	Maximalprinzip
Principle of minimum means	Minimalprinzip
Principle of rationality	Rationalprinzip
Principle of solidarity	Solidaritätsprinzip
Principle of value consistency	Prinzip der Wertgleichheit
Priority of financial goals	Geldzielpriorität
Priority of substantive goal	Sachzielpriorität
Procedural financing	Prozessfinanzierung
Process analysis	Verfahrensanalyse
Process comparison	Verfahrensvergleich
Process costs	Prozesskosten
Process organisation	Ablauforganisation
Process statement	Prozessbilanz
Process steering	Prozesssteuerung
Process synthesis	Verfahrenssynthese
Procurement	Beschaffung
Product development	Produktentwicklung
Product differentiation	Produktdifferenzierung
Product line analysis	Produktlinienanalyse
Product price	Leistungspreis
Product price	Produktpreis
Production cost	Herstellungskosten
Production costs	Herstellkosten
Production lot	Fertigungslos
Production materials	Produktionsmittel
Production process	Produktionsverfahren
Profit and loss account	Erfolgskonto

(continued)

Profit and loss planning	Erfolgsplan
Profit and loss statement	Gewinn- und Verlustrechnung
Profit centre	Ergebniseinheit, Profitcenter
Profit comparison calculation	Gewinnvergleichsrechnung
Profit margin	Gewinnspanne
Profit orientation	Gewinnstreben
Profitability	Rendite
Profitability	Rentabilität
Profitability calculation	Rentabilitätsrechnung
Profitable	rentabel
Profit-earning	erwerbswirtschaftlich
Property rights	Eigentumsrecht
Provision	Vorhaltung
Provisions	Rückstellungen
Provision of benefits	Nutzenstiftung
Public charges	öffentliche Abgaben
Public economy	öffentliche Wirtschaft
Public fees	Gebühren
Public needs	Allgemeinbedarf
Public sector economics	Finanzwissenschaft
Public task	öffentliche Aufgabe
Purchase	Kauf
Purchase cost	Anschaffungskosten
Purchase invoice	Einkaufsrechnung
Purchase price	Anschaffungspreis
Purchasing power	Kaufkraft
Pure science	reine Wissenschaft
Purposeful	effizient, zweckmäßig
Purveyor	Lieferant, Zulieferer
Quantity structure	Mengengerüst
Quotation price	Angebotspreis
Range of products and/or services offered	Leistungsangebot
Ranking	Rangfolge
Ratio analysis	Kennzahlenanalyse
Ratio calculation	Kennzahlenrechnung
Raw materials and supplies	Roh-, Hilfs- und Betriebsstoffe
Reason	Begründung
Receipt of payment	Einzahlung
Receivable	Forderung
Recurring payments	laufende Zahlungen
Redemption	Rückzahlung
Regional economy	Regionalwirtschaft
Regularity	Gesetzmäßigkeit, Regelmäßigkeit
Relation figure	Beziehungszahl

(continued)

Relief from harmful effects	Entlastungen
Remuneration	Bezahlung
Rendering of services	Dienstleistungserstellung
Renewal investment	Erneuerungsinvestition
Rent	Miete
Replacement cost value	Reproduktionswert
Replacement investment	Ersatzinvestition
Replacement value	Ersatzgröße
Reserve (fund)	Rücklage
Residential home for the elderly	Altenheim
Residual value	Restwert
Resource conservation	Ressourcenschonung
Responsibility	Verantwortung
Restructuring	Sanierung
Result of ordinary business activity	Ergebnis der gewöhnlichen Geschäftstätigkeit
Result statement	Ergebnisrechnung
Retained earnings, retained income	Gewinnrücklage
Retained profit	einbehaltener Gewinn
Return	Verzinsung
Return on equity	Eigenkapitalrendite
Return on investment	Kapitalrentabilität
Return on sales	Umsatzrendite, -rentabilität
Revenue	Einnahme, Erlös
Reward	Belohnung
Sale	Verkauf
Sales	Umsatz, Umsatzerlöse
Sales invoice	Verkaufsrechnung
Sales market	Absatzmarkt
Sales region	Absatzregion
Sales revenues	Umsatz, Umsatzerlöse
Salesperson	Verkäufer
Sampling analysis	Stichprobenanalyse
Scale of plant/operation	Betriebsgröße
Scarcity	Knappheit
Schedule of responsibilities	Geschäftsverteilungsplan
Scheduled costs	Plankosten
Scientific doctrine	wissenschaftliche Lehre
Scope of business	Betriebszweck
Search for the truth	Wahrheitssuche
Secondary business	Nebengeschäft
Secondarycost centre	Nebenkostenstelle
Secondary effect	Nebenwirkung
Securities	Wertpapiere

(continued)

Self-financing	Selbstfinanzierung
Self-fulfilment	Selbstentfaltung
Self-realisation	Selbstgestaltung/-verwirklichung
Self-realisation	Selbstverwirklichung
Senior staff	Führungskräfte
Servicecost centre	Hilfskostenstelle
Service life	Nutzungsdauer
Set of accounting figures	Rechnungsstoff
Set-up costs	Rüstkosten
Shadow price	Schattenpreis
Share capital	Grundkapital, Stammkapital
Shareholder	Gesellschafter
Shortage of resources	Güterknappheit
Sight funds	Sichtguthaben
Single product firm	Einproduktbetrieb
Single-line system	Einliniensystem
Size of order	Auftragsgröße
Skilled labour/personnel	Fachkräfte
Skilled worker/specialist	Fachkraft
Social accounting	gesellschaftsbezogenes Rechnungswesen
Social adjustment	sozialer Ausgleich
Social balance sheet	Sozialbilanz
Social benefit	Allgemeinnutzen
Social contribution	Sozialleistung
Social economic enterprise	gemeinwirtschaftliches Unternehmen
Social economy	Gemeinwirtschaft
Social insurance	Sozialversicherung
Social management	Sozialmanagement
Social order	Sozialordnung
Social sciences	Sozialwissenschaften
Social state principle	Sozialstaatsprinzip
Sole proprietorship	Einzelfirma
Sources of funds	Mittelherkunft
Span of control	Leitungsspanne
Special direct costs	Sondereinzelkosten
Specialised knowledge	Fachwissen
Special-purpose balance sheet	Sonderbilanz
Spokesman	Sprecher
Sports association	Sportverein
Staff	Personal
Staff turnover rate	Fluktuationsrate
Stakeholder	Anspruchsgruppe
Standard costing	Plankostenrechnung
Standard costs	Plankosten
Start-up loss	Anlaufverlust

(continued)

State duties	staatliche Aufgaben
Statement of assets	Bestandsrechnung
Statement of flows	Stromrechnung
State-owned enterprise	staatliches Unternehmen
Stock account	Bestandsrechnung
Stock on hand	Warenbestand
Stock size	Bestandsgröße
Stocktaking	Inventur
Storage costs	Lagerkosten
Striving for the common welfare	Gemeinwohlstreben
Structural financing	Strukturfinanzierung
Structural policy	Strukturpolitik
Style of thought	Denkstil
Subgroup	Teilkonzern
Subordinated work	nichtselbständige Arbeit
Subscribed capital	gezeichnetes Kapital
Subsidiary	Tochtergesellschaft
Subsidised operation	Zuschussbetrieb
Subsidy	Beihilfe, Subvention
Subsistence economy	Bedarfswirtschaft
Substantive goal	Sachziel
Sub-unit	Teileinheit
Superior target	Oberziel
Supervisory board	Aufsichtsrat
Supplier	Lieferant, Zulieferer
Supplementary costs	Zusatzkosten
Supplementary investment	Ergänzungsinvestition
Supranational economy	Großraumwirtschaft
Surplus	Überschuss
System of direct power	Weisungssystem
Tangible asset	Sachwert
Tangible asset liability	Sachverbindlichkeit
Tangible asset receivable	Sachforderung
Tangible assets	Sachvermögen
Tangible goods	Sachgüter
Tangible assets	Sachanlagen
Target	Ziel
Target capacity	Soll-Kapazität
Target concept	Zielkonzept
Target costing	Zielkostenrechnung
Target costs	Soll-Kosten, Zielkosten
Target orientation	Zielorientierung/-vorschrift
Target output	Soll-Leistung
Target-performance relation	Soll-Ist-Relation

(continued)

Target price	Zielpreis
Target range	Zielkorridor
Target setting	Zielsetzung
Target system	Zielsystem
Target value	Zielgröße
Task	Aufgabe
Task analysis	Aufgabenanalyse
Task assignment	Aufgabenstellung
Task fulfilment	Aufgabenerfüllung
Task synthesis	Aufgabensynthese
Tax adviser/consultant	Steuerberater
Tax audit	Betriebsprüfung, Steuerprüfung
Tax balance sheet	Steuerbilanz
Taxation	Besteuerung
Territorial public institution	Gebietskörperschaft
Theory of public finance	Finanzwissenschaft
Theory of utility	Nutzentheorie
Thought process	Denkprozess
Time of retrieval	Wiedergewinnungszeit
Timeline	Zeitachse
Time-series analysis	Zeitreihenanalyse
Total cost method	Gesamtkostenverfahren
Total costs	Gesamtkosten
Total operating performance	Gesamtleistung
Total revenue	Gesamtumsatz/-erlös
Trade goods, commodities	Waren
Trading company	Handelsgesellschaft
Transfer costs	Umlagekosten
Transferability	Übertragbarkeit
Truthfulness	Wahrheitsgehalt
Turnover	Umsatz, Umsatzerlöse
Type of transfer pricing	Verrechnungsart
Uneconomic	unwirtschaftlich
Uniformsystem of accounts	Kontenrahmen
Union	Gewerkschaft
Unit costs	Stückkosten
Unit-of-output costing	Kostenträgerstückrechnung
Unit-of-output profit statement	Stückergebnisrechnung
Unused capacity	Kapazitätsreserve
Usability	Brauchbarkeit
Usage	Usance
Usage right	Nutzungsrecht
Use of goods	Verwendungszweck
Use of resources	Mittelverwendung
Used capacity costs	Nutzkosten
Utilisation fee	Benutzungsgebühr

(continued)

Utility value	Nutzwert
Utility-value analysis	Nutzwertanalyse
Validity relation	Geltungszusammenhang
Valuation	Wertansatz
Value added calculation	Wertschöpfungsrechnung
Value adding process	Wertschöpfungsprozess
Value chain analysis	Wertkettenanalyse
Value consistency	Wertgleichheit
Value dimension	Wertdimension
Value for money	Preis-Leistungs-Verhältnis
Value-free science	wertfreie Wissenschaft
Variance in capacity utilisation	Beschäftigungsabweichung
Veil of money	Geldschleier
Venture	Wagnis
Verifiability	Prüfbarkeit
Verification	Prüfung
Vertical integration	Fertigungstiefe
Warehousing	Lagerhaltung
Waste disposal security	Entsorgungssicherheit
Waste rate	Abfallquote
Weak-point analysis	Schwachstellenanalyse
Wealth	Wohlstand
Welfare	Wohlfahrt
What if relation	Wenn-dann-Beziehung
Whole group	Gesamtkonzern
Willingness to learn	Lernbereitschaft
Work plan	Arbeitsplan
Work safety	Arbeitsschutz
Work target	Arbeitsziel
Working out a budget	Budgeterstellung, Budgetierung
World economy	Weltwirtschaft
Write-up	Zuschreibung
Writing-back of provisions	Auflösung von Rückstellungen
Year-end audit	Jahresabschlussprüfung
Yield	Ergiebigkeit
Yield from contributions/ premiums	Beitragsaufkommen

Glossary German—English

Abfallquote	Waste rate
Ablauforganisation	Process organisation
Abnehmer/Käufer	Buyer, purchaser
Absatz-/Konsumentenrente	Consumers' surplus
Absatzmarkt	Sales market
Absatzmix	Marketing mix
Absatzregion	Sales region
Abschlussprüfer	Annual auditor
Abschreibung	Depreciation
Aggregationsprinzip	Principle of aggregation
aktivierbare Eigenleistungen	Capitalisable company-produced outputs
Alimentationsprinzip	Principle of alimentation
allgemeine Deckungsmittel	General financial coverage
Allgemeine Kostenstelle	Generalcost centre
Allgemeinbedarf	Public needs
Allgemeinheit	General public
Allgemeinnutzen	Social benefit
Allgemeinwissen	General knowledge
Altenheim	Residential home for the elderly
Alternativ-/Opportunitätskosten	Opportunity costs
Amortisationsrechnung	Payback calculation
Anderskosten	Outlay costs
Anfangsbestand	Opening balance
Anfangsinvestition	Initial investment
Angebotspreis	Asking price, quotation price
angewandte Wissenschaft	Applied science
Anlagegüter	Fixed assets
Anlagenintensität	Capitalisation ratio
Anlagevermögen	Fixed assets, permanent assets
Anlaufverlust	Start-up loss
Annahme	Assumption
Annuitätenmethode	Annuity method

(continued)

© Springer International Publishing AG 2018

P. Eichhorn, I. Towers, *Principles of Management*, Springer Texts in Business and Economics, https://doi.org/10.1007/978-3-319-70902-4

Anschaffungskosten	Purchase cost
Anschaffungspreis	Purchase price
Anspruchsgruppe	Stakeholder
Äquivalenzprinzip	Principle of equivalence
Äquivalenzziffer	Equivalence coefficient
Äquivalenzziffernrechnung	Equivalence coefficient calculation
Arbeitgeber	Employer
Arbeitnehmer	Employee
Arbeitsbesetzung	Allocation of work
Arbeitsplan	Work plan
Arbeitsschutz	Work safety
Arbeitsteilung	Division of labour
Arbeitsvereinigung	Pooling of work
Arbeitsverteilung	Distribution of work
Arbeitsziel	Work target
Aufbauorganisation	Organisational structure
Aufgabe	Task
Aufgabenanalyse	Task analysis
Aufgabenerfüllung	Task fulfilment
Aufgabenstellung	Task assignment
Aufgabensynthese	Task synthesis
Auflösung von Rückstellungen	Writing-back of provisions
Aufsichtsrat	Supervisory board
Auftragsführung	Managing an order
Auftragsgröße	Size of order
Auftragslage	Order situation
Aufwand, Aufwendung	Expense
Aufwandsausgabe	Operating expense
Ausbringungsmenge	Manufacturing output
Auseinandersetzung	Dissolution (e.g. of a partnership)
Ausgabe	Expenditure
Aussage	Assertion
Außenfinanzierung	Externalfinancing
Außenhandel	External trade
außerbetrieblich	Non-operational
außerordentlicher Aufwand	Extraordinary expense
außerordentlicher Ertrag	Extraordinary income
außerwirtschaftlich	Metaeconomic
Auswahlkriterium	Criterion of identity
Auswirkung	Outcome
Auszahlung	Outpayment
Bankguthaben	Bank deposit
Bargeld	Cash
Barwert	Cash value
Basisforschung	Basic research

(continued)

Bauamt	Building authority
Bedarf, Bedürfnis	Need
Bedarfsdeckung	Fulfilment of needs
Bedarfslenkung	Needs control
Bedarfsweckung	Needcreation
Bedarfswirtschaft	Subsistence economy
Bedarfswirtschaftlichkeit	Economy of needs
Begriffspaar	Pair of concepts
Begründung	Reason
Beihilfe	Subsidy
Beitrag	Contribution
Beitragsaufkommen	Yield from contributions/premiums
Bekanntheitsgrad	Level of familiarity
Belastungen	Harmful effects
Belohnung	Reward
Belohnung	Compensation
Benutzungsgebühr	Utilisation fee
Beschaffung	Procurement
Beschaffungsrente	Buyers' surplus
Beschäftigung	Employment
Beschäftigungsabweichung	Variance in capacity utilisation
Beschäftigungsgrad	Capacity utilisation rate, level of activity
Bestandsaufnahme	Assessment of current position/situation, audit
Bestandsgröße	Stock size
Bestandskonto	Asset account
Bestandsrechnung	Balance sheet, stock account, statement of assets
Bestätigungsvermerk	Audit, auditors' certificate
Bestellmenge	Order quantity
Besteuerung	Taxation
betrieblich	Operational
betriebliche Altersversorgung	Employee pension scheme
betriebliche Kosten	Internal costs, operating costs
betriebliche Nutzenrechnung	Operating benefit calculation
betriebliche Sozialleistung	Fringe benefit
betriebliches Rechnungswesen	Business accounting
Betriebsprüfung	Tax audit
Betriebsaufwand	Operating expense
Betriebsertrag	Operating income
Betriebsabrechnung	Cost apportionment to cost centres
Betriebsabrechnungsbogen	Overhead allocation sheet
Betriebsaufwand	Operating expense
Betriebsbuchhaltung	Internal cost accounting
Betriebserfolg	Operating result, operating profit/loss
Betriebserfolgsrechnung	Operatingincome statement
Betriebsergebnis	Operating result

(continued)

Betriebsergebnisrechnung	Operating statement
Betriebsertrag	Operating income
betriebsfremder Aufwand	Non-operating expense
betriebsfremder Ertrag	Non-operatingincome
Betriebsgröße	Scale of plant/operation
Betriebsindikator	Operational indicator
Betriebsmittel	Operating resources
betriebsnotwendiges Vermögen	Necessary business assets
Betriebsprüfung	Tax audit
Betriebsvergleich	Inter-company comparison
Betriebswirtschaft	Economic unit
Betriebswirtschaftslehre	Business administration
Betriebswirtschaftspolitik	Business management policy
Betriebszweck	Scope of business
Bewegungsbilanz	Flow balance sheet
Bezahlung	Remuneration
Beziehungszahl	Relation figure
Bilanz	Balance sheet
Bilanzgewinn	Balance sheet profit
Bilanzstichtag	Balance sheet date
Bilanzverlust	Balance sheet loss
Bildungsmanagement	Educational management
Bildungsökonomie	Education(al) economics
Bindungsdauer	Commitment period
Bonität	Credit standing
Börsenunternehmen	Listed company/corporation
Brauchbarkeit	Usability
Bruttovermögen	Gross assets
Buchgeld	Book money
Buchhaltung	Bookkeeping
Buchwert	Book value
Budgeterstellung, Budgetierung	Working out a budget/budgeting
Budgetvollzug	Budget implementation
Bürokratiehemmnis	Bureaucratic restraint
Bürotechnik	Office technology
Controlling	Controllership
Deckungsbeitrag	Contribution margin
Deckungsbeitragsrechnung	Contribution costing
Deckungserfordernis	Budgetary requirement
Deckungsgrad	Coverage ratio
Deckungsmittel	Financial coverage
Deckungsverlauf	Course of coverage
Denkprozess	Thought process
Denkstil	Style of thought
Dienstleistungserstellung	Rendering of services

(continued)

Dienstplan	Duty roster
Differentialrechnung	Differential calculus
Divisionskalkulation	Output costing
doppelte kaufmännische Buchführung	Double-entry book-keeping
effektiv	Effective
effizient	Efficient, purposeful
Eigenbedarfsdeckung	Coverage of individual needs
Eigenfinanzierung	Equityfinancing
Eigenkapital	Equity
Eigenkapitalrendite	Return on equity
Eigenkapitalzinsen	Interest on invested capital
Eigentümer-Unternehmer	Owner-entrepreneur
Eigenwirtschaftlichkeit	Economy of self-interest
Eigentum	Ownership
Eigentumsrecht	Property rights
einbehaltener Gewinn	Retained profit
Einflussfaktor	Influencing factor
Einkauf	Buying, purchasing
Einkaufsrechnung	Purchase invoice
Einkommen	Income
Einkünfte	Income
Einlagen	Deposits
Einliniensystem	Single-line system
einmalige Zahlung	One-off payment
Einnahme	Revenue
Einproduktbetrieb	Single product firm
Einsatz	Deployment, input
Einwirkung	Impact
Einzahlung	Receipt of payment
Einzelfertigung	Job production
Einzelfirma	Sole proprietorship
Einzelkosten	Direct costs
Einzelwirtschaft	Economic unit
Einzelwirtschaftlichkeit	Individual economy
Einzugsgebiet	Catchment area
eiserner Bestand	Base stock inventory
Empirie	Empiricism
Endbestand	Ending balance
Endprodukt	Final product
Endkosten	End costs
Endkostenstelle	Finalcost centre
Endwertmethode	Future valuemethod
Energiebilanz	Energy balance
Entdeckung	Discovery
Entdeckungsmethode	Method of discovery

(continued)

Entlastungen	Relief from harmful effects
Entscheidung	Decision
Entsorgungsquote	Disposal rate
Entsorgungssicherheit	Waste disposal security
Erbschaft	Inheritance
erfahrene Wirklichkeit	Experienced reality
Erfahrungsgegenstand	Object of experience
Erfolgskonto	Income statement, profit and loss account
Erfolgskontrolle	Performance control
Erfolgsplan	Profit and loss planning
Erfolgsrechnung	Income statement, earnings calculation
Erfolgsspaltung	Breakdown, performance split
Ergänzungsinvestition	Supplementary investment
Ergebnis der gewöhnlichen Geschäftstätigkeit	Result of ordinary business activity
Ergebniseinheit	Performance/profit centre
Ergebnisrechnung	Result statement
Ergiebigkeit	Yield
Erhaltungsinvestition	Maintenance investment
Erhaltungsziel	Preservation target
Erkenntnisfortschritt	Cognitive process
Erkenntnisinteresse	Cognitive interest
Erkenntnismethode	Cognitive method
Erkenntnisobjekt	Object of cognition
Erklärung	Explanation
erlaubte/zugebilligte Kosten	Allowable costs
Erlös	Revenue
Erneuerungsinvestition	Renewal investment
Ersatzgröße	Replacement value
Ersatzinvestition	Replacement investment
Erstellungskosten	Costs of rendering
Ertrag	Income
Ertragseinnahme	Operating income
Ertragskraft	Earning power
Ertragswert	Earning capacity value
Ertragswertverfahren	Earning capacity value method
Erweiterungsinvestition	Expansion investment
erwerbswirtschaftlich	Profit-earning
Erwerbswirtschaftlichkeit	Economy of returns
Eventbelastungsanalyse	Event pollution analysis
externe Aktiva	External assets
externe Kosten	External costs
externe Nutzen	External benefits
externe Passiva	External liabilities
externer Nettonutzen	External net benefit

(continued)

externer Nettoschaden	External net damage
Fachkraft	Skilled worker/specialist
Fachkräfte	Skilled labour/personnel
Fachplanung	Operational planning
Fachwissen	Specialised knowledge
Faktorbedarf	Factor requirements
Faktoreinsatz	Factor input
Faktorerlös	Factor output
Faktorkosten	Factor cost
Faktorverzehr	Consumption of resources
Fehlbetrag	Deficit
Fertigung	Manufacturing
Fertigungskosten	Manufacturing costs
Fertigungslos	Production lot
Fertigungstiefe	Vertical integration
Finanzanalyse	Analysis of ends
Finanzbedarf	Finance requirement
Finanzbuchhaltung	Financial accounting
Finanzdisposition/-planung	Financial planning
finanzielles Gleichgewicht	Financial equilibrium
Finanzierung	Financing
Finanzierungsrechnung	Financing calculation
Finanzierungsregel	Financing rule
Finanzkonzept	Finance concept
Finanzkraft	Financial powers
Finanzrechnung	Finance calculation
Finanzsphäre	Financial sphere
Finanzvermögen	Financial assets
Finanzwissenschaft	Theory of public finance, public sector economics
Finanzziel	Financial goal
Fixkosten	Fixed costs
flexibles Ziel	Moving target
Fluktuationsrate	Staff turnover rate
Forderung	Receivable
Formalziel	Formal goal
Forschungsperspektive	Mode of thinking
freiberufliche Tätigkeit	Freelance work
freie Spitze	Free disposable means
Fremdbedarfsdeckung	Coverage of needs of others
Fremdfinanzierung	Debt financing
Fremdkapital	Debt capital
Fristenkongruenz	Matching of maturities
Führung	Leadership/management
Führung durch Weisung	Management by instruction
Führungskompetenz	Management competence

(continued)

Führungskraft	Executive, manager
Führungskräfte	Executive personnel, senior staff
Führungskräfteentwicklung	Management development
Führungsphilosophie	Leadership philosophy
Führungspolitik	Leadership policy
Führungsprozess	Management process
Führungsstil	Management style
Führungssystem	Management system
Führungsunterstützung	Managementsupport
Führungswissen	Leadership knowledge
Führungsziel	Management goal
gängige Kosten	Drifting costs
Gebietskörperschaft	Territorial public institution
Gebrauchsgüter	Durables, durable goods
Gebühren	Public fees, charges
Gegenbuchung	Cross-entry
Gegenleistung	Consideration, counter-performance
Gegenwartswert	Present value
Geldbestand	Monetary holding
Geldkapital	Monetary capital
Geldschleier	Veil of money
Geldvermögen	Financial assets
Geldwirtschaft	Money-based economy
Geldzielpriorität	Priority of financial goals
Geltungsdauer	Period of validity
Geltungszusammenhang	Validity relation
Gemeinkosten	Overhead costs
Gemeinkostenwertanalyse	Overhead-value analysis
Gemeinlastprinzip	Principle of common burden
Gemeinschulden	Common liabilities
Gemeinvermögen	Common assets
Gemeinwirtschaft	Social economy
gemeinwirtschaftliches Unternehmen	Social economic enterprise
Gemeinwirtschaftlichkeit	Economy of common interest
Gemeinwohl	Common/public welfare
Gemeinwohlstreben	Striving for the common welfare
Genehmigungsverfahren	Approval procedure
Generalversammlung	General meeting
Genossenschaft	Cooperative
Gerichtsverfahren	Law suit
Gesamtkonzern	Whole group
Gesamtkosten	Total costs
Gesamtkostenverfahren	Total cost method
Gesamtleistung	Total operating performance
Gesamtumsatz, -erlös	Total revenue

(continued)

Gesamtwirtschaft	Overall economy
Gesamtwirtschaftlichkeit	Aggregate economy
Geschäftsverteilungsplan	Schedule of responsibilities
Gesellschafter	Shareholder
Gesellschaft mit beschränkter Haftung	Limited company
gesellschaftsbezogenes Rechnungswesen	Social accounting
gesetzliches Gebot	Legal ban
gesetzliches Verbot	Legal imperative
Gesetzmäßigkeit	Regularity, rule
Gestaltungszusammenhang	Formative relation
Gesundheitsmanagement	Healthcare management
Gesundheitsökonomie	Health economics
Gesundheitsschutz	Health safety
Gewerkschaft	Union
Gewinn- und Verlustrechnung	Profit and loss statement
Gewinnausschüttung	Distribution of profits
Gewinnrücklage	Retained earnings/income
Gewinnschwellenrechnung	Break-even calculation
Gewinnspanne	Profit margin
Gewinnstreben	Profit orientation
Gewinnvergleichsrechnung	Profit comparison calculation
gewissenhaft	Conscientious
gezeichnetes Kapital	Subscribed capital
Gläubiger	Creditor
Gliederungszahl	Classification figure
Grenzkosten	Marginal costs
Grenznutzen	Marginal utility
Größenordnung	Dimension
Großraumwirtschaft	Supranational economy
Gründungskosten	Initial costs
Grundbuchamt	Land registry office
Grundkosten	Basic costs
Grundleistungen	Basic outputs
Gründungsinvestition	Founding investment
Grundkapital	Share capital
Güter	Commodities
Güterknappheit	Shortage of resources
Handelsbilanz	Commercial balance sheet
Handelsgesellschaft	Trading company
Handelsgesetzbuch (HGB)	German commercial code
Handelsrecht	Commercial law
Handelswaren	Merchandise
Handlungsprinzip	Principle for action
Handwerksbetrieb	Craft business
Hauptfunktion	Principal function

(continued)

Hauptkostenstelle	Primarycost centre
Hauptprodukt	Primary product
Hauptversammlung	General meeting
Hauptwirkung	Primary effect
Haushalt(ung)	Household
Hauswirtschaft	Domestic unit
Hebelwirkung	Leverage effect
Herstellkosten	Production costs
Herstellungskosten	Production cost
Hilfskostenstelle	Service cost centre
Humanschulden	Human liabilities
Humanvermögen	Human assets
Humanvermögensrechnung	Human capital accounting
Hypothese	Hypothesis
ideeller Zweck	Ideal purpose
immaterielles Vermögenswert	Intangible asset value
Implikation	Implication
Indexierung	Indexing
Indexzahlen	Indexes
Industriespionage	Industrial espionage
Innenfinanzierung	Internal financing
Innenrevision	Internal audit
innerbetriebliche Leistungen	In-house goods and services
innerbetrieblicher Vergleich	Intrafirm comparison
Insolvenz	Insolvency
Instanz	Management unit
Institutionalprinzip	Institutional principle
interne Zinsfußmethode	Internal rate of returnmethod
Inventur	Stocktaking
Investitionsentscheidung	Investment decision
Investitionsgut	Capital good
Investitionskontrolle	Investment monitoring activity
Investitionsplanung	Investment planning activity
investitionspolitische Frage	Political-investment question
Investitionsquote	Investment ratio
Investitionsrechnung	Capital budgeting
Investivlohn	Investive wages
Ist-Kapazität	Actual capacity
Ist-Kosten	Actual costs
Istkostenrechnung	Actual costing
Ist-Leistung	Actual output
Jahresabschluss	Annual financial statement
Jahresabschlussprüfung	Year-end audit
Jahresfehlbetrag	Loss for the year
Jahresüberschuss	Annual profit

(continued)

Kalkulationsverfahren	Costing method
kalkulatorische Kosten	Imputed/implicit costs
kameralistisches Rechnungswesen	Cameralistic/governmental accounting
Kapazitätsauslastung	Capacity utilisation
Kapazitätsreserve	Unused capacity
Kapitalbedarf	Capital needs/requirements
Kapitalbedarfsrechnung	Capital requirements calculation
Kapitaldeckung	Capital coverage
Kapitalerhaltung	Preservation of capital
Kapitalflussrechnung	Capital-flow statement
Kapitalfristigkeit	Capital maturity
Kapitalgeber	Capital provider/financier/investor
Kapitalgesellschaft	Joint-stock company
Kapitalnehmer	Capital acquirer/seeker
Kapitalrentabilität	Return on investment
Kapitalrücklage	Capital reserve
Kapitalumschlag	Asset/capital turnover
Kapitalvermögen	Capital assets
Kapitalwert	Capital value
Kapitalwertmethode	Capital value method
Karriereplanung	Career planning
Kassenbestand	Cash on hand
Kauf	Purchase
Kaufkraft	Purchasing power
kaufmännisches Rechnungswesen	Commercial accounting
Kausalanalyse	Causal analysis
Kausalnexus	Causal relationships
Kenntnis	Knowledge
Kennzahlenanalyse	Ratio analysis
Kennzahlenrechnung	Ratio calculation
Kerngeschäft	Core business
Knappheit	Scarcity
kommunaler Zweckverband	Municipal special-purpose association
kommunales Unternehmen	Municipal enterprise
Konkurrenzprinzip	Principle of competition
Konsum	Consumption
Kontenplan	Chart of accounts
Kontenrahmen	Uniformsystem of accounts
Konto	Account
Kontrolle	Check
Konzernarchitektur	Group structure
konzernpolitisch	Groups policy
Kooperationsprinzip	Cooperation principle
Kostenabweichung	Cost variance
Kostenarten	Cost types

(continued)

Kostenartenrechnung	Cost type accounting
kostendeckender Preis	Cost covering price
Kostendeckungsziel	Goal ofcost coverage
Kosteneinflussgröße	Cost determinant
Kostenersparnis	Cost saving
Kostenführerschaft	Cost leadership
kostengünstig	Cost-effective, economic
Kostenkontrolle	Cost check/monitoring
Kostenplanung	Cost planning
Kostenrechnung	Cost account/accounting, costing
Kostenrechnungssystem	Cost accounting system, costing system
Kostenremanenz	Cost stickiness
Kostensatz	Cost rate, cost unit rate
Kostenstelle	Cost centre
Kostenstellenrechnung	Cost centre accounting
Kostensteuerung	Cost steering
Kostenträger	Cost unit
Kostenträgerrechnung	Cost unit accounting
Kostenträgerstückrechnung	Unit-of-output costing
Kostenträgerzeitrechnung	Cost unit period accounting
Kostentragfähigkeit	Cost absorptioncapacity, cost carrying capacity
Kostenvergleichsrechnung	Cost comparison calculation
Kostenverlauf	Cost trend
Kostenverrechnung	Cost allocation
Kostenwirksamkeitsanalyse	Cost effectiveness analysis
Kostenwirtschaftlichkeit	Cost efficiency
Krankenquote	Illness rate
Kreditvorgang	Credit transaction
Kreditwürdigkeitsprüfung	Credit standing investigation
Kreislaufwirtschaft	Circular economy
Kulturmanagement	Cultural management
Kulturökonomie	Cultural economics
Kunde	Customer
Kundenakquisition	Customer sourcing
Kundenbindung	Customer retention
Kundenorientierung	Customer orientation
Kuppelkalkulation	Joint production costing
Kuppelprodukt	Joint product
Kuppelproduktion	Joint production
Kurs-Gewinn-Verhältnis	Price-earnings ratio
Lagerhaltung	Inventory/materials management, warehousing
Lagerkosten	Storage costs
laufende Zahlungen	Recurring payments
Laufzeit	Lifespan
Lebensweganalyse	Life cycle analysis

(continued)

Lebenszyklusanalyse	Life cycle analysis
Leerkosten	Idle capacity costs
Leistung	Output, performance
Leistungsangebot	Range of products and/or services offered
Leistungsanreiz	Incentive
Leistungsarten	Output types
Leistungsbereitschaft	Motivation
Leistungsbeurteilung	Performance appraisal
Leistungsfähigkeit	Performance capacity
Leistungskontrolle	Output check
Leistungskonzept	Output concept
Leistungsplanung	Output planning
Leistungspotenzial	Potential capabilities, level of performance
Leistungspreis	Product price
Leistungssphäre	Performance sphere
Leistungssteuerung	Output steering
Leistungsstrom	Flow of goods and services
Leistungszentrum	Performance centre
Leistungsziel	Performance goal
Leistungszulage	Performance bonus
Leitbild	Mission statement
Leitungsspanne	Span of control
Lenkungsinstrument	Instrument of control
Lernbereitschaft	Willingness to learn
Lernfähigkeit	Ability to learn
Lernprozess	Learning process
Lieferant	Supplier
Lieferung	Delivery
Liquidationswert	Liquidation value
Liquiditätsplan	Liquidity plan
Liquiditätsplanung	Liquidity planning
Liquiditätsrechnung	Liquidity calculation
Losgröße	Lot size
Manager-Unternehmer	Manager-entrepreneur
Marktdurchdringung	Market penetration
Marktwert	Market value
Marktwirtschaft	Market economy
Materialaufwand	Cost of materials
Maximalprinzip	Principle of maximum result
Mehraufwendungen	Additional expenses
Mehrliniensystem	Multiple-line system
Mehrwertschöpfung	Creation ofadded value
Mengengerüst	Quantity structure
Methodenvielfalt	Multiplicity of methods
Miete	Rent

(continued)

Minimalprinzip	Principle of minimum means
Mitarbeiter	Employee
Mitgliedsbeitrag	Membership fee
Mitteilung	Notification
Mittelbewirtschaftung	Management of financial resources
Mitteleinsatz	Deployment of means
Mittelherkunft	Sources of funds
Mittelverwendung	Use of resources
Mittelwert	Average/mean value
mittleres Axiom	Intermediate axiom
Mitwirkung	Participation
Modellbildung	Modelling
Nachwuchsplanung	Junior management planning
Naturschulden	Nature liabilities
Naturvermögen	Nature assets
Naturwissenschaften	Natural sciences
Neben-/Rahmenbedingung	Accompanying condition
Nebenfunktion	Auxiliary function
Nebengeschäft	Secondary business
Nebenbedingung	Accompanying condition
Nebenkosten	Incidentals, incidental costs
Nebenkostenstelle	Secondarycost centre
Nebenprodukt	By-product
Nebenwirkung	Secondary effect
Nettonutzennebengeschäft	Net benefit
Nettoschaden	Net damage
Nettovermögen	Net assets
neutrale Erfolgsrechnung	Non-operatingincome statement
neutraler Aufwand	Non-operating expense
neutraler Ertrag	Non-operating income
nichtselbständige Arbeit	Subordinated work
nichtwirtschaftlich	Non-economic
Niederlassung	Branch
Nonprofit-Organisation	Non-profit organisation
Normalkostenrechnung	Normal costing
Nutzen	Benefit
Nutzen-Kosten-Analyse	Cost-benefit analysis
Nutzenrechnung	Benefit calculation
Nutzenstiftung	Provision of benefits
Nutzentheorie	Theory of utility
Nutzkosten	Used capacity costs
Nutzungsdauer	Economic/operating/service life
Nutzungsrecht	Usage right
Nutzwert	Utility value
Nutzwertanalyse	Utility-value analysis

(continued)

Oberziel	Superior target
öffentliche Abgaben	Fiscal/public charges
öffentliche Aufgabe	Public task
öffentliche Wirtschaft	Public economy
Ökoeffizienzanalyse	Eco-efficiencyanalysis
ökologische Buchhaltung	Ecological book-keeping
operativ	Operative
Ordnungsmäßigkeit	Compliance
Ordnungspolitik	Policy of economic order
Organisationskultur	Organisational culture
örtliche Wirtschaft	Local economy
pagatorisch	Payment-based
pauschales Entgelt	Flat fee
Periodenerfolg	Accounting period result, net income of a given period
Periodenrechnung	Accruals accounting
Personal	Personnel, staff
Personaleinsatzplanung	Manpower planning
Personalentwicklung	Personnel/management development
Personalführung	Human resource management
Personalpolitik	Human resource policy/management
Personengesellschaft	Partnership
Personalsteuerung	Human resource management
Personalwirtschaft	Human resource management
Pflegeheim	Nursing home
Plankosten	Standard/predicted/forecast/budget/scheduled costs
Plankostenrechnung	Standard costing
Planung	Planning
Planungsrechnung	Planning calculation
Planwirtschaft	Planned economy
politisches Ziel	Policy goal
Potenzialanalyse	Analysis of potential
Prämisse	Premise
Preis-Leistungs-Verhältnis	Value for money
Preisuntergrenze	Lower price limit
Prinzip der Wertgleichheit	Principle of value consistency
Produktdifferenzierung	Product differentiation
Produktentwicklung	Product development
Produktionsmittel	Production materials
Produktionsverfahren	Production process
Produktpreis	Product price
Produktlinienanalyse	Product line analysis
Profitcenter	Profit centre
Prognose	Prediction

(continued)

Prognoserechnung	Forecast calculation
Prozessbilanz	Process statement
Prozessfinanzierung	Procedural financing
Prozesskosten	Process costs
Prozesskostenrechnung	Activity based costing, activity based accounting
Prozesspolitik	Policy of economic process
Prozesssteuerung	Process steering
Prüfbarkeit	Verifiability
Prüfplan	Inspection plan
Prüfung	Audit, auditing, verification
Prüfungsbericht	Audit report
Rahmenbedingung	Accompanying condition
Rangfolge	Ranking
Rationalprinzip	Principle of rationality
Raumgestaltung	Design of work spaces
Rechenkategorie	Arithmetical category
Rechenschaftslegung	Accountability
Rechenverfahren	Calculation method
Rechnungsabgrenzungsposten	Accruals
Rechnungslegung	Accounting
Rechnungsstoff	Set of accounting figures
Rechnungswesen	Accounting system
Rechtmäßigkeit	Lawfulness
Rechtsform	Legal form
Regelkreis	Control circuit
Regionalwirtschaft	Regional economy
reine Wissenschaft	Pure science
Reinvermögen	Actual assets
Rendite	Profitability
rentabel	Profitable
Rentabilität	Profitability
Rentabilitätsrechnung	Profitability calculation
Reproduktionswert	Replacement cost value
Ressourcenschonung	Resource conservation
Restwert	Residual value
Rhythmenabstimmung	Coordination of rhythm
Roh-, Hilfs- und Betriebsstoffe	Raw materials and supplies
Rückkopplung	Feedback
Rücklage	Reserve (fund)
Rückstellungen	Accruals, liability reserves, provisions
Rückzahlung	Redemption
Rüstkosten	Set-up costs
Ruhezeitenabstimmung	Coordination of rest periods
Sachanlagen	Tangible/fixed assets
Sachforderung	Tangible asset receivable

(continued)

Sachgüter	Tangible goods
Sachverbindlichkeit	Tangible asset liability
Sachvermögen	Tangible assets
Sachwert	Tangible asset
Sachziel	Substantive goal
Sachzielpriorität	Priority of substantive goal
Saldo	Balance
Sanierung	Restructuring
Schadensverhinderung	Damages prevented
Schadensverursachung	Damages incurred
Schattenpreis	Shadow price
Scheingewinn	Fictitious profit
Schulden	Liabilities
Schuldner	Debtor
Schwachstellenanalyse	Weak-point analysis
Schwerpunktstrategie	Nichestrategy
selbständige Arbeit	Autonomous work
Selbstentfaltung	Self-fulfilment
Selbstfinanzierung	Self-financing
Selbstgestaltung/-verwirklichung	Self-realisation
Selbstkosten	Prime costs
Selbstkostenrechnung	Cost price accounting
Selbstverwirklichung	Self-realisation
Sichtguthaben	Sight funds
Solidaritätsprinzip	Principle of solidarity
Soll-Ist-Relation	Target-performance relation
Soll-Kapazität	Target capacity
Soll-Kosten	Target costs
Soll-Leistung	Target output
Sonderbilanz	Special-purpose balance sheet
Sondereinzelkosten	Special direct costs
Sorgfalt	Diligence
Sortenfertigung	Flow production
Sozialbilanz	Social balance sheet
sozialer Ausgleich	Social adjustment
Sozialleistung	Social contribution
Sozialmanagement	Social management
Sozialökonomie	Economies of social care
Sozialordnung	Social order
Sozialstaatsprinzip	Social state principle
Sozialversicherung	Social insurance
Sozialwissenschaften	Social sciences
Spartenorganisation	Divisional organisation
Spende	Donation
Sportverein	Sports association

(continued)

Sprecher	Spokesman
staatliche Aufgaben	State duties
staatliches Unternehmen	State-owned enterprise
Staatsverbund	Community of states
Stabliniensystem	Line-and-staff system
Stammkapital	Share capital
Standortwahl	Choice of location
Stellenausschreibung	Job advertisement
Stellenbewertung	Job valuation
Stellenbildung	Job formation
Steuerberater	Tax adviser/consultant
Steuerbilanz	Tax balance sheet
Steuerprüfung	Tax audit
Steuerung	Governance, control
Stichprobenanalyse	Sampling analysis
Stiftung	Foundation
Stiftungsunternehmen	Foundation company
stille Reserve	Hidden reserve
Stoffbilanz	Materials balance
Stromgröße	Flow variable/unit
Stromrechnung	Statement of flows
Strukturfinanzierung	Structural financing
Strukturpolitik	Structural policy
Stückergebnisrechnung	Unit-of-output profit statement
Stückkosten	Unit costs
Substanzerhaltung	Preservation of assets
Substanzwert	Net asset value
Taktabstimmung	Coordination of timing
Tatsachenerkenntnis	Cognition of facts
Tauschwert	Exchange value
Tauschwirtschaft	Barter economy
Teileinheit	Sub-unit
Teilkonzern	Subgroup
Teilkostenrechnung	Marginal costing
Teilmarktbetrieb	Partial market entity
Teilwert	Going concern value
Teilziel	Partial target
Tochtergesellschaft	Subsidiary
Treiber	Driver
Umlagekosten	Allocated costs
Umlageschlüssel	Allocation formula
Überlassungsdauer	Assignment period
Überschuldung	Overindebtedness
Überschuss	Surplus
Übertragbarkeit	Transferability

(continued)

Überwachung	Monitoring, supervision
Umgangssprache	Colloquial language
Umlagekosten	Transfer costs
Umlageschlüssel	Allocation formula
Umlaufvermögen	Current assets
Umsatz	Turnover, sales, sales revenues
Umsatzerlöse	Turnover, sales, sales revenues
Umsatzkostenverfahren	Cost of sales method
Umsatzprozess	Operational sales
Umsatzrendite, -rentabilität	Return on sales
Umsetzungsplanung	Operational planning
umweltbezogenes Rechnungswesen	Environmental accounting
Umwelterklärung	Environmental statement
Umweltgüter	Environmental commodities
Umweltgutachter	Environmental expert
Umwelthaftung	Environmental liability
Umweltkosten	Environmental costs
Umweltmanagement	Environmental management
Umweltökonomie	Environmental economics
Umweltordnung	Environmental order
Umweltrisikoanalyse	Environmental riskanalysis
unentgeltlich	Free of charge
Ungüter	(External) diseconomies
unterjährig	During the fiscal year
Unternehmen/Unternehmung	Enterprise, firm
Unternehmensbewertung	Company valuation
Unternehmensinnere	Inside of a company
Unternehmenspolitik	Corporate policy/strategy
Unternehmensrechnung	Management accounting
Unternehmensumfeld	Environment of a company
Unternehmer	Entrepreneur
Unternehmung	Enterprise, firm
Unternehmungsführung	Management of a company
Unternehmungspolitik	Corporate policy/strategy
unwirtschaftlich	Uneconomic
Ursache-Wirkungs-Zusammenhang	Cause-effect relationship
Usance	Usage
Verantwortung	Responsibility
Verbindlichkeiten	Liabilities
Verbrauchsgüter	Commodities, consumer goods, consumables
Verein/Vereinigung	Association
Verfahrensanalyse	Process analysis
Verfahrenssynthese	Process synthesis
Verfahrensvergleich	Process comparison
Verkauf	Sale

(continued)

Verkäufer	Salesperson
Verkaufsrechnung	Sales invoice
Vermögen	Assets
vermögensunwirksam	Non-asset-effective
vermögenswirksam	Asset-effective
Verrechnungsart	Type of transfer pricing
Verschmelzung	Merger
Versicherung	Insurance
Versicherungsverein auf Gegenseitigkeit	Mutual insurance association
Vertriebsweg	Distribution channel
Verursacherprinzip	Polluter principle
Verwaltung	Administration
Verwaltungsgebühr	Administrative fee
Verwaltungsgemeinkosten	Administrative overheads
Verwaltungsziel	Administrative goal
Verwendungszweck	Use of goods
Verzinsung	Interest, return
Volkswirtschaft	National economy
volkswirtschaftliche Gesamtrechnung	National accounting
volkswirtschaftliche Vermögensrechnung	National balance sheet
volkswirtschaftliches Rechnungswesen	National accounting
Volkswirtschaftslehre	Economics
Vollkostenrechnung	Full costing
Vorauszahlung	Advance payment
Vorhaltung	Provision
Vorkostenstelle	Preliminarycost centre
Vorleistung	Intermediate input, advance delivery
Vorprodukt	Initial product
Vorrat	Inventory
Vorsitzender	Chairman
Vorsorge	Precaution
Vorsorgeprinzip	Cautionary principle
Vorstand	Management board
Wachstumsziel	Growth target
Wagnis	Venture
Wahrheitsgehalt	Truthfulness
Wahrheitssuche	Search for the truth
Wahrnehmung	Perception
Waren	Trade goods, commodities
Warenbestand	Stock on hand
Weisungssystem	System of direct power
Weltwirtschaft	Worldeconomy
Wenn-dann-Beziehung	What if relation
Werbeerfolgskontrolle	Evaluation of advertising effectiveness
Werbung	Advertising

(continued)

Werkstoffe	Materials
Wertansatz	Valuation
Wertdimension	Value dimension
wertende Wissenschaft	Evaluating science
wertfreie Wissenschaft	Value-free science
Wertgleichheit	Value consistency
Wertkettenanalyse	Value chain analysis
Wertpapiere	Securities
Wertschöpfungsprozess	Value adding process
Wertschöpfungsrechnung	Value added calculation
Wertzuwachs	Increase in value
Wettbewerbsfähigkeit	Competitiveness
Wettbewerbsverbot	Non-competition obligation
Wiedergewinnungszeit	Time of retrieval
Willensbildung	Decision making
wirksam	Effective
Wirksamkeit	Effectiveness
Wirkungsanalyse	Efficiency analysis
Wirkungsbestandsrechnung	Outcome-impact-balance sheet
Wirkungserfassung	Measurementof operation
Wirkungsergebnisrechnung	Outcome-impact-result statement
Wirkungsforschung	Impact research
Wirkungsrechnung	Effect/outcome-impact statement
wirtschaftlich	Economic
Wirtschaftlichkeit	Economic efficiency
wirtschaftlich vertretbar	Economically justifiable
Wirtschaftseinheit	Economic entity
Wirtschaftskraft	Economic power
Wirtschaftspädagogik	Economic pedagogics
Wirtschaftsprüfer	Chartered/certified public accountant
Wirtschaftssubjekt	Economic subject
Wirtschaftssystem	Economic system
Wirtschaftsverfassung	Economic constitution
Wirtschafswissenschaften	Economic sciences
Wissen	Knowledge
wissenschaftliche Lehre	Scientific doctrine
Wohlfahrt	Welfare
Wohlfahrtsoptimum	Optimum welfare
Wohlstand	Wealth
Wohlstandsmehrung	Growth of wealth
Zählbarkeit	Countability
Zahlungsfähigkeit	Ability to pay
Zahlungsmittelabgänge	Outflows of liquid funds
Zahlungsmittelbestand	Liquid fund balance
Zahlungsmittelzugänge	Inflows of liquid funds

(continued)

Zahlungsstrom	Payment flow/stream
Zeitachse	Timeline
Zeitreihenanalyse	Time-series analysis
Zeitvergleich	Comparison of time
Ziel	Aim, goal, target
Zielbeziehung	Goal relationship
zielbezogen	Effective
Zielbildung	Formation of goals/targets
zielführend	Effective
Zielgröße	Target value
Zielkonzept	Goal/target concept
Zielkorridor	Target range
Zielkosten	Target costs
Zielkostenrechnung	Target costing
Zielorientierung	Goal/target orientation
Zielpreis	Target price
Zielsetzung	Goal/target setting
Zielsystem	Goal/target system
Zielvereinbarung	Goal agreement
Zielvorgabe	Defined goal/target
Zielvorschrift	Goal/target orientation
Zinsfuß	Interest rate
Zinskosten	Interest charges
Zulassungsrecht	Approval right
Zulieferer	Supplier
Zusammensetzung	Composition
Zusatzkosten	Additional/supplementary costs
Zusatzleistungen	Additional outputs
Zuschlagskalkulation	Job order costing
Zuschreibung	Write-up
Zuschuss	Allowance/grant
Zuschussbetrieb	Subsidised operation
Zuschussfinanzierung	Allowance financing
Zustiftung	Endowment
Zuwendung	Allowance
Zweck	Objective/purpose
Zweckaufwand	Operating expense
Zweckertrag	Operating income
Zweckforschung	Functional research
zweckmäßig	Efficient, purposeful
Zweckmäßigkeit	Efficiency
Zweck-Mittel-Beziehung	Means-end relationship
zwischenbetrieblicher Vergleich	Interfirm comparison
Zwischenholding	Intermediate holding
Zwischenprodukt	Interim product

Bibliography

English

Arrow, K. J. (1951). *Social choice and individual values*. New York: Wiley.

Berk, J., & DeMarzo, P. (2016). *Corporate finance*. Harlow: Pearson Education.

Boddy, D. (2016). *Management: An introduction* (7th ed.). London: Prentice Hall.

Brealey, R., Myers, S. C., & Allen, F. (2016). *Principles of corporate finance* (12th ed.). New York: McGraw-Hill.

Clegg, S., Kornberger, M., & Pitsis, T. (2015). *Managing and organizations: An introduction to theory and practice* (4th ed.). Thousand Oaks, CA: Sage.

de Wit, B. (2017). *Strategy: An international perspective* (6th ed.). London: Cengage.

Dessler, G. (2012). *A framework for human resource management* (7th ed.). London: Pearson.

Gerber, J. (2017). *International economics* (7th ed.). Harlow: Pearson Education.

Gill, R. (2011). *Theory and practice of leadership* (2nd ed.). Thousand Oaks, CA: Sage.

Harrison, W. T., Horngren, C. T., Thomas, B., & Suwardy, T. (2013). *Financial accounting: International financial reports standards* (9th ed.). Harlow: Pearson Education.

Heizer, J., Render, B., & Munson, C. (2016). *Operations management: Sustainability and supply chain management* (12th ed.). New York: Prentice-Hall.

Hill, C. W. L. (2014). *International business: Competing in the global marketplace* (10th ed.). New York: McGraw-Hill.

Hillier, D., Ross, S., Westerfield, R., & Jaffe, J. (2013). *Corporate finance* (3rd ed.). New York: McGraw-Hill.

Hofstede, G. (2001). *Culture's consequences: Comparing values, behaviors, institutions, and organizations across nations*. Thousand Oaks, CA: Sage.

Horngren, C. T., Datar, S. M., & Rajan, M. V. (2017). *Cost accounting: A managerial emphasis* (16th ed.). New York: Prentice Hall.

Kaplan, R. S., & Norton, D. P. (1996). *The balanced scorecard*. Boston, MA: Harvard Business School Press.

Kotler, P., & Armstrong, G. (2017). *Principles of marketing* (17th ed.). New York: Prentice Hall.

Krugman, P., & Wells, R. (2012). *Microeconomics* (3rd ed.). Basingstoke: Palgrave Macmillan.

Maslow, A. H. (1954). *Motivation and personality*. New York: Harper.

McLaney, E., & Atrill, P. (2017). *Accounting and finance* (10th ed.). New York: Prentice-Hall.

Mintzberg, H., Ahlstrand, B., & Lampel, J. (2010). *Management? It's not what you think!* London: Prentice Hall.

Musgrave, R. A. (1959). *The theory of public finance: A study in public economy*. New York: McGraw-Hill.

Popper, K. (1959). *The logic of scientific discovery*. London: Routledge.

Porter, M. (2004). *Competitive strategy: Techniques for analyzing industries and competitors.* New York: Free Press.

Radcliffe, S. (2012). *Leadership: Plain and simple.* London: FT Publishing.

Rainey, H. G. (2014). *Understanding and managing public organizations* (5th ed.). San Francisco, CA: Jossey-Bass.

Richard, G. (2014). *Warehouse management* (2nd ed.). London: Kogan Page.

Robbers, G. (2012). *An introduction to German law* (6th ed.). Baden-Baden: Nomos.

Robbins, S. P., DeCenzo, D. A., & Coulter, A. (2014). *Fundamentals of management* (9th ed.). New York: Prentice Hall.

Rushton, A., Croucher, P., & Baker, P. (2014). *The handbook of logistics and distribution management: Understanding the supply chain* (6th ed.). London: Kogan Page.

Schulz, M., & Wasmeier, O. (2012). *The law of business organizations: A concise overview of German corporate law.* Heidelberg: Springer.

Slack, N., Brandon-Jones, A., & Johnston, R. (2016). *Operations management* (8th ed.). London: Pearson.

Solomon, M. (2017). *Consumer behavior: Buying, having, being* (12th ed.). New York: Prentice-Hall.

van der Wal, Z. (2017). *The 21st century public manager.* London: Palgrave.

German

Balderjahn, I., & Specht, G. (2016). *Einführung in die Betriebswirtschaftslehre* (7th ed.). Stuttgart: Schäffer Poeschel.

Bamberg, G., Coenenberg, A. G., & Krapp, M. (2012). *Betriebswirtschaftliche Entscheidungslehre* (15th ed.). Munich: Vahlen.

Bea, F. X., Dichtl, E., & Schweitzer, M. (Eds.). (2006–2011). *Allgemeine Betriebswirtschaftslehre (3 volumes).* Stuttgart: Gustav Fischer.

Beschorner, D., & Peemöller, V. H. (2006). *Allgemeine Betriebswirtschaftslehre* (2nd ed.). Herne: NWB Verlag.

Brockhoff, K. (2016). *Betriebswirtschaftslehre in Wissenschaft und Geschichte: Eine Skizze* (5th ed.). Wiesbaden: Springer Gabler.

Corsten, H., & Reiß, M. (Eds.). (2008). *Betriebswirtschaftslehre (2 vol).* Munich: Oldenbourg Wissenschaftsverlag.

Domschke, W., & Scholl, A. (2008). *Grundlagen der Betriebswirtschaftslehre: Eine Einführung aus Entscheidungsorientierter Sicht* (4th ed.). Berlin: Springer.

Eichhorn, P., & Merk, J. (2016). *Das Prinzip Wirtschaftlichkeit: Basiswissen der Betriebswirtschaftslehre* (4th ed.). Wiesbaden: Springer Gabler.

Hutzschenreuter, T. (2015). *Allgemeine Betriebswirtschaftslehre: Grundlagen mit zahlreichen Praxisbeispielen* (6th ed.). Wiesbaden: Springer Gabler.

Jung, H. (2016). *Allgemeine Betriebswirtschaftslehre* (12th ed.). Munich: De Gruyter Oldenbourg.

Lechner, K., Egger, A., & Schauer, R. (2008). *Einführung in die Allgemeine Betriebswirtschaftslehre* (24th ed.). Vienna: Linde.

Mellerowicz, K. (1976). *Unternehmenspolitik.* Freiburg: Haufe.

Neus, W. (2015). *Einführung in die Betriebswirtschaftslehre aus institutionenökonomischer Sicht* (9th ed.). Tübingen: Mohr Siebeck.

Olfert, K. (2013). *Einführung in die Betriebswirtschaftslehre* (11th ed.). Herne: NWB Verlag.

Pepels, W. (Ed.). (2015). *Allgemeine Betriebswirtschaftslehre* (5th ed.). Berliner Wissenschafts-Verlag: Berlin.

Peters, S., Brühl, R., & Stelling, J. N. (2005). *Betriebswirtschaftslehre: Einführung* (12th ed.). Munich: Oldenbourg Wissenschaftsverlag.

Sandig, C. (1966). *Betriebswirtschaftspolitik.* Stuttgart: Poeschel.

Schierenbeck, H., & Wöhle, C. B. (2016). *Grundzüge der Betriebswirtschaftslehre* (19th ed.). Munich: De Gruyter Oldenbourg.

Schmalen, H., & Pechtl, H. (2013). *Grundlagen und Probleme der Betriebswirtschaft* (15th ed.). Stuttgart: Schäffer Poeschel.

Steinmann, H., Schreyögg, H. G., & Koch, J. (2013). *Management: Grundlagen der Unternehmensführung Konzepte – Funktionen – Fallstudien* (7th ed.). Wiesbaden: Springer Gabler.

Straub, T. (2014). *Einführung in die Allgemeine Betriebswirtschaftslehre* (2nd ed.). Munich: Pearson.

Thommen, J.-P. (2016). *Betriebswirtschaft und Management: managementorientierte Betriebswirtschaftslehre*. Zürich: Versus.

Thommen, J.-P., & Achleitner, A.-K. (2016). *Allgemeine Betriebswirtschaftslehre, Umfassende Einführung aus managementorientierter Sicht* (8th ed.). Wiesbaden: Springer Gabler.

Töpfer, A. (2007). *Betriebswirtschaftslehre: Anwendungs- und prozessorientierte Grundlagen*. Berlin: Springer.

Ulrich, H. (1978). *Unternehmenspolitik*. Bern: Haupt.

Ulrich, P., & Fluri, E. (1995). *Management*. Stuttgart: UTB.

Vahs, D., & Schäfer-Kunz, J. (2015). *Einführung in die Betriebswirtschaftslehre* (7th ed.). Stuttgart: Schäffer Poeschel.

von Colbe, B., Coenenberg, A. G., Kajüter, P., Linnhoff, U., & Pellens, B. (Eds.). (2011). *Betriebswirtschaft für Führungskräfte* (4th ed.). Schäffer Poeschel: Stuttgart.

Wöhe, G., & Döring, U. (2016). *Einführung in die Allgemeine Betriebswirtschaftslehre* (26th ed.). Munich: Vahlen.

Zangemeister, C. (1972). Nutzwertanalyse. In G. Tumm (Ed.), *Die neuen Methoden der Entscheidungsfindung* (pp. 264–285). Munich: Verlag moderne Industrie.

Index

A

Accounting
  corporate social, 199, 200
  ecological, 198, 199, 201, 203–205
Added value, 40, 107, 212, 228, 241
Administration
  environmentally aware, 255
Advertising goals, 256
Aggregate economic welfare, 108
Aggregate social welfare, 108
Analysis
  ABC environment, 202
  eco-efficiency, 202
  environmental risk, 203
Annuity, 232
Assets
  external, 201, 212, 213
  types, 132
Associations
  tasks, 281

B

Balance sheet
  external, 213
  outcome-impact, 205
Balanced Scorecard (BSC), 286, 307, 308, 312
Benchmarking, 224, 280, 286
Benefit calculations, 195–207, 212
Break-even, 106, 116
Budgeting, 11, 15–17, 47, 48, 67, 72, 79, 80,
    85, 118, 141, 166–168, 212, 225–232,
    234, 240, 254, 256, 262, 274, 276, 277,
    281, 285, 290, 291
Business administration
  concepts, 14
  related disciplines, 14–18
  taxonomy, 12, 13

Business ethics, 19, 119
Buyers' surplus, 194

C

Capacity, 9, 68, 118, 120, 122, 132, 142, 143,
    169, 178, 180, 182, 188, 225, 228
Capital budgeting, 166–168, 212, 225–232, 240
Capital planning, 234
Cash conversion cycle, 169
Cash flow, 104, 119, 123, 162, 165, 166, 175,
    216, 231, 309
Circular economy, 55, 121, 252, 253, 262
Cognitive methods, 26–29
Company valuations, 177
Compensation principle, 47
Consumers' surplus, 194, 205
Controllership, 17, 43, 133, 276, 280–282, 284,
    285, 287, 290, 291, 293–295, 297–299,
    302, 303, 305, 312
Corporate policy, 162, 267–271, 273, 281, 297
Cost allocation, 184, 187
Cost centre, 74, 184–187, 189, 191, 193, 220,
    233, 271, 290
Cost coverage, 105, 106
Cost management, 182
Cost monitoring, 182, 191
Cost planning, 182, 302
Cost types, 137, 180, 182, 184, 186, 189, 219, 294
Costing methods, 188, 190, 192
Costing systems, 191, 192
Costs
  operational, 43, 85, 91, 118, 121, 128, 131,
    134, 139, 147, 170
  transport, 83
Costing methods, 188–190, 192, 193
Coverage ratios, 163, 164, 215, 216
Current assets, 124, 131, 140, 163, 209, 215, 216

D

Debt capital, 9, 100, 124, 131, 140, 161, 168, 209, 226, 268

Decision, 2, 5, 7, 9, 10, 14, 15, 17, 20, 21, 23, 25–28, 30, 33, 39, 43, 45, 46, 49, 59, 63, 68, 72, 75, 76, 78, 129, 133, 143, 151, 166–168, 170, 182, 192, 221, 222, 225, 226, 232, 234, 245, 252, 256, 258, 259, 261, 264, 267, 268, 271–276, 278, 280

Decision making, 49, 56, 80, 96, 107, 143, 182, 225, 274, 276, 292, 294, 295

Demand, 11, 15, 17–19, 36, 37, 40, 42, 47, 48, 50

Diseconomies, 18, 40, 135, 136, 138, 139, 145, 146, 154, 194

E

EBIT, 175

EBITDA, 175, 244

Eco-Management and Audit Scheme (EMAS), 204

Economic agent, 63, 66–74, 76, 80–85
  legal form, 68
  typology, 65–67

Economic efficiency, 2, 3, 5, 14, 18, 29, 36, 64, 95–101, 103, 107–110, 112, 113, 141–143, 146, 149–151, 158, 159, 181, 182, 197, 243–262, 264, 281, 291, 301, 303

Economic order quantity, 244, 245, 250, 259, 260, 262

Economic system, 7, 15, 49–53, 55, 73, 102, 119

Economic welfare function, 46

Economies of scale, 79, 142, 245, 250, 288

Economy
  behavioural, 18, 94, 96, 112
  local, 5, 6, 30, 195
  market, 5, 8, 15, 16, 45, 49, 50
  mixed-market, 49
  national, 5, 7, 195, 209
  planned, 51
  regional, 4, 6, 7, 9, 10, 38, 39, 107
  social market, 50
  socialist market, 50
  supranational, 5, 7, 8
  world, 5, 8, 9

Effectiveness, 2, 3, 5, 14, 18, 29, 36, 45, 64, 75, 79, 84, 98

Efficiency, 2, 18, 45, 79, 95

Emissions, 108, 118, 121, 145, 146, 201, 203

Employees, 14, 37, 40, 48, 54, 67, 76, 105, 117, 124–126, 138, 139, 141, 142, 144, 149, 158, 170

Environmental law, 58, 202

Equity capital, 140, 209, 226, 304

Equivalence coefficient, 188, 201, 227, 228

Expenditures, 16, 72, 82, 105, 167–171, 173, 178, 179, 220, 276, 298

Expenses
  non-operating, 74, 172, 174

External effects, 18, 48, 59, 134, 135, 150, 180, 197, 200, 201, 203, 205, 213, 246, 247, 249, 277

F

Factors of production
  capital, 85
  combination, 132–134, 141–143, 145, 158, 232
  energy, 85, 132
  legislation, 133
  material, 85
  nature, 85
  procurement, 261, 280
  service, 132
  universal factor system, 129

Financial management, 85, 169, 174, 298, 299, 305

Financing, 7, 11, 16, 17, 43, 68, 78, 83, 86, 87, 102, 105, 106, 121, 124, 140, 163, 165, 167–169, 217, 220, 245, 250, 287, 298, 303

Firms
  orientation, 123

Flow balance sheet, 210

Forecasts
  moving average method, 238
  regression analysis, 238
  simple average method, 238
  weighted average method, 238

Foundations, 5, 12, 55, 68, 78, 86, 94–96, 106, 107, 133, 168, 264

Future value, 230–232, 239, 240

G

General theory of marginal utility, 44

German commercial code, 175, 210, 248

Global reporting initiative (GRI), 205

Goals
  formal, 102, 119, 121, 122, 154, 299
  substantive, 66, 80, 95, 96, 102, 103, 112, 119, 121–123, 125, 154, 181, 210, 287
  substantive ecologic, 120, 121

substantive economic, 120, 121
substantive social, 120, 121
types, 154
Goods
types, 67, 159, 160, 246
Green marketing, 257

H
Hospitals, 4, 5, 9, 12, 17, 38, 48, 65, 67, 73, 74, 79, 85, 87, 105, 118
Households, 6, 7, 11, 15, 18, 19, 37, 43, 50, 64, 66, 68, 70–73, 78, 86, 91, 104, 107, 116, 123, 125, 128, 131, 162, 169, 170, 178, 264, 283
Human resource management, 4, 12, 14, 18, 139, 252, 278, 295–298, 312

I
Immissions, 121, 146
Impacts, 99, 113, 121, 146, 195, 201
Income
households, 11
non-operating, 172–174, 179, 181, 187, 190
Income statement, 74, 79, 165, 174, 177, 178, 181, 192, 195, 200, 202, 220, 228, 304, 305
Indicators, 17, 45, 108, 146–148, 154, 196
Indicators of benefits, 45
Institutional principle, 107
Internal rate of return, 231, 232
Inventory management, 247–249, 258, 261, 267
Investment types, 166
ISO, 202, 205

L
Learning processes, 22, 23, 33
Legal system, 53
Leverage effect, 124, 168
Liabilities
external, 213
Linear programming, 233
Liquidity, 104, 118–120, 123, 131, 140, 162–166, 168, 215, 219, 224, 276, 291, 298, 299, 301
Liquidity management, 162
Liquidity planning, 123, 162, 164, 166
Location, 9, 16, 19, 30, 35, 66, 123, 133, 134
Lot size, 182, 250, 262

M
Management
activity circuit, 275
auditing, 301, 303–305
execution, 118
execution phase, 274, 275
feedback, 306
knowledge, 11
monitoring, 193
non-profit, 11
organisation, 68, 293
planning phase, 275
process, 294, 295
public, 81
reporting, 302
skills, 279
structure, 293
styles, 293
supervision, 280
supervision phase, 275, 276
support, 274, 281
system, 269, 270, 272–274, 280
tasks, 272–274, 276
Management philosophy, 125, 126
Management system, 269, 270, 272–274, 280, 312
Marketing mix, 256, 257
Measurement, 108, 146–151, 158, 224, 271, 294
Mission statement, 115, 124–127, 140, 154, 268, 306, 307

N
Needs
creation, 38–40
types, 32

O
Objects of cognition, 3, 5–9, 14, 18, 29
Operational planning, 274, 275, 287–289
Optimisation calculations, 232, 233
Ordinal utility theory, 45
Organisational culture, 125, 126, 272, 274
Outcome-impact balance sheet, 205, 213
Outcome-impact result statement, 207, 208, 213
Outcome-impact statement, 205
Outcomes, 2, 18, 28, 74, 99, 113, 121, 128, 145, 146, 150, 201, 203, 205, 213
Outpayments, 74, 161–167, 179, 214, 227, 229, 231, 234

Output concept, 124
Outputs, 2, 3, 5, 14, 16, 18, 40, 41, 55, 60, 64,
    65, 73, 76, 84
Overheads
    administration, 253

P

P/E ratio, 175
Payback period, 227
Payment streams, 131, 161, 162, 164, 220, 244
PESTLE analysis, 283
Present value, 165, 167, 180, 212, 229–232,
    234, 239, 244
Prices, 6, 20, 30, 36, 48, 49, 60, 74, 83, 96, 103,
    105, 106, 110, 124
Principle of aggregation, 107–108
Principle of alimentation, 106
Principle of competition, 103–104
Principle of equivalence, 104–106, 113
Principle of maximum result, 3, 96, 97, 111, 112
Principle of minimum means, 3, 97, 98, 111, 112
Principle of rationality, 94
Principle of solidarity, 101, 102, 113
Procurement, 4, 6, 11, 12, 17, 18, 29, 43, 78,
    82, 83, 85, 96, 103, 117, 118, 136, 141,
    142, 154, 193, 194, 234, 244–246, 248,
    252, 255, 259, 261, 262, 280, 295, 297
Productivity, 52, 120, 122, 130, 142, 146, 151,
    152, 182, 224, 255, 274, 288, 295, 307
Profitability, 96, 100, 101, 103, 110–113,
    118–120, 123, 162, 166, 168, 205, 207,
    219, 226, 227, 230, 232, 240, 241, 285,
    299, 304
Profitability calculation, 226, 241
Public charges, 81–83, 105
Public tasks, 12, 44, 61, 62, 80–84, 87, 91,
    103, 121
Public-private partnerships, 43, 66

R

Rationality
    meta-economic, 2
Ratios, 18, 140, 163, 164, 182, 189, 214–217,
    220, 222
Receipt of payments, 161

Resources
    households, 6, 71
Return on investment, 104, 218, 219, 223, 226
Revenues, 2, 16, 61, 67, 69, 71, 73–75
    associations, 76–80
    firms, 265
Risk analysis, 203, 234, 238

S

Scales, 149
Self-employed, 42, 71, 73, 85, 86
Social welfare function, 45
State, 5–10, 15–17, 19, 24, 30, 37, 38, 44, 45,
    49–55, 58, 59, 62, 65, 66, 69, 72, 73,
    76–78, 81, 83, 88, 91, 94, 102, 103, 106,
    119, 121, 122, 132, 163, 164, 169, 209,
    218, 248, 268, 269, 279, 283, 294, 295
Stocktaking, 249
Strategy, 20, 80, 120, 194, 247, 282, 284, 285,
    287, 295, 307–310
Sustainable development, 50, 55, 118
SWOT analysis, 40, 284, 309, 310
System of accounts, 184
Systems theory, 268, 306

T

Theory of public goods, 42
Theory of public tasks, 42
Theory of value, 44
Time-series analysis, 234, 235, 241

U

Utility-value analysis, 195, 196

V

Valuation, 150, 151, 160, 173, 175, 177, 179,
    194–197, 200, 202–204, 209, 210, 256,
    301, 303, 305
Vector analysis, 233, 241

Z

Zero-based budgeting (ZBB), 254, 308

Printed by Printforce, the Netherlands